SOUTHAMPTON

PROVINCES OF EARLY MEXICO

UCLA Latin American Studies
Volume 36

Series Editor
Johannes Wilbert

PROVINCES OF EARLY MEXICO

Variants of Spanish American Regional Evolution

Edited by
Ida Altman and James Lockhart

UCLA Latin American Center Publications
University of California, Los Angeles
1976

UCLA Latin American Center Publications
University of California
Los Angeles, California

Library of Congress Catalog Card Number: 76-620055
ISBN: 0-87903-036-4
Printed in the United States of America

To the scholarly generation of
Borah, Chevalier, and Gibson

Preface

Before synthesis, panorama. In recent years historians, historical geographers, and anthropologist-ethnohistorians have been producing an impressive number of excellent studies on individual regions of Latin America in the early modern period. This activity has a good deal of cohesion in respect to both results and methods of investigation. However, strong and spontaneous though it is, the movement is still quite fragmented. The scholarly public is insufficiently aware of these studies, and even the writers of them too rarely show awareness of their colleagues' work, reacting instead to the monuments of the preceding wave of scholarship.

A bringing together is called for. Understandably, no one seems presently prepared to undertake full-scale comparative analysis on the basis of the kaleidoscopic picture now before us—some region of nearly every country but all the regions of none; huge gaps in coverage of time and topic (while studies keep pouring out to fill the gaps). Also, the writers in this vein have rarely meant to concentrate on regional history per se; usually they have been interested in some special aspect or segment of the total social-economic complex, and their works, at times, offer little in points of direct comparability with each other.

In this volume we take an intermediary step toward synthesis and integration. The chapters of the volume represent a large sampling—not all—of the regional studies, recent and still in progress, on one important country, Mexico. Mexico not only exemplifies unusually well the range of principal regional variants of mainland Spanish America, but it also seems to have a stronger regionally oriented historical literature than any other single country. In this case as in hardly any other, the corpus of recent sophisticated studies is thick enough to give some idea of the overall interaction of the parts of the larger or protonational entity. Our interest, then, is by no means primarily in "Mexican history," but in a better understanding of Latin America's constituent processes, and we hope the book will be interpreted correspondingly. Inside these covers are studies of several kinds—some drawing on well-known work, here made succinct or augmented as the case may require, others drawing on work now going on (dissertations, books-to-be, dissertations in progress)—each adjusted to the purpose of attaining an overview of a Mexican region from a certain perspective at a certain time.

Our thanks and acknowledgments go in general to the many scholars who since about 1950 have had the perspicacity and industry to seek general patterns in the specifics of Latin American reality. The editors of the volume especially thank the authors of the chapters for the wealth of their contributions, which, had expense not made brutal excisions necessary, could have filled two volumes like this one.

I.A. and J.L.

CONTENTS

PROVINCES OF EARLY MEXICO

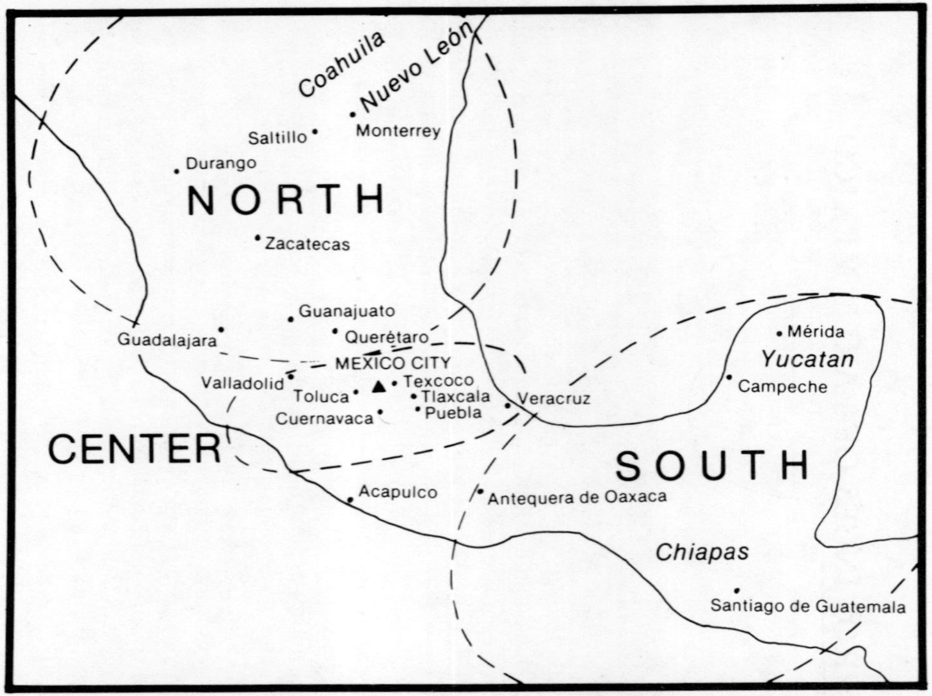

Colonial Mexico: Macroregions and Some Principal Centers

Introduction

James Lockhart

The Framework

South, Center, and North.—That the local environments of Spanish America—the totality of physical features, resources, and indigenous population—have had enormous shaping power is as obvious as the strikingly different characteristics of human society and economy in different Spanish American regions at any time from the sixteenth century to the present. On the other hand, one cannot accept environment, even in this broad sense, as the sole determinant of evolution, or there would be no explanation for the fact that things were so different after the Spaniards arrived than before.

Once the initial explorations were carried out, the Spanish (i.e., European) factor was, though crucial, potentially the same everywhere, and differences in development from that point can be attributed ultimately to differentials in the local situations. (Before long, of course, the Spanish presence in a given area, its strength or weakness, became an additional environmental determinant, and often the crucial one.) Yet even taking the Spanish component as a constant, it would probably be artificial to work out a standard course of evolution of a Spanish American region regardless of environmental peculiarities. What would the Spaniards do where the environment could truly be disregarded, as on a desert island? Stay away, no doubt. It is more immediately instructive and easier to deal with variants—with principles and expected ranges of variation—than with an imagined standard.

The regional variations under consideration are not those of whole countries. No nation-sized unit in all Spanish America is or has been uniform as to the primary characteristics of its subregions.[1] The local variety is exuberant, but not chaotic; rather the constituent parts repeat themselves. Entire subregional types recur time and time again: the dry, flat, thinly occupied livestock regions; the inaccessible Indian mountain areas; the complexes around the capitals; and many other types and subtypes—with the result that the peculiarity of a given country usually consists largely in the distinctive distribution of elements common to Spanish America as a whole.

In the present anthology of chapters on parts of early Mexico, we have adopted the common rough classification of the Mexican regions as South, Center, and North. The South is principally Yucatan and Oaxaca (Guatemala and Chiapas could well be included). The Center consists of everything from the Valley of Mexico to Veracruz, with the Toluca and Cuernavaca basins, the area north of Mexico City as far as Tula, and in some respects Michoacán to the west.[2] The North is everything beyond that, to both north and west. This type of organization is accepted a bit reluctantly, because historians and others are already too prone to think in terms of purely individual, geographical regions. The reader may be deterred from a literal interpretation by considering that parts of our "South" lie north of Mexico City, while parts of the "North" are hardly out of sight of the Valley of Mexico.

The intention is to point to three types of situations common in Spanish America. The three divisions may be thought of as a symmetrical arrangement according to only two variables: type of Indian population and strength of European immigration. In general, the South had a dense, sedentary indigenous population and experienced relatively slow, weak Spanish immigration; the Center had the same kind of indigenous population, with much greater Spanish immigration; whereas the North had a thin, mobile Indian population combined with Spanish penetration often as strong as in the Center or stronger, at least relatively speaking. Much of the reason for the spatial distribution of the Europeans was the distribution of deposits of silver, long the chief export commodity and sole ultimate basis for a European-style Mexican economy. The Europeans went to the North because the great mines were there. They went to the Center at first because it contained Mexico's largest, most populous, and wealthiest imperial agglomerate, and later for even stronger reasons: the area was on the way from the mines to the sea, with some more mines of its own, and there was a snowballing effect as Spaniards congregated near the capital where the most Spaniards already were. They avoided the South because it was off the main line of the silver economy and had no strong economic motor of its own, in addition to its being in good part hot and unhealthy for them.

Though Spaniards are an indispensable variable in our tripartite division, in some ways all three components of the schema existed in preconquest times. The sedentary South and Center stood in strong contrast to the North, as the peoples of the Center were well aware. Also, two or three times the Nahua peoples of the Center had invaded and conquered large parts of the South, which thus had at times something of the aspect of a peripheral, remote, and subordinated area that was to characterize it after the conquest. The Center had a more temperate climate than the South as well as, at conquest, larger political organizations and apparently a larger population; although these were all things differentially attracting Spaniards, they were also longstanding regional distinctions characteristic of both preconquest and colonial periods.

What was said above of the heterogeneity of Spanish American countries applies also to the macroregions of South, Center, and North. Each of these had internal diversity, and meaningful generalizations phrased in terms of them are hardly to be expected and rarely attained. For example, the rate of Spanish acquisition of land is not uniformly one thing in the South, another in the Center, another in the North: the actual picture from locality to locality is much more complex. The principles determining the rate, however, are more unitary, being a single set of variables applying to all situations. The rate of Spanish land acquisition is determined in any local situation by a series of closely interacting factors of which one may mention especially (1) number of Spaniards present, (2) proximity of markets and profitability of agrarian production, and (3) number of Indians using the land intensively. If it is true, *generally speaking,* that land acquisition was relatively slow in the South, this is only because certain crucial conditions such as position off the silver trunkline, few Spaniards, a weak local market, and numerous Indian maize-growers all happened to obtain in so much of the area. When these characteristics chance to occur together in a reasonably fertile and populated but out-of-the-way locality of the near North such as Metztitlan,[3] one expects and in fact sees the same result; this in no way constitutes an exception to a properly constructed generalization. On the other hand, in a Southern locality like Campeche, in which these conditions did not obtain, one expects and sees a different result. Accepting the actual diversity of the great Mexican regions is important for another reason as well: in order to grasp where further research is or is not needed for drawing conclusions. To map the regions of Mexico accurately and fully as to rate and absolute chronology of Spanish land acquisition, a great deal more research is needed. To understand the significant question of what determined the rate at which Spaniards acquired land, plenty of basic research has already been done.

The three hundred years of elapsed time before Mexican political independence (this being the period within which our studies fall) appear to make for additional difficulties of interpretation, especially since the chapters here, like the entire literature of which they are a part, concentrate on different time blocks. Actually, however, the temporal element can help us to understand and mentally organize the growing mass of Spanish American regional data. A great many of what appear to be regional-spatial distinctions are differences in timing or tempo only. (It is true that as a consequence of such temporal layering, one cannot hastily draw static comparisons and contrasts on the basis of treatments of different time periods.) The variation in tempo is strongly patterned. Wherever wealth and Europeans congregated, things happened quickly; wherever they did not, slowly. The Valley of Oaxaca in 1750 looked a great deal like the Valley of Toluca in 1580.

The consolidation of landholding, to take one regional variable that has already enjoyed considerable attention, is not something that takes place everywhere at once, whether in the sense of a definitive establishment of estate units and tenure patterns, or the sense of accompanying formal surveys and clearing of title. But it is something that invariably occurs in a locality at a certain level of the profitability of agriculture and a certain stage in the constitution of the region as a Spanish province; the differential dating of the phenomenon in, say, the Valley of Mexico, the western Bajío, or Nuevo León, tells us the times at which these areas attained a comparable state in some important respects, and therefore something about the rhythm of the whole. In many cases the time differential means early development near Mexico City, later development on the periphery. But this need not be so; the mining areas, for example, led the way in types of labor arrangements that would not be a majority phenomenon in the area near the capital for centuries and, in parts of the far southern interior, may never be.

Mexico City and the provinces.—With this we broach a topic basic to the makeup of Mexico at any time since the fifteenth century and also crucial to the intent and organization of the present book. From beginning to end of the colonial period, New Spain's capital of Mexico had a position of even greater predominance and more widespread influence than the Aztec capital of Tenochtitlan that preceded it on the same site. The growth of a more European Mexico at times takes on the aspect of a spread outward from this center, though neatly concentric zones fail to result, since activity from the capital leapt great distances to areas of interest, leaving closer ones relatively isolated and unaffected. There is no reason to believe, in general, that the provincials were directly and deliberately imitating Mexico City. The source of the uniformity is much deeper: the culture and technology of Spain and Europe in the early modern period; the behavior of human beings in new areas; the international economy of the time; the relationship between Europe and the peoples of the western hemisphere.

The nature of a given region's ties to Mexico City often places it in a context better than any other single factor, and the sum total of these ties goes far to define the structure of New Spain as a whole, revealing for example not only the relatively separate status of the South, but other facets less expected (though by no means anomalous), such as the orientation of parts of the near-northern Bajío more toward the capital than toward the silver mines. In fact, the set of ties between individual regions and the area of the capital came very near to being the structure of the country, far stronger than most other interregional connections, though these of course existed.

Mexico City was also a major center of organization, distribution, and consumption related to the movement of people and goods along a route stretching between the source of wealth (the silver mines) and the source of what was bought with it (the sea and Europe). A sort of trunkline led from the great mining sites—Zacatecas, later also Guanajuato, and some others at times—to Mexico City, then on through Puebla to Veracruz. Other things equal, any place lying on this trunkline would experience livelier economic activity and more intense change than a place off it. The silver mines were remote, embedded in the outlying regions, but Mexico City–Puebla–Veracruz constituted a metropolitan complex which in a number of ways stood apart from the rest.

The present volume omits this capital-to-port complex and concentrates on the generality of what in the book's title we call the provinces—regions all of them in some sense removed from the center. Even so, in a way the book is about Mexico City and Puebla, about their far-reaching impact and the limits of it, telling much about them that a direct study could not. We strongly hope that another book like this one, devoted to the metropolitan complex, will come into existence in due time, and that when it does, it will also in the same fashion shed light back on the provinces.[4]

A complex interplay went on at all times in which the capital, whether by its action or lack of action, affected the autonomy and self-containedness to which each province in and of itself tended. A seeming paradox was central to the relationship. Economic growth and the concomitant creation of a local European nucleus caused a province to become (in terms of the European-Mexican world) socially and economically self-contained and a relatively complete and integrated regional entity. The action of Mexico City in providing people, skills, and capital to those areas with export resources, and serving as the all-important market for those areas without them, promoted exactly the kind of growth and in-migration that would cause the province to mature. But this very intervention retarded at the same time it stimulated; the provinces were overwhelmed by investment funds they long could not generate themselves, goods and services they could not duplicate, and a flow of people in and out without regard to internal needs, so that local society, despite the impetus, was prevented from developing in some directions and left incomplete. The result was that in some things independence and maturity were best fostered by neglect. Two important basins near Mexico City, Morelos and Toluca, saw the rise of impressive European-style social-economic complexes, but never attained even the minimal autonomy of a local Spanish city council, and they remained weak in the professions and crafts, while a good portion of their wealthiest citizens were residents of Mexico City. Relatively neglected areas such as Guadalajara or Yucatan might long have less wealth and a less impressive European social web, but more of their prominent people stayed home, and they had their own Spanish municipalities, lawyers, artisans, bishops, institutions of government and education. Distance alone is very important here, of course. Distant Zacatecas had a quite autonomous and complete society despite Mexico City's strong interest and crushing commercial predominance. On the other hand, no amount of distance could insulate a region until it had in one fashion or another managed to attract some settlers and build up a minimal social-economic base; witness the long time period during which the greatest estate-owning family of Nuevo León and Coahuila were Mexico City aristocrats.

Each province, if its European base grew indefinitely, might theoretically tend to become a metropolitan center replacing Mexico City, at least within some part of the country; if the coefficients of size, wealth, and distance came together at the right level, serious movements in this direction could take shape, as in Puebla in the seventeenth century or Guadalajara as independence drew near. Usually, long-lasting compromises eventually imposed themselves: in Toluca, near-total dependence on the capital in political and professional matters, along with strong market orientation toward it, but a local Hispanic society quite stable and self-contained except for the allegiance of its very highest level to Mexico City; in Yucatan, a far more complete independence, even a separate outlet to the sea, but with still, it appears, a partial dependence on the shipping of Indian products to central Mexico. It is not yet the time to write a complete history of Mexican capital-province relationships; for that, more research *is* needed. The intention here is mainly to point to this never-ending dialectic as a major temporal and regional constant. A defined trend is so far not apparent. One region after another attained the rock-bottom independence of a reasonably stable local Hispanic society, regional integration, meaningful local markets, and some generation of investment capital; this much is clear, and important. The late eighteenth-century establishment of several "intendancies" in different parts of the country can be seen as recognition of their maturation as Hispanic subsocieties. But at other levels—high finance, mercantile networks, family alliances, migration trends, recruitment of officials, and operation of institutions—things went back and forth and were never settled. What Mexico City lost in one region in one decade it would gain the next in another region; again and again the capital city would return to dominance at a new and higher level. When new European demands and shipping capacities generated such fresh regional opportunities as the eighteenth-century cochineal boom, the agents of Mexico City could come crashing down on an isolated and somewhat archaic situation like that of Oaxaca, changing it drastically for a time. In the end, one is impressed with the concentrating, nucleating power of prosperity.

In using the word "province" we are more concerned with studying processes of evolution in nonmetropolitan situations than with defining a regional unit. The region, in other words, is for us primarily a means of emphasizing diversity and studying the pattern therein. Our authors treat entities of different orders of size and internal complexity. Although this is the result of chance, it is enlightening and appropriate because it tends to show an important fact: like the principles of the behavior of molecules or bodies in space, the principles of regional evolution apply at several levels, on a smaller and smaller or larger and larger scale, both sequentially and at the same time. Every unit from the huge quasi-continental viceroyalties to the tiniest submunicipality—anything with a nucleus and a periphery, or merely some degree of cohesiveness and interaction—constitutes a region, and acts like it. The small units replicate the larger ones, or so it seems in the New World situation, where the larger ones appear first and the smaller ones gradually fill in the empty spaces. And of course the Indian sector was richly articulated in regional terms. The Nahuatl-speaking world; the large ethnic groups inhabiting the Valley of Mexico, like the Tepaneca or the Acolhuaque; the individual city-states; their constituent subject towns—regional units like these persisted all over the South and Center and parts of the North. It is initially quite amazing in how many respects the city-state of indigenous central Mexico was built like the Iberian municipality-province. And again and again, in the Center-South and certain northern pockets, Spanish regions built upon Indian ones, in great detail. Yet Indian regionality was something apart, existing in itself regardless of whether the Europeans had yet given an area their attention; even in areas of most intense settlement and transformation, the Indian divisions never came to overlap entirely with Spanish ones. Thus the Spanish-Indian contrast gives Mexican regional organization a potentially strong second dimension (though the reality was nowhere near as sharply dichotomized as the potential). As to provinces of whatever size and type when seen as Spanish entities, our authors all tend to agree on the indivisibility of the whole unit, including both the more urban and the more rural parts of it, since these were socially and economically intertwined, the raison d'etre of the rural parts being to serve as a support system for the towns; the whole flourished or declined as one, and the same processes, procedures, and ambitions obtained in all parts of it.

Despite the notion of multilevel regionality, there is a certain uniformity in the "province" of which our authors write. It is a large building block, an area of a size and importance, as to population or resources, such that the Spaniards might have been expected to establish there at an early time a Spanish city, the headquarters of encomenderos and perhaps a bishop, drawing on a hinterland measured in scores or hundreds of miles. Because of local conditions, neither the city, the encomenderos, nor the bishop always eventuated, but this can serve to indicate the general order of size. Sometimes a pronounced physical feature like a basin (Oaxaca, Morelos, Toluca) or a peninsula (Yucatan) or in one case a major silver deposit (Zacatecas) gives the ultimate basis of the unit. One author is interested in two basins (Valleys of Mexico and Toluca), another in a large portion of one (Querētaro), and another in one of the several major subareas of one (Texcoco). The units dealt with are generally of the type that might be Mexican states today, as several in fact are.

Some General Themes

Our chapters, despite somewhat different emphases, cover much common ground, facilitating the differentiation of constants from variables and pointing to pattern where variation exists. Possible themes for discussion are many. One might begin with, indeed one might dedicate this volume to, the figure of the muleteer, who appears in chapter after chapter, clearly a constant in early Mexican history, his function to expedite interregional trade, his status and capital investment both marginal, and he himself finding a place on the margins of the Hispanic world, whether he was a mulatto of Yucatan, a Tolucan Indian taking supplies to the mines, or a Spaniard carrying sugar from Cuernavaca to Mexico City. The carter was a similar type.

Of the many conceivable topics, I will briefly treat a few, centering first on the role of certain ethnic groups and second on estate forms; this will give occasion to consider respectively the society and the economy in a provisional way.

The authors seem impressed with the internal heterogeneity of ethnic groupings and the fluid boundaries between them; indeed much of the thrust is to bypass ethnic groups as primary categories of analysis. Meanwhile, a good deal can be said to refine the categories and put them in perspective, a useful enterprise in view of the fact that the scholarly public still tends to think of Spanish American society in terms of ethnic divisions.

The Spanish sector.—The distinction which our authors find most real is that between an Indian world, dominated by preconquest continuities and tending to be more locally oriented, and a Spanish world, less obviously connected with preconquest phenomena and more interregional and international in orientation. This division is well known, and I do not wish to emphasize it unduly; indeed the chapters here tend to show Indian towns, villages, and barrios as internally varied, characterized by mobility and many kinds of contact with the outside. The main point is rather the converse, that the other, "Spanish" half of postconquest society *is* a unit in a great many ways. It is surely not monolithic, this conglomerate of all the occupations known to man, located both in cities and in the country, containing Spaniards native-born and new, mestizos, blacks, mulattoes, and even some town Indians and Indian nobles. Nevertheless, it is so intertwined, interdependent, with so many goals and techniques common to the whole, that any division within it must be considered partial and severely limited in significance, of an altogether lesser order than the distinctions and cleavages that exist between separate societies. Chroniclers and census-takers of the seventeenth and eighteenth centuries were perfectly justified in their frequent procedure of speaking in terms of only two groups, Indians and all the others; the others were often specified as Spaniards, mestizos, and mulattoes, but even this was only a kind of shorthand for a complex body with nearly endless subtle internal distinctions and fluidities.

Within the Spanish world the role of the "creole-peninsular" distinction is far from what earlier generations of scholars imagined. There is little apparent regional variation in this respect; the more important dimension is time. Both "creole" and "peninsular" are very late categories. *Criollo* long mainly referred to non-Europeans; though there are some examples of its use to denote native-born Spaniards as early as the seventeenth century, usually in restricted or derogatory senses, it was still not in common or official use even at the end of the colonial period. The "creoles" were generally described, by themselves and by others, simply as "Spaniards." The term "peninsular" does surface in censuses and other records in the latter eighteenth century.

Before that time, it is not always easy for the historian to find out which Spaniards were born in Spain, which in Mexico. From their aims and actions, there is no distinguishing them. In many situations, one searches for the newcomer among the humble outsiders making their beginnings on the edge of things. In other words, the newly arriving Spaniard was like immigrants to many other areas of the world, and the term "immigrant" is the one several of our authors prefer to use for him, as tending to put him in a proper light. Most of the immigrant lore familiar to us from United States history is directly applicable to him. Often he came to join relatives or people from his home town.[5] In region after region there appears the figure of the humble immigrant, starting at the bottom in whatever activity takes least capital, attempting to emulate, join, and marry into the group of locally prominent people; after the first generation or so, the latter are mainly locally born. Being new from Spain in itself carried little or no prestige in a society where from the beginning seniority had counted for so much, and the most noble and best established families were the oldest ones. From the time when a second Spanish generation came to maturity, native-born Spaniards in most regions made up the heart of the corps of owners of large estates and of the membership of the Spanish town councils; they quickly went into the professions, soon becoming a majority of the secular clergy, advancing also in the various religious orders, and in governmental positions to the extent of penetrating the Royal Audiencia itself.

The question of the stability of leading families, which, outside international commerce and at times mining, were usually on the surface "creole," does not lend itself to a simple answer. In the core area and in other parts of the country there were *some* families which passed large and valuable properties from heir to heir, maintaining the family name and high social position, from mid-sixteenth century or earlier to the end of the colonial period. It is clear, however, that from North to Center to South, estates changed hands frequently. Nevertheless, this is not quite the same thing as family instability. There was manipulation, consolidation, and retrenching as well as seizure and loss, and the unit which mattered to the people involved was a quite broadly conceived family clan, not any one individual or father-son line. Nor was the continual quick perdition of individual silver mining enterprises quite tantamount to the ruin and disappearance of mining families—though no one is inclined to doubt a quick turnover at the mining camps. With rural estates, there is also the phenomenon that after a certain point individual complexes—ranches, farms, haciendas—took on a life of their own and might be seized, sold, or incorporated into larger holdings without losing their social-economic continuity at all levels beneath ownership.

The other way to measure continuity is to use the evidence of family names, a reasonable but hazardous method because of naming patterns and constant intermarriage of new and old families. If doña Maravilla de Peñasgrandes y Castilla, third cousin of a third cousin of the main line of an old encomendero family, marries Pedro Pérez, new small merchant, and the Pérez family never makes any further such marriages, yet it will soon be calling itself Peñasgrandes y Castilla, in which case a new and marginal family will tend to look like an old established one, and continuity will appear to reign. More serious, though, is the opposite situation. Established families made alliances with new wealth; usually the match was between a daughter of the older family and a male of the new one. In cases like this, where the new name already meant something, it would be the one to be retained, and an entirely new family seems to arise, to be followed by yet others as the process is repeated every two or three generations. Only a view which concentrates exclusively on the male line can see this as sharp discontinuity.

What emerges in those studies here which touch on such things at all is that at almost any time most prominent Spanish Mexican families in a given area were a combination of new and old. On one side they would go back to the beginning, to conquerors and encomenderos, or the first miners of the region, or the first settlers; on the other side they would be quite new, and the renewal might be carried out frequently. This is as true of the aristocracy of the far North and the Zacatecas silver miners as it is of the plebeian ranchers and farmers of Tlaxcala and the noble encomendero families of Yucatan—the latter being the only sizable group studied thoroughly in these terms and over some time. One can emphasize either the continuity or the renewal; both are indispensable elements in the evolution of the society. Since the newcomers were outsiders seeking to assimilate and become part of the established group, and all the children of such alliances had relatives in it, grew up under mothers who were of it, and were in close touch with its mores, I myself feel that some emphasis may properly fall on the continuity so essential to the development and preservation of Mexican and Spanish American subcultures.

As to regional variation, the commonsense perception that stability is less where there is wealth and centrality, more where there is poverty and isolation, seems quite well borne out, though in an impressionistic way. Turnover is quickest on the trunkline, quickest of all at the silver mines. In Yucatan it is much slower. For Toluca, I take the situation to have had much familial permanence, to judge by the great stability of the first two or three generations and the persistence of the same family names, prominent and humble, over centuries. Oaxaca, which was long one of the most isolated and poorest of regions and then was opened up in a large way in the eighteenth century, offers a mixed picture, with great stability among a small group of old leading families and much flux for the rest.

At any rate, the role of newcomers from the outside is a vital element in the growth of Hispanic Mexican society, at the center and even more on the edges. Not all were immigrants; in Yucatan or other distant regions, the person from Mexico City was just as much an outsider and could play a similar role. But many in fact *were* new immigrants, flowing past a Mexico City that could not hold them and out into the provinces near and far. For most of the colonial period the immigrant—often humble, but not necessarily so—was a familiar figure participating in a conventional process integral to local society. Since he was so frequently the nephew of someone already in Mexico, he could have excellent connections, especially in the Mexican branch of the far-flung world of international commerce.

This type of relationship between local-born Spaniard and new immigrant held true for the bulk of the colonial period; indeed it never ceased to be the underlying situation. But there were some major additional developments toward the end of the period. Part of what happened can be seen as challenge and response. The natural course of Mexican society's growth led by about 1750-1770 to a commanding position for the upper elements of local Spanish society, mainly "creoles": as always, they dominated the economies of most of the regions, urban society, and the town councils, but by now also ecclesiastical, newly meaningful military, and governmental posts, except for the very highest, to the point that they were a strong majority on the basic organ of Spanish American government, the Royal Audiencia. If Mexico was to continue to be a colony, action was called for, and it began, just at the point when creole institutional majorities were becoming monopolies. If the Spanish government had the motivation to act, it also had new means to do so, provided by the Industrial Revolution: better ships, more goods and capital, an economic and demographic upsurge in the north and east of Spain. The crown reversed the creole majorities on the Audiencia; it sent several waves of new types of representatives (treasury officials, tobacco monopoly administrators, and so on) and, in the intendants, a viceroy for every province—all Spaniards born.[6] At the same time, large-scale commerce, the one sector that had always remained thoroughly immigrant-dominated, had been gaining ground over the entire colonial period—not because of any change in Spanish or Mexican attitudes, but because, with the direction the economy took, commerce loomed ever larger as a source of wealth. Since society was highly sensitive to wealth, the Mexican social position of large merchants constantly improved, until by the eighteenth century some of them were acquiring large landed properties and titles of nobility, and had no farther up to go.[7] In addition, the Industrial Revolution rendered a far broader range of Mexico's products exportable and profitable, with consequent activity of immigrant merchants in parts of the country where they had rarely been seen. By the latter eighteenth century, in other words, the picture familiar to us, of the resented, dominant, unintegrated "peninsular" had taken on a certain substance, though as a crisis phenomenon, and in certain areas of life only.[8]

With mestizos and mulattoes, let the reader brace himself for a dreary uniform preachment from the authors. One after another of us proclaims that the "mestizo vagabond" is not to be found in that particular region and time—perhaps later, perhaps somewhere else. Everyone is aware that many mestizos elude detection, while the mulattoes and blacks leap to the eye in the records. With regard to the latter, one is impressed with how strong an element they continued to be at least through the seventeenth century in almost any area that had the wealth to support it. Both groups, insofar as they can be located and characterized, are intermediaries, auxiliaries. An important insight and general truth for both is formulated by Super: their patterns of activity are Spanish, but their contacts are Indian. They are of the Spanish world, but they face the world of the Indians.

As far as mestizos are concerned, these words apply only to those more or less openly so labeled. Many people who were biologically mestizos, having formal recognition by Spanish parents or some kind of connections or wealth, were simply treated as Spaniards of varying degrees of marginality, like the poor or the newly arrived, and generalizations about "mestizos" do not apply to them in any real sense. Although it is not wrong to take the mestizo as the symbol of marginality, it does not follow that mestizos are to be found mainly in distant fringe areas. They were indeed often pushed outward, but they originated at the center, where the most Spaniards met the most Indians. The chapter in which mestizos play the largest role is the one on Texcoco, just outside Mexico City.

Demography.—At this point, having touched on Europeans and before saying a word on Indians, we may briefly survey the demographic aspect of the studies. One regional distinction stands out sharply, an essential difference in the trend of the thinly populated North and the originally populous South and Center. The South and Center lost vastly in overall numbers during the first two centuries of the colonial period, then recouped some of the loss on a different basis.[9] The North simply grew, though not necessarily steadily or in all parts. Moreover, the entire category or general demographic-structural description of much of the North changed. If we think of demography in somewhat functional terms and set up two categories, one containing areas with a population which is not dense enough to man cities, specialist production, and intensive agriculture, and the other containing areas with population sufficient for those purposes, then we find that the condition of the South and Center was in a sense stable, in that, except for coastal regions, they never fell out of the second category, while in the North there was a true revolution as one subregion after another passed into the second category and out of the first.

All the authors represented in this book believe in the importance of demography to the extent that it is one large and congruent part of an interacting social-cultural-technological-economic continuum. We all phrase generalizations in terms of larger or smaller, increasing or decreasing numbers of certain human elements. There is some difference of opinion as to the causative weight that is to be assigned to demographic movements. Some weigh them very heavily as a cause; some (like myself), while seeing the interaction, tend to see the demographic phenomena as the precipitation of other factors, from disease to technology to social-cultural conventions, and their further repercussions as side effects. Some would say that the primary reason for Spanish occupation of certain lands was their emptying through Indian population loss. I would say that the greatest Indian population loss and land-emptying commonly preceded definitive Spanish land occupation in a given area by a generation, and often much more, and that occupation of land came at the time when its direct exploitation became profitable.

Regional studies reveal that for many purposes relative proportions are more indicative than absolute numbers of people. Except in one very important aspect, namely as a market, the North tends to act like an area of many Spaniards, that is, "many" compared with the Indians there, though the absolute numbers were not impressive. The trend with the greatest overall explanatory potential is that of the changing proportion of Indians to others; it is much more simple and one-directional than the aggregate trend, resulting by the end of the colonial period in a picture in which the Indians were a minority of the population on a countrywide basis. Seen in this light, there was no Indian demographic resurgence, for when the Indians began to increase, the others increased even more.[10]

Further, specific studies of local societies teach us that secular trends in the size of human groups have explanatory value largely to the extent that cultural coefficients can be given to the numbers. From census data and general knowledge alone one can see, for example, that the general eighteenth-century decline in the employment of blacks and mulattoes in inland areas was related not to the now-increasing number of Indians per se, which was still not as great as it had been in the sixteenth century, but to the increased number of humble people with Hispanic skills and traits among both the mestizos and the Indians of that time—people who could carry out those functions well and at lower expense. Rarely, however, does one find trends for which whole ethnic groups can so nearly be treated as blocks as in this matter, and the same is true for the broad occupational groupings found in the late eighteenth-century series of censuses; the truly functional categories are not usually seen there.

Emphasis in early Mexican demography was long given, and properly so, to Indians and to the great decline in their numbers. Much that occurred correlated with that decline, it seemed, from the rise of the hacienda to bad economic conditions in parts of the seventeenth century. Detailed study of individual regions, however, often shows that a great many aspects of provincial and general Mexican life did not depend on numbers of Indians, as long as the situation did not change in respect to the two basic categories just mentioned. Whereas the Indian population went through drastic decline through the sixteenth and into the seventeenth centuries, followed by relative stability and eventual growth (from the reduced base), there are important aspects of Mexican colonial evolution that have a far more linear pattern, or at least one not correlating with Indian demographic trends: aspects as diverse as the profitability of certain crops and consequent Spanish involvement with them; the state of *obrajes* (textile shops) and artisan production; the relative amount of permanent and skilled labor compared with short-term unskilled labor; changes in the role of blacks (already alluded to); even changes taking place in the Nahuatl language. With these matters the relevant factor is not Indian decline, but rise in numbers of Spaniards, or more properly considered, in the whole Spanish sector including the ethnically mixed and Indians beyond a certain degree of Hispanization. The correlation of such trends with the demographic growth of the Spanish sector as measured by censuses is quite good, but the real explanation lies in the increase of numbers of people with certain cultural, social, and economic attributes. This can be seen most clearly in those aspects where only Indians are involved. For example, the Indians of the Valley of Mexico were becoming a more meaningful maize and cacao market at the very time (the late sixteenth century) when they were declining steeply, because more of them were participating in some way in the Mexico City silver economy. Or to take Spanish linguistic influence on Nahuatl, there was, after the first wave of introduction of cultural elements, a steady accretion of loan words until, in the mid-seventeenth century, a new and definitive stage was reached, involving morphological and syntactic influence of a type that can only be attributed to an increased body of Indians bilingual in Nahuatl and Spanish. Thus in the time around 1640–1660, which was surely no high point in the Indian demographic curve, the number of bilingual Nahuatl speakers passed a critical point, bringing on a set of basic adaptations in Nahuatl. These adaptations did not, by the way, change much after 1700.[11]

Another factor often strongly influencing general developments counter to the Indian demographic trend, in addition to the more or less linear progress of Hispanization, is the international economy. Whenever a commodity emerged that was salable in Europe at a clear profit, developmental trends would go in the face of demographic trends if necessary. In general, Spaniards of the sixteenth century avoided the empty dry plains areas of America. That the Mexican North was a partial exception is owing almost entirely to the commodity role of silver. The ups and downs of silver production (vastly different at different sites) relate to deposits, techniques, finances, and supply of mercury (mainly from Europe)—not to aggregate demographic trends. The fact that silver was so long dominant in the Mexican economy was a reflection of the then obtaining state of European technology and markets. Europe intervened again, and mightily, in the latter part of the eighteenth century, when it had developed new demands, new means of transport, and new productivity. Many of the effects of the European developments coincided with the rising internal Mexican demographic curve of the late colonial period in a straightforward way, but in some respects the distinction between the two thrusts becomes clear. Thus obraje production grew, matured, and throve as the number of poor people interested in European-style products grew over the first two postconquest centuries; yet that number was still growing, even faster, when in the late colonial period the obrajes fell on hard times because Europe could now produce and deliver comparable goods at competitive prices.

Naborías.—In the Caribbean islands, the first part of America occupied by Spaniards, there existed the indigenous social type of the *naboría,* a commoner who was the direct dependent of a noble and who therefore did not participate fully in the general community obligations and privileges. With their extreme need for auxiliaries, the Spaniards found the naborías most useful as their own personal dependents, and soon they were turning them into an Indian servant and employee class outside the encomienda and Indian community life; they continued to consider them "naborías," though it is doubtful that most originally were that. In Mexico the institution flourished, since not only did the larger-scale and more permanent Spanish presence render the need even greater, but the Indian societies of the Center and South already knew the type, probably in a more fully developed form than in the Caribbean. Still called "naborías" by the Spaniards at first, these Indians-among-Spaniards quickly became a fixture, one step below the blacks in every imaginable intermediary, domestic, or semiskilled position in Hispanic Mexican society. Working for one master led to working for several, and the naborías were the first Indian free wage workers. Many of the subtleties and apparent puzzles of Mexican history have to do with the generally constant strengthening of this Indian element in and around Spanish cities and estates (later in Indian towns and villages too) as a function of the growth of the Spanish sector and regardless of current trends in the Indian world more broadly speaking. The word "naboría" itself, alas, before long fell out of use—primarily, I think, because of the great variety of functions the group carried out. We see the term still in use in seventeenth-century Yucatan. It also appeared in the North as the first general term for the Indian mine-workers, but before long the latter were being called *barreteros* ("pick-men") and *tenateros* ("bag-men"). For a while there was the hybrid term *laborio*. There is something of the naboría in many terms that appear in the later colonial centuries: *gañán,* "hired man"; *criado,* "servant" or "employee"; in a different way *indio vago,* "errant Indian," that is, one not attached to an Indian town or district.[12] But the general type and its function transcended all of these, and indeed a very large part of the late-colonial mestizo population must have been descendants and relatives of naborías, as well as inheriting their role.

The naboría was often displaced from his home area, a short distance or a long one. In the earliest time, the patterns of conquest and settlement left many central Mexican auxiliaries in the South, in both Oaxaca and Yucatan, on the edges of Antequera and Mérida. The same was true in the North, and far more so. In the later years this displacement becomes harder to trace, but so often does one see town Indians who were born elsewhere, or Indian employees of Spaniards being taken with them to new residences, that it is clear that the trend continues to some extent.

Though the type was ubiquitous and the inherent function not greatly different from North to South, there was strong regional patterning in the distribution of naborías. The primary distinction is between the North on the one hand and the Center and South on the other. In the latter, society consisted of the Spanish sector, naborías, and Indians of pueblos; in the former, it consisted practically of the Spanish sector and naborías alone. The naborías of the North, nearly all from the Center or its buffer zones, were a far, far greater proportion of the entire social fabric than elsewhere. Being that, they long retained their own weight as a certain kind of Indian community; on the other hand, lacking the constantly renewed contact with Indian towns and corporations that existed in other parts of the country, in the long run they became much more fully and evenly Hispanized. As to the Center-South, it would be surprising if the naboría element were not much stronger near Mexico City and along the trunkline than to the south and the west, but this remains to be demonstrated in detail. Even at the end of the colonial period, the majority of those inhabitants of the entire Center-South region who were considered to be Indians at all had an affiliation with some Indian corporation.

The Indian world.—The internal life of the various types of Indian entities of Mexico is a nearly limitless topic, of strong interest to several disciplines; several of our authors are, apart from the present book, in some sense engaged primarily in the study of Mexican Indians. Moreover, as emphasized earlier, the Indian societies of Mesoamerica had created a culture area which in the preconquest period already had most of the dimensions that characterized it afterward. Nevertheless, during the time with which we are concerned, most of the connections holding the larger regions together, and the various regions to each other, were realized through some facet of the Hispanic sector, whether social, economic, or official. Since these large regions and their interconnections are the primary arena here, our attention in almost all cases has gone to the Spanish sector in an Indian context rather than vice versa. In the above pages, with their frequent discussion of the implications of the Indian factor for the local Hispanic subsocieties, most of what there is to say for the moment on the topic is covered.

Let me, however, emphasize a few points. The preconquest Indian societies of the Center and South dictated the constituent units of the area in the postconquest period as well. It is one thing to realize this in a general way, another to follow more closely how in one region after another not only the larger centers, but the secondary and later arising ones, as well as the smaller jurisdictions and parishes, all go back to structures already existing. Even new Spanish additions, from the town of Puebla to the sugar haciendas of Cuernavaca, were located in relation to some Indian entity. And all this was determined not by mere traces of something that had gone before, but by local Indian groups which maintained a great deal of corporate vigor and self-assertiveness to the end of the colonial period—a self-assertiveness directed at other Indian groups as much as at Spaniards. Such retention of vigor and consciousness characterized not only areas where there was less outside intrusion, but also towns within a few miles of Mexico City itself, despite all the kinds of loss, restriction, and engulfment that these towns had undergone. Many aspects of decline were real enough, but to the picture of decline must be added the element of stability and long-maintained integrity. Comprehended within the integrity was a substantial European cultural component that before long was as much a part of life as elements accepted in previous centuries from other Indian groups. Both from necessity and from self-interest, Indians in their corporate life made a series of creative, viable adaptations, preserving the old as much as possible, adjusting the new to it, in every branch of life from language through technology to politics.[13] We only begin to glimpse these adjustments, as well as an aspect of Indian community life in the late preconquest and early postconquest time which is even newer to us: the extent to which the Indian world was characterized by the activity and mobility of individuals as individuals. Much that we have taken to be Hispanization may be continuation and growth of preconquest trends.

Speaking much more specifically now, there is one pattern our authors find everywhere from Yucatan to Querétaro: the direct participation of local Indian nobles, *principales,* in whatever branch of the Spanish economy impinges on their area, whether obrajes in Tlaxcala, pig raising in Toluca, or petty commerce in Texcoco. The principales stay within the context of Indian community life, using their leverage there, employing Indian personnel except for an occasional manager out of the Spanish sector, but otherwise such economic activities are in the local Spanish style and act as part of the local Spanish economy. Given the state of research on the internal Indian world, this does not mean that the principales were the only Indians in Spanish-style commerce and production; indeed there are already several glimpses of commoners engaged in a smaller-scale activity that may have just as much overall cultural-social importance. At any rate, the enterprises of the principales catch the eye.

A secondary but still an important aspect of the imprint of the sedentary societies of the Center-South on postconquest Mexico is the way they were reflected in the North. It has already been said that the bulk of the Indians in the towns and camps of the North were originally migrants from the Center. This fact of itself meant considerable direct cultural influence at the lower levels of Northern society and economy, visible in such things as the many mining terms and Northern geographical names derived from Nahuatl words. In the North the regional subgroups from the Center congregated and reconstituted themselves as communities. But more than this, the whole Spanish-Indian combined effort in the North took the shape of a conscious or unconscious attempt to replicate the Center—Spanish towns within a cocoon of transplanted sedentary Indians to be hired like the naborías to the south and to be governed through the familiar machinery of the colonial Indian municipality as known in the Center-South. Of course the new context brought change, but there did arise in the North such facets of the South as the semiautonomous Indian town council keeping records in Nahuatl, or, as in Nuevo León, the familiar spectacle of a pueblo (of transplanted Indians) in conflict with a Spanish estate owner over land and water.

Estate forms.—Most forms of colonial Spanish American agrarian and industrial endeavor can usefully be considered under the rubric "estates." One may equally well call them simply "enterprises," though in fact most of the more industrial variants did branch out into agricultural support activity. This includes not only the sugar mills of Morelos, but also the Northern silver-mining businesses, which, as Bakewell shows, were built around a refining plant suggestively entitled *hacienda de minas,* and also commonly included an ancillary rural hacienda. Even the obrajes were sometimes part of a complex including sheep ranches. Among the more clearly rural enterprises were the encomienda estates of the sixteenth century (in central Mexico; later as well in Yucatan and some other areas); the smallish farms growing wheat or other products for town markets and often going by the name of *labor,* or later *rancho*; the livestock estancias of the middle years; the full-blown combined stock-raising and agricultural hacienda with a well-defined plant or *casco,* characteristic of the (latter) seventeenth and the eighteenth centuries in the Center, North, and parts of the South. The important thing is that all these organizational types shared important common traits of motivation and structure and varied systematically according to the same principles, within a single set framework.

The clearest constant, the thing they all shared and the factor which, in interaction with local conditions, most determined the shape of regional and temporal variants, was profit motivation and market orientation. The broader function of estates was to mediate between a Spanish town and its environment, whether that environment was a silver deposit or an Indian countryside, by growing, producing, or extracting anything region-specific that would produce a meaningful revenue for the town-dwelling owners. A stepped social hierarchy of decreasing wealth, status, urbanity, and Hispanization constituted the personnel of the estate and reached out into the country to achieve its ends. The priority of profits and markets does not preclude additional motives, from the desire for security to the prestige drive, nor does the wealth-producing function preclude the importance of supply, nor the vast cultural and ethnic transformation as the estate system took more and more of the population within itself, even though this was an unintended effect.

The profit-market nexus was there from the very beginning.[14] Encomienda estates were highly sensitive to it as far back as they can be traced.[15] On their heels came humble wheat farmers who sold their entire crop to Mexico City and Puebla. The sixteenth century was precisely the time of the greatest thrashing about, in all parts of Mexico, in search of products and techniques of production, hoping first for something salable in Europe; failing that, something salable in Mexico City; failing that, then something to sell locally (the preference being simply for larger and more powerful markets over smaller, weaker ones). If in the end some estates in some places appear to be selling very little to anyone, that is because they lack a product and a market; they are still market-oriented, having adjusted to the local market situation in the only way they could.

A corollary of the profit orientation is that investment varies with the expectation of profits. Investment never lagged too far behind proven opportunities to realize a substantial gain; on the other hand it never took place without the reasonable expectation of such gain. Therefore the absolute amount and type of investment is a major regional and temporal variable. High, and then even higher, in the silver mines, it was quite substantial in the Morelos sugar industry; in the run-of-the-mill agrarian activity in the orbit of Mexico City it was much less, though not insignificant, and it increased as markets and range of salable products increased; in remote areas with neither a large local market nor any external one, investment could be at a minimum. At the level of the individual, simple lack of capital could be the main determinant. Immigrants and other marginal individuals would go into small-scale agrarian activity or the shoestring operation of an obraje because they lacked connections and credit, not out of unwillingness to invest.

It is within this framework that one best understands the process of land acquisition. There was a movement to acquire (i.e., invest in) land for estates whenever, but only when, something profitable could be done with said land. All over the Center and South, as long as nearby wheat- and meat-consuming Spaniards were few and the Indian maize market not yet too lucrative, Spaniards were content to have only enough wheat-growing and stock-raising enterprises to meet the need and to acquire maize for resale mainly through tribute or purchase from the Indians who grew it. This continued to be the situation in much of the hinterland of Mexico City for the entire sixteenth century, and in more remote areas of the Center-South it was still the state of things as the colonial period ended. The apparent land-grabbing that took place in parts of the North will bear some discussion in this context. I do not believe that this activity violates the general principles of profit-motivated investment. First, the land being empty, the investment in its acquisition was practically nothing. Second, as Altman points out, since the land was so dry, remote, and plagued with other difficulties, operations could be truly profitable and stable only if they were on a vast scale and indeed on a near-monopoly basis. Precluding competitors made economic sense even if one was not oneself using all the land. That Nuevo León-Coahuila could support but one dominant, estate-owning, governorship-holding family is seen by the way the Marqueses de Aguayo, when they finally fell of accumulated weight, were succeeded by just one other equally dominant family.

The Spaniards brought with them from Europe principles of estate organization which characterize all forms of colonial Mexican enterprise at all time periods and in all regions. No change is observable in these principles, only adaptations to varying situations. The encomienda estates of the sixteenth century were as full an embodiment of them as the eighteenth-century conglomerates, except for the usual lack of the high-level general administrator, and even he was present in the early Cortés estate.[16] Some forms specific to America appear at the lower levels because, though the categories of permanent and temporary worker were already known, in the American context they were strongly influenced by the new categories of the naboría and the Indian townsman. The structure which tends to appear whenever an enterprise reaches a certain size, stability, and wealth is something like the following:

1. Ownership
   A. The owner, prominent in city society, allied to other important families, a little removed from the enterprise, not that he is necessarily an "absentee owner"; he directs things at the level of strategy rather than tactics, with the overall family welfare in mind.
   B. The owner's relatives, who may act partly as co-owners, partly as trusted administrators.
2. Management[17]
   A. The *administrador,* appearing where there is a conglomerate of separate enterprises, a high-level figure in charge of overall operations and sales.
   B. The majordomo, a more modest figure in charge of the day-to-day management of a single enterprise or of several which are close together and interrelated.
   C. Foremen and technicians, another step down the social scale. The labor bosses-tax collectors-stock supervisors of the early encomienda belong here, as well as the estancia and hacienda foremen with such titles as *capataz,* and people like those supervising the individual processes in an obraje, the sugarmaster in a sugar mill, and the *azoguero* or amalgamation expert at a silver-refining plant.
3. Permanent workers, often resident. As few or as many as are required for maintenance, tertiary supervision, and performing skilled tasks related to production and processing. This group was long nearly coterminous with the naborías, and it was the best paid and most Hispanized part of the labor force.
4. Temporary workers, for the most part from Indian towns in the general area, performing unskilled tasks, especially at times of peak work load. At first they came through encomienda obligation or ad hoc administrative orders, then through the longer-lasting draft rotary labor provisions or *repartimiento*; increasingly they were simply hired when needed on a day-to-day or week-to-week basis.

The reader will quickly see how and why such a structure varies. This crowded book is not the place to enter into detail, so I will merely give a few illustrations. None of the forms are really "early" or "late" in an absolute sense, but continue strong as long as conditions are right, like the encomienda estates of Yucatan. Much of the variation of forms is truncation, either enforced by conditions or desirable because of the special nature of the enterprise. A *labor,* or wheat farm, is an estate cut off at the majordomo level by its owner's lack of capital and connections. Socially the owner is at level 2B or 2C, and just like the people in those positions, he lives in the country, acting as his own majordomo. If successful enough, the *labrador* will extend his holdings, hire a majordomo, and move to the city. If he is unsuccessful, his property may become part of a larger estate, and he a majordomo in it. In general, the owner and management levels tended to collapse into each other in modest or beginning enterprises. The holders of the smaller early encomiendas were often both "owner" and majordomo, though they usually managed to live in town.

In a sheep-raising estancia of the seventeenth century, there might be owner, majordomo, foremen, and shepherds (level 3), but no temporary workers (level 4) at all, not because they could not be hired, but because they simply were not needed. Obrajes, so dependent on skills, also had little use for temporary laborers. On the other hand, the North was largely forced to do without level 4, in both mines and agrarian enterprises, because of the absence of a hinterland of Indian towns. In successful mining ventures, the separation of the owner from the enterprise often failed to appear. Instead, he would live at or close to his refinery and continue to act as a high-level administrator; in such a technical business, the special expertise of the owner was too important an element to sacrifice.

The ethnic makeup of estates varied with place and especially with time. Although it is true that blacks and mulattoes were to be found overwhelmingly at levels 2C and 3, static generalizations of this type cannot be expected to hold true generally. Rather the estate structure responded to position in Spanish society and level of Hispanization; the highest and most Hispanized at the top and the lowest and least Hispanized at the bottom. As Hispanic Mexican society grew and embraced a broader ethnic spectrum, level 2C, for example, broadened from the special province of newly arrived, humble Europeans to include more blacks and mulattoes, then mestizos, and eventually Hispanized Indians as well; but the relative social-cultural position of all of these people in their respective times and places was the same.

A key to comprehending the dynamics of Hispanic Mexican society is the changing proportion of permanent to temporary labor. The more industrialized an enterprise, that is, the more it has to process its product, the higher a proportion of skilled permanent workers it needs. This is an atemporal constant, as true in 1550 as in 1800. However, the proportion of permanent workers gradually, slowly, but generally rises. On the one hand, this expansion is a social, quasi-demographic phenomenon vital to the overall cultural evolution of the country; it is another side of what was discussed in previous pages as the growth of the naboría class. On the other hand it is a reflection of the growth of a larger Hispanic Mexican society and a stronger internal market, which made the relatively intensive production and processing of an increasing range of products profitable (external markets also have their relevance here, of course). Thus the rate of expansion of permanent labor specifies usefully the tempo of general development; everywhere in Mexico, except in the North for lack of alternatives, and in mines and obrajes because of their specific characteristics, enterprises still tended to have more temporary unskilled than permanent skilled workers. Study of the changing temporary-permanent proportion further points to areas of continuity stretching forward through the nineteenth century, during the entirety of which time the trend continued, accelerating in the second half.[18]

In sixteenth-century central Mexico the naboría stood out sharply against the temporary worker from the villages. Then as time went by, variations, gradations, and intermediary types arose, though in fact the root distinction between long-term and short-term, skilled and unskilled, never lost its importance. For example, in the North there grew up the type of the temporary permanent worker, that is, the person who was generically a naboría or permanent worker at level 3, without connection to an Indian corporation, quite skilled at, say, underground mine work, but going quickly from one job to the next according to employers' needs or his own desires, and relatively less skilled than the more permanent workers in the refineries. On the other hand, in the Mexico City orbit by the late colonial period, haciendas and Indian towns had lived side by side for so long and pressed so close upon each other that they were greatly intertwined. Some of the level 2 and 3 personnel of the estates had taken the villages as a base. Most intriguing, however, was the by then common type of the permanent temporary worker, essentially at level 4—a person who spoke Nahuatl and was a member of an Indian corporation where he in principle resided, but who did short-term work stints at haciendas for so much of the year that he approximated an all-year hacienda worker.

There are other specific trends of continuity and change to be found in the areas of estate mortgages, types and amounts of estate products, the profitability of estates, and their relative continuity. These movements are in constant interplay not only with purely economic factors, but also with the cultural, social, ethnic, and demographic variables I have touched on in preceding pages, plus many more matters I have not touched on. The whole constitutes a vast and rich fabric of meaning, with a few strong, bright-colored threads that articulate it, hold it together, and make it potentially easy to understand. Detailing the relationships, however, becomes a lengthy task, and further exposition here would lead us too far. Instead, I now refer the reader to the many related discussions, some of them formulated in quite general terms, which will be found in the individual chapters below.

NOTES

1. There are some former provinces, such as Uruguay or El Salvador, which have become independent nations through fortuitous circumstances.

2. West-central Michoacán, however, as a remote area of populous city-states has much in common with the South (see the introduction to Part II).

3. See Wayne S. Osborne, "Indian Land Retention in Colonial Metztitlan."

4. Persons doing work which might find a place in such a volume include Richard Boyer, Louisa Hoberman, John Kicza, and Alejandra Moreno Toscano.

5. See James Lockhart and Enrique Otte, eds., *Letters and People of the Spanish Indies, Sixteenth Century,* and D. A. Brading, *Miners and Merchants in Bourbon Mexico, 1763–1810.*

6. This entire set of developments occurred simultaneously in many, if not most, parts of the Spanish Indies. Much of the relevant bibliography is given in D. A. Brading, "Government and Elite in Late Colonial Mexico," p. 401. See also Paul B. Ganster, "A Social History of the Secular Clergy of Lima During the Middle Decades of the Eighteenth Century," and Leon G. Campbell, *The Military and Society in Colonial Peru, 1750–1820.*

7. This had often happened before in the Hispanic world: in Seville, for example, at least from the sixteenth century forward.

8. It begins to appear that there is a somewhat similar trend with church organizations, that is, that whereas ecclesiastical careers and endowments originally and long thereafter occurred within the framework of the overall strategy and self-interest of (mainly influential) secular families, at the end of the colonial period, with the growth of the number and size of endowments, their long extension through time, and the dying out of some family lines, institutionalization and consolidation of *capellanías* and the like became necessary, leading to a partial alienation of the secular patrons from the administration of funds, the more independent economic weight of church entities, and some tension over their economic role, which had surely not been the case for the period as a whole. For Peru, Ganster, "A Social History," documents in detail the standard family-dominated picture as late as the mid-eighteenth century.

9. Trends, methodological discussions, and bibliography are all in Sherburne F. Cook and Woodrow Borah, *Essays in Population History: Mexico and the Caribbean.*

10. This fact alone should be enough to keep us from imagining that increasing Spanish numbers were inverse to Indian numbers in any causative relation. For the rest, however, this simultaneous upswing in all aspects makes it very hard to demonstrate which variables are more relevant to any given change.

11. For an extended technical discussion of the nature and timing of the linguistic adaptations see Frances Karttunen and James Lockhart, *Nahuatl in the Middle Years: Language Contact Phenomena in Texts of the Colonial Period.*

12. The term *peón* is emphatically not one of these partial synonyms. Rather, to the end of the colonial period it denoted a worker paid by the day, on a temporary rather than a permanent basis.

13. I know of no place where the importance of this development is as fully expressed, nor the process so properly placed in the light of being the natural, positive human reaction that it is, as in Woodrow Borah's "Race and Class in Mexico."

14. The favorite illusion of the historian of Mexico has been that commercialism first appeared in the century and region he happens to be studying.

15. See José Miranda, *La función económica del encomendero en los orígenes del régimen colonial.*

16. For a fuller treatment of the relation between encomienda and hacienda as organizational types and social-economic components of the city-country complex, see my "Ençomienda and Hacienda: The Evolution of the Great Estate in the Spanish Indies."

17. When estates are profitable and large enough and great investment is required, the figure of the financier regularly appears and becomes increasingly involved, not quite belonging to the estate, but taking over some higher management functions and likely to enter at the owner level as well. The phenomenon is seen in the present book in the merchant-*aviadores* of the silver mines and the Mexico City agents of the sugar haciendas.

18. Friedrich Katz's fine article "Labor Conditions on Haciendas in Porfirian Mexico: Some Trends and Tendencies" can serve to illustrate. One point, minor and peripheral in that context, major and crucial in this one, deserves a word of discussion. On pp. 40–41 Katz seems to give the impression that permanent labor became the main type in the seventeenth century, and the predominance of temporary labor of the eighteenth century, as seen by Gibson and others, was a change back. On the contrary, I believe, and the studies here tend to confirm, that permanent labor was the minority in the seventeenth century as well, and that its proportional weight in the late colonial period was the greatest up to that date. Katz bases himself on Borah's *New Spain's Century of Depression,* written in 1951, before Gibson's *Aztecs* and before the entire wave of specific regional scholarship, at a time when Borah and Chevalier still tended to equate the hacienda with permanent labor, not thinking in terms of the internal articulation of the labor force. I doubt that Borah would maintain the position of 1951 in quite that form today.

Part I: The South

This section's chapters on Yucatan and Oaxaca treat, at somewhat different time periods, two of the main components of the Mexican South (actually Southeast). Here, Mexico City and the Center play a less prominent role than anywhere else in the country. Not that that role is negligible. The conquering expeditions of both Southern regions branched out from the Center; from there they brought Spaniards and central Mexican Indian auxiliaries who created the first nucleus of the respective Hispanic Mexican provinces. The South is non-Nahua Mexico, the home of cultures outshining the Aztecs in some ways, even if later subordinated to them in other ways. During the colonial period, these areas were to a large extent off the main track of export-import wealth, but they retained a great deal of their own proud preconquest culture and supported a local Hispanic complex of considerable dimensions.

It was something of a surprise to several of us involved in the preparation of this volume to discover that for a long time the rate of development was quicker in Yucatan than in Oaxaca. That Oaxaca is nearer to the Center turns out to be of little importance compared with Yucatan's location on the principal sea route, putting it in steady contact with the outside and facilitating trade with both the Center and the Caribbean. Also, Yucatan had lowland tropical products which found a better market among the people of central Mexico (especially among the Indians, who had long been accustomed to this trade) than did the products of the temperate Valley of Oaxaca. Oaxaca's turn came when the incipient Industrial Revolution made textile dyes increasingly valuable and exportable, and Oaxaca (or actually, for the most part, its farther outlying dependencies) proved especially propitious for cochineal, bringing on many changes in the region in the course of the eighteenth century.

The third major part of the South was Guatemala, which then included Chiapas and indeed for a short time threatened to include Yucatan as well. Although it had its own high court with the chief judge as governor, it came within the governmental sphere of Mexico City and New Spain to some extent. Its indigenous peoples had elaborate sedentary societies like those of other Southern regions, and many spoke languages related to Yucatecan Maya. To get a conception of the many things the region had in common with Oaxaca and Yucatan, the reader may wish to consult Murdo MacLeod's large book on Guatemala in the sixteenth and seventeenth centuries.[1] As in the rest of the South, Spaniards in early Guatemala searched for an export product and, finding none, looked to Mexico City as a market. Parts of Guatemala, like Yucatan, had indigenous tropical products potentially salable to the Indians of temperate central Mexico. In fact, the high-grade cacao of the western coast of Guatemala was a product with a greater reputation and higher specific value than Yucatan's cotton textiles. As the central Mexican silver economy grew, and especially as the Indians of that area began to participate in it more in the latter sixteenth century, a cacao boom came to Guatemala; the market was strengthened even more by the growing consumption of the product by Mexican Spaniards. As with Yucatecan cotton, production of cacao was in the hands of Indians, and local Spaniards acquired it for resale through encomienda tribute obligation, other local administrative pressures, and petty trade (Oaxaca's much later cochineal business was similar). By the early seventeenth century the boom was over, not from lack of a market but from inability to produce, for reasons too complex and little understood to go into here. After that, Guatemala settled into relative isolation and poverty; its remoteness and inaccessibility hurt its competitive position in the tropical export business that was gradually taking shape in the Caribbean, and then too, much of its populated area was temperate highland like the Valley of Oaxaca. Even so, indigo production was quite successful for a time. Santiago de Guatemala dominated its area as Antequera and Mérida did theirs; with its university, institutions of government, encomenderos, and governors intermarrying with them, it appears to resemble Mérida more than Antequera.

Both our chapters are broad-gauged treatments of large regions in a multitude of aspects. A study of the trajectory of a single one of the South's Indian city-states, with considerable attention to the internal functioning of institutions, is Borah and Cook's article on the Mixtec town of Santiago Tejupan.[2] Much of what is seen there has extremely close parallels in Indian towns of the Center.

J. L.

NOTES

1. Murdo J. MacLeod, *Spanish Central America: A Socioeconomic History, 1520–1720*. Devoted in large part to macroeconomic, macrodemographic and

administrative history, the work contains relatively little of the more specific entity-and-pattern oriented social and economic investigation so prominent in the present volume, making comparisons difficult. The cacao merchants of Guatemala were probably close cousins to the *tratantes* of Yucatan; but the entire internal organization of cacao production and marketing remains to be studied.

2. Woodrow Borah and Sherburne F. Cook, "A Case History of the Transition from Precolonial to the Colonial Period in Mexico: Santiago Tejupan." See also Cook and Borah, *The Population of the Mixteca Alta 1520–1960.*

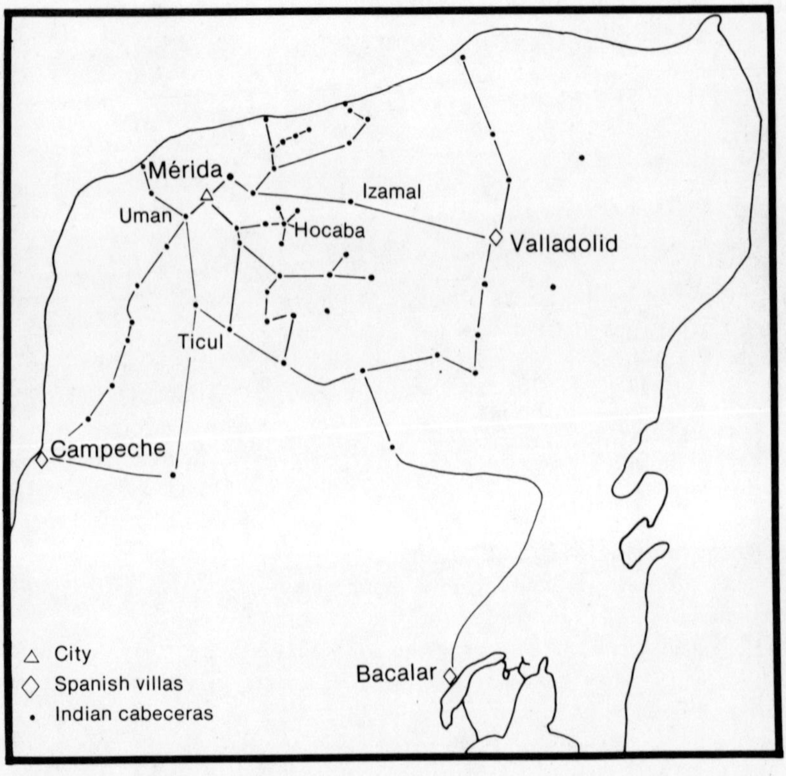

Yucatan: Spanish City and Villas and Principal Indian Cabeceras, with Communication Routes—Seventeenth Century

1. The Processes of the Development of Yucatan, 1600–1700

Marta Espejo-Ponce Hunt

The lowland peninsula of Yucatan, situated south and east of central Mexico, was not an area likely to attract quick, massive Spanish settlement.[1] Its soils were dry and shallow, it lacked mineral deposits, and it was far removed from New Spain's capital. On the other hand, Yucatan did have certain advantages. Lying directly in the path of ships between Veracruz and Havana, it was far more accessible than neighboring Oaxaca and Chiapas. The area's numerous and highly sophisticated Indian population, the Maya, were a major asset. Though in a state of decline and political disarray when the Spaniards arrived, the Maya had products and a tribute system that would make the implantation of a Spanish settlement possible and profitable.

Between 1542 and 1547, after the conquest of the core area of Mexico but early for a secondary region, a small group of Spaniards occupied the most important Indian centers of Yucatan and went about the creation of a Spanish city and two small *villas* (towns). Within a few years an institutional framework had been established, and the newcomers were engaged in all types of activities that would permit them to live as Spaniards. They had also begun to expand outwards, simultaneously drawing from the countryside in terms of human and economic resources.

The object of this chapter is to examine the processes of growth and development of Yucatan as a Spanish province after the initial phase, mainly in the early period, about 1600–1700.

Society, Economy, and Government

For a relatively poor region, Yucatan had a wide repertory of Spanish social and economic types, the same ones now familiar from other parts of

Spanish America. The inability of settlers to draw on the distant centers of New Spain favored the existence of fairly numerous artisans and the relatively wide representation of trades. Similarly, Yucatan achieved early independence in matters of education with the establishment of schools, a seminary, and a university, and did not rely on Mexico City for its priests and lawyers.

The Encomenderos

The encomenderos were at the top of provincial society, a dominant element originating at the time of the conquest and persisting almost through the entire colonial period. Among this group the major resource of the region, the Indians' tribute, was divided. The institution of the encomienda not only governed relations between Spaniards and Indians, but among the Spaniards themselves. All Spaniards were either encomenderos, their dependents, or their employees. The only others were bureaucrats and merchants, and they too in some sense served the encomenderos' needs.

During the heyday of the encomienda, 1542–1630, the encomenderos retained first claim to the Indians' surplus. Almost the total population at conquest, they had come to represent only 18 to 20 percent of the Spanish heads-of-household in 1630; but they were only three or four generations removed from the original conquistadors and still able to support directly their numerous kin. During this period, the representatives of the encomenderos were usually the only Spaniards or Spanish auxiliaries in the pueblos, collecting the *mantas* (cotton cloth), chickens, and maize that made up the tribute items. The remaining sectors of society received their share of the wealth by fulfilling whatever function was theirs in serving the encomenderos.

The first half of the main period of the encomienda, 1542–1580, was a time of great activity, as encomendero-entrepreneurs tried desperately to find an export or cash crop to trade for Spanish goods. But after 1580 the realization set in that Yucatan had only the tribute items plus some salt from along the coasts and the dyewoods and hardwoods of the southern interior. It was precious little, but a market began to develop for these basic supplies, eventually to encompass Veracruz, Havana, Puerto Rico, Cartagena, and other points in the Caribbean, aside from the old Indian trade between Tabasco and Yucatan in salt and cacao beans. The encomenderos settled down to living within their means, selling to the long-distance merchants whatever Indian surplus remained at their disposal after they had taken care of their own needs.

The following period of 1630–1688 was roughly comparable to that of 1580–1620 in central New Spain. It was a time of change and of a rapidly growing urban population. The 70 encomenderos in the city became a small minority among an estimated 400 heads-of-family by 1639 (perhaps half that many more by 1688), and there were too many worthy descendants of conquistadors for the encomienda vacancies. The authorities solved the problem by granting pensions on existing encomiendas, undercutting the encomenderos. At the same time, there were new taxes imposed on the encomienda, some of them related to Caribbean defense. To make matters worse, a series of famines and epidemics affected the Indian population and resulted in the diminution of the tribute, particularly in the period between 1648 and 1660. The income from a good-sized encomienda dropped to half what it had been.

Total dependence on the encomienda was no longer desirable if the encomenderos were to maintain their position as leaders of society. The increased demand for food and goods caused by the growth of the population of Mérida represented a substantial opportunity for them. The conquistadors had had the first livestock enterprises, located on the outskirts of the urban nuclei, particularly Mérida. The encomenderos, their heirs, were now able to expand these estates to supply meat, hides, and beasts of burden to the city and villas. Moreover, trade was stimulated by the rise in the Hispanic population. As interior and exterior trade began to flourish, the encomenderos were in a unique position to participate, because of their close connection with long-distance merchants who had heretofore supplied them and purchased grain and mantas from them, and because of their traditional control of the countryside.

During the final period of the encomienda in the seventeenth century, the years 1688 to 1720, income was further eroded by the imposition of a 2-peso tax for military purposes, and vacant encomiendas were kept in the royal treasury for long periods of time. Also, the process of granting pensions on encomienda income had advanced yet further.

There are many well-documented figures of the late seventeenth century who were nominally encomenderos but received most of their income from commercial activities or a livestock estate. In Campeche, the major outlet for goods from Yucatan and the principal importing center, there are innumerable examples of daughters of encomenderos marrying merchants, while their children became merchants or merchant-encomenderos. If the latter, they were encomenderos mostly in name; their trading activities were paramount.

In the late seventeenth century and the beginning of the eighteenth the encomienda thus ceased to be the main system of the Spanish economy of Yucatan, although the encomenderos continued to be the nominal leaders of society. The Hispanic population had grown to such a point that it was no longer possible for it to depend on an inelastic Indian tribute. Internal and external trade and the landed estate superseded tribute as the sources of wealth for the settlers.

Churchmen

In the seventeenth century the church in Yucatan became largely an extension of the dominant social group. Rural parishes were an integral part of the encomienda from the start, but during the period in question the church became one more vehicle by which the encomenderos branched out into other endeavors as the net proceeds from the Indian tribute diminished. From the first, a priest operating in a village received a percentage of the tribute and a direct stipend from the Indians in cotton cloth. Thus the priests were second encomenderos in a village. After 1600 the two groups were virtually one and the same, since the priests were invariably the sons, brothers, or nephews of the encomenderos. The first son inherited the encomienda and the second son inherited the means to become a priest (the family *capellanía* or clerical endowment).

During the peak period of the encomienda the amount collected by the priests may not have been more than a third of encomenderos' official revenue. As time went by, however, the ratio in favor of the priests was to increase. After 1688, many a benefice was twice as valuable as an encomienda in terms of cotton cloth received. Although the encomenderos were plagued by the problems of increased taxation and partitioning of encomiendas, church benefices remained essentially untouched, though there was some sharing of income where deputies were hired.

Related to the higher relative worth of the benefices as time went by was a struggle between the Franciscan order (which first controlled the country parishes) and the rising diocesan clergy, the offshoot of a growing creole population.[2] The rivalry was expressed in the systematic containment of the friars to a narrower and narrower circle of influence in the countryside, while the secular priests took over all the benefices left vacant in the enforced retreat. Between 1600 and 1750, the Franciscans were deprived of the most important parishes in Yucatan.

The economic base of the clergy.—The rivalry between the regular clergy and the seculars had economic roots. It was impossible for local society to benefit from a Franciscan benefice, because all monies collected were deposited in a common Franciscan fund. On the other hand, the diocesan posts essentially represented one more employment opportunity for the creoles. Except for the vows of chastity and obedience, the secular clergymen were members of the local community and hardly distinguishable in their actions from others. What enriched them—their benefices—enriched their famiiies, for they could accumulate and bequeath wealth without restriction.

A further problem had to do with the capital expended in the education and ordination of a priest, as well as his *congrua* or assured source of income. In the case of the Franciscans, the money was an outright donation and the capital was lost to the family. In contrast, the diocesan priest was educated and later supported by the capital provided by his family in the form of a capellanía or private clerical endowment under family control. He would later usually hold a job for which he was further remunerated as an individual, be it a benefice, an assistantship, or a post in one of the diocesan churches in the Spanish city or villas.

The device of the capellanía was crucial to the rise of a local clergy, and it was the main economic link between provincial society as a whole and the diocesan church; its absence in any of the regular orders assured a certain detachment of society towards them, in spite of the fact that many of the priests or friars were sons of locally prominent families, or relatives from New Spain or the mother country.

The capellanía.—The capellanía was capital put at interest by an individual or family in perpetuity for the purpose of supporting a succession of priests. The priest received only the interest, and the family, in the person of the patron, retained control of the capital; the priest's duty was to recite a certain number of masses for specified souls. In this manner the capellanía served a family's religious welfare and prestige and maintained generations of its members as secular priests, while the family continued to use the capital for its own economic purposes.

Capellanía monies were used to finance the acquisition of real property, to add improvements to an existing investment, and at times even as venture capital. In the last third of the seventeenth century almost every house in the city of Mérida and villas of Campeche and Valladolid was mortgaged with funds procured from capellanías. In fact, the majority of houses were mortgaged up to their full purchase price at any given time.

When the Spanish population of Yucatan began to expand in earnest after 1650–1660, clerical endowments financed the expansion of the original cattle estates around the city and villas, and later the exodus into the countryside for the purpose of establishing new ones. The capellanía monies, the accumulated wealth of the creole population, were responsible for the growth of many estates from a negligible money value to many thousands of pesos. This factor cannot be overemphasized, for it has particular bearing on the expansion of the Spanish population outwards into the Indian areas. The middling people being squeezed out of the city in search of a living after midcentury were often creoles, poor relatives of encomenderos. In many instances, these people had a claim on capellanía funds through some patron relative. Persons of the next degree of marginality, however—blacks, mestizos, or poor immigrants—could not hope to tap capellanías for their purposes, and their enterprises were always to remain small through lack of capital.

Some venture capital for the financing of trade activities came from capellanía monies. Although this was not the usual way of employing these funds, yet in one way or another their availability made it possible for many an encomendero in tight financial straits to become an active merchant.

Contrary to common belief, then, the capellanías were not a way in which a pious and superstitious population transferred control of its worldly goods to the church. In Yucatan, the evidence is that these clerical endowments were not part of the wealth of an institution but the accumulated capital of the creole population, established in times of surplus wealth in any one family, available to the Spanish population of Yucatan, but especially to those families of encomendero background who had had the means to institute the endowments in the first place.

All religious bodies in Yucatan—the orders, the various *cofradías* or religious brotherhoods, the cathedral chapter, the bishop—placed capital at interest. The amount from this source, especially from the Jesuits, may conceivably have totaled as much all together as the capellanías. But whatever the amount, other church entities limited themselves to loaning money on the same basis as the patron of the capellanías discussed above. Neither the individual priests nor the lending institutions seem to have had any control over the properties from which they derived income.

Altogether, the evidence is that the church as an institution did not have a very strong grip on the economy of Yucatan. Such a situation is reminiscent of some other peripheral areas in Hispanic America, though it may also reflect a more general state of things.

Merchants and Traders

There was active commerce in Yucatan from the earliest times, along with the encomienda. One was the vehicle of the other; merchants and traders distributed incoming merchandise to the city and villas, and eventually to the countryside as well. The reverse was also true, as goods from the villages and country estates moved to the city or were shipped out via Campeche and other minor ports. The prosperity of the commercial group was keyed to the growth and development of Yucatan's Spanish society. It became more complex in its makeup and much more numerous and well-to-do as a result of increased opportunities after 1650.

Merchants.—Only one class of people was called "mercader," and this was the long-distance merchant. The group began to become a recognizable social force first in Campeche, then in Mérida and Valladolid as well. From a respected few in the late sixteenth century, servicing mainly the limited group of encomenderos, the role and numbers of merchants grew until, after 1650, they became a new element destined to parallel their clients, first in terms of economic influence and eventually in social prestige and strength in the local councils.

The items exported were whatever Yucatan had to offer, mainly the tribute items plus dyewoods and hardwoods. After 1650, some products from the cattle estates were added. In return, the merchants imported luxury items and a few necessities from the mother country and New Spain.

The growth of the port of Campeche, where nearly all trade with the exterior was transacted, is testimony to the increasing importance of the commercial group. Maps of the seventeenth century show Campeche's development from a hamlet in the early years to a fortified town in the 1660s. The port had contained a mere 40 to 50 Spanish men in the sixteenth century, and by the 1660s there were more than 300 men with their families. In the 1680s one of the notaries of Campeche had to pay 2,200 pesos for his office, whereas such a post sold for a mere 250 to 300 pesos in Mérida.[3]

As to the wealth of individual merchants, our documentation is from Mérida, where merchant activities took second place to those of the encomenderos, and when a merchant moved to Mérida it was often because he was in the process of becoming something else. Nevertheless, some of Mérida's largest dowries were those of merchant families. Other individuals lived in expensive houses, and some of their capellanías, larger and more numerous in the seventeenth century compared with the declining number and size of those of the encomenderos, were impressive.

Individuals involved in long-distance trade were usually immigrants from the mother country or other places in Europe and arrived as factors of a trading company based outside Yucatan. Some came on their own, but these were more apt to be creoles from New Spain or the Spanish Main. In addition, as the encomenderos faced diminishing returns, some of them, as well as other elements of local society, also entered into activities that involved long-distance operations and set up their own factors in such places as Campeche, Veracruz, Tabasco, and points in the Caribbean. The close connection between merchants and encomenderos was thus reinforced, resulting eventually in merger along the edges of the two elements (especially susceptible to entering local society were merchants who had come as individuals to Yucatan and had little prospect of becoming representatives of a firm in an important port or city). It was in Campeche where the line first began to blur; here encomenderos engaged in trade came in contact with merchants on the rise.

The merger of the two groups was the logical development of a convergence of interests; it was also a key element in the acquisition of honors and recognition commensurate with the merchants' growing importance in the Yucatan economy. The first honor available to them was military title, so that almost every merchant had "captain" or "ensign" before his name. Any bureaucratic post was also welcome, and these were forthcoming through commercial connections with powerful encomenderos and administrators. A merchant on his way up would then marry a descendant of conquistadors, as close to encomendero status as possible (though, in practice, almost always along the fringes of the group). The next step was usually a move to Mérida, where the successful merchant involved himself in the affairs of the city and eventually purchased a seat on the cabildo. The hope was that public exposure and relations with the governor in time would bring him the coveted title of encomendero, always granted through the merits of the creole wife. The process did not always go all the way in the first generation; the children of the merchant might complete the transition from merchant to encomendero. A tell-tale sign of social advancement from father to son was the use of the "don." Invariably the father had a military title only; the son, an encomendero, was called "don."

After the third decade of the seventeenth century, almost half the alcaldes of Mérida were immigrants of merchant background. By the close of the century, they had gone beyond the position of alcalde to the council proper, and half the body of councilmen were first-generation Spaniards, merchants by origin.[4] In the core areas, these offices were often reserved for the most powerful members of society. In Yucatan, however, the encomenderos of conquistador background (and later the estate owners) were not necessarily in the majority on the cabildo but, as in many peripheral and near-peripheral areas in Hispanic America, they appear to have run things without the need of a formal structure. The cabildo almost invariably reflected their views, since the merchants or other immigrants on it were not advancing their own group but merely attempting to achieve the prestige that went with encomendero status. It should thus be noted that membership in the cabildo in an area removed from the centers of power is not necessarily drawn directly from the dominant social and economic elite. Rather the composition of a cabildo must be viewed along with its actions, which always point in the right direction.

Retail tradesmen.—Retailers were known as *comerciantes* or *del comercio.* They were a different group from the merchants, and their social inferiors. Ethnically many were immigrants, although there was a heavier admixture of creoles than among the merchants, and there were probably some creole-mestizos in business. Most retailers seemed to start with very little capital—usually money saved from their dealings with the Indians in the countryside. Some also appear to have started as craftsmen. Still others were descendants of conquistadors who were quite far removed from an encomienda and inherited the money or means to establish a retail outlet.

Most of these individuals were ambitious, hard-working, and stable, part of a growing social and economic middle group, sometimes marrying poor relatives of the encomendero class. For the most part they owned their own stores, although some retail outlets were the property of long-distance merchants (particularly those selling clothing) and were manned by hired personnel.

Retail tradesmen occupied a position intermediary between the merchant and the individual who dealt in the pueblos, the *tratante.* The merchant dealt with the encomendero directly in buying the products of the encomienda and in selling him imported silver, cloth, wine, chinaware, and so on. What was left over was purchased by the retailer, who then supplied both the retail trade in the city and the tratante. The latter went into the countryside with Spanish goods that he bartered or sold in exchange for mantas, corn, and cotton, and brought these back to the comerciante. Each tradesman had his own sphere of influence and activity, although the edges were blurred at times, and successful tratantes regularly became retailers.

Tratantes.—The tratante or Indian trader had his own niche socially and especially ethnically. The proportion of creoles, creole-mestizos, mestizos, and Indians increased here, while that of the Europeans decreased. There were also many blacks and mulattoes in the business, since they were the first in the pueblos as assistants to encomenderos, priests, and bureaucrats, and eventually struck out on their own. The wealth generated by these individuals varied. Those who worked for others, such as the black slaves and mulattoes, probably made very little for themselves. Yet there is evidence that they were able to save something; they were able to collect their own purchase price or accumulate enough to buy a piece of land on which to keep bees, chickens, and pigs. Semi-independent mestizos and creoles in this kind of work sometimes managed to amass capital worth several hundred or a thousand pesos.

The importance of the trader or tratante is that he provided a link between the city and the countryside in his person and function. Not only was the tratante the bearer of goods from the Spanish sector into the Indian, but his constant consorting with Indians generated closer personal ties. Marriage to an Indian woman was common if the tratante was mestizo or mulatto; concubinage was more likely if the tratante was creole or creole-mestizo (since these individuals usually returned to live in the city and considered their activities in the countryside of a temporary nature). The activities of the traders, whatever their background, were among the first real observable bonds of a social and biological nature between the city and the Indian world, for the mestizos or *pardos* (mixed persons of African descent) who were born of these unions stayed in the countryside and were usually mestizos in the fullest sense, that is, individuals able to function in both worlds, that of the father and of the mother.

Blacks, Mestizos, and Indians

Up to now most of the people described have been *españoles,* either from Spain or Spanish-born in the province. The humbler elements of society, the "castes," were the bulk of the population. We have already seen mixed bloods and blacks in the more humble Spanish pursuits of artisan, retail tradesman, and tratante, spheres where Indians too had begun to appear.

Blacks.—The role played by blacks, present since the conquest, is a familiar one. They were invariably skilled individuals, in responsible positions in some particular endeavor, or, at the very least, domestic servants for wealthy encomenderos (though considering the availability of Indians this was not typical).

By the seventeenth century, most persons of African ancestry in Yucatan were pardos or mulattoes. That is, they were individuals of mixed black and Indian blood. Mixtures of white and black were rare and were called "mulato blanco." The majority were *criollos* (creoles) born in Yucatan or the Caribbean. By that time also, a large proportion seem to have been freemen, the results of practices of manumission and self-purchase common to all of Spanish America. Free blacks and mulattoes are mentioned much more often in the documents of the time than are slaves.

Just how many blacks or mulattoes were present in Yucatan at any one time is very difficult to tell. One is struck in the records by the fact that the overwhelming majority of artisans in the city seem to be of African ancestry, and that out in the pueblos and estancias pardos were always in larger numbers than Spaniards. By the time of the first full census of the province in the late eighteenth century, the number of blacks and mulattoes matches the number of whites in the city of Mérida almost one to one.[5] At what point this state was reached we do not know.

Though blacks and mulattoes continued to be the majority of artisans in the city of Mérida throughout the seventeenth century, contemporary documents show that by 1680–1690 they had competition from the Indians, who seemed to constitute a good third of the artisan corps. In fact, it was very often the case that Indian children were apprenticed to mulatto artisans; in this manner a large enough succession of Indians had been trained to begin supplanting the blacks in skilled pursuits. Another area where blacks and pardos were indispensable was in the countryside, collecting tributes and manning livestock estates at the middle management level, although there too they were being slowly supplanted by creole-mestizos, mestizos, and Hispanized Indians. Yet the partial census of 1688 shows blacks and mulattoes as still constituting the majority of the outsiders in the Indian pueblos.[6]

This was the traditional Spanish American role of the person of African descent, that of an intermediary between the Spaniard and the Indian. The blacks were supervisors and instructors of the Indians, carriers of Spanish material culture into the countryside, among the first to move into the pueblos on a permanent basis and mix their blood with that of the indigenous people. They were, in a word, the avant-garde of the Spaniards ethnically, socially, and culturally.

Mestizos.—Few people are designated as mestizos in the records of the cathedral of Mérida in the sixteenth and seventeenth centuries, although a large racially mixed segment of society was in the process of formation. The rate of miscegenation stepped up, if anything, after the first few decades of the seventeenth century. Yet the incidence of the word "mestizo," though it increases, is still minimal in the late seventeenth century. Apparently children born in a Spanish household, though racially mixed and illegitimate, were brought up as Spaniards and functioned as such. They were really creole-mestizos, that is, persons of mixed descent called Spaniards because they were that culturally. On the other hand, the mixed children of Indian mothers who belonged to a village were brought up as Indians. There was no shiftless population of half-castes running loose about the country in seventeenth-century Yucatan.

The true mestizos, however, did exist. These were people in the middle who would grow up in the city or in a subprovincial town, straddling the two worlds culturally and biologically; they might or might not bear the label. One of them, son of an Indian woman of noble birth and founder of one of the first larger estancias of cattle and horses outside of the immediate area around Mérida, was so much a part of both sectors that Indian village elders (and he himself) were prepared to consider him an Indian, whereas a priest entering him in the census of 1688 called him a Spaniard.

True mestizos of this kind were entering fields of endeavor which had been the preserve of the blacks and pardos for generations. In the late seventeenth century, mestizos are found increasingly in the trades, running estancias for their encomendero relatives, collecting tributes, managing encomiendas, and also as tratantes, petty officials, and interpreters. Though mestizos were in constant touch with the Indians of the countryside, they were part of the Spanish world. If the blacks may be considered the spearhead of the movement of Spaniards into the countryside, the mestizos were the result of increasing contact between the two sectors.

Indians. —Indians in seventeenth-century Yucatan were either villagers subject to a pueblo corporation in the countryside or individuals not so attached, for the most part *naboríos* (Indians working for Spaniards). The latter ran the gamut from those who for one reason or another had recently left their village to work in the city, Spanish villa, or subprovincial town, to *ladinos en lengua castellana,* Indians who spoke Spanish and who could be very well versed in Spanish ways.

Contact between urbanized Indians and Spaniards took a variety of forms. Some town Indians were skilled artisans on a par with the blacks and pardos; many were domestics; a fair portion provided the permanent labor in stock-raising operations, were stable boys, orchard workers, or just plain help around house and estate; still others helped to transport goods between the residences of Spaniards and their other holdings, and had become independent muleteers on a small scale. A select group were the nobles or *principales* who by the seventeenth century had been in contact with Spaniards in the city long enough to function on almost the same basis as persons of European background. There were gradations of Hispanization among this group, of course, but in the latter seventeenth century there was at least one person called a merchant (and taken as such by his peers) who was an Indian; two noblemen who owned an important cattle estate; two Indians with a high military title who served as governors of their pueblos and afterwards returned to the city to live; and one Indian woman from a pueblo near Mérida who had extensive holdings in the city.

Altogether, in 1688, the number of Indians in Mérida and vicinity was an estimated 8,000 to 10,000, and the figures had more than doubled 100 years later. Nevertheless, throughout the colonial period (as even now) a vast majority of the Indian population of Yucatan were people living inside rural village corporations.

These Indians, an average of 200,000 under the encomienda for most of the seventeenth century, were relatively protected from the immediate intense effects of Spanish cultural factors for the very reason that they lived in an organization of their own and not in a Spanish entity. Moreover, it was in the interest of the Spanish population to preserve the integrity of these corporations. Since wheat could not be raised, and the Indians retained a monopoly of raising maize, they helped to feed the Spanish population both through the encomienda and through direct sales. The village was also responsible for the delivery of Yucatan's main exportable item, the cotton cloth that made up the greater part of the tribute. It is thus understandable that both the encomenderos and the general population of the Spanish sector should support the existence of the villages.

Even so, villagers were not immune to Hispanization. They did not suffer the disruption occasioned by major outside labor demands, but they were affected in direct proportion to their proximity to Spaniards and to the number of Hispanized individuals present. Villagers near the city and the Spanish villas were the first to experience Spanish cultural influences, and felt them most acutely. The number of Hispanized people and the concentration of Spanish institutions was greatest in Mérida, Campeche, and Valladolid (in that order). Indians from the pueblos flocked there in search of work, and they were called upon by the city people to fill all kinds of tasks, whether they were encomienda Indians or not; it was difficult at times to tell who was a villager and who was a naborío.

In the countryside those villages where the most Spaniards congregated, such as the subcenters growing out of once important Indian *cabeceras,* were the places where the Indians experienced the greatest Spanish influence. Spaniards with smallish livestock enterprises usually had a house in the cabecera; the military officer (the equivalent of the alcalde mayor elsewhere) would have his headquarters there; the priest, of course, would have his church in the main village; petty traders or tratantes flocked to the subcenters with their wares. Spaniards were not numerous, but they were there, and the Indians came in contact with them in a variety of ways.

Farther away, in remote regions and in secondary villages or *sujetos,* contact was less. Valladolid, the Spanish outpost to the east, was peopled mostly by individuals engaged in encomienda activities, along with a few merchants and traders; as late as 1688 it had fewer than 150 Spaniards and their families, probably a third the number in Campeche and a fifth of those in Mérida. Consider the status of the pueblos in the southern Cupul area as revealed in the *Titles of Ebtun,* a collection of documents showing the situation in five pueblos for most of the colonial period. Spaniards were few and far between, and the life of the villagers seemed hardly touched by alien ways. In these places acculturative factors worked slowly indeed.[7]

Altogether it may be said that the humbler elements of society, mixed bloods, blacks, and Indians, were constantly in a state of flux. Just as blacks were increasingly turning into African-Indian mixed bloods, and affecting the Indian population biologically and culturally, so the mixed bloods of European and Indian were acquiring a function of their own as they spanned the bridge between their relatives in the city and those in the countryside. At the same time the Indians themselves, the majority of the population of Yucatan, were undergoing a transition such that some (the naboríos mainly) approached mestizo status without being so biologically, while others, though nearly imperceptibly, were affected in the villages.

Councilmen and Local Crown Bureaucrats

As elsewhere in Spanish America, the government of the province was divided into two tiers: municipal government run by local elements, and government at the provincial level directed by officials from Spain or New Spain. The system reflected the divergent interests of the crown and the local people; it also worked to resolve normal conflict by institutionalizing such factors as checks and balances, neglect, ill-defined lines of authority, and time and distance. The only aspect special to Yucatan was the relative strength of the antagonists, reflecting the rather low degree of importance of the region in the eyes of the imperial government and its distance from the principal centers of power.

The cabildo, the organ of local government, had jurisdiction over both the city and the surrounding territory. The council was controlled mainly by the encomenderos, though as we have seen, nearly half of the councilmen were merchants by 1680–1690. Nevertheless, for reasons suggested in previous pages, there was little difference in the outlook of the two elements, and the community of interests expressed itself in a single viewpoint on the cabildo.

Local officials of the crown.—The imperial government, represented by the governor, his deputies, and the agents of the royal exchequer, pulled in the opposite direction. They served as official links to the outside world and as reminders to the local population that they were part of a greater whole with needs and interests on a global scale. In contrast to the cabildo, however, the imperial government representatives did not present a united front. Cohesiveness was hampered by competition arising from the blurred lines of authority in the Spanish system and the officials' separate personal interests and career ambitions.

The idea that officials of the crown, except for the governor himself, opposed encomendero interests, can be dismissed outright. Treasury officials invariably intermarried with encomendero families, forming substantial social and monetary alliances. The same may be said for the lieutenant governor, who was second in command to the governor and had significant judicial functions; the encomenderos always soon captured the individual. A marriage alliance was again the usual device, and almost to a man the lieutenant governors ended their bureaucratic careers in Yucatan. The lives of all these officials followed the same pattern as that of any immigrant of important position: consorting with encomenderos, marriage to a descendant of conquistadors, and an encomienda in the end.

The governorship.—The sole force checking the encomenderos was the governor. He represented the legitimate interests of the Spanish government, but more than anything he worked for himself. The post was usually a step in a long career in the bureaucracy; it was also an opportunity—limited to no more than four or five years at a stretch—to advance materially.

The two objectives of the governor, personal gain and official duties, were not mutually exclusive. Individual economic activity by officials was the corollary of a system notorious for underpaying its agents. The governor's salary was only half that of the secretary of state of the province. It is not surprising that the chief executive attempted to supplement his income, especially through exactions on and trade with the Indians, who were the most subordinated element in the population as well as the producers of Yucutan's chief items of export and of internal consumption.

Using every subterfuge imaginable, and under the pretext of the need to control the interior and protect the coastal areas from pirate attacks, the governor delegated authority there to an increasing number of cohorts in the course of the seventeenth century. These agents had the official duty of acting as Spanish administrators and military officers in the pueblos. Their appointment met the resistance of the encomenderos, who succeeded periodically in having them banned from service, on the grounds that they were not needed in active encomienda regions.

If the merchants were exponents of long-distance external trade, then the military officers must be seen as their counterparts in the lucrative internal trade in the subregions of the province, with the governor as head trader in the city. The officers gravitated to the subcenters of the countryside as these became important. There they set up their headquarters, usually directing a number of subagents who were functionally the same as the tratantes already covered in previous pages. They bartered and traded with the Indians, giving them Spanish items in return for cloth and maize.

The fact that the military district officers acquired more official duties as time progressed did not disguise the reality that they were in the pueblos primarily in order to tax and trade with Indians already in encomienda. Since this matter touched the encomenderos (and the priests) to the quick, it was the main subject of the unending quarrels between the cabildo and the many governors who arrived in Yucatan throughout the colonial period. The conflict boiled down to competition for the rights to Indian products.

From a broader perspective, one can see that the special interests of the governors meshed quite well with the need of the crown for more direct control of the colony, as well as with the real situation in the subregions, which, as will be recalled, were maturing with the passage of time and developing into more complex socioeconomic entities with interests other than those of the encomenderos. The play of personal interests, the unofficial system of checks and balances which pitted one faction against another, and the relative degree of independence of the governor from local society, made an essentially weak governorship function effectively with a minimum of interference from the greater powers abroad.

To achieve his personal and professional objectives, the governor had relatively few recourses. Essentially he had no coercive power with which to enforce his actions and decisions. The colony did not have a standing army, except for a few paid men at arms in Campeche after 1677. The militias of Mérida, Valladolid, and Campeche were simply companies of citizens led by the encomenderos as captains.

The governors also suffered from two other basic problems: a tendency to get entangled with local society after all, and lack of support for their policies and actions from the imperial government. In the early period, when governors were of noble birth or high standing, they sought alliances with the then rich encomenderos, who usually had their way in anything they wanted. After the second half of the seventeenth century, the problem was lack of backing from abroad. Spain saw Yucatan as devoid of importance and resources, and the men chosen for the governorship were seldom very far up the ladder in influence or position.

The main factor in the chief executives' favor was patronage. Governors named people to all the vacancies in the church, military, and civilian posts, including the filling of vacant encomiendas. Although they had to respect local interests, and the appointments were subject to approval by king and council, yet this was a powerful weapon, particularly as the Hispanic population expanded from 1600 to 1700 and those worthy of office became more numerous. Since the encomenderos, especially as the seventeenth century progressed, had urgent demands related to their privileges, incomes, and status, the governor's bargaining position was not inconsequential. Whoever was willing to help the governor the most received the most. In the end, the governors and the encomenderos always somehow managed to compromise their respective positions.

The state as an institution must be seen as inert in Yucatan. Problems were usually resolved in terms of defining spheres of influence, rarely with involvement of powers outside the peninsula. The general unimportance of the region made it easier for authorities to look the other way. From the latter sixteenth century through the seventeenth, before Yucatan developed a self-generating economy of a great enough intensity and scale to interest the crown, the province enjoyed a wide autonomy in governmental matters. This corresponds well with the findings of scholars for other less than wealthy regions of Spanish America, from Paraguay to Popayán.[8]

Immigrants

In Yucatan as elsewhere, immigrants began to arrive as soon as the conquest was completed, though not in the floods that some areas attracted. Upper-level immigrants before 1650 were in large part bureaucrats, sometimes lesser sons of prominent creole families in New Spain. After 1650, the majority were merchants from Spain. There was also a continuous heavy admixture of men from the mother country who came without resources or connections to seek their fortunes in Yucatan; these entered society at their own level. Women also contributed their share, though they were less numerous than the men. Wherever they came from, and whatever their social and functional origins, immigrants to Yucutan formed an important and steady stream that revitalized the Spanish strain, renewing the cultural bond between colony and mother country and freshening Hispanic values and outlooks.

Penetration and recruitment.—The behavior of the immigrants is strikingly uniform, representing a pattern of penetration of a new society on the one hand and of recruitment on the other. From the standpoint of penetration, a type emerges which concurs with that seen by David Brading in Guanajuato and is probably universal in Hispanic America. The immigrant goes about his business with a degree of dedication and single-minded purpose which shows strong ambition to succeed socially and financially. Penetration from the social standpoint occurs either in a single generation or over several; the immigrant himself or his children approach the ultimate goal of identification with the descendants of the conquistadors. Since the latter effect is usually achieved through marriage to the female line of a prominent local family, it is not surprising that the daughters of the immigrant merchants usually marry other merchants, while the sons obtain an encomienda through the merits of their creole wives (or their creole mothers), or failing this, they manage livestock enterprises and their descendants marry further into encomendero society. The pattern may be compared to Brading's model of a merchant handing over the business, as well as his daughter in marriage, to an immigrant from his home town in Spain, while his son inherits an estate and title and marries into a prominent family in Guanajuato or Mexico City.[9]

On the other side of the ledger was the absorption or recruitment of new elements by local society. Penetration was deemed desirable also from the receiving end, because of the economic (and occasionally social or political) benefits which the immigrants brought, particularly as the encomienda began its long and gradual decline. A proof of this is that merchants usually made their first move up at the fringes of encomendero society; that is, they married into families that had already lost their encomiendas, were on the verge of losing them, or had too many marriageable daughters and not enough money to go around. The economic boost provided by the alliance propelled the family back onto center stage, though since the change occurred through the female line, the result is not discernible at first sight. If the immigrant happened to be a bureaucrat, penetration usually took place at or near the top of local society, because that is precisely where the influence was most needed and desired. As the encomienda decreased in importance, of course, the wealthier merchants were ever more readily welcome and married into progressively higher echelons of the encomendero group.

Creole–peninsular rivalries.—Immigrants, then, seemed to fit quite well into the host society. The question of rivalries or competition between "creoles" and "peninsulares" does not arise or have any reason to arise in seventeenth-century Yucatan. The creoles considered themselves Spaniards and were so called by all. The newcomer had only one ambition: to follow the example of the man who already had a certain social and economic position in local society. It was not a matter of energetic immigrant versus indolent creole, but of the difference between those who are established and those who seek to be established. Immigrants at the low end of the scale appear to have been more numerous than those at the top, to judge from the records at the cathedral of Mérida, a fact paralleled in the findings of others.[10]

The only area where antagonisms showed themselves between the local population and those considered outsiders was in the monasteries, and between the secular and regular clergy. But for Yucatan the categories "insider" and "outsider" are very vague, and not coterminous with "creole" and "peninsular."[11]

Social Change and Social Mobility

Though Yucatan's patriarchal, encomendero-dominated society remained outwardly unchanged for the better part of 300 years, by the early seventeenth century economic pressures had begun to build up which were altering the internal balance. The date 1630 may be viewed as the equivalent of 1580 in central New Spain in regard to this phenomenon. In central Mexico the encomienda was largely finished as the prevailing socioeconomic arrangement by the first quarter of the seventeenth century. A comparable state of things was detectable in Yucatan by 1700, though the skeleton of the institution continued to exist for three-score more years, until it finally faded away. The lag was from 50 to 75 years all along.

As it happened, though, the prestige of the encomenderos did not come to an end in spite of the decline of the encomienda and the economic predominance of cattle estates and long-distance trade, which superseded the encomienda by the close of the seventeenth century. The normal transference of prestige to a new dominant economic institution took place to some extent, but the effect was largely erased by the fact that encomendero, estate owner, and entrepreneur were often one and the same person. This adaptation to new conditions was possible because it was the man at the top who had the best opportunity to move into new pursuits and promising economic activities. At the same time, the fact that in the end wealth rather than birth determined social status meant that the door to social advancement was open to those who had accumulated capital. The situation was comparable to New Spain proper, where encomenderos became mine owners or the owners of great estates. The only difference was that in New Spain events occurred at a more rapid pace, and one institution had almost disappeared before the full emergence of the second.

The phenomenon described made for a great deal of social stability. One group did not challenge another; rather, the group on the rise sought to join the one at the top. Moreover, social mobility was not confined to the wealthier elements. Though it was nearly impossible for the lower and middle ranks to reach the top, there was much movement between contiguous groups.

Expansion of the Spanish Commonwealth

Expansion of the Spaniards as an organized social, economic, and political community was geared to the growth in population of the city and villas. The first spurt of growth was experienced before 1650; by that time what was called the *traza* or core of Mérida, plus the first circle of pueblos around the city, had begun to fill up. Occupation of the countryside was limited to the immediate area beyond these pueblos. After this there was a pause of some twenty years (1648-1660) when Yucatan suffered its greatest attacks of plague and famine. From about 1660 to 1700, however, a second spurt of population growth of the Spanish sector, nearly tripling the preceding rise, helped push people farther out to absorb a second circle of pueblos, and carried enough momentum to cause a massive move outwards that encouraged the establishment of new cattle estates, as well as medium-sized and marginal properties—this time not only by the encomenderos, but also by middling people of creole background and many of the more humble elements. These individuals invaded previously exclusively Indian areas, settling in and near the cabecera villages (head towns) closest to the urban centers or along the major routes of communication. The result was that by the close of the seventeenth century the important business of incorporation of the Indian hinterland into the Spanish commonwealth had begun to take place in earnest.

The Growth of Mérida

During the seventeenth century, then, the Spanish city expanded beyond the original layout determined at the time of conquest. It burst out of the traza or inner core, and by the first decades of the eighteenth century it included all the original pueblos around the early city, no longer as separate corporate structures but as *barrios* or *arrabales* (suburbs) of the city.

Initially the tiny Spanish nucleus was implanted in the midst of a thriving cluster of Indian villages, supplanting the cabecera or head town of T-Ho, a Maya cultural and religious center. Expansion then took place in the form of a double current between the Spanish core and the outlying pueblos. One went outward from the city in the form of Hispanized individuals penetrating the villages (blacks in the service of Spaniards, mulattoes and other mixed bloods establishing artisan businesses on their own and bartering with the village Indians, or other poor Spaniards who found Mérida too expensive to live in); the second returned to the Spanish nucleus in the form of Indians seeking work and consorting with the city population. After a certain period of time the Indians who had migrated to the city were transformed culturally and perhaps racially; the nearby pueblos suffered alteration, becoming increasingly non-Indian, and eventually retained only traces of having once been pueblos. By then the second circle of pueblos around the city had undergone an initiation to Spanish ways by means of their own double current in relation to the villages closer to the city. These outer villages served as feeders to those closer in. At the same time they had developed a dependency on the villages near the core which prepared them for succeeding Spanish penetration and ultimate incorporation into the Spanish urban entity.

As early as 1600–1620 both San Juan pueblo, to the immediate south of Mérida, and Santa Lucía, to the north, seem to have been in an advanced state of incorporation. Three other pueblos in the immediate vicinity of Mérida had undergone vast changes by mid-seventeenth century—Santiago, San Cristóbal, Mejorada—but the process was arrested because of the setback experienced by the Spanish population between 1648 and 1660. Nevertheless, in the last third of the century, with the second spurt in growth of the Spanish population, the pace of change resumed.

Behind each of these nearly assimilated pueblos lay another, with its own Indian cabildo, but dependent on the nearer village for ceremonial purposes and in other ways. Many people from the outer ring married citizens of neighboring pueblos in the inner ring and moved in permanently. By the end of the seventeenth century the villages of the second ring had already experienced a great deal of infiltration by mestizos, poor Spaniards, and blacks as property owners, and the evidence points further to a number of Indians involved in crafts and other pursuits geared to the Spanish market. Moreover, the parish records of these feeder pueblos show not only considerable intermarriage toward Mérida, but also intermarriage with individuals arriving from pueblos even farther out. This indicates a third circle of villages affected by urban growth, but not due to be assimilated for another fifty or more years in what was a continuous process limited only by the size of the Spanish or near-Spanish population of Mérida.

Development of Subcenters

The rise of subregional Hispanic centers in all directions from Mérida was due to the same process described above. As we have seen, Spanish elements with business among the Indians congregated in the cabeceras or head villages more than in the smaller sujetos. There they exerted the same kind of pull for individual Indians as they did in the city. The result was for the minor villages to lose population to the major ones, and for the greater centers to receive Indians in a type of relay system that ultimately included the Spanish nucleus of Mérida as the main point of attraction. For the countryside, all this meant eventual concentration in the main villages of both Indian and Spanish elements.

The cabecera village of Hocabá, southeast of Mérida, for example, won out over all its sujetos. The parish records of the village show movement of Indians towards the cabecera throughout the seventeenth century. Estate records also indicate a great deal of consorting between Spanish and Indian elements. In fact, there was so much contact between Hocabá and people from Mérida in terms of cattle estates and internal trade that eventually the area gravitated towards the city from the standpoint of Spanish administration.

Whether or not a cabecera was to develop into a subregional Spanish center had to do with where it was most convenient for the Spaniards to operate. The village of Ticul, for example, at the entrance of the Xiu district, had not crystallized as yet into a subregional capital in the seventeenth century, but being on a well-traveled path, it eventually came to be favored as a base by Spanish officials and traders over competing cabeceras. By the first half of the nineteenth century, when Stephens visited Ticul, he called it a Spanish town with no sign of ever having been Indian, though we know it had been.[12]

Movement inwards to the Spanish center by Indians, and outwards to the villages by Spaniards, was accomplished either physically (actual migration) or biologically (intermarriage), and it could take anywhere from one generation to several to complete the process. Indian nobles and employees of Spaniards gravitated from the villages to the local Spanish subcenter, then perhaps towards Mérida. The parish registries of the Mérida barrios occasionally record deaths of individuals who had come from very far away. In the Xiu district to the southeast, and along the road to Campeche from Mérida, there was a significant element of Indian travelers and temporary residents in the villages who were not counted among the tributaries.

The movement to the interior by Spaniards was similar. Waves of them went outwards whenever it was propitious, first as agents of the encomenderos; then as more and more people from the city traded with the Indians, they formed liaisons in the villages, or bought land to establish livestock enterprises; ultimately the influx of Spaniards was recognized in the formal establishment of a new administrative and military jurisdiction and the permanent appointment of an agent of the governor.

This was the manner in which Yucatan was becoming more Spanish. Probably it is the way all Indian-Spanish areas experienced the process; consider the similarities between the above Indian migration patterns and those seen in Karen Spalding's work on the Huarochirí province of Peru.[13] The movement of Indians along a continuum from lesser villages, to major ones, to the Spanish nucleus, appears to be a constant.

Development of the Country Estates

The push into the countryside also took the form of land acquisition for the purpose of establishing Spanish enterprises. These, in seventeenth-century Yucatan, were limited to estates for cattle and other livestock, for there were none of the usual *labores* (small farming properties) that were to be found in much of the rest of New Spain by then or earlier. (One of the bases for that form of investment was lacking, since wheat could not be grown successfully in Yucatan.) Like the rise of subcenters, or the absorption of pueblos as barrios of Mérida, development of rural properties was tied to the size of the Spanish population in a given area—with the added element that the accepted Spanish outlook tended towards the creation of the great estate and a patriarchal, aristocratic ordering of society. What and how much the estates produced depended on the population they had to satisfy; how they produced it was a function of size and the practices of Spaniards everywhere.

The first estates to develop were those of encomenderos around the city and villas, which from the earliest times provided meat for the citizens. After mid-seventeenth century, with a tripling of the original population, the same properties became larger, while smaller enterprises began to appear near the Indian cabeceras and along major arteries of communication. Changes were also evident in the ownership of the estates. Encomenderos and merchants centered their attention on the larger enterprises near the major urban nuclei, while properties farther out in the countryside were established mostly by secondary individuals unable to maintain themselves in the city. The more important of these outlying estates were set up by creole relatives of higher-ups in the city: priests, women, second sons, nephews and brothers of encomenderos, merchants in the early stages of penetration, and others. The more marginal enterprises were the property of almost any Hispanized individual (pardo, mestizo, or even Indian), who might manage to acquire a little land and raise anything from bees to chickens and pigs or, if he was relatively well off, a few horses and mules.

Since the key factor in estate activity was the size and distribution of the urban population, Yucatan's great estates clustered about Mérida, Campeche, and to a much lesser extent Valladolid; few were in the interior, where there were fewer Spaniards. After 1650, when the urban population grew beyond 400 families, and later perhaps double this number, the cluster of estates around Mérida expanded to include a much larger area, approximately twenty to thirty miles in radius. Estates thinned out the farther one proceeded from Mérida, except that some were located around important cabeceras. However, along the great arch from Mérida to Campeche, including the coast to the west, a significant number of enterprises were distributed more or less evenly, in a state of development commensurate with the commercial importance of both Campeche and Mérida. In this case, along a constantly traveled road, fairly large estates existed beyond the orbit of the Spanish city and villa; several cabeceras were becoming Spanish subcenters, and many Spaniards and Hispanized people made their home there.

As the population expanded in the Spanish centers, changes also occurred in the structure and makeup of the estates. The tendency was for the older enterprises to become larger, at first by acquiring adjacent land, and later by annexation of smaller, less efficient units in the vicinity and farther out. This was especially true for properties around Mérida. Along the route to Campeche another transformation was taking place: country estates were beginning to raise maize for the port-villa, an area growing at a rapid pace after 1650 because of commercial activity, and apparently without a large nearby Indian population to supply it with grain. Diversification and hiring of seasonal agricultural labor became more apparent as one approached Campeche on the route from Mérida. While estates contained the usual livestock, maize was gaining importance as a cash crop. Moreover, the census of 1688 lists in some villages noncitizen Indians in large numbers working for a wage, sometimes more than those listed as paying tribute, an unheard-of thing in any other section of the peninsula. It seems evident, then, that by the close of the seventeenth century, though the livestock enterprise still predominated, the full-fledged inclusive great estate had begun to take shape in Yucatan, and that the pattern of development was to be similar to that of older, more mature areas in New Spain. After all, the very purpose of the estates was to provide the urban centers with the products they needed. These needs were to expand beyond what Indians in encomienda could supply, so that eventually the estates would provide not only meat and beasts of burden but grains as well.

The same almost inevitable situation could be discerned in matters of personnel structure. A three-step hierarchy of those associated with ownership, management, and production developed, the result in part of the organizational practices of Spaniards generally. The elaboration of the structure depended on the size of the enterprise, but all rural properties tended towards the same arrangement, whether the properties of wealthy individuals, of persons of much smaller means, or even those of acculturated Indians.

As long as the estates of encomenderos were small, they themselves managed as well as owned them. An incipient division of these two functions was present all along, however, since the owner lived in the city most of the time and inspected the enterprise only sporadically, while at the estate lower-echelon overseers fulfilled the management function in part. Back in the city, poorer relations or the sons of the owner did some of the managing on that end. When the estates grew, it was an easy step for these secondary relatives to assume all the management, and for the overseers at the estate to sink to the level of foremen. Caring for the livestock, the production level, was done by naborío Indians, not villagers.

The smaller enterprises in the countryside followed a similar pattern. The owner usually lived in an Indian cabecera and managed his enterprise from that point, going out to his estate occasionally. The immediate running of it was in the hands of an overseer, very often an Indian rather than the black slave or mulatto common among the enterprises of the encomenderos. Villagers probably watched the herds, since sometimes only four or five people were needed. Of course, the smaller the estate, the more all three functions were concentrated in the same few people.

It is interesting to observe that Indian enterprises were also being run on the Spanish model. There were some large estates, including one near Mérida and another near Abalá to the west of the city. More often than not, however, Indian estates that appear in the records were medium-sized or very marginal. Usually they had an animal or two, but concentrated on the keeping of bees for wax and honey (a traditional Indian activity). In these latter cases the Indian owner took care of all functions, managerial and otherwise. In the larger estates, though, the owner lived in the city, some relations managed it, and, at least in one case, there were village Indians fulfilling tasks at the production level. In all the cases seen by this writer, there was no difference in management between Indian estates and property owned by Spaniards.

In summary, the estates of Yucatan, large and small, with various ownership, though not as developed as in some other areas of New Spain in the seventeenth century, appear to have been following an established course that, given the further growth of the colony, increasingly would approach the form of the full-fledged great landed estate.

The Indian Village

The Spanish occupation of Yucatan took place in various stages, and the effect on the village varied accordingly. Spanish settlement occurred in the midst of the largest Indian groups, and incipient Spanish towns developed in the head villages. Yet it seems that the Indian factor was more important when Spanish institutions were youngest. Eventually a point was reached when the Spaniards were no longer guided by the Indian element. Their economy and institutional development became inner-directed and self-propelled. The village then receded in at least two ways: wherever it was near a Spanish center it underwent the transformation described before, whereby it became more Spanish than Indian; those villages far away from the city and villas then receded from Spanish interest, and the time for their eventual transformation was pushed back to await the effects of future urban advance, a process that is still going on.

In the first stage, under the encomienda, actual Spanish occupation of the countryside was at a minimum, and the local villages remained essentially undisturbed. A feeling for this situation can still be obtained in the census of 1688; in remote villages the priests were sometimes the only Spanish individuals, or at most there were two or three mulattoes, mestizos, or secular Spaniards.

The next stage came when the urban population expanded and the encomienda was no longer an adequate framework. The population pushed outwards to trade with the Indians, congregate in cabeceras, and occupy some of the land physically with their livestock enterprises. The village, though still not greatly affected (because the nature of Spanish enterprise left the growing of grain to the villages and required few Indians to man the estates), was increasingly exposed to alien culture elements and to an advancing Spanish economy. This era, for the most part, lasted throughout the seventeenth century for greater Yucatan.

The third and final stage arrived with the political incorporation of the subregions by the urban nuclei, particularly Mérida. This was the end result of continued varied activity that had focused from the beginning on the major Indian centers close to the city and villas or along the main roads. Gradually the local agent of the governor acquired an official status as military district officer, a post like the one known in other areas of New Spain and South America as the *corregimiento* or principal rural administrative office. The offical recognition of the military officer occurred only when his area had made considerable advances towards social and economic incorporation into the Spanish community. Attaining this stage took a long time, but two to four such districts crystallized by mid-seventeenth century, eight by 1688, and finally twelve by the time of further redistricting during the Intendancy in the eighteenth century.

In general, the economic and political boundaries of Yucatan followed almost exactly the older Indian divisions; each *cacicazgo* or Maya state of the sixteenth century eventually became a district, and almost every important head town, especially along the most traversed roads, became a Spanish subregional center. Even so, though the Spaniards superimposed their organization on the Indian layout, the extent and timing of development were always dependent on the Spanish impetus and direction; the Indians of Yucatan at this time were a relatively passive factor, a group being acted upon. The Spaniards advanced relative to the Indian village no matter what was happening there, in good times or bad. They paused, as during the plague of 1648 and for twenty years afterward, because the catastrophe affected the Spanish population as much as the Indian. After that, the thrust outward continued with renewed vigor. The Indians actively cooperated in the process when not undergoing hardship. In times of stress, when disease and famine struck, they retrenched and fled the city, suburbs, and cabeceras. If things were bad enough, they would abandon completely the settled areas, a common enough complaint of officials and encomenderos ever since conquest times. Very often the records show that bad times coincided in the Indian and Spanish communities. If the Spaniards were spared, however, as apparently on at least two occasions of epidemic outbreaks (1631 and 1670–72), conditions in the Indian villages hardly affected the rate of the Spanish advance.

The general outline of the Spanish colony was developed early. The frontier was delineated at the time of the conquest and remained fixed for the duration of the colony and beyond. The rise in the Hispanic population, rather than causing expansion towards the Indian community, after a point prompted a change in the direction of activity, toward itself and toward the greater Spanish world. The result was that the villages far away from these centers of activity all but lost contact; those nearby were engulfed. Spanish filling in of the boundaries laid out at conquest would have to await the growth of the city and other institutions, not in a movement directed toward the Indians per se, but out of processes generated in the Spanish community itself.

Conclusions

The underlying theme of this chapter is that growth in numbers at the Hispanic urban core determined the intensity and course of Spanish activity. Such a theme contrasts with the thesis, first advanced by Woodrow Borah, that the fortunes of the Spaniards in New Spain were predicated upon the health of the Indian population. According to this view, when the Indians suffered decimation, particularly after the epidemic of 1576–79, New Spain went into a prolonged depression from which it did not recover until the end of the seventeenth century, when the Indian population began to recuperate. For Yucatan there was a seventy-five year lag, but the implication is that a similar set of circumstances existed when that society experienced what appears to have been its own Indian population decline, approximately 1648–1736.[14]

The Spanish society and economy of Yucatan did not experience a depression; the Indian population does not seem to have been a determining factor after the early era of the encomienda. The Spanish sector grew and prospered in the seventeenth century, and institutions developed along lines similar to the central areas. Spanish society did experience setbacks due to epidemics, but this was primarily because they affected the Spanish as well as the Indian population, and they were only episodes, the effects of the longest one lasting about twenty years. Rather than depression, Yucatan experienced prolonged development: the growth of Mérida, the development of the cattle estates, the growth of commerce and therefore of Campeche, and the emergence of subregional centers that were concrete testimony to the advance of the Spaniards into Indian territory.

Neither did Yucatan suffer a reduction of agricultural production and trade. A constant number of Indians in encomienda (their numbers were replenished after every epidemic by raids into frontier areas) provided food for a growing population in the city plus, apparently, shipments of maize to points outside the colony. When Spaniards became too many in a given area, the Indian grain-growing monopoly was broken (as along the road to Mérida from Campeche), and Spanish enterprises partially took over grain production, on a different technological basis. In the matter of trade, a net of commerce with the outside developed, including

Veracruz, Havana, and other points in the Caribbean such as Cartegena. Indians of central Mexico may have been an important part of the market for mantas. The growth rather than slowdown of trade is shown by the expansion of the port of Campeche, particularly after 1650.

A second theme in this chapter is that there was an underlying similarity of development between Yucatan and the core of New Spain, and that any differences were the result of a slower pace rather than departures from the norm. According to this view, development may have taken place in slow motion, so to speak, but the direction of that development followed the pattern in the core areas. The similarities had to do with the shared Spanish culture and the general economy and technology of the time; dissimilarities, on the other hand, were the result of mainly economic peculiarities of the region and its position relative to the outside. Any catching up later on was due to changed circumstances, mainly new outside demands which rendered Yucatan's situation more like that of central Mexico.

The establishment of the encomienda, for example, was the basic response of Spaniards to sedentary Indians. In Yucatan the institution lasted almost the entire colonial period, whereas in central Mexico it gave way much earlier to other forms of exploitation of land and labor. The demise of the encomienda was retarded in Yucatan—as in Chile and many other remote areas—because the Spanish population of the colony was not as large as that in central New Spain and therefore exerted relatively little pressure on the system for a long time. Moreover, it took time for secondary systems of trade to develop, linking the regional economy with that of the greater Spanish community. When these factors changed, the same pressures and circumstances that brought about the end of the encomienda in New Spain prevailed in Yucatan. The duration of the encomienda in this region, then, was not a departure from the normal course of events. Rather it is an indication that for a very long time Yucatan remained several steps behind central Mexico in economic development.

NOTES

1. General antecedents to the present chapter are to be found in Marta Espejo-Ponce Hunt, "Colonial Yucatan: Town and Region in the Seventeenth Century," which contains detailed figures and maps, as well as many illustrated career patterns and descriptions of types of holdings, all fully referenced. Methodology and sources are there discussed in the prologue, pp. 1-23. Primary materials came mostly from local repositories, of which the notarial archives, the parish office registries of the Archbishopric of Yucatan, some documents in the land registry office, and collections in private archives are perhaps the most important. Some significant documentation, however, came from the Archivo General de

Indias (AGI) in Seville: *residencias, visitas,* encomienda grants, petitions, and census figures. Of almost equal importance was the Archivo General de la Nación (AGN) in Mexico City, where use was made of documents in the sections Inquisición, Historia, and Civil. Mention must also be made of the "chronicles," eyewitness accounts of observers of everyday life in Yucatan, which date from 1588 to 1701. Among the chroniclers one may include Yucatan's foremost historian, J. F. Molina Solís, whose *Historia de Yucatán* is a chronology of events taken mostly from primary documents, many of which are now lost.

2. I use the word "creole" to mean a person of Spanish descent born in America, in order to have a term for the local Spanish population in distinction to outsiders. In fact, of course, no distinction of category was commonly made in the sixteenth and seventeenth centuries between Spaniards born in America and those born in Spain, both being *españoles.* The Spanish word *criollo* was still most commonly used for Africans born in the New World.

3. For pictorial descriptions of the stages of growth of Campeche, see *Planos de ciudades iberoamericanas y filipinas sacados del Archivo de Indias.*

4. J. Ignacio Rubio Mañé, *Alcaldes de Mérida de Yucatán,* lists the origins of most of Mérida's alcaldes.

5. Rubio Mañé, *Archivo de la historia de Yucatán, Campeche y Tabasco,* I:207-11.

6. AGI, Contaduría 920, Matrícula de 1688, expedientes 1 and 2. This important document is a census of the parishes of Yucatan under diocesan control in 1688, including the names of and tribute received by the encomenderos. It is partial in that all those in the care of the Franciscans were not tabulated. However, since the diocesan parishes were, by this date, the more numerous and scattered throughout Yucatan, the data have general validity for certain purposes and for deriving trends. The census included Indians, blacks and mulattoes, Spaniards, and mestizos. All mentions in this chapter of the late seventeenth-century census refer to this document. See also Sherburne F. Cook and Woodrow Borah, *Essays in Population History: Mexico and the Caribbean,* II:75-96, especially for estimates of the size of the non-Indian population and its spread throughout the peninsula.

7. Ralph L. Roys, ed., *The Titles of Ebtun.*

8. See Elman R. Service, "The Encomienda in Paraguay," 230-52; Peter Marzahl, "The Cabildo of Popayán in the Seventeenth Century: The Emergence of a Creole Elite," and "Creoles and Government: The Cabildo of Popayán."

9. D. A. Brading, *Miners and Merchants in Bourbon Mexico, 1763-1810.*

10. See Rubio Mañé, "Gente de España en la ciudad de México, año de 1689." Rubio Mañé shows that the greater number of immigrant Spaniards in Mexico City in 1689 were following humble pursuits, and that those who were officials, wealthy merchants, or noblemen were very much in the minority.

11. For example, the *alternativa,* a method whereby creole and peninsular Spanish friars alternated in the leadership posts within their order in the Americas, was adapted to local conditions of Yucatan. Creoles from other provinces were also considered outsiders for alternativa purposes, so that antagonisms were not quite "creole" vs. "peninsular."

12. John L. Stephens, *Incidents of Travel in Yucatan,* I:154–59.

13. Karen Spalding, "Indian Rural Society in Colonial Peru."

14. Woodrow Borah, *New Spain's Century of Depression.* Again, in the *Essays in Population History,* II:1-179, the implication by Cook and Borah is that their estimated drastic decline in the Indian population of Yucatan, which began after mid-seventeenth century and reached its nadir in 1736, had an adverse effect on the development of the economy of the peninsula, which did not, in this view, begin to prosper and grow until after mid-eighteenth century, when the combined effects of a burst in the Indian population (doubling in the 58 years from 1736 to 1794) and the free trade policies under the Intendancy began to make themselves felt.

2. Town and Country in the Valley of Oaxaca, 1750–1812

William B. Taylor

Oaxaca is a vast, richly varied region. Mountains dominate the landscape, carving out at least four major geographical and cultural zones: the Mixteca Alta and Baja, the Sierra and Norte, the coast and Isthmus of Tehuantepec, and the central valleys.[1] The province was one of the most thickly peopled Indian areas of New Spain, with a count of 477,267 tributaries or about 16 percent of the Indian population of the viceroyalty in 1548. As late as the 1790s, nearly 90 percent of the 411,000 inhabitants were listed as Indians.[2] Dense Indian settlement was concentrated in the central highlands. Dramatic peaks and troughs mark the demographic history of colonial Oaxaca—the Mixteca Alta and the coast were especially hard hit by epidemics—but the central valleys were always especially populous. Of the provincial Indian population of approximately 250,000 in about 1740, the valleys accounted for 29.5 percent of the total. The Sierra and Norte, over two and a half times the area of the central valleys, had 31 percent of the population, followed by the Mixteca Alta with 20 percent.[3]

The major linguistic groups were the Zapotecs and Mixtecs, though at least fourteen other indigenous languages were spoken. Ronald Spores has distinguished three types of Indian settlement patterns in pre-Columbian times, corresponding roughly to geographical zones: (1) diffuse, vacant-center settlements, found among the Mixe and Chinantec groups in the eastern Sierra; (2) compact settlements, found mostly in the Zapotec central valleys and among the southern and mountain Zapotecs; and (3) sparsely occupied political centers surrounded by dispersed hamlets, found primarily in the Mixteca.[4] Although families and towns were the basic units of Indian society, regional states had developed in many parts of the province before the Spanish conquest.

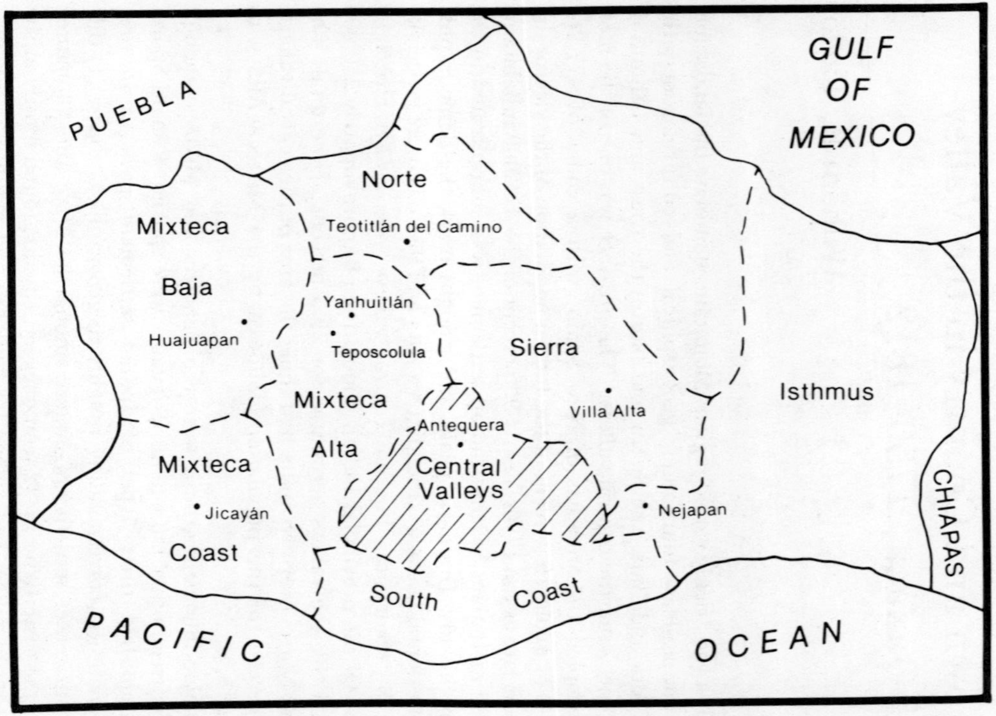

The Province of Oaxaca

Except for the coastal zone and isolated pockets elsewhere, the non-Indian population was in the minority throughout the province. The Spanish population clustered in Antequera (over 10,000 "Spaniards" in 1790), in towns along the Mixteca Alta trade route connecting Mexico City and Puebla with Antequera, and in the small settlements of Villa Alta, Nexapa, and Tehuantepec. The black and free mulatto group was not unsubstantial, totaling nearly 17,000 in the late eighteenth century,[5] but nearly 75 percent of it was concentrated in the coastal jurisdictions. Smaller pockets of black people resided at Antequera and in the low-lying sugar- and cotton-producing areas.

Because mestizos were not separated for purposes of taxation, the importance of this group is more difficult to document than that of the black or Indian populations. Detailed census records for 1777 and 1804–1806, however, suggest that *mestizaje* (the mixture of peoples) was a slow, irregular process in the region's most populous Indian zones. In the colonial period it was confined largely to new urban centers such as Antequera, towns along the trade routes, the coast, and the sugar-producing areas where Indian communities were small and dispersed.

While not forgetting the larger provincial context, this essay centers on the region of the Valley of Oaxaca, where the major non-Indian settlement of Antequera was located and where occupation of the land by Indian communities was most concentrated. Within this regional focus, the main emphasis is placed on major social groups and their economic and cultural bases in the late eighteenth century.

The Valley of Oaxaca

The Valley of Oaxaca is a wide alluvial plain roughly 700 square kilometers in area. Mountain ranges divide it into three subregions with colonial Antequera at the center. The Valley of Etla extends to the northwest, the Valley of Tlacolula to the southeast, and the Valley of Zimatlán to the south. The Valley has a tropical highland climate—temperate, warm, and fairly dry, with some sectional variations. Etla was the most productive section of the Valley during the colonial period, extensive irrigation permitting some towns to harvest two or three crops annually. Although successful maize agriculture was widespread in the Valley, Etla's alluvial plain and the northern half of the Zimatlán valley were the most intensively cultivated areas.

The array of European and native crops grown reflects the variety of ecological niches in the Valley and their general suitability for agriculture. Native crops harvested in the colonial period were maize, maguey, beans, fodder, and all the usual Mesoamerican auxiliary plants, including tuna cactus (which nurtures the cochineal insect). European crops grown were white and yellow varieties of wheat, sugar cane, grapes, and the common fruits and vegetables.[6] The Etla valley was best suited for the cultivation of wheat, and from early in the colonial period wheat fields abounded there.[7] The cultivation of wheat was attempted elsewhere in the Valley with only limited success.

Because of the Valley's temperate climate, broad alluvial plain, perennial rivers, and high water table, it could support a large population dependent on the land. During the colonial period Indians, Spaniards, and small numbers of blacks, mestizos, and mulattoes lived in the Valley. In 1568 the native population was approximately 150,000, and at its lowest point in the 1630s dwindled to perhaps 40,000 or 50,000. The Spanish population, as we have seen, was concentrated in Antequera. Although it is difficult to determine the total population of the Valley at any one time, the Indian population always represented a sizable majority. In the first half of the seventeenth century, the Valley probably had fewer than 50,000 inhabitants, or fewer than 71 inhabitants per square kilometer. By 1740, the total had risen to nearly 70,000, and by the 1790s to 110,000. In 1959 the Valley had some 290,000 inhabitants, or 414 per square kilometer.

Antequera

Late colonial society in the Valley of Oaxaca included one important urban center at Antequera and a patchwork hinterland of small to medium-sized private estates and semiautonomous rural communities. Strictly speaking, most of the landed estates represent economic rather than social units, since few embraced permanent communities of any size, leaving the city and the rural villages as the two major types of communities. Each of these three units—city, communities, and estates—receives separate treatment in the following pages.

The Spaniards' conception of civilization in terms of ordered town life ensured that focal points of colonization such as Oaxaca would have to support substantial urban centers. A permanent settlement of Spaniards at Antequera in the center of the Valley dates from 1529, eight years after the first expedition into the region. Hernando Cortés's interest in the populous and fertile valleys of central Oaxaca drew the attention of the crown and of rival Spanish colonists as well. City life and provincial administration were quickly set in order. By 1533, the settlement of several hundred Spaniards was elevated to the noble status of *ciudad* or city, and two years later the bishopric of Oaxaca was created, with headquarters in Antequera.

During its first two hundred years, Antequera was largely a patrimonial capital rather than a center of production and redistribution. Activities

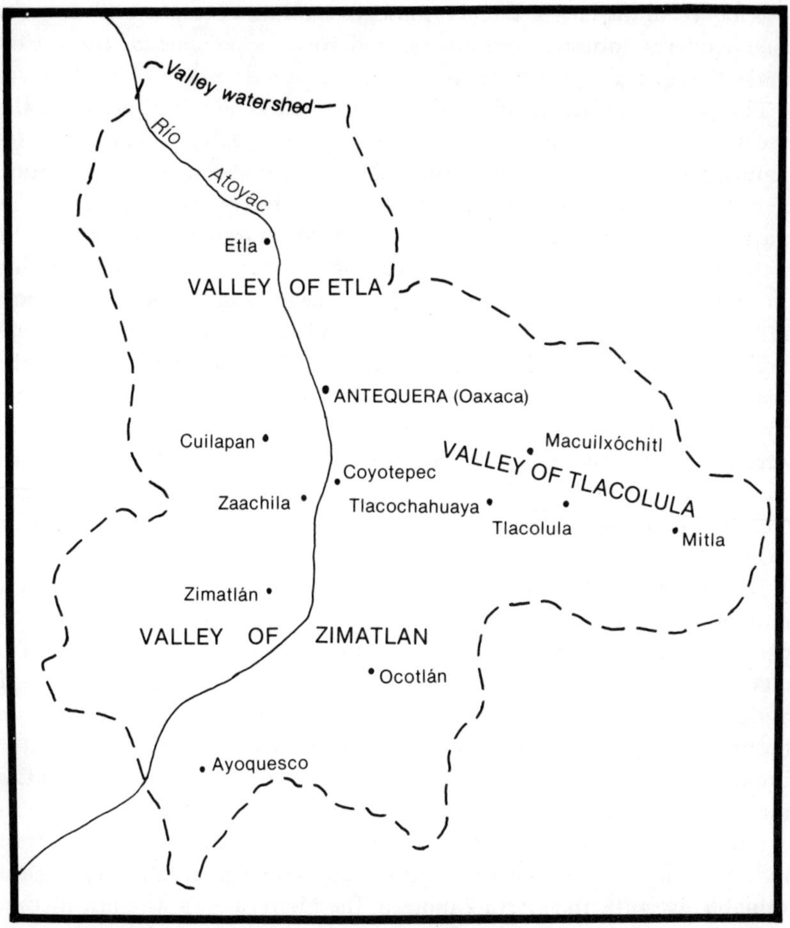

The Valley Of Oaxaca

such as grain shipments to Chiapas and Guatemala, or silk production and weaving in the Mixteca Alta, stimulated some short-lived commercial activity, but in general, trade and commerce were of little importance in Antequera before the eighteenth century. Antequera was essentially an administrative center and a haven for ecclesiastical, office-holding, and landowning Spaniards from throughout the province. From its inception, Antequera was the only important settlement of Spaniards in the central valleys, and despite efforts to promote such towns as Villa Alta and Nexapa, it was also the only important organized city in the province. Except for some Spaniards with interests in the Mixteca Alta and Baja who looked to the city of Puebla, most sixteenth- and seventeenth-century encomenderos, priests, landowners, and royal appointees of the region made Antequera their permanent base.

The population of the city, which remained at about 3,000 from the late sixteenth to the mid-seventeenth century, created new market demands, but commercial capitalism and a firm social-economic integration of city and countryside developed slowly. Although Antequera had its marketplace, the city was not sustained by margins of profit in the exchange of goods and services. It fed off the surplus of the countryside through the prerogatives of political rule: head taxes, tithe, draft labor, and, to a lesser extent, the operation of landed estates by the church and individual Spaniards. The lower classes—in 1571, roughly a third of the non-Indian urban population was classified as mestizo or mulatto—were probably service-oriented (domestic service, repairmen, and so on) or were craftsmen and petty vendors strictly oriented to the local urban market. In addition to the mestizo and mulatto groups, an estimated four hundred Indians were occupied in domestic service in the city in 1571.[8]

During the eighteenth century, Antequera grew dramatically and developed a more elaborate colonial economy, with the expansion of capital formation, trade and manufacturing, and economic classes. The older complex, built on taxes from the rural peasantry, plus regional agriculture and ranching, persisted, but it gave way in importance to the cochineal trade and textile manufacturing aimed at outside markets; this brought the regional economy into the sphere of influence of Mexico City merchant firms and the now more centralized government of the viceregal capital. The cochineal trade made Antequera a genuine provincial capital. The city formed new ties with remote outlying areas producing this valuable dyestuff: the Sierra Zapoteca, the Mixteca Alta, the jurisdictions of Miahuatlán-Zimatlán, and Jicayán in the coastal zone. Severe financial setbacks disturbed the early years of the eighteenth century (crop failures; rising indebtedness and defaults on loans; buildings and public services in disarray; a high incidence of vagrancy and robbery, suggesting high unemployment), but by the 1770s the urban population had topped 19,000, and new wealth was obvious in building activities and the flow of goods and services.

The most important single factor in urban development was the booming cochineal industry. From 1758 to 1777, over 45 million pesos worth of cochineal were registered at Antequera. Incredible fortunes could be made in the dye trade, but the investment prospects were highly speculative. David Brading's comparison between the opportunities in silver mining and an open hoist, which might raise men at dizzying speed or dash them to ruin, applies to the cochineal trade as well.[9] Both were boom and bust industries. In years of poor harvests or slack demand, a merchant who invested heavily in cochineal futures could find himself facing an overdue loan of 100,000 pesos and have his entire estate sequestered. Demand and production were strong from the 1750s to the early 1780s, but were followed by some deep troughs in years thereafter and the steady decline of the industry after independence. The initial decline of cochineal in the 1780s was attributed by contemporary observers to the crown's order against the use of the *reparto de efectos* (forced distribution of goods) to guarantee future production of the dyestuff.[10] The reparto had involved large advances of money, livestock, and goods to the communities engaged in producing cochineal. The pattern of the cochineal trade also appears to coincide with Antequera's population changes, with a peak in the 1770s and slight decline in the years preceding independence.

A second major ingredient in the growth of Antequera in the late eighteenth century was textile manufacturing. Raw cotton from the coastal zones was shipped to obrajes or textile shops in Antequera for processing, weaving, and shipment to other regions of the viceroyalty. One source estimates eight hundred cotton looms in operation in the city in 1796, plus seven looms producing silk fabric. By 1828, however, the textile industry had declined dramatically. In that year only fifty looms were said to be in use.

Some idea of status and occupation groups in this urban society after the period of rapid growth is provided by summary census lists for 1790 and property records from the last two decades of the eighteenth century.[11] Some of the data from these lists are organized in Tables 1 and 2. Not surprisingly, this city of 18,000+ was very complex in structure and cannot be described adequately in a few pages. Two keys to the operation of Antequera, however, deserve special emphasis: (1) the total society was not rigidly stratified in any series of endogamous racial groupings; and (2) economic and political power were concentrated on the one hand in the church, closely connected with the native population, and on the other hand among peninsular merchants and officeholders, who had greatly increased in number and influence with the eighteenth-century cochineal boom.

The census summaries divide the population into five ethnic groupings: peninsular, Spaniard, Indian, mulatto, and "other castas." These categories should be thought of as status groupings seen from a Spanish vantage point rather than as an accurate description of a racially-based

TABLE 1. THE POPULATION OF ANTEQUERA IN 1790

Category	Males	Females	Total
Peninsular	266	14	280
Spaniard	4,923	5,500	10,423
Indian	2,886	2,213	5,099
Mulatto	921	1,065	1,986
Other Castas	248	201	449
Total	9,244	8,993	18,237

society. They rely more on cultural distinctions—the individual's wealth, values, and lifestyle—than on physical appearance or clear lines of descent.

The Spaniard or "español" category (what is today often called "creole") reflects this status consideration in particular. A very large proportion of the urban population is classified as "español" (10,423, or over 57 percent of the total) whereas only two minor categories account for people of mixed racial ancestry (mulatto and other castas). The mestizo designation is not included at all in this five-part scheme, although as early as the late sixteenth century the mestizo population is reported to have accounted for a third of the non-Indians in Antequera. If we were to take the census categories literally, only 13 percent of the population was not Spanish or Indian. The suspiciously large "español" category hides many people of mixed racial ancestry. The number of "españoles" and the lack of a mestizo category supports John Chance's hypothesis, based on marriage patterns, that by the late colonial period "español" was the rank of upward social mobility in Antequera, a status to which lighter-skinned mestizos and mulattoes could aspire through wealth, marriage, and lifestyle.[12]

The incidence of "passing" as an "español" is reflected in the age-group distribution for the mulatto category. Compared with the standard age pyramid, the mulatto age distribution shows a marked under-representation of children under the age of seven (15.5 percent of the total). Age distribution for the population as a whole does not indicate that low fertility was a general trend at this time. The most likely explanation for the abnormally low number of mulatto children is that a significant number of mulatto adults were marrying "up," with the result that their children would be classified as "españoles." A demographic factor as well as the increasing social mobility of wealth helps to account for such a trend at this time: there was a substantial imbalance of the sexes in the "español" category among different age groups. Of the group under sixteen years old, there were 2,248 males and 1,620 females; over sixteen, the distribution was reversed, with 3,880 females to 2,675 males. This left many males in the under-sixteen age group and many females over sixteen likely to marry outside their category. With these trends in mind, we would expect that the mulatto category would disappear altogether from social rankings in Antequera by the mid-nineteenth century.

The Indian category remained large at the end of the colonial period. It appears that most "españoles" saw the urban society in dualistic terms of Spaniards and Indians, the division being partly cultural in content, since many of the "españoles" were of mixed racial ancestry. Chance has demonstrated that Valley Indians residing in Antequera in the early eighteenth century were a very tightly bonded ethnic group, and we would expect that the Indian category would come much closer to defining a separate social unit rather than either "mulatto" or "español."

The most distinctive and exclusive status category was the immigrant "peninsular." The nature of the "español" group left the peninsulares as the only city-dwellers who could claim uncontestedly to be "pure" Spanish. Ninety-five percent of this substantial group (only Mexico City and Guanajuato had more peninsulares at this time[13]) were adult males, and the majority of them were unmarried. Perhaps intending to return to the mother country, and often tied to organizations in Mexico City or elsewhere, these people did not sink deep personal roots in the Oaxaca soil, yet they occupied a preeminent position in the local society. Most of the high political officials and the successful merchants in the export trade were peninsulares.

The occupation breakdown in Table 2 gives a very rough idea of employment patterns in the late colonial period and underlines the preindustrial quality of the economic groups, the legacy of Antequera as an administrative center, and the concentration of nonagricultural employment in the city. The significant merchant, mining, and artisan groups suggest the greater economic diversity of the city at the end of the colonial period, whereas the large numbers in the literate professions (clergy, bureaucrats, lawyers, notaries, physicians) recall the more traditional kinds of high-status employment. The cultivator and Indian tributary groups continue a traditional link between city and countryside. The military payroll category is difficult to interpret because many men with small military salaries would also be artisans, government officials, and so on.

The very large presence of the church in Antequera—over six hundred resident clergy in 1790—cannot be ignored. The political and social

TABLE 2. EMPLOYMENT PATTERNS IN ANTEQUERA, 1790

Trade			
Merchants	209	On military payroll	398
Mining		Skilled and semiskilled labor	1,824
Miners	29		
Professional and Managerial		Unskilled labor	537
Secular clergy	104	Cultivators (includes land owners as well as farm laborers)	396
Regular clergy	493		
Royal officials	172		
Letrados	19	Indians (476½ tributaries)	ca. 2,000
Notaries	5		
Students	150		
Physicians	5		

influence of the Antequera clergy was largely informal in nature and escapes measurement, but the documented wealth of the secular and regular branches of the church gave it considerable direct economic power. By the late eighteenth century religious corporations and individual priests residing in Antequera owned most of the best rural estates in the central valleys. Title to much of the urban center itself was held by the regular orders. In 1792 monasteries and convents owned 870 buildings in Antequera, most of which were rented out. The cathedral church and major monastic establishments were the important credit institutions, holding large mortgages on many rural estates in the province and financing some of the large repartos de efectos. Along with the town council, the church was the one stable source of creole influence in Antequera, for although the bishop was usually a peninsular, the local priesthood was overwhelmingly "español."

The cultivator group is especially difficult to interpret, since it lumps together holders of entailed estates, large landowners, small holders, sharecroppers, and farm laborers. Even a list of landowners from the 1792 census does not provide an easy answer to the status of the landholding group in the urban society. Some owners of rural estates were prominent figures in the government and society of the city. But except for the few who came from the wealthiest or oldest families and owned other property or productive capital, they were dependent for their prominence exclusively on the productivity of their land—a most precarious foundation. Since many estates were sold on the death of their owners, the prestige of a family was rarely ascendant for more than a generation.

Yet unlike most Valley landowners, whose prominence in political affairs was transient, the holders of the Valley's six entailed estates remained in the political and social limelight even when their estates were in decline. Members of the Güenduláin, Ramírez de Aguilar, and Bohórquez families in particular receive frequent mention in colonial records as "leading citizens," thanks to their perpetual membership in the military orders and the town council of Antequera. Not only did the entails of these families and that of the Laso de la Vega family carry with them the title of *regidor perpétuo,* but from time to time individual holders of these estates secured other political and religious offices as well. Some were positions of substantial authority such as corregidor, chief constable, alcalde, and *promotor fiscal del obispado*, an important office in managing the affairs of the bishopric; others, such as *alférez real* or royal ensign were largely honorific. The social rank of holders of entailed estates gave them subtle influence in political matters beyond their tenure in office. Their friendship and advice frequently was sought by political officials of lower social standing. In 1711, for example, the community of Teotitlán del Valle complained that Joseph de Güenduláin's favor with the local alcalde mayor had resulted in a faulty measurement of the boundary between Teotitlán and the Güenduláin hacienda.

Owing to the modest size, heavy indebtedness, and frequent sale of estates owned by non-Indians, the landowning class of Antequera was not a closed, homogeneous, self-perpetuating or especially powerful group. Most new owners, like their predecessors, were not wealthy men. Their investment might be as little as 1,000 pesos on a heavily mortgaged estate worth over 20,000 pesos; the estate was likely to be their only valuable possession and its productivity their sole means of livelihood. Many of Oaxaca's hacendados and farmers were creoles. Of the 133 landowners and tenant farmers in Antequera in 1792, 88 were creoles, 34 were mestizos, 9 were peninsulares, and 3 were mulattoes. This alone suggests that landowners were not a uniform social and economic class in Oaxaca; and furthermore, the creole group, as elsewhere in New Spain, spanned the social spectrum from vagrants, beggars, and impoverished sharecroppers to the wealthiest landowners.

Greater integration of city and countryside accompanied the urban growth of the late eighteenth century. Valley farmers long had met the food demands of the city, but by the second half of the eighteenth century we can begin to speak of contacts between town and countryside that did not depend on taxation, forced labor, and colonial authority. Market demands and large cash reserves bought Adam Smith's "invisible hand" into play, bringing more areas of Oaxaca under the urban influence and modifying production in some peasant communities with the incentive of substantial cash income. Indian-produced pulque supplied the burgeoning public taverns of Antequera, and the famous Saturday market there became a great entrepôt and meeting place for rural people with goods to sell. Utensils, pottery, nuts, fruits, vegetables, livestock and feed, charcoal, wool, hides, grains, and lime: all this and more found its way from rural communities into the city. The flow of people as well as goods from rural areas also increased. Some Valley Indians found steady employment in the city and established permanent residence, whereas for other villagers in the Valley the city became a source of seasonal employment. This pattern of peasants becoming part-time residents of Antequera in the late eighteenth century is well documented for Macuilxóchitl and Tlacochahuaya in the Tlacolula valley. According to an 1801 report, thirty families from Macuilxóchitl resided in Antequera during the post-harvest months. The adult men were employed as weavers and carpenters. In 1803, the parish priest of Tlacochahuaya reported that a number of local men worked in Antequera as carpenters during part of the year. He noted that these men were relatively wealthy and prone to spend heavily on newly acquired vices.[14] In short, the economic expansion of Antequera after 1740 brought qualitative changes to the urban setting. Administration and regulation were to remain important, but they were no longer the overwhelming reasons for the city's existence. Trade, commerce, and manufacturing assumed new importance, and the city and countryside of the central valleys had begun to form a stronger regional system.

The network of contacts between Antequera and the more remote parts of the province grew more extensive at the end of the colonial period, though even then the interrelationships were primarily administrative or economic and did not include many of the areas operating outside the export economy. Antequera had long been the hub of communications in Oaxaca. Mule trails were ordered cleared from Antequera into the Sierra and coastal regions in the 1570s. The main roads led north through the Mixteca Alta to Puebla and southeast to the Isthmus of Tehuantepec and on to Guatemala. The Guatemala and Puebla connections had been especially important in the sixteenth century, when grains, livestock, silk, and cochineal were traded to these neighboring areas. In several important ways, the Mixteca Alta and Baja were more within Puebla's sphere of influence than within Antequera's. Some of the Mixteca priests, merchants, and landowners maintained permanent residence in Puebla, and labor for the obrajes of the city of Puebla in the sixteenth and seventeenth centuries was sometimes recruited from peasant villages in the Mixteca.

Rural Society in the Valley

Most of the inhabitants of the more than two hundred rural communities in the Valley of Oaxaca can be considered a special type of colonial peasantry. Although students of rural sociology still do not agree on the meaning of "peasant," all of the attempts at definition would comprehend the communities of rural Oaxaca.[15] There are four areas of agreement in the various definitions of a peasantry: (1) the peasant is a rural cultivator; husbandry is an important part of the livelihood of the peasant family and community, meeting the major part of local consumption needs; (2) "peasant" implies a specific traditional culture related to the way of life of small communities; (3) the peasant has a dual orientation (*a*) to family and community and (*b*) to markets and a social system beyond the community; and (4) within the larger social system, peasant communities occupy a subordinate position; they normally do not participate in the exercise of political power outside the community, yet there are important points of contact with the larger society. For settled Indian areas of Mexico in the colonial period, the following definition of peasant society is appropriate: a peasant society is composed of settled rural peoples, engaged for the most part in agricultural production on their own lands, whose productive activities, utilization of surpluses, and culturally distinct characteristics are influenced or determined to a significant extent by powerful outsiders.[16]

This general conception of peasantry can help to clarify the position of rural communities in the Valley. Certainly the land-based village was the most striking social group in the Oaxaca countryside. Only a short distance beyond the confines of Antequera, rural communities were visibly discrete clusters of buildings accommodating from a few hundred to a few thousand residents, separated from each other by stretches of plowed fields and grazing land. Local people belonged to their villages in ways that they belonged to no other social group. Heavy emphasis was placed on responsibility to the community, and while private property was common, the peasant family was careful not to flaunt personal wealth. The wills of landholding peasants in colonial Oaxaca regularly contained a disclaimer to the effect that "I am extremely poor" before listing often impressive quantities of privately held land.

In addition to birth, marriage arrangements, and an ethos of "community first," a strong sense of solidarity was supported by territorial consciousness and landholding. One of the striking features of the land system in the Valley during the colonial centuries is the extent of the holdings retained by rural villages and their individual citizens. During the final one hundred years of Spanish rule, they controlled about two thirds of the Valley's agricultural land. Connection to alien landlords thus did not characterize the Valley peasantry. The community's territory was and remained much more than a purely economic or administrative area. The land was symbolic of village identity, and boundary violations were often tantamount to a declaration of war.

This firm link between peasant communities and land ownership under colonial rule was forged in the sixteenth century by Indians sensitive to formal property rights, combined with a crown interest in supporting the means of production of tax-paying subjects. Hard upon the founding of Antequera and the establishment of colonial government in the late 1520s, native nobles and communities began to seek and receive formal title to the lands they had occupied before the conquest, as well as new grants to previously unclaimed grazing land. These same communities willingly incurred the burden of litigation over territorial boundaries. They financed costly trips by their representatives to Mexico City or even to Spain to establish their claim to a disputed boundary. For some of the larger communities, hardly a year passed without a boundary dispute or pending litigation. Sometimes, like other Indian towns of New Spain, they would even engage a permanent legal representative in Mexico City to see to their affairs. The costs of litigation could be very great, often exceeding the value of the land under dispute; yet the lawsuits continued, because more was at stake than a parcel of productive land. This was the very flesh and bone of the community. In the eighteenth century, litigation was accepted as a way of life by many communities, bordering on a costly ritual, the price paid for renewing a certain level of cohesiveness and harmony among their members.

The Valley peasantry retained a definite Indian flavor. Zapotec and Mixtec were the languages of Valley communities, and many communities had a distinctiveness of local speech so strong that they claimed to be unable to understand their neighbors. Racial mixture proceeded slowly in rural Oaxaca. A 1686 investigation to identify non-Indians living in rural communities of the Etla valley located only sixteen individuals in an area with more than 850 Indian tributaries. No more than five of the sixteen resided in any one community. Even in the late eighteenth century, many of the largest communities in the Valley were entirely Indian. A 1777 census lists non-Indians in only forty-two of the eighty-eight towns surveyed; and in 1804 five Valley towns, with 805½ tributaries, recorded only seven Spanish and mestizo residents.[17]

The survival of a hereditary native nobility at the community level is another example of the Indianness of rural Oaxaca. The status and wealth of the *cacicazgo* (hereditary estate of an Indian ruler) experienced a much less complete disintegration in the Valley than in areas of central and northern New Spain that have been studied. The position of a hereditary *cacique,* or ruler, was still a rank of prestige and authority at the end of the eighteenth century, despite signs of decline in wealth and formal political power. There were still unwritten sumptuary laws distinguishing nobles from commoners in some communities, and caciques remained the largest Indian landowners in Oaxaca throughout the colonial period. The cacicazgos of Cuilapan and Etla were the largest individual estates, Indian or Spanish, in the Valley of Oaxaca.

The land-rooted sense of identity of these people depended on the fact that most of the communities were pre-Columbian settlements projected into a colonial setting, thus allowing a long, continuous identification between the community and its territory. Few rural communities in the Valley were new towns, and the Spanish policy of congregation bore very limited fruit in the Valley. Such *congregaciones* as took shape in the Valley were remarkably short-lived. Most of the nine documented examples had broken down into their constituent communities before the end of the seventeenth century.[18]

The ability to provide for basic necessities and the high value placed on village solidarity combined to limit the need for contact among villages and often led to open hostility between the villagers and outsiders. Villages were differentiated from one another not only by each community's solidarity, but also by more tangible distinctions, in things such as accepted weights and measures and clothing styles. Rebellions against local Spanish authorities and bloody battles between communities occurred regularly and are well documented in records for the eighteenth century.

These rural uprisings have several distinctive features which underscore the importance of the peasant community and its cultural distance from the outside, whether from its neighbors or from the urban center at Antequera. First, rural disturbances often involved entire communities, without distinction of age or sex. Startled Spanish witnesses describe mobs of women cradling rocks in their huipiles and small children with sticks in hand fighting alongside the adult men. Second, uprisings provided another means of reaffirming village solidarity and traditional values. Descriptions of two of the better known cases suggest that perceptions about community values could play an important role. In depositions following mob action in Zimatlán in 1772, Indian witnesses said that they hated the Spanish schoolmaster for trying to keep their children from speaking Zapotec. In Tlapacoya in 1784, the local citizens hounded the priest and alcalde mayor out of town with flying rocks and shouts of "We alone are sovereign in this town." Third, the delicate questions of taxation and subordination to Spanish authorities often were involved in many of the short-lived peasant revolts. Priests, alcaldes mayores, and schoolmasters—the local representatives of Spanish authority—were frequently the objects of attack. Especially in the late eighteenth century, the immediate cause of these local uprisings was usually the collection of new church fees or higher state taxes on local products. Fourth, along with the problems just mentioned, boundary disputes were the most frequent sources of collective action. Mob kidnappings, lynchings, and destruction of livestock are all documented, but the most frequent type of mass disturbance over land pitted one village against another in pitched battle. Fifth, the community was the primary unit of revolts. No regional rebellions bringing several towns together in a common movement are known for the Valley in the eighteenth century.[19]

My emphasis on the independent aspects of peasant communities in the Valley does not deny the existence of a web of political and economic connections among villages and between them and the colonial rulers. The peasant communities were not completely self-contained systems, but neither do they represent the "nation-oriented groups" described by anthropologist Eric Wolf, who concludes that Indian communities were qualitatively reconstituted and utterly dependent as a result of Spanish colonization.[20]

Connections between peasant communities and the outside world were numerous. Economic exchange was constant and lively, through regional Indian markets at four secondary centers, as well as the weekly market at Antequera. Working the land was the primary activity of the villagers, but a variety of craft specialties supplemented farming and ranching and promoted market connections, especially in the Tlacolula valley. The potentially coercive side of a colonial economy was softened by the fact that, in contrast to neighboring subregions, the Valley was not suited to cash crops such as sugar cane, cotton, and the cochineal dyestuff, mainly because of its high altitude and temperate climate. The failure of cash crops was not for lack of trying. Sugar cane was planted in every part of the Valley at some time during the colonial period, but always with very modest results. The cultivation of cotton and silkworms was attempted with even less success. During the height of the cochineal boom in the second half of the eighteenth century, small quantities of the cactus mite were raised in the southern and eastern portions of the Valley, but several of the 1777 Relaciones Topográficas declared the cochineal harvest to be poor in quality and yield.[21]

Production of cochineal and maguey (a more important commercial crop in the Valley at this time) was largely confined to Indian lands. Only three of the forty-nine estates for which eighteenth-century inventories have been examined had *nopaleras* for cochineal, and only one on a large scale (6,000 plants). Only two estates listed maguey as an important crop, one with 3,000 plants and another with 100. By comparison, an 1806 report on the cultivation of maguey in peasant communities of the Tlacolula valley lists nearly 50,000 plants in 25 communities.[22] Production figures from San Bartolo Coyotepec, another important maguey-producing village in the Zimatlán valley, have not been located, but one enterprising citizen of nearby San Martín Tilcajete owned approximately 10,000 plants in the late 1760s.

Formal and informal transfers of Spanish culture had been taking place in the Valley from soon after the founding of Antequera. On the formal side, institutions of local government in the peasant communities took on the Spanish cabildo form, with a "gobernador" and alcaldes elected annually. A hierarchy of new local offices was also associated with the church, which, by the end of the sixteenth century, had baptized most Valley residents and constructed church buildings in nearly every town. New offices could, of course, mean that old functions were being continued in a new guise. The hereditary nobility which exercised special power in most communities at the time of the conquest continued to dominate the Indian cabildos in the sixteenth and seventeenth centuries, and many important decisions were made by consensus of the community at large rather than through the formal political channels.

The encomienda as a labor institution was of limited importance in the central valleys. The nominal authority of the Marqués del Valle in the Valley during the early years of the colonial period meant that few Valley towns were available for encomienda grants to individual Spaniards. As the crown reduced the territory and powers of the Marqués in Oaxaca after 1532, it refused to assign many Valley towns to private citizens. By 1590, only six towns in or near the Valley were still held in encomienda. Thus the Valley hardly experienced a phase that was often an important episode in the history of settled Indian areas surrounding organized Spanish municipalities. This contrasts with other regions of the province of Oaxaca, where encomiendas were still numerous at the end of the sixteenth century.

Taxation and labor service were not new to Valley communities, although under Spanish rule they lost much of their former moral and spiritual significance and became obligations imposed from outside. Evasion and resistance to these demands were common. Whole towns were occasionally abandoned to avoid labor service; communities understated their tributary populations to reduce tax and service obligations; and local rebellions frequently accompanied new or higher taxes. Though the encomienda was weak and short-lived, the tribute tax, repartimiento labor drafts, ecclesiastical fees, and later the reparto de efectos still brought the colonial economic system directly into the village.

The labor drafts from rural communities were most important to the sixteenth century, being used to man major construction programs for Antequera. In 1609, 162 Indian residents of the Valley were serving in repartimiento. Forced service in the modest nearby mines of Chichicapa and Magdalena amounted to approximately the same number of Valley Indians as the city repartimientos (213 Indians from eleven Valley towns in 1578), but it appears that the mining drafts endured longer, at least into the 1640s. Smaller labor drafts for service on Valley estates lasted well into the eighteenth century.

The technology of peasant cultivators underwent some important changes during the colonial period. Machete, oxen, and plow replaced the digging stick and stone cutting tools. New crops such as wheat and sugar cane were introduced, if not widely adopted. Animal husbandry—sheep, swine, goats, cattle, poultry—became an important activity in most villages, modifying the diet and providing new raw materials such as wool and hides. Although communal lands were important in Indian villages throughout the period, private ownership took on a larger role as a result of Spanish rule. The development of private property was usually associated with lands acquired after the conquest. For example, two colonial grants of grazing sites to the community of Macuilxóchitl in 1553 and 1573 were divided up by the citizens and held into the eighteenth century as private family plots.

Some villagers learned to speak Spanish, and most dressed in modified Castilian fashion. The one group in native society that became most acculturated to Spanish ways was the nobility. Colonial authorities encouraged Indian caciques and principales to assume the trappings of Spanish nobility. They were usually the first Indians to learn to speak and write in Spanish and to assume Spanish habits of food, dress, and demeanor. Some nobles established permanent residence in Antequera, divorcing themselves physically as well as culturally from their communities. The special status of the Indian nobles gave them access to membership in elite groups that were closed to Indian commoners, and even to the clergy, a rare situation in most parts of New Spain. Access to status in the colonial society was sometimes sustained by the encumbrance of cacicazgo estates. A series of priests drawn from the Indian nobility of Etla was supported in the eighteenth century by an endowment of 2,000 pesos from the cacicazgo of San Juan Guelache.[23]

The acculturation of Indians in the Valley had an important spatial as well as a class dimension. Indian communities within a few kilometers of Antequera normally underwent the most drastic changes. Many of these communities were new foundations to begin with. Several were reported to be transplanted settlements of Nahuatl speakers introduced by Cortés in the 1520s. Trinidad de las Huertas, a nearby settlement, was formed in the early 1530s as a labor pool of Indians for construction work in the city. Lacking ancestral lands or extensive grants, and increasingly hemmed in by urban growth, these Indian communities readily came under the city's influence. Jalatlaco, for example, was gradually engulfed, losing its farmland and water resources, and the residents of Jalatlaco became tied to the economy of the city. As early as the 1630s, men from this community were known as the bakers of Antequera. Other residents of the town worked as tailors, hatters, and cobblers in the city. Jalatlaco's location and its political and economic dependence on Antequera encouraged an intermingling of ethnic groups that gradually undermined the Indian character of the community. In this same time period of the 1630s, Indians in Jalatlaco were complaining of blacks and mulattoes moving in and abusing the earlier residents. By 1777 Jalatlaco was no longer predominantly Indian, 162 of its 294 residents being non-Indians.[24]

Older Zapotec and Mixtec communities within an hour's walk of Antequera were also dependent on the city in many ways. The Antequera marketplace and wage labor opportunities attracted these nearby residents well before the cochineal boom of the eighteenth century. A most intriguing relationship between close-in peasant villages and the urban center is suggested by the business establishment of one Ana María de Santa Cruz, española. During the late seventeenth century, she made a successful career of renting "traditional" costumes (wooden horses, masks, *negritos* outfits) to nearby Indian communities for their feast day celebrations.[25]

Rural Estates

Eighteenth-century records distinguish three types of rural estates in the Valley: haciendas, ranchos, and labores. Haciendas—combined ranching and agricultural enterprises—were the largest and most labor-intensive; ranchos were modest ranching estates; and labores were small farms. Haciendas and ranchos were numerous in the Zimatlán valley, where thirty-nine haciendas and ten ranchos have been identified by name. Haciendas in the Tlacolula valley, fifteen in number, were generally larger in size than those in Zimatlán, and few bordered on one another. Etla, the smallest arm of the Valley, had thirteen haciendas as well as a number of labores. Most labores (48) were located within a radius of seven kilometers of Antequera.

With two exceptions, Valley estates were comparatively small. Valley haciendas in the late eighteenth century generally encompassed two or three cattle estancias and about five *caballerías* of farmland (a total of roughly 4,500 acres). Some haciendas in the Zimatlán valley whose size we know had from two to four estancias (4,000 to 8,000 acres) plus small amounts of farm land. Estates were generally smaller in the Etla valley but encompassed proportionately more arable land. The Hacienda de Guadalupe, for example, owned one "estancia de ganado menor" and at least ten caballerías of arable land (3,000 acres). The largest haciendas were located in the southern portion of the Zimatlán valley and in the Tlacolula valley: San José Progreso and Valdeflores each encompassed seven estancias and two labores (20,000–30,000 acres), and two other estates were not far behind them.

The most important factors determining an hacienda's worth were the amount of arable land, the number of livestock it owned, and the amount of money advanced to laborers. With few exceptions, the larger haciendas relied more heavily on livestock than the smaller ones, which emphasized farming. In the eighteenth century, several of the smaller estates in the Etla and Zimatlán valleys were among the most valuable, worth from 20,000 to 60,000 pesos.

The *casco,* or plant, was the main feature distinguishing the major estates in the Valley from the minor ones. The Hacienda de Guadalupe in the Etla valley had one of the more elaborate building complexes, consisting of a main house, a chapel, a stable, and a granary. The main house was made up of a vestibule, a carriage house, a patio, a main living room, four bedrooms, an oratory, a kitchen, three other rooms, and two *miradores* (places with a view).[26] The casco represented one of the few signs of greater capital investment by the largest estates. Significantly, it was not an investment designed to increase productivity. Haciendas were usually labor intensive rather than capital intensive. The equipment needed to operate an estate was usually worth less than 200 pesos, while the cost of labor, even at the modest rate of two reales per man-day, often exceeded 2,500 pesos annually.

The Valley's labores usually consisted of one to four caballerías of arable land, sometimes irrigated. Because of their small size and the nature of their holdings, farms of this type were viable only when cultivated intensively. They grew several crops, including maize, wheat, beans, fodder, maguey, cactus, and various fruits and vegetables. Although the emphasis was on farming, many enterprises combined it with other kinds of land use, especially orchards and pastureland. The following 1773 inventory of Joseph del Castillo's farm, located on the Jalatlaco River near Antequera, is fairly typical:

3 caballerías of irrigated land (315 acres)
19 oxen
21 horses

1 mule
9 sheep
1 buggy drawn by two mules
various plows, hoes, and other farm implements
80 *fanegas* of corn
150 *zontles* of fodder
2 *fanegas* of corn sown
4 *fanegas* of beans
637 pesos, 6 reales owed to the owner by "various servants"
95 pesos, 5 reales paid in advance to rent water from the Jalatlaco River.[27]

Such an enterprise had the appearance of a small family farm, but its system of labor resembled that of an hacienda. The inventories of labores indicate clearly that the Spanish owners performed little if any of the physical labor on their estates. Day laborers, transient workers, and resident workers prevailed there just as they did on haciendas. Then too, the number of livestock on some labores suggests that the owners considered their estates miniature haciendas rather than farms.

One of the striking features of Spanish land ownership in the Valley was its instability. Although many rural estates grew noticeably, they did so in spite of a weakness in hereditary succession. As elsewhere in the Hispanic world, Spanish landowners in the Valley showed no strong tendency toward primogeniture in the transfer of nonentailed estates; thus estates, especially those consisting of various holdings throughout the Valley, were often divided up among several relatives.

The history of the eight nonentailed haciendas for which we have fairly complete records indicates that sale was a more common means of transfer than inheritance. During the colonial period these eight estates changed hands a total of 89 times. Only 13 of the 89 transfers were by inheritance; the remaining 76 (over 85 percent) were by sale. Sales were especially frequent in the years 1699–1761, when the eight estates were sold a total of 36 times, including seven each for two of them and six each for two others.

The growth of mortgages on rural estates from the late seventeenth century through to the end of the colonial period, both in value and in number, helps to explain the frequency of sales.[28] The church was the major source of credit, normally charging 5 percent interest. Since monasteries, convents, and secular priests generally considered interest payments a desirable fixed income, they did not encourage estate owners to pay off the principal. In fact, most borrowers could not afford to do so anyway. Heavily mortgaged estates paid as much as 1,000 to 1,500 pesos in annual interest, which might exceed the hacienda's income in a year of poor harvests or disease. Foreclosure occasionally followed a failure to meet interest payments, but more often a debt-ridden hacienda would be sold at the death of the owner. Buyers could be found more readily for heavily mortgaged estates, since the initial capital investment, or the difference between the estate's assessed value and the principal of the mortgage, was small. The larger the mortgage, the less capital the new owner needed. However, a vicious circle of sales had been initiated, for the hacienda was quite likely to be sold again if the profits still did not exceed the interest by a safe margin.

Mortgages on rural estates were common throughout New Spain in the late colonial period, but their effect on land transfers was especially great in an area like the Valley of Oaxaca where the value of mortgages was already high and rising. Of 27 eighteenth-century estates for which sufficient information is available, 20 were mortgaged to over 80 percent of their value, 10 to over 90 percent. The average was 76.8 percent for 25 of the 27 estates and 66.9 percent for all 27.[29] The sample shows a strong relationship between large mortgages and sales. All twenty estates mortgaged to over 80 percent of their value were sold on or before the death of the owner.

Production and labor on valley estates.—Production on Valley estates can be characterized as primary to semicomplex. By definition, haciendas combined agriculture with ranching, usually with an emphasis on ranching. The best farmland throughout the colonial period was controlled by Indian communities and native individuals. The marginal lands of many haciendas, combined with the ranching focus of their economic activities, generally made for extensive rather than intensive land use. There were, however, some important exceptions. Several haciendas in the Etla and Zimatlán valleys constructed waterworks and consistently irrigated a large portion of their cultivated fields.

Valley haciendas produced a much less varied group of crops than did the Indian communities. On many estates in the Zimatlán and Tlacolula valleys the only crops were maize, beans, and fodder. In the Etla valley and on lands near Antequera, haciendas and labores concentrated on the cultivation of wheat. The few other hacienda crops were also generally produced for sale: sugar cane (Zimatlán), maguey (Tlacolula and Zimatlán), chick peas (Zimatlán), tomatoes (Etla), and melons (Zimatlán). Small stands of cactus for the production of cochineal are occasionally mentioned in hacienda inventories. Of the nonagricultural hacienda products, salt and lime were the most important. The market for hacienda produce was within the region and heavily concentrated in the city of Antequera. During the mid-sixteenth century, Valley wheat was occasionally shipped to Tehuantepec and Guatemala, but by the early seventeenth century virtually all agricultural trade was regionalized.

Although rural estates relied to a certain extent on indebtedness to insure a reliable supply of permanent labor, resident peonage was not widespread. Still, advances of cash and goods to laborers were a regular feature of the hacienda economy in the eighteenth century, and worker indebtedness consistently exceeded the legal limits set by the crown. In a sample of debts for 475 resident laborers on fourteen Valley estates in the eighteenth century, the average individual debt was 35.5 pesos.[30] With monthly wages generally set at 3.2 pesos, this represents roughly eleven months' work. Individual debts ranged from 1 real to 425 pesos, with 79.6 percent of them exceeding the legal limit of 6 pesos set in 1755. Although debt labor in Oaxaca had coercive overtones, the large debts may actually indicate that rural laborers enjoyed an advantageous bargaining position. Certainly 35.5 pesos was much more than necessary to perpetuate a laborer's indebtedness. This suggests that the estate laborer could and did demand special advances and luxuries from his master. When the Audiencia enforced the 6-peso rule for resident peons on one hacienda in 1791, the owner complained that he would not be able to find Indians to work for him regularly if he could not advance them more than this.

The majority of resident laborers living inside the casco on Valley haciendas in the late eighteenth century were Indians, though there were also significant numbers of mulattoes and mestizos. Of 1,499 non-Spanish residents on Valley haciendas recorded in 1777, 966 were Indians, 411 were mulattoes, and 122 were mestizos.[31] The records indicate that haciendas and labores in Oaxaca had modest numbers of resident workers during the eighteenth century, ranging from 1 to 99. Of the 56 Valley estates included in the 1777 census, 12 had no resident workers, 33 had 1 to 3, and only 4 had more than 50. The mean average was 11; the median was 3.

It seems likely that most haciendas relied more heavily on day labor by Indians from nearby communities than on resident peonage. The repartimiento labor drafts also persisted in the Valley to the end of the colonial period to supply haciendas. Such grants usually went to estates claiming to face ruin from a shortage of voluntary laborers. The temporary, stopgap nature of eighteenth-century repartimientos in the Valley is indicated by the fact that termination dates were clearly stated in the grants.

When repartimientos and voluntary recruitment methods failed, some hacendados resorted to coercion to retain laborers. Several hacendados refused to allow debts to be repaid, attempting to make them hereditary. (But in contrast to nineteenth-century practice, debts could not legally be passed on to heirs in the colonial period. The Audiencia once returned two young children to their Indian grandmother after an hacendado had taken them from her, claiming they were responsible for the debts of their deceased father.) Workers might be threatened with physical harm if they attempted to leave. In a practice reminiscent of the reparto de efectos, some hacendados literally forced money and goods on reluctant Indians in order to establish a legal bond of obligation. At the local level, the Spanish government supported involuntary hacienda labor in several ways. During the 1790s, natives of Zaachila who were unable to pay their tribute were sometimes forced to work on local haciendas in lieu of going to jail. Native lawbreakers might also be sent to haciendas, as in the case of Indians from the rebellious town of Soledad Etla, who were arrested and sent to the Hacienda de Güenduláin when they tried to sell goods at the market in Antequera without permission.

The operation of a valley estate.—Annual account records summarizing costs and value of production comprise one of the fullest sources for describing the operation of colonial estates. These records are as scarce as they are important to understanding the characteristics of production on landed estates. In searching for Oaxaca hacienda documentation, I have located only four sets of account records. By contrast, estate inventories, snapshots of assets and liabilities at a specific moment in time, are relatively abundant. A set of four accounts for the San Juan Bautista hacienda has survived, covering five and a half years within the time span 1789-1795.[32]

Before discussing production at San Juan Bautista, I will briefly describe the estate itself. By 1790, the San Juan Bautista hacienda, one of the two or three most valuable estates in the Valley, included roughly 1,470 acres of farmland (fourteen caballerías) and 2,000 acres of pasture (one *sitio de ganado menor*) in the Zimatlán valley west of San Bartolo Coyotepec and San Agustín de las Juntas. In the early 1640s the property of the estate was consolidated, and the permanent casco and outbuildings began to take shape. By the mid-eighteenth century San Juan Bautista had been sold on six separate occasions. The final transfer during the colonial period was to the Carmelites of Antequera, who purchased the property in 1745 for 60,000 pesos. The Carmelites apparently regretted their purchase, for they later twice unsuccessfully attempted to sell the estate at 5 percent below its appraised value.

Unlike most haciendas in the Valley, but like others among the most valuable, San Juan Bautista drew its basic worth from its farmland. The land was appraised at more than half the value of the estate in 1745. No other Valley hacienda could match fourteen caballerías of good arable land; after 1733, when a ditch 4,300 *varas* long was dug, ten caballerías became choice irrigated land (a *vara* is a little less than a yard). On the other hand, San Juan Bautista was one of the least important ranching haciendas in the Valley. Of the livestock recorded there in the eighteenth century, a large proportion were draft animals used in farming. A 1794 inventory recorded 271 oxen, 16 horses, 7 mules, 512 sheep, and 50 swine. A 1741 inventory reported even fewer sheep, goats, and dairy cattle: 55 goats, 71 sheep, 23 cows, 145 oxen, 21 horses, 42 mules, and 1 burro. (In contrast, an important ranching hacienda would have sheep, goats, and cattle by the thousand and far fewer service animals.) Only one type of production for outside markets which is not specifically agricultural—extracting and processing lime—appears in the inventories or on the account books for San Juan Bautista. And although the hacienda had operated a lime kiln in the mid-seventeenth century, this activity was of virtually no importance to San Juan Bautista's market economy between 1789 and 1795.

The casco of the hacienda in 1745 was composed of a principal building (*casa grande*) valued at 6,156 pesos, plus corrals, chicken coops, a granary, and a separate storage bin for corn. Tools, plows, carts, and other farming and ranching equipment were valued at less than 500 pesos, roughly the same as the religious paintings and chapel furnishings on the estate. Other important categories in the 1745 inventory were draft animals (1,672 pesos), other livestock (618 pesos), expenses for irrigation works, building improvements, and clarifying land titles (3,685 pesos), value of grain in the mow (1,170 pesos), and the accumulated debts of thirteen resident workers (503 pesos). The only major technological improvement on the hacienda before 1745 was the long irrigation ditch. Water from this *zanja* probably powered the flour mill which was constructed on the estate in 1788 and which made an important contribution to income during the years of the account records.

The production figures for the estate are consistent with San Juan Bautista's strength in farm land. The value of crops produced over the five and a half years was roughly eight and a half times the value of livestock and dairy products sold or exchanged; 27,791 pesos 7½ reales for crops, 3,380 pesos 4 reales for livestock of all types, milk, and wool. Most of this 5,053 pesos worth of average annual farming output was sold or exchanged in the city of Antequera. The emphasis on farming over ranching is especially evident in the fact that fodder was produced for sale (951 pesos 2 reales worth) by San Juan Bautista rather than used to expand local ranching activities. Furthermore, the hacienda's one ranching site was rented out during part of this period.

Corn, wheat, and beans were consistently the most important crops on the estate. Over the period of the accounts, the value of corn production totaled 13,330 pesos 3 reales; wheat and flour, 8,900 pesos 4½ reales; and beans, 2,138 pesos 6 reales. In contrast to most haciendas in the Zimatlán valley, which cultivated only maize and beans, San Juan Bautista produced a variety of other crops in small quantities: chickpeas, watermelons, cochineal, reed grass, hay, and barley. Sugar cane was not produced in

1789 to 1795, but was reportedly grown in 1694 (18 *surcos,* "rows," "furrows") and 1848 (50 surcos). Predictably, there was considerable fluctuation in production figures for each crop even over this short period. The value of corn production, for example, varied from 600 pesos to 6,565 pesos; flour, from 890 pesos to 2,244 pesos; beans, from 297 pesos to 1,000+ pesos; and watermelons from 7 pesos ½ real to 289 pesos 4 reales.

On the debit side of the ledger, mortgage payments and labor costs occupied a commanding position (see Table 3). Interest charges and labor, together, account for nearly 80 percent of total expenses over the five and a half years. Since the mortgages were capellanías administered by the Carmelite monastery, the Carmelites were in the curious position of being both owner and major creditor of the estate. Interest charges on the mortgages were the last expenses to be paid by San Juan Bautista and were consistently in arrears. As a result, labor amounted to an even larger share of paid up expenses than the 37.8 percent figure computed from the accounts. If we exclude mortgage payments altogether, labor amounts to 64.6 percent of the remainder. The cost of labor is somewhat inflated by the fact that workers seem to have been charged exorbitant prices for grain produced on the estate. In 1790, for example, workers were charged 3.87 pesos per *fanega* of corn (a fanega being something more than a bushel), when the market value of San Juan Bautista's corn was approximately 2.14 pesos per fanega. The meager cost of equipment, construction and maintenance (8 percent of expenses), and livestock purchased

TABLE 3. EXPENSES OF THE SAN JUAN BAUTISTA HACIENDA: JULY 1789 TO DECEMBER 1792, JANUARY 1794 TO DECEMBER 1795

Type of Expense	Amount	Percentage of Total
Mortgages	15,056p 2½rr	39.4
Labor	14,319p 1½rr	37.8
Supplies, construction costs	2,977p 5rr	7.8
Household	2,172p 3½rr	5.5
Livestock	2,356p 3½rr	6.1
Tithe	906p	2.3
Water use	40p	.1
Cost of sowing wheat and beans, 1791	181p 4½rr	.4
Cost of cochineal harvest, 1791	252p 1r	.6
Total	37,211p 5½rr	100.0

(6.3 percent of expenses) provides further evidence of San Juan Bautista's labor-intensive operations. Rather than maintaining a community of resident workers, the hacienda largely recruited labor from nearby villages on a seasonal basis. During 1793, fifty-eight individuals worked at San Juan Bautista for an average of 4.3 days each. The only important capital investment on the estate during the Carmelite ownership was the flour mill constructed in 1788. A hidden expense for the estate was the apparently adverse balance of exchange with the monastery. The accounts (probably incomplete) register 4,866 pesos 4 reales worth of goods and cash passing to the monastery compared with 4,043 pesos 5 reales in cash provided by the Carmelites. The goods sent to Antequera suggest that the hacienda supplied the basic foodstuffs required by the monastery: flour, milk, beans, and corn.

Matching costs against production, it appears that San Juan Bautista operated at a loss throughout the period covered by the account books (see Table 4). Losses totaled 6,386 pesos 5 reales for an average of 1,161 pesos per year. Since the average loss was well within the 2,715 pesos owed to the convent in interest each year, the losses on paper did not create an urgent need to sell the estate even though the Carmelites could have invested its value in more profitable 5 percent loans. To a casual reader, the finances of the estate were deceptively favorable. The accounts for 1791 and 1792 were carefully juggled, deleting mortgages and several other key expenses to give the impression of substantial profits. In fact, the period of these accounts, despite the losses, was one of the brighter spots in the economic history of San Juan Bautista under Carmelite ownership. The administrator calls the years 1791 and 1792 "very good

TABLE 4. PROFITS AND LOSSES, SAN JUAN BAUTISTA HACIENDA

Time	Expenses	Value of Sales and Exchanges	Probable Profit or Loss
July 1789–Dec. 1790	11,081p 6½rr	10,159p 1r	- 922p 5½rr
Jan. 1791–Jan. 1792	7,828p 5rr	6,909p 3½rr	- 919p 3½rr
Feb. 1792–Dec. 1792	6,366p 4rr	5,971p 4½rr	- 394p 7½rr
Jan. 1794–Dec. 1795	12,203p 6rr	8,054p	- 4,149p 6rr
Total losses			- 6,386p 5rr

harvests," whereas earlier attempts to sell the estate in the 1740s and 1760s imply heavy losses.

Town, Country, and Attitudes toward Independence

The distinction between urban Antequera and the surrounding countryside involved more than material wealth and physical appearances. Despite longstanding economic ties, both Spanish city folk and Indian peasants perceived the differences in moral and ethnic terms. To villagers, Spaniards were outsiders who could not share in the meaning of their community except through the exercise of raw power or through participation in the recognized overarching authority of church or state. To Oaxaca's Spaniards, rural Indians were "niños con barbas" or perpetual minors, cowardly, drunken, and vice-ridden by nature. The idea of order in each of these societies widened the cultural gap between them. In trying to uncover the cause of a major rebellion in Zimatlán in 1772, their Spanish parish priest made this difference quite clear. He considered the uprising the end product of the Indians' "wicked" style of government. Drawing a parallel to Spain's arch-rival England, he warned that continual uprisings could be expected in Indian villages because "everyone rules"; women and children had a voice in Zimatlán's community decisions, as he noted with some disgust. Consensus decision-making in rural Oaxaca received little sympathy from Spaniards imbued with the idea of a natural order based on highly stratified hierarchies.

Developments in the thirty years preceding the independence movement sharpened social and political divisions, including those existing within the capital city of Antequera itself. Fresh tensions in the urban society appeared in the mid-1780s as the cochineal trade fell off and old problems of food, water supply, and epidemic disease returned. The decline of cochineal roughly coincided with the inception of Bourbon political and tax reforms in Oaxaca. The complex causes of crisis in the cochineal industry seemed simple to the peninsular merchants and high churchmen of Antequera whose futures were most directly affected by it. They attributed everything to the new politics of free trade and laissez faire. The intendants and their associates, they thought, were far too tolerant of Indian vices and too naive in their belief that Indian producers would respond to laws of supply and demand. And in fact, the termination in 1783 of the reparto de efectos, which had forced Indians in the cochineal districts to produce the dyestuff in return for cash advances, undoubtedly cut deeply into dye production.

These were tense times in the city. The local representatives of the crown were blamed for a host of problems, old and new. Panic in the city in 1797 over the possible spread of a smallpox epidemic from the Tlacolula valley gave rise to an ultra-conservative political movement in the name of "Death to bad government, long live the Law of God!" Antequera's economic and social elite blamed weak government for unrest among artisans, priests, overtaxed merchants, debt-ridden landowners, and litigious Indians.

The dissatisfaction of the peninsular merchants and priests with the provincial government came to a head in 1809 when the stridently Hispanophile bishop of Oaxaca, Antonio Bergoza y Jordán, went to the Audiencia with charges of corruption, moral laxity, and weak leadership against the acting intendant, Antonio Izquierdo, and other royal officials. As a result of his actions and neglect, said Bergoza, Indians were in revolt, unrest was general, and the city suffered under a food shortage because the Indians were insolent and refused to work on the haciendas or to pay their debts. He claimed that one of the Valley's best farming estates had been virtually abandoned by its owner because he could not find laborers, and the ill-willed Indians of Zaachila prevented new workers from entering the estate. The investigation into Izquierdo's performance lasted over two years, leaving a cloud over the city's public affairs as the emotion-charged events leading to independence gathered momentum.

This enthusiasm of the merchants and prominent priests for reactionary politics as a solution to their problems skated over the surface of the more deeply imbedded sources of conflict in Oaxaca. There were important and complex divisions between rural peasants and urban rulers, between creole Spaniards and colonial government, and divisions also within the landholding class of Spaniards, within the church itself, and between the peninsular elite and the current royal officials; these would not disappear with a change of local politicians and tax collectors. The declaration of independence in September 1810, and the preparations in 1811-1812 for the defense of Antequera against the forces of José María Morelos, set these divisions in bold relief.

A detailed list of donations for the defense of Antequera against the independence forces in July 1812 allows us to identify the social groups which actively supported the continuation of Spanish rule. Merchants, priests, military officers, and state functionaries—mostly peninsulares—account for nearly all of the 44,617 pesos collected from 223 individuals, 4 revenue agencies, and an unknown number of convents and sodalities. The merchants in particular rallied to the crown's side: 147 of them contributed 21,182 pesos, or 47 percent of the funds raised. Twenty-one merchants contributed 400 pesos each or more. The church was the other major donor, with 12,113 pesos (27 percent of the total), of which 3,410 pesos were contributed by 48 individual priests (the bishop headed the list with 500 pesos), 7,814 from the regular orders, and 889 pesos from sodalities. Six military officers contributed 3,464 pesos, and various state employees contributed 5,835 pesos. The last group donating to the loyalist cause was local landowners, and their share of the total amounted to less than 5 percent (2,023 pesos). Only 19 landowners contributed, and only 5 of them accounted for more than 66 pesos each.[33]

The guiding spirit behind the military and political defense was Bishop Bergoza, who proclaimed the excommunication of Father Hidalgo, mobilized church support for the loyalists, formed the Provincial Batallion from priests, sacristans, artisans, merchants, and a few wealthy hacendados, and directed the Junta de Defensa in 1812. The few creole landowners who supported the loyalists in 1812, or in 1814 when the city was recaptured, were members of the economic elite—holders of entailed estates such as Captain Manuel Güenduláin, José María Laso, and José Jimeno Bohórquez, or especially prosperous hacendados such as Francisco Monterrubio and Juan José Ruiz.

Beyond this narrow slice of Antequera society—the economic elite and an important part of the priesthood—the urban population was passive or openly hostile to the loyalists. It is not surprising, then, to learn that it took less than two hours for Morelos to overcome the half-hearted defense of the city on November 26, 1812. A number of artisans belonged to the ranks of the loyalist batallion, but as early as July 1811 they complained that they could not make more financial sacrifices in the king's service. As preparations for defense of the city became an urgent matter in August 1812, Antonio González, a principal loyalist organizer, complained bitterly of the slow progress being made, the public criticisms, and the general lack of enthusiasm for the loyalist cause in the city.

The creole population, clinging to a precarious gentility while the benefits of Bourbon politics and the mid-eighteenth-century boom largely eluded them, had little to gain by supporting the loyalists. They account for many of the active as well as the passive resisters who welcomed the Morelos forces and delighted in driving the peninsular merchants, bureaucrats, and high ecclesiastics from the city. The hatred of urban creoles for the peninsular elite was the most sharply defined division in provincial politics in 1812 and goes far to account for Oaxaca's part in the independence movement—limited by regional interests but still most active politically. As Brading has noted, it was the creoles—in Oaxaca, the small landholders in particular—who generally descended the social ladder and found new political opportunities closed to them in the last generations before independence, while the peninsular immigrants dominated the lucrative export industries and occupied the powerful official positions.

The Dominicans, being closely identified with Oaxaca from the earliest stages of Spanish settlement and largely staffed with *oaxaqueños,* felt the creole predicament acutely at the end of the colonial period.

Throughout the eighteenth century, the Dominicans were locked in a bitter struggle with the secular church for control of the populous rural parishes they had administered since the sixteenth century. This was an unequal and unsuccessful struggle for the Dominicans, since the peninsular bishops of Oaxaca represented the crown's interests quite closely and had direct influence with the metropolitan decision-makers. With their spiritual and temporal authority eroding, the Dominicans in Antequera cast their lot with the independence forces in 1812. The order's provincial superior, fray Francisco Aparicio, placed nearly two million pesos of Dominican assets at the disposal of the Morelos government.

Sentiments about independence in the countryside especially underline the politically negative, separatist spirit of rural communities in Oaxaca. Rural support for Morelos was concentrated in pockets of northern Oaxaca, the districts where cochineal and cotton textile traders had penetrated most intensively during the fifty years preceding 1810. There appears to be a close connection between political unrest and the pressure for export production. The criminal records for the district of Teposcolula evince growing tensions after 1775 between royal officials and Indian communities, over payment of tribute and production of cochineal and cotton huipiles. Imprisonment of Indians for reneging on commitments to produce cochineal touched off at least three rebellions against merchants and royal officials in northern Oaxaca in the 1780s and 1790s.

In most of rural Oaxaca, however, the peasantry did not choose sides. Villages in the central valleys were suspicious of all outside authority. It made little difference whether the intruders were constitutionalists or monarchists. The issues over which Oaxaca's peasants could be driven to rebellion were local—usually land disputes, kidnappings, cattle rustling, abusive governors or priests, and high taxes—and the battles were fought at home. The loyalist governors in Antequera in 1811–1812 appreciated this fact and tried to exploit it to their advantage with a strategy of settling as many land disputes as possible, always in favor of the largest community involved.

Conditions in Oaxaca at the end of the colonial period were ripe for an urban creole rebellion sparked from outside and supported by rural areas in the north of the region, where export products had recently been developed with ruthless efficiency. Of the groups that could mobilize for a political cause, the decisive split in Oaxaca was between the peninsular elite on the one hand and creole landowners, intellectuals, and skilled artisans on the other. Oaxaca's Indian villages were shielded from the risks and rewards of a general provincial struggle by their militant xenophobia, relative wealth, and urge toward self-sufficiency. The tradition of fierce local identities, extensive (if decreasingly adequate) community landholdings, and bloody battles between rural villages over territory survives to this day. Nearly one fourth of Mexico's 2,344 modern *municipios* are located in the state of Oaxaca. Every village, no matter how small, and with little regard for the financial burden of operating a municipality, still wants to govern itself. Most have succeeded, though today the price has become very dear.

NOTES

1. The present chapter, a panoramic treatment of the society and economy of the Oaxaca region, may be supplemented by my *Landlord and Peasant in Colonial Oaxaca,* which concentrates more rigorously on aspects related to land tenure, as well as going into greater detail on the physical and narrative background. Specific references are not given for material here which draws on *Landlord and Peasant.* Neither are individual archival documents cited, except when the document directly supports a significant and previously undocumented point. The illustrations used can be multiplied indefinitely from the rich documentation available. For demographic aspects, John K. Chance and I are presently engaged in a more systematic study of Antequera's society at the end of the eighteenth century, based on the detailed manuscript census of 1792 and related documentation; that publication will be exhaustively referenced.

2. Ronald Spores, "The Zapotec and Mixtec at Spanish Contact," p. 964. Enrique Florescano and Isabel Gil, eds., *Descripciones económicas generales de Nueva España, 1784–1817,* p. 146.

3. By 1799, the central valleys' percentage of the provincial Indian population had declined slightly to 26.7 percent. Archivo General de la Nación (Mexico City) (AGN) Criminal 309 segunda parte, exp. 1.

4. Spores, "The Zapotec and Mixtec," p. 986.

5. AGN Tributos 43, exp. 9, fol. 8r.

6. José María Murguía y Galardi, "Extracto general que abraza la estadística . . . del estado de Guaxaca . . . 1827," manuscript, University of Texas, passim.

7. Francisco del Paso y Troncoso, *Epistolario de la Nueva España, 1505–1818,* IV:141.

8. Archivo General de las Indias (Seville) (AGI), México 357.

9. D. A. Brading, "Government and Elite in Late Colonial Mexico," p. 394.

10. For this and similar points see Brian R. Hamnett, *Politics and Trade in Southern Mexico, 1750–1821.* This book is largely devoted to the administrative aspects of the cochineal trade, including the role of the alcaldes mayores and of Mexico City commercial interests. There is also information on the textile industry. For the present discussion see especially pp. 127–29 and 187.

11. AGN Historia 522.

12. See John K. Chance, "Race and Class in a Colonial Mexican City: A Social History of Antequera, 1521–1800." Especially pp. 219, 229, and 266 are drawn upon in the following pages.

13. Brading, "Government and Elite," p. 393.

14. Archivo del Estado de Oaxaca (AEO), Juzgados, bundle labeled 1801. Collección Castañeda Guzmán (Oaxaca), typescript of report by Lic. Juan José de Echarri, April 29, 1803.

15. A spirited ongoing discussion of definitions appears in *Peasant Studies Newsletter,* I-III (1972-74).

16. See Teodor Shanin, ed., *Peasants and Peasant Societies,* pp. 14-15, and Henry A. Landsberger, ed., *Latin American Peasant Movements,* pp. 1-3.

17. AGN Hospital de Jesús 163, exp. 48, fol. 46r; ibid., 63 passim; AGI México 2589-91 passim.

18. In spite of the dispersion of people back to their former townsites, the congregation policy had an interesting long-term impact in areas near the Valley, similar to Orlando Fals Borda's findings in rural Colombia. The Indians abandoned the congregation center, but did continue to go there several times a year for ceremonial occasions. Biblioteca Nacional (Madrid), MS 2450, fol. 30r, Relación de Lachixijo.

19. Impressive regional rebellions did occur in other parts of the province in the seventeenth century, especially in Tehuantepec during the 1660s and the Sierra Zapoteca in the 1690s.

20. Eric Wolf, "Aspects of Group Relations in a Complex Society: Mexico," in Shanin, *Peasants and Peasant Societies,* pp. 50-68.

21. Biblioteca Nacional (Madrid) MSS. 2449-50.

22. Colección Castañeda Guzmán, "Instrucción para los visitadores de magueyes de la comprehensión de la Receptoría de Teutitlán del Valle, 1806."

23. AGN Bienes Nacionales 553, exp. 8.

24. AGI México 355 and 2589.

25. AEO Juzgados, bundle labeled 1612-1683.

26. AGN Hospital de Jesús 330, exp. 1, fol. 7r (1699).

27. Archivo Público de Notarías del Estado de Oaxaca, volume for 1733, fol. 54r.

28. We know of six haciendas that were mortgaged in the seventeenth century. The total was 20,760 pesos or 46.4 percent of the estates' value of 44,719 pesos. For the years 1700-1750 we know of nine mortgaged haciendas whose total mortgages were 74.7 percent of their value.

29. The total value of the twenty-seven estates was 346,456 pesos with mortgages of 231,855 pesos. For twenty-five estates (excluding Santa Cruz and San Juan Bautista) the totals were 252,711 pesos and 194,057 pesos respectively.

30. Figures from the sample: 1-6 pesos, 97 laborers; 7-30 pesos, 170 laborers; 30-60 pesos, 112 laborers; 61-90 pesos, 56 laborers; over 91 pesos, 40 laborers.

31. AGI Mexico 2589-91 passim.

32. Colección Castañeda Guzmán, titles and account records of the Hacienda San Juan, Bautista.

33. For this and much else on these matters, see AEO Juzgados, bundles labeled 1810-1812, and Colección Martínez Gracida, Biblioteca Genaro V. Vásquez (Oaxaca), Vol. 25.

Part II: The Center

In this section we have four chapters on the hinterland of Mexico City and one on that of Puebla; three studies concentrate on the earlier part of the colonial period, two on the later. Thus the world of the central Mexican countryside and small towns is well represented. As might be expected in an area at the hub of interregional movements both before and after the conquest, complexity is great; there is a dense population not only of human beings but of structures and countervailing forces. The groups and tendencies seen here do not differ in kind, in and of themselves, from those of the South, but they jostle each other more in their closeness. The Hispanic and Hispanized elements of the countryside, a topic central to all the chapters here, existed between what were perhaps the two strongest social forces in the whole country: the metropolis of Mexico City above, and the web of Nahua states, provinces, and towns below, each in its own way shaping and directing the course of development.

As to the capital, a macrocosmic embodiment of all that was Spanish Mexico, let it be portrayed for the moment by its drastic repercussions in its hinterland and by the Hispanic provincials there, who were but its reflection. As to the Indian world of the Center, we are just beginning to have a sense of its internal cultural and social life, and how this bears on the whole; such things enter into our chapters to some extent, and there are also some sketches of local Indian corporate entities in the postconquest context. But for the Indian corporation, the reader should consult Charles Gibson's *Aztecs under Spanish Rule,* which contains massive treatments of how the Indian towns of the Valley of Mexico maintained themselves and exerted strong influence on the nature and boundaries of Spanish provincial institutions, economic as well as governmental and religious. Political and religious offices within the community, as well as many aspects of labor and economic activities, are also discussed extensively in this rich book. Most of the descriptions are applicable to surrounding valleys as well.

One would be inclined to include western Michoacán as part of the Center, since it was a contiguous temperate area with sedentary peoples in fixed provincial units, and it experienced enough in-migration to have a very substantial Spanish sector by the end of the colonial period. Much of the region's historical literature, however, belongs to the genre of ecclesiastical romance, and, though the jurisdictional-institutional aspects are well enough known, the social-economic evolution of Michoacán is a lacuna. Our most useful knowledge comes from people and things leaving the area. We know that Tarascan migrants to the Bajío and the Northern mines acted, in general, like their Nahua counterparts. We know that wooden artifacts in Spanish style, produced in Michoacán, were reaching the Center in the sixteenth century, a typical attempt of an out-of-the-way region to gain a hold on the silver economy. And we know that Toluca pig dealers treated Michoacán as a backwoods area where they could buy animals cheap for ultimate sale in Mexico City. Thus Michoacán seems to have some of the attributes of the Valley of Oaxaca as an area temperate and attractive in itself, with agricultural, nucleated Indians, able to support a bishopric and a Spanish municipality, but remote, isolated, and without products strongly profitable in interregional or export trade. Yet at the end of the colonial period the proportion of the Spanish to the Indian sector in terms of census categories was more like the Center than the South, in fact veering toward the high proportions of non-Indians seen in the North.

J.L.

3. Capital and Province, Spaniard and Indian: The Example of Late Sixteenth-Century Toluca

James Lockhart

Indians of Central Mexico

In central Mexico, Indian entities, practices, and products survived the conquest in an important way.[1] Spanish actions there took place against this background, and were often directly built upon and determined by it. If the Indian stratum was a crucial determinant in the region overall, it was even more so in the specific subareas, where shapes, sizes, and trends of colonial-period structures often followed minutely the contours of preconquest phenomena. By rights, then, any treatment of a part of this region should start with a close characterization of that particular area's Indian sector as it existed around the time of conquest. The time for this order of specificity, however, has not yet come, and we must count ourselves fortunate if we can piece together some notion of relevant general characteristics for the entire region.

The root characteristic of Indian central Mexico (not unique to the region—very little was) was a productive maize agriculture, with its concomitants, a dense population and settlement sites whose permanence must be reckoned by the century. The area's peak phenomenon, on the other hand, was the Aztec empire, whose great metropolis of Tenochtitlan drew people and tribute from its own valley and from the surrounding ones. Preconquest Tenochtitlan, in fact, had social-economic relationships with areas like Toluca and Cuernavaca that hardly differed from ones obtaining between its successor Mexico City and those same regions during the colonial period. The preconquest precedents of imperial tribute, migration, subordination, and superordination were important. Yet in

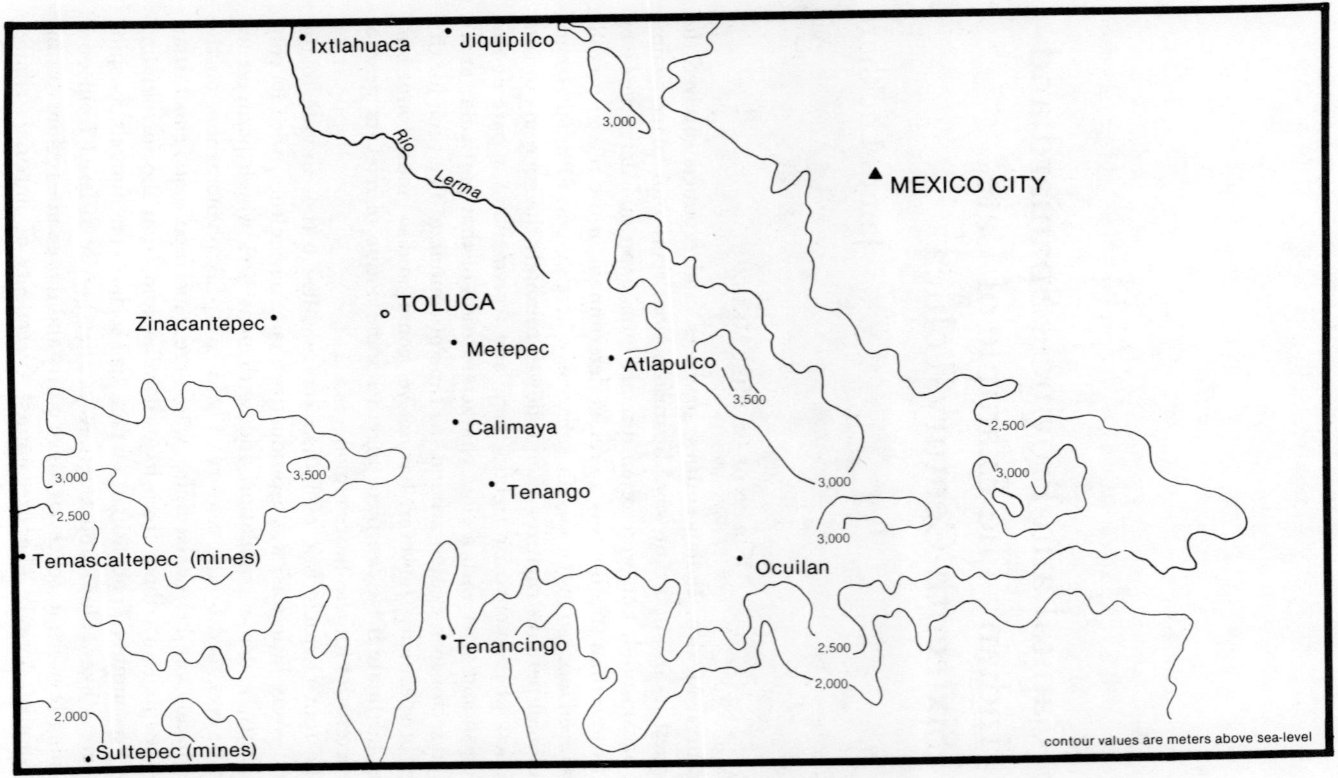

The Valley of Toluca

many senses the empire was destroyed, and the relationships arose anew, partly out of geographic-demographic realities and the logic of the behavior of a dominant group taking the preconquest location as its own capital.

The unit that had preceded the empire in time and survived as a living entity into the colonial period, still asserting itself, maintaining its integrity and its traditions, was the town or subprovince, the county-sized unit, in Nahuatl the *altepetl,* larger than a hamlet and smaller than a valley basin, with some consciousness of itself as an independent group or people. "Altepetl" usually translates as "city" or "town," but like its Spanish counterpart it was basically less an urban complex than the association of a group of people with a given extended territory. If the word's primary effective reference was to the people as an organized body, yet it was, by origin, a territorial metaphor, "water and hill." The entire central Mexican landscape and population was articulated in terms of these city-states.[2] Internal organization varied a good deal. Some units had four territorial subdivisions; others had some form of dual organization, either territorial or of the moiety type. Sometimes individual dependencies of the unit were located at some distance from the home territory. But in most cases there was a single large settlement, the city proper ("cabecera" in Spanish colonial usage, as seen in previous chapters), located more or less centrally to the area, with subject villages (called "sujetos" by the Spaniards) lying all around as far as the city-state's borders extended. In the cabecera was a *tlatoani,* "king" or "ruler," a dynast who adjudicated and decreed for the entire unit and who received tribute and labor from all his subjects. He was surrounded socially and aided officially by a proud, self-conscious noble class of which he himself was a member.

Each outlying village was a *calpulli,* a community in its own right with its own territorial dimensions (calpulli names were things like "in the marsh," "below the hill," and so on); it had its own headman and hierarchy, for internal self-regulation on the one hand and performance of duties to the city-state on the other. The cabecera itself consisted of several wards, each a calpulli. The city-state was an economy as well as a society and a polity. There were merchants and craftsmen. The complementary agricultural and craft specialties of the different sujetos were traded in the cabecera market. As to land, the main regime was a patrimonial one mixing elements of the private and the communal. The bulk of the good land belonged residually to the calpulli; in practice it was held by individual families as long as they survived, the only limitation on tenure being that they could not alienate the land. The body of commoners holding and working productive maize lands in this way, and paying tributes as a function of it, represented the lasting strength of the calpullis and the city-state. Although individual sujetos might have memories or ambitions of independence, and the whole unit was not necessarily inward-looking, it was quite self-contained, complete, and capable of sustaining itself.

From the above considerations, one can readily see how these city-states could deliver tributes and labor to the Spaniards through the tlatoani's prerogatives, yet otherwise remain, initially, quite untouched. Indestructible, highly conscious of their group identity, they, more than any other factor, dictated colonial jurisdictional boundaries and population clusters. But this corporate weight, the permanent underpinning of central Mexican society, should not hide from us another aspect of the Indian world: patterns of individual action and mobility which had much in common with those of the Europeans and were to meet the Spaniards half way in the region's social-economic evolution.

In the oldest postconquest Nahuatl documents there is evidence that Indians did not adhere strictly or exclusively to systems of patrimonial-communal land. When they felt impelled to leave such land for any reason, they simply did so; the plot might lie vacant a while, or someone else might come and start cultivating it, entirely on his own initiative, hoping that formal permission would come later. Even more importantly, there was much land, dry or hilly or rocky, with which the calpulli did not concern itself, and individuals took this up, abandoned or traded it as they saw fit, with no limitation and without paying taxes on it. Many of the rulers and nobles also had fully private lands in addition to patrimonial ones, and these were extensive and fertile.

The most interesting aspect of the lands of the powerful is that they were worked by persons who, though they were like the commoners in most respects, did not belong to a calpulli and did not have calpulli land or perform calpulli duties, but were the permanent direct dependents of the nobles. Scholarship has often elevated these dependents into a separate class of serfs, but in the sources they usually receive the same denomination as other commoners, *macehualli.* Though systematic research on the topic lies ahead of us, everything suggests that the dependents were mainly people in a marginal position because of recent change of status, whether conquest by another group, or their own movement as individuals from one group to another. In Tlaxcala and Huejotzingo, the proportion of such dependents was greatest in the areas most recently acquired.[3]

But the individual movement is the most suggestive. Large-scale individual migration from one city-state to another must be postulated as a major constituent process of preconquest central Mexico. Only on this basis, for example, is the rise and apogee of Tenochtitlan intelligible. Such migration gave the corporations the flexibility necessary to their survival, allowing inevitable demographic and economic shifts to take place without destroying the life and identity of the city-states. When a household grew too large, the younger members often went elsewhere: to another calpulli, to be with the tlatoani, to another city altogether. The servants, slaves, and other direct dependents of Indian noblemen were often familyless young people from distant areas. Mobility among the rulers' dependents can be deduced from the uniformity and smallness of their families and of the plots they worked, as compared to the rich variety seen in more established situations.

The upshot is that the people of central Mexico were fully accustomed to leaving their calpullis and city-states (not necessarily to the detriment of those organizations), either pushed by overcrowding and destitution or attracted by opportunity, and going to other areas where they expected, at least as an interim measure, to become dependents of well-situated people in the new location. Thus they would be prepared to move toward the new centers of wealth of colonial Mexico, the Spanish towns and estates, and to provide the Spaniards, the new wealthy, with the permanent helpers, outside the corporate encomienda arrangement, of whom they stood greatly in need and whom, after their experience in the Caribbean with the *naborías,* they expected to find or create.

The Toluca valley, our present specific concern, is by no means the best known area of central Mexico in respect to preconquest society.[4] For centuries it had been the preserve of Otomi-related peoples not sharing the full panoply of Nahua culture. But in the last centuries before conquest there had been a Nahua incursion, indeed a specifically Aztec one, on a large scale. The proximity of the high Toluca basin (even if behind a mountain barrier) and its excellent maize lands led to a thorough occupation by Nahuatl speakers, probably involving both corporate and individual immigration. At any rate, by the time the Spaniards saw the valley, it contained, in its moister, more fertile southern and central areas, several semisovereign Indian units of the type we have discussed; the northern part was drier, emptier, with a less sedentary and nucleated population.

The Encomienda and Its Offshoots

As in the entire central region, the first approach of the Spaniards to the countryside of Toluca was through the encomienda. Except for the holdings of the Cortés estate, which may be viewed as one large encomienda, the Toluca valley was originally divided by the Spaniards into encomienda grants, each typically including one (sometimes two) of the provincial units we have been discussing, that is, a single large Indian settlement with its outlying dependent villages and surrounding territory. The essence of the encomienda in areas of this type was to build on the Indian entity, accepting its boundaries and dealing with it as one unit which could deliver goods and services through its own traditional internal mechanisms. The encomienda channeled goods and labor in the direction of Mexico City, the capital, where the Spanish encomendero himself was headquartered. This was the first form taken by Toluca's continuing orientation toward Mexico City in the colonial period. The Spaniards in a given part of the valley, whether involved in tribute collection, agriculture, or other things, would practically all be dependents of that region's encomendero, so that the encomienda provided the general framework for Spanish intrusion into the country, and for Spanish-Indian relationships. Church activity was included within this framework, for although the Franciscans who carried out most of it at first had their own strong corporate organization and were not simply the encomenderos' dependents, yet their monasteries in the valley were placed in the cabeceras of the largest encomiendas, served an area coterminous with the encomienda, and received their principal income from the encomendero, as a percentage of his. Encomienda structure expressed in very pure form the principles of strong city-country ties and city dominance, with the heads gathered in Mexico City and their underlings scattered through the valley, working to support them.

The encomienda also gave the Spanish society of Toluca its first generational continuity. Up to around 1600, or into the third Spanish generation, the same families continued to hold the valley's grants. These families became fixtures of Mexico City society, some of them (those originally better connected and of nobler birth, with the largest grants) belonging to the high circle staffing the Mexico City council and close to the viceroy.

Before long there was one substantial modification of the classic encomienda "system," in that a secular provincial administrator, the alcalde mayor, entered the picture, collecting tributes in areas that were vacant of an encomendero either temporarily or permanently, and exercising legal jurisdiction over both Indians and Spaniards of the area. But the system was capable of absorbing this new element. Like the encomenderos, the alcalde mayor came from Mexico City; he would be either a noninheriting member of the encomendero group, or someone from the entourage of the viceroy. Like the encomenderos, the administrator dealt in terms of entire Indian units. And although there were two and sometimes more alcaldes mayores functioning in the Toluca valley, encomenderos retained their hold on their individual areas. Since their positions were permanent and that of the administrator only for a few years, he had to accommodate to them. And since they were mainline inheritors, family heads, and he was not, he was all in all their social inferior, even their poor relative.

Since the sixteenth century was a time of quick change, it is hard to convey what is basic and what is incidental to the encomienda as an all-encompassing unit of provincial exploitation. Many of the important ties were of kinship, and it took two generations to develop them in their fullest form; yet by that time other elements had already entered the picture. Let us look at the standard procedure of the larger encomenderos of the Toluca valley in the last quarter of the century. Their main official asset was tribute in maize, the Indian towns' most meaningful surplus product. Encomenderos, indeed Spaniards in general at this time, left maize-bearing lands and maize production largely in the hands of the Indians, acquiring maize through tribute or sale for urban supply. Maize was in a sense a secondary crop from the point of view of the Spanish economy, since wheat was the Spanish food and Spaniards had the most money, but there was a more numerous Indian lower group in the cities (and in the silver mines off to the south, the valley's second market) that ate maize, paying for it either directly or through their Spanish employers. The encomenderos of Toluca sold some of their maize for the direct supply of the Mexico City market; another part of it went, immediately or after sale, to fatten the pigs which flourished in the valley and then also found their way to the capital. The steady maize revenue was also a major source of credit for various purposes. Encomenderos of this time had only modest farms for general agriculture, to supply their own establishments both in the valley and in Mexico City. They were prone to lease out even these. For direct enterprise, their emphasis was on livestock, especially cattle and sheep, which they raised in large numbers on loosely defined estancias located in their encomienda jurisdictions, staffed by some Spanish, mestizo, and mulatto employees and black slaves, along with somewhat more numerous permanent Indian herdsmen. But the direct labor demands which the encomienda estates made on the Indian towns at this time were not great.

The social hierarchy of the encomienda estate was a finely adjusted system whose members occupied a lower rank and a more rural position the more marginal they were to Spanish society. The main inheritors, though retaining their Toluca interests, were not only primarily citizens of Mexico City, but were increasingly remote from Toluca physically, socially and culturally, being educated in the most recent metropolitan style and sheltered from the province by various kinds of intermediaries. The closest relatives of the encomendero were also creatures of Mexico City, but they might be propelled toward the province in various ways: as owners of additional estancias in the encomienda area, as secular priests in charge of rural parishes there (as well as seeing to family business), as alcaldes mayores—all tending to remain citizens of the capital in principle. Then there were more distant relatives, often illegitimate (or mestizo), without the noble aura of the encomienda line; these settled in the valley more permanently, in effect as high-level supervisors for the estate, though seeking their own fortunes as well. In addition to these two types, the richer encomienda families also had a more professional estate manager who was frequently on the move between Mexico City and Toluca. In an archetypal situation, the encomendero would be on the council of Mexico City, his noninheriting uncle would be the alcalde mayor of the district of the encomienda, his younger brother a secular priest somewhere near, his illegitimate brother settled there permanently, involved in estate management, and an unrelated Spaniard of modest pretensions would be majordomo. No single family may have achieved all this simultaneously, but the Sámanos (Zinacantepec) and the Altamiranos (Metepec, Calimaya) came very close at times.

At the next lower level, that of Hispanized people serving the estates for a modest yearly wage as foremen or agriculturalists (*labradores*), the direct tie to Mexico City was lacking. These people were true residents of the valley, and they gave Toluca's local Spanish community a markedly plebeian stamp from the first. Although ethnically quite diverse, they shared the common characteristic of belonging on the margins of the Mexican Spanish world. We see the marginality clearly in the new immigrant from Spain, without Mexican ties and low in the seniority that the Indies worshipped; or in the Portuguese so often found in these positions; or in the free mulattoes and black slaves who were spread around the valley's estates, one or two to an estancia. It equally characterizes the many unlabeled mestizos doing work of this kind. The hierarchy also embraced Indians; the permanent workers for the estates were a large step further into the Spanish world than the Indians connected with them only through corporate duties and perhaps seasonal, temporary work.

This system, in which very nearly the entire yield of an area in surplus maize and livestock products was channeled toward the encomendero in Mexico City, contained within itself the seeds of growth and fragmentation. Only a small part of it, the maize tribute and the inherited title of encomendero, was inseparable from the encomienda proper. It was natural that all the noninheriting Spaniards involved would aim for properties, stock, and employees of their own. By the third Spanish generation, this process had already gone quite far. It did not, however, break the system, nor was it by any means always opposed by the encomenderos. Younger sons of important families sometimes managed to acquire holdings with nearly all the characteristics of encomienda estates, including their own citizenship in Mexico City. But why should an encomendero object? If his brother or cousin did not somehow manage to make a living, he himself would have to feed him. Independent estates for cadet relatives relieved the encomendero of a burden and provided him with substantial allies.

Other kinds of relatives of the encomendero proceeded a bit differently. When the illegitimate brother in the valley or the cousin who was parish priest got land and stock in their own names, acquired partners, or hired their own employees, they made no attempt to establish a full complex with its own connections to Mexico City. Rather they relied on the encomienda network; their employees were also the encomienda estate's employees. What they gained was for themselves, but for the family too, and the priest's property would one day be bequeathed back formally. And the only alternative to letting the estate majordomo branch out for himself was to pay him a higher salary.

If the encomienda estate gained as much as it lost through such quasi-independent expansion on the part of its higher-level associates, the same was true for its humbler middle-level agriculturalists. Encomenderos coexisted with small-scale pig farmers, often previously their employees, in the area of their grant; they could sell tribute maize to them, and later they could help market their pigs for a consideration. The small farmers needed the encomendero's favor in order to have, in turn, the favor of the alcalde mayor and of the authorities of the nearest Indian town. To the encomendero these freeholders remained in effect dependents. Already somewhat alienated from the province, faced with a quite limited market, the encomendero's best interests were served by taking as small a direct part in local enterprises as was consistent with a steady revenue. We find encomenderos of this time actually selling land grants of their own to employees. An even more favored device was the lease of lands, equipment, or stock to humble Spanish locals, assuring a fixed income with no direct involvement. The encomienda areas could look like a crazy quilt where scattered Spanish property units varied wildly between large property with employees, estate on lease, and small freehold, while properties and individuals changed status frequently. But the encomienda employees and the small freeholders were the same kind of people, or even the same people literally, and shifts in tenure made little difference, for the time being, to the system or to the individuals.

Markets and Marginalization

There is no doubt that the encomienda was in fact the principal framework of the early Spanish occupation of areas like Toluca, that it so remained considerably longer, even here in the center, than it has been given credit for, and that the process of the growth and branching out of Spanish rural activity took place in close relation to the encomienda system's own internal changes and characteristics. If we look at the several locally-based processors and traders (in valley products for Mexico City) who were active in late sixteenth-century Toluca, we find that many were in the second generation of existence, that behind the tolerably educated provincial merchant or obraje operator of 1580 or 1590 was an illiterate immigrant father, the very type of the encomenderos' employees. In other words, the first independent opportunity the encomienda offered to local Spanish residents of small resources was to become involved in the preparation and handling of encomienda estate products. Only after this encomienda-related opportunity was exhausted did humble residents begin to go into agriculture and stockraising for themselves; the majority of the humble farmers and stockmen of Toluca at the time of the third encomendero generation were the first local generation to be in that business, many of them immigrants from Spain and Portugal. And the most successful of them were often not so much independent estate owners as lessees of stock and shearers of sheep belonging to the encomienda estates. Or if one considers the increasing creation of parishes which were administered by secular priests, in addition to the original ones held by the Franciscans, one finds that this development corresponds to the appearance of a second generation of the encomendero class, well educated and in need of adequate employment.

Yet for all its pervasiveness in regions of dense Indian settlement, the encomienda was in some ways a means and channel rather than a primary phenomenon. It gave expression to forces which were even deeper and more universal than itself, forces which were felt also in the substantial parts of central Mexico that never came under encomienda and which continued to operate after the specific encomienda form became obsolete, on through the entire colonial period and until today. Given an intrusive dominant group in Mexico as large as the Spaniards, in as close contact with Europe as they were, the expansion of European cultural, social, and economic components, with the relative contraction or arrest of Indian ones, was predictable. Since Spaniards were originally mainly in the cities and Indians in the country, the process was bound to follow pronounced and classic lines of urban-hinterland, capital-province relationships. The growth in numbers and complexity of Mexican Spanish society was fed by biological reproduction, by European immigrants attracted to Mexico's silver economy, by Indians, blacks, and ethnically mixed people entering the Spanish sector in one way or another—forces in no way necessarily connected with encomiendas or even large estates of other kinds. Then there was the element of silver, mainstay of the export economy and sole base of the entire Spanish and interregional aspect of Mexico's internal economy; in Mexico the main silver mining settlements were remotely located with respect to the densely populated areas, outside the encomienda's domain and even too small and distant to be the primary markets for estate products.

The mines, then, in themselves remained secondary attractions, while their silver poured into New Spain's capital of Mexico City, far and away the country's largest concentration of Spaniards (and especially the wealthy and important ones). Thus in many ways—economically, socially, organizationally, even numerically—Mexico City was the core of the Spanish world in New Spain, and it was no accident that the country came to be named after its capital. Looming large over all Mexico, the capital exercised even vaster influence on the central region more narrowly defined. This populous and highly organized countryside had its own strong life, with internally generated integrity and continuity, but change came from Mexico City. What the capital wanted, and only that, the countryside produced according to its capacity. Anyone who could succeed in the capital was there; those whom the capital rejected were propelled into the countryside. Once given environmental determinants, the capital largely dictated the economic activities of the hinterland and the nature of city-country migration. The flow back and forth of goods and people took on a special character. Since for Toluca the capital was the overwhelmingly significant market, with some small silver mines to the south being a very poor second and the valley itself hardly to be considered, nearly all movement of goods was from the province to the capital, and nearly all activity for profit by Europeans in the valley had to do with supplying Mexico City. This situation was not necessarily permanent, since the activity of supplying the capital in the long run brought a certain prosperity and much Hispanization to an area like Toluca, transforming it into a real, if still secondary, market. In the sixteenth century Toluca's alcaldes mayores concentrated on hides and maize for the capital; not until much later, when the people of the countryside had more money and needs more adjusted to European-style products, would the administrators get into their famous business of selling cheap goods from the capital locally. Just so, Toluca estates of the sixteenth century sold only toward Mexico City or the mines, and had no counterpart of the company store which developed in the eighteenth century and later.

If the flow of goods was unbalanced in one direction, that of people tended to be so in the other. Although without a doubt there was significant movement of all types of people toward the capital at all times, the proportions and trends varied with the situation, according to where the pressures on opportunity, the overcrowding, were the greatest. In the first several generations the capital, which was beyond measure the most desirable place of residence in Mexico, fed by immigration from Spain, by natural growth on its large base, by the return of successful Spaniards from distant provinces, by migration from the dense population of its own valley, was forever filling up beyond the capacity of Mexico's economy to support. Therefore the marginal members of the capital's Hispanic society were pushed outward, both to the edges of town where property values were lower, and to the provinces, where there were still opportunities not taken up and activities not demanding great capital. We have already seen the types: cadets of wealthy families, new immigrants from Europe, and the ethnically mixed. As a result of the country's social-economic structure in the first century or more after conquest, Mexico City held the greatest concentration of people of all three types. Their more or less forced exit from the capital, their marginalization, was one of the primary movements shaping Toluca and areas like it. If the capital was overcrowded, there was still need and economic reward in the surrounding area for permanent, skilled, Europeanized personnel in humble intermediary or auxiliary positions related to supplying the capital, a need illustrated graphically by the continued presence in such positions, well into the seventeenth century at least, of expensive black slaves. This situation, however, was no more permanent than that related to markets. Ultimately the movement of marginal Hispanic people to the province, combined with Hispanization, and ethnic mixture of the local indigenous population with the ever larger local Hispanic nucleus, led to overcrowding in provincial intermediate positions, with consequences such as, by the eighteenth century, something on the order of mestizo vagabondage, indebtedness, and proletarianization, as well as movement back towards the capital. For the early period the most conspicuous movement in the direction of the capital was that of those who were fully successful both economically and socially; this element tended to be permanently lost to the province, reinforcing the double equation of capital with wealth, prestige, nobility, and province with poverty, humbleness, commonness.

The Local Spanish Community

In the light of this dichotomy let us consider the local Spaniards of Toluca in the late sixteenth century. Though they often emerged from or depended on the encomienda in one way or another, their patterns of action also responded to social imperatives of the more general nature just discussed. Based in Toluca proper, a community had grown up of Spaniards who were in some way involved with processing and handling the products of the valley's estate economy. There were two or three operators of obrajes producing woolen textiles on a reasonably large scale (one of them bought over fifteen tons of wool one year); there was also a tannery or two. The best location for such operations was in Mexico

City or Puebla, where more skilled labor and capital were available, and also there was greater proximity to the market; wool itself was cheap as dirt, and hides hardly less so. But the very fact of the relative unattractiveness left some room for less capitalized enterprises in places such as Toluca. In the same way, the valley's nullity as a market, and its unexceptional agrarian products (merely those of central Mexico generally and far less profitable than Zacatecas silver or Spanish cloth), made sixteenth-century Toluca a place of small interest to the great commercial combines of the capital and allowed local Spaniards to dominate Toluca's commerce. Only one or two traders were specialized enough to receive the label "merchant"; others combined trade with some production of their own. But it was in fact through Toluca-based dealers of one sort or another that most valley products reached Mexico City at this time. Alongside a few well-established figures who often made large sales and even became involved in helping finance valley estates, there were more numerous small dealers: pig traders, who might go as far as Michoacán to buy and to Mexico City of course to sell; muleteers, who took valley products to the capital and the mines, often investing in what they carried. Once again, this situation was subject to change. To the extent that Toluca became a better market and its products more central to the supply of a larger Mexico City, commercial interests from the capital could be expected to become more directly involved in the valley.

In addition to the commercial element there was also a small group of officials based in the town of Toluca, staffing the provincial administration under the alcalde mayor.[5] They had much in common with the others, for they too largely served the valley's Spanish estate economy, attending to its legal needs and adjudicating its disputes with Indians; they too, both in an official capacity and for their employer as an individual, were involved in collecting, buying, and selling maize for the capital, and in such things as tannery operation. The alcalde mayor was a quickly shifting figure, while his subordinates were long-term local residents, working under many successive administrators over the years. Though they had no standing appointments, the lack of alternative candidates imposed their choice again and again. They provided continuity, allowed de facto traditions to develop, and helped valley interests to assert themselves in an unobtrusive way.

True to his social affinities with the encomenderos, the alcalde mayor was often in Mexico City, sometimes for months at a time, leaving the underlings to carry on by themselves. During the frequent intervals between alcaldes mayores, the local figures had an even freer hand. The staff was not large or impressive: a "deputy" (*teniente*), notary by trade, who was second in command, taking the alcalde mayor's place in his absence, and often presiding in court even when the superior was in town; a chief constable, of humbler extraction; two or three notaries who both acted as secretaries and prepared documents for the public; a lawyer without degree, who represented parties of every description in the alcalde mayor's court, and would also serve as deputy or secretary when needed; an official interpreter for translating Indian testimony (during much of this time the interpreter was an Indian himself, Juan Serrano, who was literate in Spanish and owner of an estancia near Toluca).

The third element among the Spanish residents of Toluca proper was that of the nonencomendero estate owners of the valley. Though they tended to be their own stewards, some of the small pig farms they held in the central part of the valley were close enough that the owners could go back and forth from a home in town. Others, raisers of sheep or sometimes horses (cattle still being largely for encomenderos), were beginning to develop staffs of their own, and could leave a junior partner, son-in-law, or black slave foreman in charge of the estancia while they maintained a Toluca residence.

Spread among these Spanish (as well as many Portuguese) residents were mulattoes and an unknowable proportion of mestizos. The mulattoes stand out in the records: generally they were in someone else's employ, usually with some special trade or skill and earning pay on the level of a poor Spaniard; usually they were free. Many were scattered around the valley's estates, but some lived in Toluca itself, even owned houses there. Mestizos are much harder to trace. At this time they were doubtless most numerous in Mexico City, where Spaniards and Indians met in greatest numbers, and though many must have come to the provinces, they did not yet come to Toluca *as* mestizos. The only people labeled "mestizos" were the lame, the destitute, the abandoned. Local Spanish residents did have many otherwise unidentified natural daughters whom they married off to newly arriving single males from the outside, whether new from Spain or merely from Mexico City. Thus despite the lack of firm information, one can discern a situation already well on its way to what it would be in the seventeenth and eighteenth centuries, when chroniclers would report the size of Toluca's population in terms of two numbers, one for Indians and the other for Spaniards, mestizos, and mulattoes all together.

By the latter sixteenth century the local Spaniards and the Hispanized had given the town of Toluca a social organization essentially like that of Mexico City despite the fact that Toluca still had only an Indian town council and retained the status of Indian town to the end of the colonial period. The traders, producers, and estate owners of whom we have just been speaking owned houses and maintained homes in the center of town; these were no mansions, but some had paintings and tapestries on the walls, silver cups on the table, and some books on the shelves. To judge by descriptions of contiguous properties in house sales, the Spaniards had taken over much of the central area around the square and the Franciscan monastery, which was becoming a Spanish religious and ceremonial establishment as well as one for the Indians. As in Mexico City, in Toluca too wealth was concentrating near the square, and the town was increasingly Spanish at the center, Indian at the edge, though in both cases much petty Indian market activity took place in the very midst of things. And this almost clandestine Spanish urban nucleus was beginning to play for the plebeian valley residents a little of the role that Mexico City did for the aristocrats; even those estate owners whose interests were located too far into the dry northern region for them to live in Toluca often visited there and began to establish social and marriage ties there. They were also beginning to make pious donations and request burial at the monastery in Toluca rather than at the Mexico City cathedral. Church architecture and statuary in outlying areas were modeled on those of Toluca.

Of course this long remained an incomplete and markedly humble subsociety. It did not include the encomenderos or the ecclesiastics, not even those who lived in the valley for a long period of time. There was no one in it more than a generation away from quite lowly status. In the late sixteenth century there was not a Spanish man entitled "don," when nearly all the encomenderos had that title; nor more than a Spanish woman or two with the "doña," which was borne by half the women in Mexico City. The professions and trades were abysmally weak in Toluca. There was not a titled lawyer or physician in the valley, nor a sculptor or architect, nor even a tailor to whom mending the alcalde mayor's trousers could be entrusted. But this could all change as the Spanish base grew, and there were already some signs of it. Around 1600 the daughters of a few of the most prosperous of the local estate-owners began to sport the "doña," and their fathers began to seek some aura of nobility for their children's marriage partners. Eventually, by the nineteenth century, this process gave an aristocratic tone and legends of noble origin to some prominent local families which descended from a first generation of illiterate, enterprising Tolucan sheep-shearers. The main local merchant family already maintained a general store in Toluca, and a Venetian kept something like a tavern. Such enterprises would increase, as would craft production for local consumption. But the commercial as well as the social manifestations of self-containedness would be held within a tight limit and be clearly marked as second-ranking because of Mexico City's proximity.

Indian Adjustments

What was going on in the Indian world, now that the Toluca valley was teeming with Spanish people and structures? To do justice to continuity and change among the Indians, one must make a distinction between corporate phenomena and patterns of action of individuals. Of course such a distinction cannot be maintained rigorously, since all the members of the corporation were to some extent already acting as individuals in the preconquest period, as we have seen. But it is useful to differentiate between, on the one hand, the mass of the Indian community whose main interactions were with each other, who shared common characteristics and were served by common institutions and, on the other hand, those Indians who had important daily contacts outside the community, mainly with elements of the Tolucan Spanish society we have just been describing, to the extent of belonging there more than within an Indian entity.

With corporate phenomena, the predominant note was an overwhelming continuity in the main departments of life. In each branch some rather major adjustments and adoptions had taken place, quite quickly, but in nearly every case the additions were in the nature of upper-level modifications to an already existing Indian core; these modifications were soon quite fully integrated, and after that change proceeded very slowly indeed. The sixteenth century saw practically no change in the general distribution of the Toluca valley's population. The area ended the century with the same clusters, provincial units, relative densities, boundaries, even place-names, as when it began. The steady and heavy loss of Indian population characteristic of all such regions had many effects, including that of making the expansion of Spanish livestock estancias easier, but it did not alter relative distribution, nor even change the character of the central and southern parts of the valley as an area of dense population relative to many other sections of the country. Some widening of plazas and straightening of streets went on, and even the moving of towns off hills and onto the plain, as in the case of Tenango. But the very few truly new settlements ever to arise in the valley, such as Lerma, were creations of a time somewhat later than the one we are considering here.

Maize agriculture remained the root activity, practiced mainly by commoners on their plots under arrangements seemingly little different than before the Spaniards came. European animals—the valley's ubiquitous pigs, and oxen for plowing—were gradually finding their way inside the village economy, at first through the nobles. The Indian community still spoke Indian languages, a fact of the utmost importance, both symptomatic of the relative integrity and isolation of the provincial units and itself serving to insulate and give corporate strength. Even among the nobles, even in Toluca proper, few could yet speak Spanish. On the other hand, as one can deduce from the few remaining Nahuatl documents written in the valley of this time, the Indians' language, here as in the entire central region, had accepted many Spanish words for plants, animals, tools, clothing items, offices, administrative and religious concepts, and other things which had been introduced and now were being integrated into the Indian world. Once again, however, after a great initial impact, change was slow. Thus Spanish words for "shirt" and "trousers" were quickly adopted throughout central Mexico, as well as the items to which the words referred, yet in the latter sixteenth century in Toluca as elsewhere there was a distinctive Indian manner of dress, partially because of the indigenous items and materials still retained, partially because Indian dress was more conservative and did not modify the European items it adopted at the same rate as such things changed in the Spanish world.

Looking to the Indian world's economic, political, and religious institutions, the picture remains the same—a successful graft onto living stock, then relative stasis. The markets changed least. There continued to be village markets, a staggered schedule of larger markets in the several valley centers, and one largest of all in the square of Toluca proper. One presumes that here as elsewhere the preconquest specialties and staples continued to be traded, and by the same people, in addition to some European items of common use and local manufacture, like metal knives, candles, or shirt collars. The schedule had to be readjusted to the seven-day week; the market in Toluca town soon came to be Friday, as it still is. Money circulated in the markets, though in small amounts (*tomin,* "1/8 of a peso," soon grew into the Nahuatl word for "cash, money"). Actually, cash sales and the idea of a currency may have been nothing new for Mesoamericans. Neither was the idea of individual commercial activity, which had always been the basis for the market system, nor the presence of full-time professional traders. The latter element, indeed, may have diminshed. Trade toward Mexico City was in the hands of Spaniards rather than *pochteca,* though there were some Indian pork butchers of Mexico City who bought in the valley (from Spaniards). In the Toluca market there were Indian traders in maize, *rescatadores,* who would seem to have bought up maize from individuals in the smaller markets to sell in Toluca, sometimes to Spaniards. Sale of pulque—which was to beverages what maize was to grains, the Indian staple—took place more often in individual homes than in markets. It was sold, a pitcher at a time from large jars, to the Indian public for cash, and often by community leaders. Thus the two basic Indian products were to some extent being sold for money by individuals of the Indian community, maize partly to the outside, pulque mainly internally, so that some direct connection to the Spanish economy existed at the same time that Indians kept their primary activities in their own hands. Also, some portion of the products of the Spanish estate economy was beginning to find its way into Indian hands, sometimes surreptitiously or through mulatto intermediaries.

Another major set of institutions had to do with the reorganization of the indigenous altepetl as a Spanish-style municipality. Established first in the main cabecera towns, these municipal corporations included all the offices of the usual Spanish town council (alcaldes or judges, councilmen, a chief constable), presided over by a "governor" who differed from the equivalent Spanish figure only in that he was generally a local person rather than from the outside. And in fact, this assemblage went through most of the formalities of a Spanish council, including record keeping, for an Indian notary kept minutes and accounts in Nahuatl, as well as recording wills and important transactions for the local public. All this did not happen immediately at conquest, but by the second or third generation thereafter the Indians had fully accepted the reorganization, astoundingly thorough on the face of it, and they maintained the offices and practices quite autonomously. Behind this easy acceptance and further flourishing was the fact that in many ways Spanish and Indian municipal organization coincided, and pre-Columbian traits could be long maintained in new forms. In preconquest times office holding of all kinds had been the prerogative of a self-declared but generally acknowledged set of nobles, repositories of all the higher things. This continued to be the case. Descriptions of Indian councils in action are unanimous in referring to them as *principales,* the word Spaniards used for the Indian nobility in general. At first the governor was usually the tlatoani, often formally recognized as *cacique* (the Spaniards' general word for Indian ruler); the cabecera town of Zinacantepec had a "cacique and governor" well into mid-century. By late sixteenth century the term "cacique" was no longer being much heard, and the governorship was (in places) rotating every few years, but its holders were still members of the ruling dynasty, which usually took the surname of the encomendero, of the Cortés family, or the like. Those nobles pertaining to the ruling families bore the title "don," while the others tended not to, at this time.

The altepetl had had some judge-like officials who were right-hand men of the tlatoani and sometimes were also powerful in their own right. They found a reasonably close equivalent in the Spanish alcaldes. There had been nothing, however, quite like the restricted corporate body of councilmen that was the core of Spanish municipal organization. Rather a larger body of all important nobles, the "elders," took part in decisions in times of crisis or dynastic succession. This background reflects itself clearly in the scattered surviving records from late sixteenth-century Toluca. On many occasions there would appear not a full council representing a town, but only two or three figures, usually the governor, an alcalde, and perhaps a chief constable—the tlatoani and his judges. Or on the other hand, there would be the governor, alcaldes, "and the other noblemen" of the town, a much larger group than a council proper. As to the municipal notary, he too was sometimes a noble. In any case, he continued the preconquest tradition of scribes and record-keepers associated with the altepetl's tribute collection, land records, and so forth; some pictographic elements continued to appear in the mainly Nahuatl prose texts of the valley's Indian notaries on into the seventeenth and eighteenth centuries.

At the lower levels the continuities were even more transparent. Ordinary constables were called by the Aztec word *topile* as often as by the Spanish one *alguacil.* At the level of district headmen and those responsible for yet smaller units, the traditional word and office of *tepixqui,* "guarder of people," was the main one used, even by Spaniards when referring to them.

The machinery just described functioned within a local autonomy to keep the peace, collect tribute for the encomendero or alcalde mayor, deliver temporary labor for community or outside purposes, maintain a community treasury, help with the financing and organization of church functions, often raise crops which were sold as community assets or paid out as tribute, sometimes run a local "hospital" or infirmary. The *caja de comunidad* or corporation treasury and the Spanish hospital were new in their specific forms, but the old altepetl had already carried out nearly all these functions, and was well prepared to do so under the Spaniards.

With religious institutions, the change was more apparent than with economic and political ones, and the continuities were more subterranean. The office of priest, which had been important, was no longer held by anyone from within the community. The radically different religious content and overall organization of Christianity are more than apparent; on the other hand, that old beliefs and practices survived surreptitiously or in syncretic form is equally well known, though difficult to demonstrate for a specific subregion. Taking for granted both a sharp break and many hidden survivals, let us look for a moment at those aspects where local continuities can be readily seen. Christian churches were located where preconquest temples had been, in the center of the towns on an open square, and often literally on the former temple site. The church, like the temple, symbolized the glory of the town, and the local government of both periods took an active interest in religious construction as well as in religious festivities, which, as different as they were, richly punctuated the calendar under both systems. If there was no Indian priest, at least there was the *fiscal,* a chief steward for each church and practically in charge of day-to-day religious concerns wherever there was no Spanish priest or friar in permanent residence. This fiscal would be a local notable of the same type as sat on the town council, and in closest connection with that group. Under him was a varying staff of sacristans, church musicians, and so on. As to the *cofradía*, or religious brotherhood, and *compadrazgo,* or ritual kinship, these may not have had close equivalents in the preconquest period, but they did give scope for relatively independent Indian social-religious activity and the reinforcement of local ties. Actually for the late sixteenth century there is no evidence that cofradías had yet spread much beyond the valley's largest settlements, though they were ultimately to do so.

In general, then, Tolucan Indian corporate-institutional development closely conformed to that of the much more thoroughly studied Valley of Mexico and of other central Mexican areas. The same appears to be true for the internal social-cultural life of the Indian world, which we are only beginning to glimpse. In both respects the impact of the Spanish presence was in a sense great, but having made the adjustment and integrated the new elements, the Indian towns retained their identity, their language, their maize-growing, and the essence of local autonomy as long as they satisfied outside demands. After this, change was slower and more gradual, with the result that Indian towns of Toluca (and of central Mexico generally) reached the late colonial period still corresponding, all in all, to the description just given. If autonomous, viable Indian social entities, a majority on their own home ground, had been the entire picture, it is not likely that central Mexico would ever have become Spanish speaking and in so many other ways part of the European-Hispanic world.

Some unusual records (unusual in having been preserved) allow us to get a sense of the degree of continuity in following centuries in one part of the Toluca valley.[6] The Calimaya area, located in the south-center of the valley in the prime maize land, was characterized from before the conquest by two parallel provincial units, moieties, or *parcialidades,* one

Calimaya proper and the other Tepemaxalco, whose respective dependencies were interspersed across their common area. In the colonial period each was organized as a municipality of its own, and this division was respected into the eighteenth century. Some surviving internal records of Tepemaxalco show a pronounced tendency to ignore the existence of Calimaya. Through the seventeenth and well into the eighteenth century, a single prominent family with the surname de la Cruz repeated in the governorship, provided the church organist, the founder and then the majordomos of the cofradía, and sometimes the notary as well. They collected tributes and kept census records, notating it all in Nahuatl (in addition to the written text, some yellow-colored circles represented the pesos collected); other Nahuatl accounts dealt with church expenditures and receipts, the latter often being donations of the de la Cruz family. One family member making a will in the latter seventeenth century revealed extensive landownership, in the traditional fashion of a great number of individual fields at scattered locations, though they were worked by oxen and employees who were by now as much Spanish-style hired men as Indian-style *calpixque* (stewards) and dependents. Tepemaxalco was still alive and healthy in this form in the first half of the eighteenth century, when a new church was erected in the district of San Lucas and the following inscription placed on its stucco portal (in Nahuatl, with some by then long standard Spanish loan words; the inscription is still to be seen today):

> axca ypa yi xihuil de 1714 anos yc opec simiento axca ypa yni xihuil de 1733 anos yc otlamico yteocaltzin tt
>
> In the year of 1714 the foundation was begun. In the year of 1733 the temple of our Lord was completed.

But by no means all Indians in the valley of Toluca, nor in central Mexico generally, stayed within the confines of their communities, or strictly within the framework of its practices and social ties even if they continued to live there. The movement of individual Indians in some sense out of Indian structures and into Spanish ones became, over time, a large-scale process, and a vital one in changing the cultural attributes of the countryside. It brought about much more intense, daily, long-term contact between Spaniards and Indians, helping to shift the balance between the two communities and hastening the rate of internal change in the Indian world.

Earlier we saw that the preconquest period was characterized by frequent physical movement of people or their change of status, often resulting in their becoming direct dependents of the powerful rather than full-scale community members. It is no surprise, then, to see that in sixteenth-century Toluca many Indians who worked full-time for Spaniards, often possessing skills in some Spanish activity, came from outside the valley. This was not purely random movement; most Tolucan Indians originating elsewhere came from the country's most Hispanized centers: Mexico City, the Puebla region, and the mining camps. Others, a larger number, were from within the valley. We do not know a great deal about the group, which may be defined as Indians living in a Spanish establishment, whether a residence or shop in either Toluca or a cabecera town, or on an estancia. Most numerous were the domestic servants, doubtless as many as the entire Hispanized community of the valley, for custom demanded that every Spaniard, and even most mulattoes and black slaves, should have an Indian servant. Others in this category were Indians working in textiles and tanning, a small but potentially important group, some interpreters and aides attached to the local government, and the more numerous herders of stock and maintenance personnel on the valley's scattered estancias. This entire group had gained Spanish skills not present in the Indian population generally, and they drew correspondingly greater pay—generally half to a quarter of what a Spaniard or a mulatto doing the same thing might make, perhaps in the range of 30 to 45 pesos (the less skilled drew only about 20 pesos, and the unskilled even less than that). It may not be immediately apparent that the domestics were skilled, but the Spaniards valued their degree of acculturation, since they would bring them along from outside the valley, and take the trouble of formalizing contracts with them. Indeed in the late sixteenth century, formal contracts and advances in pay were characteristic only for this highest level of the Indian work force, and even there they were in the nature of an emergency measure for those cases where the Indian had gotten into trouble or was unusually sought after. One need not imagine instant and full acculturation even for the permanent employees, but the long-range effects, of which racial-ethnic mixture was only a part, were profound. Not all these Indians yet spoke Spanish, but nearly all in the valley who did so were of this group. It is not too much to say that they already belonged as much to Spanish as to Indian society. Both their numbers and their Hispanization would increase drastically as a function of the ever-thickening web of the Tolucan Spanish community. This in itself was perhaps the most important single mechanism in the transformation of the valley from what it was in 1550 to what it was in 1950. The growth of such a group must also have had significant back-effects on the Indian communities, especially as with time there developed the type of the Indian who worked full-time for Spaniards, but resided in the Indian community. In colonial Nahuatl generally, the time around the second half of the seventeenth century shows a stage of deeper Spanish linguistic influence that can only be attributed to a large degree of bilingualism, nurtured primarily among the employees of the Spaniards.

Not all who stepped outside the Indian world were in Spanish employ. Some were independent operators in the Spanish economy, of whom the main representatives to be seen in sixteenth-century Toluca were some muleteers carrying goods toward the mining camps to the south. This sort of activity must be considered secondary, however, because such Indians had typically started as Spanish employees; moreover their numbers were still very restricted. Expansion would come in the future, but always in the face of the reality that thoroughly profitable economic endeavors of any type were likely eventually to be taken over by Spaniards.

Another sort of independent activity was half in, half outside the Indian community; that is, it took place in the community, but was Spanish in nature and directed toward the Spanish economy. In the sixteenth century it was above all the nobles, often the governors themselves, who did this, raising pigs and using oxen to cultivate maize for resale. The commercial contacts and the technology involved were Spanish; though tenure and management were on Indian lines, these aspects too became increasingly assimilated to the valley estate economy of which they were a part, so that a seventeenth-century noble could refer to *nocayanis* (= *mi gañán*), "my hired man."

Secular Trends

In the last years of the colonial period the Toluca valley still contained the same kinds of structures as in the period we have been considering—Indian towns still retaining Nahuatl and Otomi speech and the same governance; and a Spanish community centered on Toluca proper, with estates throughout the valley oriented to Mexico City. The various processes we have observed were also still at work, but their very operation had brought about changes. With the continued arrival of the Spanish and Hispanized from outside the valley and the continued transferral of individuals out of the Indian community into the Spanish, the proportions had changed. Toluca proper, though still with an Indian council, now had more families of Spaniards, mestizos, and mulattoes than of Indians. By the same process, sizable Spanish subcommunities had arisen in all the cabecera towns, which by now were much like what the town of Toluca had been in the sixteenth century. Another change, more basic than in mere proportions, was that Spanish estates, while continuing to grow livestock, were now directly involved in maize production themselves. The underlying structure or rationale had not changed, but an expanded and evolving Mexico City now bought more maize and rendered direct intervention profitable. Though the Indian corporate entities were still vigorous in and of themselves, their overall viability in their traditional form was becoming problematical, faced as they now were with economically dominant Spaniards in force on their very home ground, along with Spanish intervention in the production of their core crops. A time was clearly coming soon when Spanish speakers, the estate owners and processors of the valley, would take over direct and formal management of the municipalities.

That this had not yet happened anywhere in the valley, not even in Toluca itself, can be attributed in the final analysis to the closeness of Mexico City (it is true that the hostility of the Cortés estate to a Spanish municipality was no help). An area with the population and resources of the Toluca valley would have been an independent Spanish municipality much earlier in the game if it had been located at a greater distance from the capital. In everything, the capital gave with one hand, took with the other. Without the stimulus of its market and the outflow of its marginal people, Toluca, being off the trunkline from Zacatecas to the sea, would have had a far thinner Hispanic society and little prosperity; in a word, it would have been like the interior of the far south. On the other hand, more distant areas could experience an earlier local development of professions and crafts because the distant practitioners lacked competition and could charge any price, whereas anyone operating in Toluca had the best in the country just over the pass, and could not charge more than Mexico City prices plus transportation, if that, since his efforts were not likely to equal in quality those originating in the country's main center for all amenities. Eventually Toluca settled down to a certain amount of self-containedness and a high degree of social stability, the same names appearing prominently over the centuries among both Spaniards and Indians. But the dialectic of push and pull, stimulus and limitation, in which the capital—the greater concentration of wealth, Hispanization, and people—played the more active role, continued, and still does today.

NOTES

1. Records of local transactions and court proceedings, preserved in Notaría no. 1 of Toluca, constitute the principal documentary base of this chapter. More specifics on the documentation, and a far more detailed treatment of social types and career patterns, especially for the Spanish community, may be found in my "Españoles entre indios: Toluca a fines del siglo XVI." The sections on Indians, written against the background of Charles Gibson's *Aztecs under Spanish Rule,* draw especially on documentation and analysis like those presented in Arthur J. O. Anderson, Frances Berdan, and James Lockhart, trans. and eds., *Beyond the*

Codices, and Frances Karttunen and James Lockhart, *Nahuatl in the Middle Years: Language Contact Phenomena in Colonial Nahuatl Texts.* A source of very special importance for its earliness, informativeness, and comprehensiveness is a set of Nahuatl census-tribute records from the Morelos region c. 1540 (Museo Nacional de Antropología e Historia [MNAH], Colección Antigua, vols. 549, 550, 551). Several aspects of these documents have been studied by Pedro Carrasco; his "La casa y hacienda de un señor tlalhuica" is representative of this work and contains additional bibliography.

2. It is gratifying to observe that Woodrow Borah, even without taking its strong micropatriotism into consideration, deems "city-state" the most natural and appropriate term for this Mesoamerican entity. See Sherburne F. Cook and Woodrow Borah, *The Population of the Mixteca Alta, 1520–1960,* p. 11.

3. These points were made in papers at a session on preconquest central Mexican social organization chaired by Pedro Carrasco at the International Conference of Americanists in September 1974. A volume of the papers is in preparation.

4. See, however, Thomas E. Durbin, "Aztec Patterns of Conquest as Manifested in the Valley of Toluca."

5. There was another, even thinner staff of this type in Ixtlahuaca. (The official in Toluca actually sometimes bore the title of corregidor, but the term "alcalde mayor" has been used here throughout for clarity.)

6. MNAH, Colección Gómez de Orozco, vols. 185, 186.

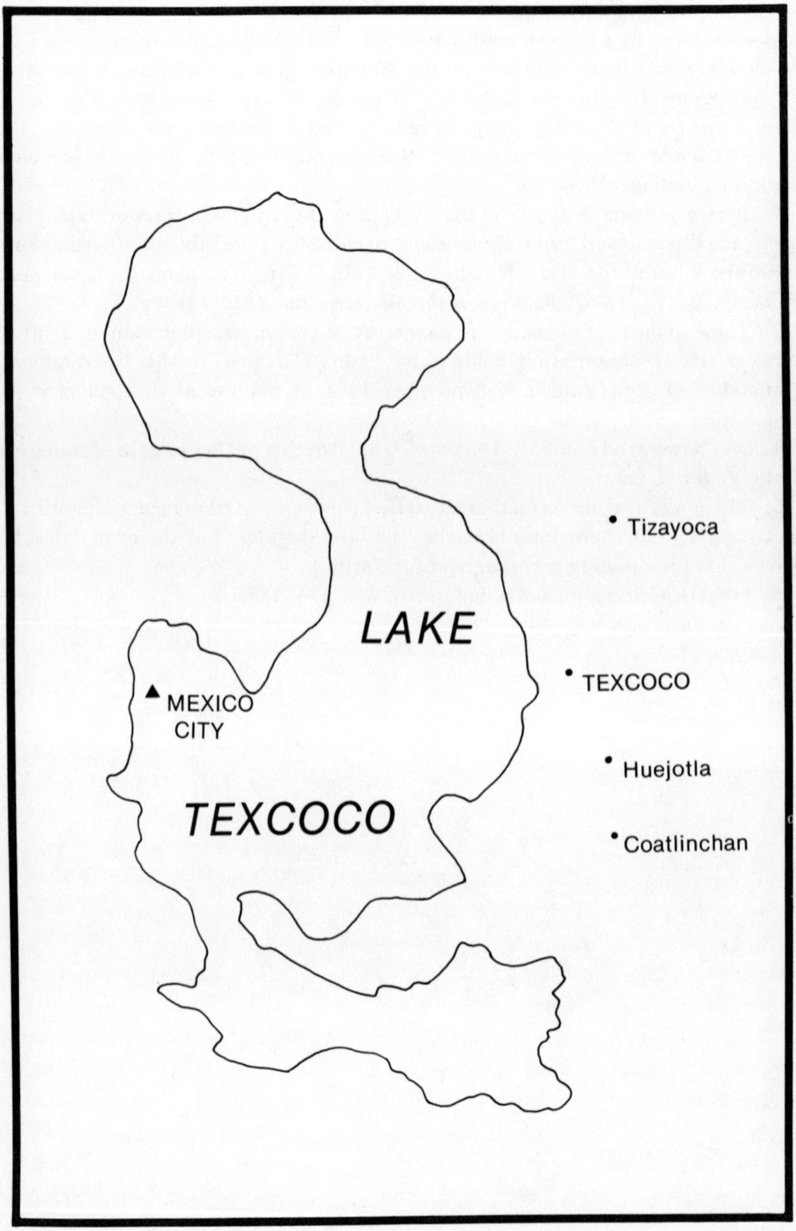

Sixteenth-Century Texcoco, with Some Subject Towns

4. In Mexico City's Shadow: Some Aspects of Economic Activity and Social Processes in Texcoco, 1570–1620

Leslie Lewis

The city of Texcoco, which lies on the eastern shore of the lake named after it, facing Tenochtitlan across some fifteen miles of water, was the capital of an ancient preconquest state of imperial stature.[1] Home of a dynasty as illustrious as that of Tenochtitlan, its reputation for cultural achievement was unequaled. Texcoco proper was a vast urban complex. It was natural, then, that Texcoco should have functioned as Tenochtitlan's equal in the great Aztec confederation. But by the time the Spaniards arrived, though it directly controlled the entire northeastern section of the Valley of Mexico and had tributaries as far south as Guatemala, Texcoco had, in relative terms, lost much ground. Although it was a large city, Tenochtitlan had outstripped it in population, wealth, and power. The Texcoco-Tenochtitlan dynastic intermarriages, which had once been for mutual benefit, became a mechanism whereby the Tenochca line imposed its relatives as rulers.

The comparative decline of Texcoco became far more pronounced after the Spaniards came. Even so, the town's prominence and Texcocan aid to the conquering Spaniards (provided especially by factions dissatisfied with Tenochtitlan's dynastic choices) gave Texcoco a somewhat favorable position. It was one of four Indian towns in the Valley of Mexico to be granted the status of "city," and as such it was one of the first to have its own town council and "governor."[2] As an encomienda it was a prize, and was so fought over that, like many other of the largest population centers, it soon came directly under the crown, though many parts of its former sphere of influence were in encomienda. But the Spaniards established only one Spanish municipality in the Valley of Mexico, precisely on the site of Texcoco's old rival Tenochtitlan. The new foundation, Mexico City, was not merely a center for the Valley, but was the metropolis, nucleus, and focal point for the entire Spanish sector of Mexico. Texcoco was now hopelessly eclipsed, yet at the same time it was too close to Mexico City not to be affected by it. This chapter examines some of the socioeconomic phenomena of Texcoco's adjustment to its situation, largely as seen among Spaniards, the Hispanized, and the Indian nobles, and including any glimpse of the general local Indian population that the records allow.

General Characteristics of Hispanic Texcocan Society

For all its eminence, Texcoco and the surrounding area lacked exploitable resources other than some agricultural products common to the entire Valley of Mexico and the Indian people who lived in the region. There was thus no strong economic motive for any local nucleation to counter the influence of the nearby capital. I find little evidence that the Hispanic community of late sixteenth- or early seventeenth-century Texcoco had attained any true local autonomy. Colonial Texcoco functioned more as a suburb of the capital than as a self-contained province with certain defined social and economic connections to Mexico City. The estate structure, so often an important link between large town and small, was missing, as were any local Hispanic aristocracy and local Spanish government. In the constant flow of individuals and goods between the capital and Texcoco, Texcoco was always the dependent partner.

The absence of the estate structure, which might have served as a stimulant of local economic activities, can be attributed to Texcoco's geographical proximity to the capital. Although the original encomienda grant of Texcoco to Cortés was revoked, several encomiendas in the area were given to other Spaniards. By the mid-sixteenth century several prosperous estates were located in the region, and they continued to exist throughout the colonial period. These estates, however, with their personnel and their direct and ancillary economic activities, functioned as an immediate extension of Mexico City, bypassing Texcoco. The people who would have formed the upper strata of resident Texcocan society, the estate owners and managers, were citizens of Mexico City and moved within the social and economic mainstream of Valley society. The owner or manager did not need to maintain or cultivate local Texcocan connections. Estate products were transported by boats or carts straight from the estate to Mexico City markets. Since most estates were located within a few miles of the capital, it was possible for estate personnel to conduct their business from Mexico City, and, when it was necessary for them to travel to the estate, they could make the round trip in less than a day.

Similarly, the province lacked a Spanish aristocracy. "Don" and "doña" were titles rarely used by Texcoco's Spanish population except among those holding the office of alcalde mayor, and these individuals were never permanent citizens of Texcoco. Usually they were related to first conquerors or to otherwise prominent Mexico City families. The alcalde mayor's aim was to further his position in the capital. The various local economic involvements of the alcaldes mayores are not yet studied in detail, but several while in office took an active part in the buying and selling of maize of Texcoco. Most of the duties of the office were carried out by a *teniente,* who was of a lower social position (never "don"); but, like the alcalde mayor, he was rarely a citizen of Texcoco.

There were no lawyers, doctors, tailors, or specialized craftsmen for a local clientele in late sixteenth-century Texcoco; Texcocans journeyed to Mexico City for these services.

Mexico City, with its far greater opportunities, acted as a magnet for Texcoco's resident population, causing constant migration out of the area to the capital. Once an individual living in Texcoco acquired a certain social and economic status, whether through a learned skill, petty mercantile activities, or a marital alliance, he or she moved to the capital. On the other hand, a much slower, sporadic movement brought marginal people out of the capital and into Texcoco.

Texcoco's lack of economic activity minimized its attractiveness even to these humble social types. From the mid-sixteenth into the seventeenth century never more than several hundred Spaniards resided in the province at any given time. The area's most lucrative and prestigious enterprises had been snatched up by the first arrivals, most of whom lived in Mexico City, and the products as well as the profits went directly there. Thus the ideal for most Spaniards living in the province remained to accumulate just enough wealth to move out and back to the capital; and in fact, this was the dominant pattern.

Another pattern of migration was the subtle but constant movement of Hispanic commoners and indigents out of Texcoco and into provinces lying farther out. These late arrivals and immigrants resettled in the outlying provinces because they lacked the socioeconomic connections necessary to gain a foothold in the Valley. Many went to the nearby areas of Tlaxcala and Puebla, but some resettled as far away as Yucatan and Guatemala. Even for these individuals, however, Mexico City remained the social and economic focal point. Persons who moved to the outlying provinces rarely severed their connections with Texcoco. In a society where personal connections often formed the basis for economic advancement, their ties with Texcoco enabled them to be that much closer to capital society. Through formal and informal trade agreements and partnerships, provincial Spaniards maintained ties with Texcocans that proved economically beneficial to both parties.

The nucleus of Texcoco's resident Hispanic population was composed of humble people, many of whom had moved there only after failing to find a place in the capital. Mestizos and new immigrants from Europe were both characteristic of Texcoco. The immigrants included not only Spaniards, but Italians, French, and Portuguese. In the seventeenth century there was an influx of Basques. But a very great portion of Texcoco's Spanish population, it seems, was mestizo. Many of the mestizos living in Texcoco proper were born there, the legitimate and illegitimate offspring of local Indians and Spaniards; in addition, illegitimate mestizos from Mexico City often attempted to establish a foothold in the province.

There was a noticeable absence of blacks in the town of Texcoco, which can be attributed in turn to the absence of wealth, craft specialization, or direct connections to the province's estates. Undoubtedly free blacks and slaves were attached in some way to the estate framework. Most of the few purchases of black slaves in Texcoco involved a Mexico City encomendero selling an infirm or maimed slave to a Texcocan Spaniard (usually for around 300 pesos). A few mulattoes did reside in Texcoco. Most were women who had migrated to Texcoco from Guatemala as a result of connections established through the long-distance cacao trade. These women functioned on the edges of Spanish Texcocan society. They lived in the Indian barrios and sometimes owned houses there which they rented to incoming Indians, but most survived economically through retail trade in maize and cacao with the local Indian population.

Low rents, land prices, and wages clearly indicate how marginal Texcocan society was. Frequently Spaniards and Indians rented or purchased houses or lots in Texcoco from Mexico City residents or from prominent local Indians. In the Indian barrios a house rented for 15 to 25 pesos a year; even houses close to the main plaza never rented for more than 45 pesos. Lots or houses on the main plaza cost as little as 300 pesos, never over 500. Wages in Texcoco were also very meager. The average for an Indian as a pieceworker in a local obraje or in personal service was about 22 pesos a year. Apprentices to local hat-makers received a yearly 12 pesos plus room and board.

Commercial Activities

Texcoco's economy was stimulated and directed by the needs of Mexico City's ever-increasing Hispanized population. Long-distance interregional trade, sale of fresh produce, livestock production, and obrajes were the backbone of Texcoco's economy. These enterprises clearly reflect the situation of the province's Indian and Spanish population. All necessitated very small initial capital outlays; yet even in these humble enterprises Texcocans exhibited astute business sense, exploiting to the fullest extent the area's available resources and New Spain's markets.

Obrajes flourished in Texcoco, since Mexico City provided a ready market for cheap cloth manufactures. Between 1570 and 1600 at least eight obrajes existed in Texcoco. There was a wide disparity in their size. Some were modest establishments located in the obrajero's home, with as few as two to four laborers. Others were prosperous enterprises which employed anywhere from ten to twenty workers. The internal organization of these larger obrajes was similar to that of the rural estate structure of owner, manager, staff, and laborers. The obrajero was often a Spaniard living in Mexico, while the manager and staff levels were occupied by resident Texcocans. The bottom stratum was filled by Indians. These laborers were never at this time bound to the obraje by debt, but were contracted on a yearly basis.

One Juan Rodríguez was a prosperous Texcocan obrajero. Rodríguez owned two obrajes in the town, both located in the barrio of Huitzcalco. Whether they were his sole source of income is not clear, but by 1578 he had prospered sufficiently to retire to Mexico City and entrust the management of his obrajes to a resident Texcocan, Pedro Bueno. Bueno, a mestizo, was an experienced manager, having previously run another local obraje for an owner who also lived in Mexico City. He was contracted on a yearly basis and received a salary of 125 pesos, small remuneration unless he had side benefits. Bueno was in charge of overall operation of the two obrajes: he purchased materials, sold finished products to Mexico City, and hired the laborers. The individual obrajes' immediate overseers were the owners of the two houses where the obrajes were located, respectively a man and a woman with Spanish names.

Almost every resident Hispanic Texcocan was involved in some form of commerce, usually of a petty nature. Most transactions involved Texcocans selling their produce and livestock directly to Mexico City merchants. Texcoco was an active supplier to the capital of sheep and of many fruits, including peaches, apricots, and muscatel grapes, as well as Indian fruits.

On the other hand, Mexico City frequently supplied Texcoco with maize. The local Indian population of course grew substantial amounts of maize, but still there seems to have been a steady local market for the grain. That the Indians of Texcoco were a meaningful market, at a time when Indians of more distant provinces were not, represents a significant difference. With the main center of the country's Hispanic economy and its liquid wealth so near at hand, even the poorest and most subordinated sector apparently had more purchasing power than comparable groups elsewhere. Maize in small quantities reached Texcoco through two sources: the Spanish estates and petty merchants from Mexico City. Spaniards, mestizos, and Hispanized Indians were all actively involved in the local maize trade. Estate maize, the single estate product that was occasionally marketed locally, reached Texcocans through a middle-level intermediary who garnered a small profit from the deal. Mexico City traders accounted for a greater volume of the maize coming into Texcoco, selling small quantities of the grain to Hispanic Texcocans who in turn sold it to local Indians.

As the Spanish and Hispanized population grew and spread out from the Valley of Mexico, Texcoco's trade patterns grew more complex. In particular, Texcocans became middlemen in the long-distance trade between the outlying provinces and Mexico City. Their commercial orientation was still toward the capital; they never sent finished products from the Valley to the distant provinces, but rather brought products from the provinces into the capital. Texcocan traders operated on a cash basis, either purchasing products outright from the provinces or working through consignment. Ephemeral partnerships between Texcocans and provincial Spaniards, who were often former residents of Texcoco, terminated as soon as the goods were delivered to Texcoco or Mexico City. In this way Texcoco maintained trade relations with provinces ranging from Querétaro to far distant Yucatan and Guatemala. The traders transported a variety of goods and raw materials. Frequently a single shipment would contain several types of goods. Textiles, wine, wool, native cotton cloth (mantas), and cacao were some of the products moved by Texcocans. Finished textiles and mantas were sold directly to Mexico City dealers, some of whom were wholesale merchants. On the other hand, the wool and cotton were sold to the local obrajes to be made into finished products, which in turn went to Mexico City.

Texcocan merchants were frequently involved in the cacao trade, a business that offers a glimpse of how the Spaniards built upon, altered, and expanded preconquest trade patterns. Prior to the Spanish arrival cacao was a favored drink of the Indian nobility, and cacao beans were also used as a basis of exchange and for tribute payment. Preconquest Texcoco's main source of cacao was Guatemala.

In the postconquest period the demand for cacao increased, and the product became a quite lucrative trade commodity within the framework of the Spanish economy. The general Indian population began to consume larger quantities of cacao, and the beans continued to be used as a means of exchange and for paying tribute. The product also began to be used by the increasing Spanish and Hispanized population. The Spaniards soon saw the profit potential and gradually became active participants in the cacao industry.

Texcoco's cacao merchants were long almost exclusively mestizos. Mestizos owned the carts and oversaw the purchase and distribution of the product to local and Mexico City markets. By 1600 mulatto women from Guatemala were also penetrating Texcoco's cacao trade, selling cacao in small quantities to Texcocan Indians. But mestizos and mulattoes never completely supplanted Indians in the cacao trade. The muleteers and carters were always Indian. Many of them were natives of Guatemala and had migrated to Texcoco through hiring on as cart drivers for Texcocan cacao traders.

Texcocans never handled enormous quantities of cacao. A shipment might vary from 8 to 300 loads (*cargas*). *Almendras* (shelled beans) and *mazorcas* (beans in the pod) were carted into Texcoco from Guatemala. Between 1570 and 1600 all of Texcoco's cacao was purchased from Soconusco, the major cacao-growing region of Guatemala until its collapse in the early seventeenth century.[3] Once the cacao arrived in Texcoco, the almendras were immediately sold either to the local market or to Mexico City merchants. It is not clear what happened to the mazorcas. Most likely they were stored and sold at a later time.

A petty merchant class began to emerge in Texcoco through long-distance trade activities. Texcoco's commercial operations were family-operated enterprises. Traders owned some carts, never more than a few, or some mules, and employed one or two Indian muleteers. Usually the male head of the family went back and forth between Mexico City and Texcoco making business agreements, while his wife, often a local-born Indian woman, oversaw the business in Texcoco.[4] The sons and sons-in-law traveled between Texcoco and the outlying provinces. There are cases in Texcoco of the wife continuing the business when the male head of the family died.

Texcoco's mercantile ventures generated related enterprises of several kinds. Many local individuals involved in the transporting of goods also produced carts, saddles, bridles, and boats. Not all these were used by the Texcocans themselves; some were sold to Mexico City traders. Texcocans also bred and sold mules.

The trade with the southern provinces was a continuation of a pre-conquest pattern based ultimately on climatic differences and a consequent regional differentiation in products. Hispanic Texcoco's involvement in the trade was nevertheless related to Mexico City in two ways. Import-export commerce, the exchange of European goods for silver, had become the principal and primary source of wealth. Dominant Mexico City took this business for itself, but some room was left for Texcoco in what had now become a very secondary branch of the economy. On the other hand, it was the Mexico City marketplace, its silver, its creation of buying power even in the Indian sector, that made the southern trade a viable part of the Spanish economy at all.

The Beginnings of Social Consolidation

Through such low-level mercantile activities, by the seventeenth century a local Hispanic community was gradually consolidating. This process never matured as fully as in provinces further out, because of Mexico City's overwhelming presence. More Europeans residing in Texcoco came to own property in the area, however, property that they often sold or rented to incoming individuals. The town square began to be filled by properties belonging to Spaniards and mestizos. Local residents assumed the guardianship of orphaned children of local families. Although most prospering male Texcocans continued to be buried in the capital, there was a strong trend among well-to-do mestizo and Indian women to be buried in the local monastery cemetery. But these women never completely severed the social bond to Mexico City; their wills always contained elaborate provisions for the saying of masses in both local and Mexico City churches.

Intermarriage between Hispanic Texcocan families also became more frequent. While these marriage patterns still need to be precisely defined, it appears that they followed the established Spanish practice of reinforcing or expanding economic enterprises through marital alliances. Many Texcocan marriages formally allied local families who were involved in diverse commercial ventures, enabling them to consolidate their resources and increase their profits.

Antonio de la Zarza is representative of a prospering late sixteenth-century Texcocan. Possibly he was a mestizo. Like most Hispanic Texcocans he was involved in a variety of interrelated humble economic ventures. The enterprises revolved around the buying and selling of urban properties and petty trade. The key to making these ventures profitable was Antonio's ability to move back and forth between the Spanish and Indian sectors. Antonio owned several properties in the Indian barrios which he rented or sold to Indian commoners. He was also actively involved in trading small quantities of maize, wool, and cacao, as well as some mules. All of Antonio's enterprises were somehow tied to Mexico City; through these trade activities he often served as the link between the Indian communities and the capital. He purchased maize from local or Mexico City Spaniards and in turn sold it to Indians, either commoners or local nobles. On the other hand, he traded wool, cacao, and mules, all purchased from local Texcocans, to Mexico City merchants.

Antonio's legitimate son and namesake participated in his father's business ventures and also served as Texcoco's official interpreter between 1576 and 1578. The father's various enterprises were never elaborate undertakings yielding large profits, but rather were based on informal, short-term agreements. At the time of his death there was just enough money left after debts were paid off to cover Antonio's burial in the local monastery and for ten masses to be said, locally and in Mexico City. Antonio's heirs received very little. The son inherited a piece of land, a house in an Indian barrio, and some money. Antonio also had two illegitimate mestizo sons by Ana de Tapia, an Indian woman of Texcoco; she and her sons, who bore her surname, received a house and the promise of money from the sale of a lot in Texcoco.

Indian Society in Texcoco

Most information on Texcoco's Indian population relates to its upper strata. Their activities clearly reveal how social and economic status often undercut ethnic origins. Hispanization of the area progressed rapidly because of Texcoco's geographical proximity to Mexico City and the movement of Spaniards back and forth between the two centers, and all levels of Texcoco's resident native population were affected. It cannot be concluded, however, that all Indian social and economic patterns were shattered by the Spaniards. Certainly, many overt social and economic practices were fragmented, but many subtle ones were sustained. The interaction between the native population and the Spaniards often took the form of accommodation between the two rather than dominance of one cultural pattern over the other.

At the time of the conquest the Spaniards recognized the native aristocracy's pretensions, and, though some noble lines died out, many prominent preconquest families survived through the colonial period. Because of considerations mentioned earlier, Texcoco's native elite received favored treatment from the Spaniards. The top level of Texcoco's postconquest nobility was composed of direct descendants of the Texcocan ruling house, but descendants of the various fragmented tlatoani regimes of the area made up the bulk of Texcoco's native elite. By as early as the mid-sixteenth century these groups gave the appearance of being highly Hispanized.

The nobles, or *principales,* owned land in the area and functioned within the social-economic mainstream of capital society. They identified with their Indian background mainly in that it served as one important buttress of their social position in the Spanish world. They increasingly adopted Spanish social and economic patterns as Texcoco's political and economic position in the Valley waned during the late sixteenth century. In some things, Spanish and Indian patterns coincided. Nothing was more Spanish than a proper attention to advantageous marital alliances, yet there was ample preconquest precedent for the Texcocan Indian elite's frequent practice of forming marital alliances with members of prominent Indian families who traced their lineage to other important regional dynasties, often of outlying provinces. In this way Texcocan native families that had fallen on bad times managed to improve their position.

The prominent Pimentel family had the greatest success with marital ties. In 1591 don Francisco Pimentel married into the dynasty of the Tlaxcalan cabecera of Ocotelulco. When all the direct male heirs died, the vacated tlatoani position fell to Pimentel. Upon his first wife's death, don Francisco married the female heir to the adjacent Tizatlan cabecera, and through this marriage he was eventually able to take control there as well. Thus, until his death he held a prestigious and lucrative dual dynastic position and linked together the elite native families of Tlaxcala and Texcoco.[5]

The principales were the Indian group most active in the Hispanic society and economy of Texcoco. They also occupied offices on the local Indian town council. Both their political and their socioeconomic activities grew out of traditional prerogatives. They never severed their relations with the general Indian population, for often the key to their local economic success was their influence in that sector, combined with their ability to mediate between the Indian and Spanish communities. In this sense Texcoco's principales were active conveyors to the outlying Indian *sujetos* of elements of Spanish culture. It is also among Texcoco's resident principales, that is, as distinct from the highest Indian nobility, that the strongest sense of local identity emerges. Often their activities were confined to the province, and they had only minimal direct contact with Mexico City.

One prosperous resident principal was Gabriel Cornejo.[6] A native of Texcoco, Cornejo was involved in a variety of local economic activities, owning property in the town itself as well as in the outlying barrios. In town he owned lots and houses on the main square, where he himself lived. In 1576 he sold a house on the plaza to a Spaniard, but he retained possession of his own lot. He also owned several houses in the Indian barrios, which he rented out to Indians on a yearly basis, at the rate of 25 pesos. Cornejo also had a house in a barrio located in the cacicazgo of Teutlan. This he rented to Gonzalo Fernández, a hat-maker, also for 25 pesos a year. Cornejo supplemented his rental income with small-scale mercantile activities; he purchased maize, livestock, and produce from local Spaniards and sold the products to Indians in the surrounding area.

In a word, Cornejo's economic activity bore a marked resemblance to that of the Spaniard or mestizo Antonio de la Zarza, portrayed above.

Information on the socioeconomic activities of Indian commoners in Texcoco is scarce. The lower strata of Texcoco's Indian population spoke only Nahuatl, and in the time period being considered, few of them even had fixed surnames. Among those who were semiacculturated were Indians who had migrated into the cabecera town from surrounding pueblos and sujetos. They often attached themselves as unskilled workers to one of the local obrajes, or became personal servants of resident Spaniards. On the other hand, there were many Indians residing in Texcoco who had migrated there from more distant regions in which Texcocan traders were active. In particular, many commoners were from Puebla, center of Mexican obrajes, and from Guatemala, the source of cacao. As might be expected, these Indians were involved in trade activities at some level. Most often they were muleteers or cart-drivers.

It can be deduced that as Texcocan Indians moved further into the Spanish world, learning Spanish and some marginal European skill, they, like their European-mestizo counterparts, moved either to Mexico City or to the outlying provinces.

There were some Hispanized commoners who remained permanent residents of Texcoco, often establishing themselves in some branch of the Spanish economy. Hat-making was one Texcocan enterprise that was almost exclusively the domain of humble Indians. Even at this level, Indians in Spanish activities followed Spanish social and economic patterns. Once a hat-maker showed even a small profit, he would take on an apprentice, usually an Indian who had just arrived in Texcoco.

In conclusion, despite much cultural change within a short period, one still is struck with the enduring sameness of the Mexico City–Texcoco relationship. The situation depicted above for the late sixteenth and early seventeenth centuries continued in its basic outline through the colonial period and until today: Texcocan expansion hinging on that of Mexico City; Texcoco as a haven of marginal social types, while the successful are lost to the capital, with the consequent lack of a sharply profiled, strongly consolidated local European-style community; the specialization in certain activities directly serving Mexico City; and more generally, the constant movement of people back and forth between the larger and the smaller urban complex.

NOTES

1. This chapter is part of my ongoing dissertation project on colonial Texcoco between 1519 and 1620. The greater part of this study is based on Texcocan

notarial records dating from 1568 to 1620. Other source materials augment the information extracted from the notarial records. Documents in the Archivo General de la Nación in Mexico City are particularly important for the study of Texcoco immediately after the conquest. The Ramos Indios, Tierras, and Vínculos yield information on early colonial Texcoco's heterogeneous population. Because of Texcoco's pre-eminent position in the preconquest Valley of Mexico, there exist several chronicles that focus on the region's Indian history. Like all similar sources the Texcocan chronicles contain numerous biases and exaggerations, but with careful use they yield important information on Texcoco's Indian elite. Among the more significant to this project are don Fernando de Alva Ixtlilxochitl's *Obras históricas* and fray Diego Durán's *Historia de las Indias de Nueva España e islas de la Tierra Firme.* Juan Bautista Pomar's *Relaciones de Tezcoco* provides an excellent description of the region in the 1580s.

2. See Charles Gibson, *The Aztecs under Spanish Rule,* pp. 32, 186. Although Texcoco together with the surrounding towns was geographically less clear-cut a region than many of the others considered in this volume and, during the colonial period, was at most a subarea of the Valley of Mexico socially and economically, nevertheless, like Tlaxcala, it bore the formal title of "province."

3. See Murdo J. MacLeod, *Spanish Central America,* pp. 68–79.

4. This combination—the marginal Spanish trader in Indian products from the south and the Indian wife—existed also in the Indian markets of Mexico City itself. See the letter of Andrés García in Enrique Otte, "Die europäischen Siedler und die Probleme der Neuen Welt," p. 28–29; also in English, with comment, in James Lockhart and Enrique Otte, eds., *Letters and People of the Spanish Indies, Sixteenth Century,* pp. 143–46.

5. Gibson, *Tlaxcala in the Sixteenth Century,* pp. 95–102.

6. Gabriel Cornejo offers an interesting example of how an Indian moving upward in Hispanic society used Indian pretensions as a means to enhance his social position within the community. Between 1570 and 1576 Cornejo used the title "principal" occasionally in his diverse business dealings. But as he prospered, his use of the title became consistent. By 1578 Cornejo not only used the term principal but also began to assume the title "don"; however, the "don" never came to be consistently used with his name.

5. New Elements in the Society of Tlaxcala, 1519–1618

David M. Szewczyk

European, African, and Indian; wealthy and indigent; master and employee; manufacturer, merchant, farmer, and rancher; native born and immigrant: by 1618 Tlaxcala contained all these and more.[1] In the hundred years following the conquest, new people and activities entered Tlaxcalan society in force, though in many basic respects the region, one of the most fertile and populous of central Mexico, remained completely unchanged (to this day Nahuatl is still heard, pre-Cortesian foods and settlement clusters abound, and maize is the principal grain crop). The Europeans coming to Tlaxcala were common folk, with no pretense to nobility or titles; since the encomienda was not introduced into the province, Spanish society lacked the one aristocratic and metropolitan element connected with the life of many areas removed from the capital. In this chapter the emphasis is on portraying several types prominent in Tlaxcala's incipient Hispanic society.

The preconquest social organization of the Tlaxcalans seems in many ways to have resembled that of their neighbors and arch-rivals the Aztecs, with whom they shared language and historical origin.[2] Much the same kinds of nobles and commoners were present, as well as the same great variety of long-distance merchants, craftsmen, scribes, vendors, and other specialists. By the time of the Spanish conquest the Otomis who had once held the area were a subordinate group. An elaborate four-part internal division and complete independence of outside domination were salient aspects of the constitution of the province. Both features were important for colonial-period Tlaxcala.[3] The four subprovinces, though each had its own *tlatoani* or dynastic ruler, had a strong tradition of unity, and they formed the basis of a single cabildo with equal representation of the four and rotation of the top position among them, holding together an entity much larger than the usual central-Mexican Indian

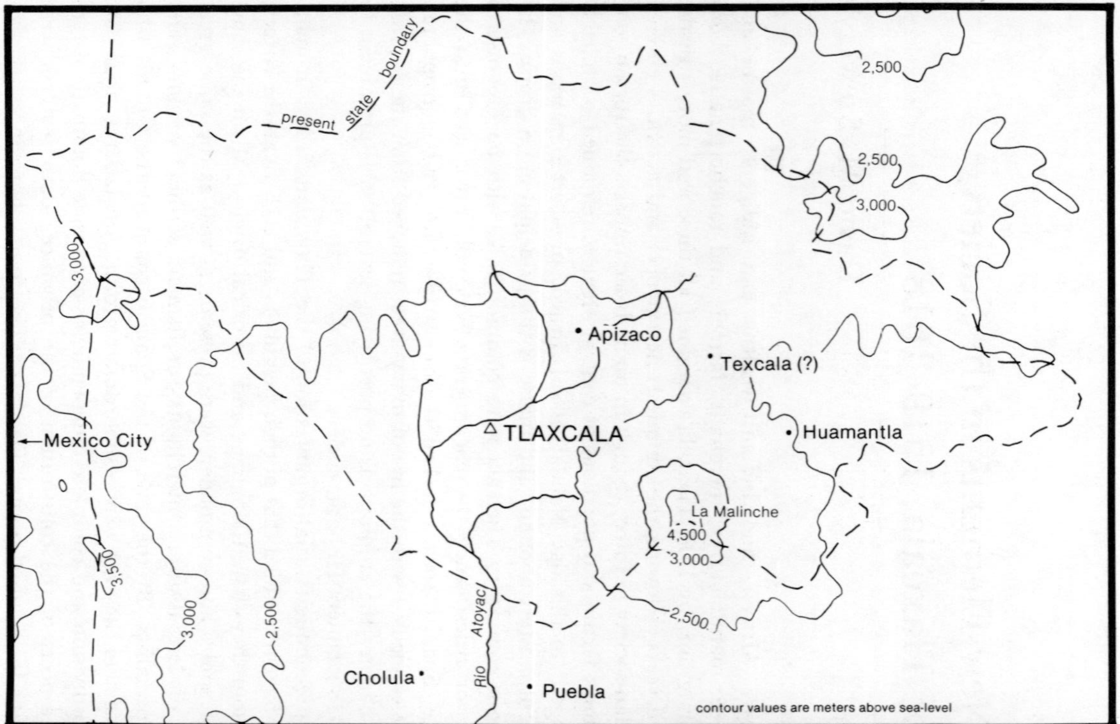

Points of Reference for Early Hispanic Tlaxcala

municipality. Since the Tlaxcalans were the largest group in central Mexico to remain independent of the Aztec empire, they were to be the Spaniards' most important auxiliaries in the conquest. This in turn meant that subsequently, aided by their own persistent propagandizing, they were to receive special treatment. Not only were they exempted from the encomienda, but the Spanish municipality which would otherwise have been established in such a center (nominal seat, after all, of the "Bishopric of Tlaxcala") was never founded. Instead, Spanish Puebla arose to the south. Being close to the country's major trade route and the markets of Puebla and Mexico City, Indian Tlaxcala was, of course, to be invaded and affected, but by a very different element and at a different rate than if it had been a Spanish town and seat of encomenderos. At the edge of Puebla's prosperity, it was infiltrated and drained rather than overwhelmed.

Against the background of an Indian society not yet vastly changed, let us look at some principal pieces in the local European or Hispanic subsociety that began to take shape in Tlaxcala. Within this community familiar social processes were at work, and the social-economic types were also not unlike ones in the better-known urban areas, but there were variants—owing partly to local idiosyncrasies, more often to the fact that Tlaxcalan Spanish society was quite marginal in its entirety and incomplete. In this environment, what was elsewhere in the middle appeared at the top; distinctions important in Mexico City or Puebla did not exist. National origin had little or nothing to do with social status among Europeans in Tlaxcala. The province had many Portuguese, and after about 1600 even Italians began to appear. Both these groups of non-Spaniards were integral parts of local European society, welcomed into its highest levels. Place of birth among Spaniards was equally unimportant. Being born in Spain did not carry the social prestige that has been so often imagined. The rankings in local European society were essentially as follows: professionals at the top; merchants, *obrajeros,* farmers, and ranchers in the middle; and carters and unskilled laborers at the bottom. There were no nobles and few artisans to flesh out the society. This ordering is far from rigid, for the most important obrajeros and merchants were on equal footing with most professionals; and the itinerant merchant (i.e., *tratante*) was really a very low-level social phenomenon.

In the 1540s and 1550s, Europeans in increasing number established themselves in the province as agriculturalists, millers, and draymen. The Indians resisted the intrusion. In the fifth and sixth decades of the sixteenth century the cabildo (the institution serving as the Indians' corporate voice) pressed several lawsuits against the larger European landowners. The results were nil. Europeans were firmly fixed in the countryside. Their residence in the city of Tlaxcala followed soon after. In 1562 the cabildo sought to prevent Spaniards from buying urban real estate.[4] Once again the effort failed. And so in one way or another numbers of Europeans were soon living in Tlaxcala (close to a hundred in 1570).

Merchants and Commerce

After the conquest proper, the first Spaniards in Tlaxcala by way of business were merchants engaged in various kinds of barter. They did not come to stay, since there were not enough resident Europeans to justify it. By 1560 the picture had begun to change, and Europeans were present in sufficient number to make local European shops profitable. Indian merchants did not, however, disappear. They even continued to travel to Mexico's periphery in search of exotic feathers (for artisans) and rare spices, stones, metals, and comestibles. On a much lower social level, the fresh produce hucksters, tamale vendors, and all the other types of retail merchants who were integral to the *tiánguiz* persisted.

The first Spanish merchants were owners of general stores. Traditionally, in provincial settings, such stores were fixtures on the town square, and the same was soon true of Tlaxcala. With few exceptions, however, the Europeans rented their stores (and trades shops), for throughout the sixteenth and early seventeenth centuries the houses ringing the square were owned by upper-class Indians. In fact, a large number of the principales, perhaps 40 percent, made all or part of their livelihood through urban real estate. Despite the fact that the merchants did not own large houses on the town square, so often a requisite for social prestige, they did command a position far up on the Spanish provincial social ladder, outranked only by the officials from the outside.

Francisco Pérez de Rua can serve as the archetype of a successful Tlaxcalan merchant. A native of Portugal, he came to Mexico with his wife (also a native Portuguese) some time after 1550. By the 1560s he was a citizen (*vecino*) of Tlaxcala City and had set himself up in business as a merchant. By 1572 he was selling dye material (cochineal and indigo) and supplies for Indian workers (cacao) to the obrajeros of Tlaxcala City. He also had good volume in selling wine. The big buyers were the most profitable side of his business, but until he died (around 1590) he continued to maintain a general goods store in the arched portico on the town square. There he sold ready-made native clothes, flour, and bread, as well as paper, ink, and the other stock items of a Spanish store.

Although he was Portuguese, Pérez de Rua was completely acculturated, speaking and writing Spanish fluently, and he was influential and respected as a member of local Tlaxcalan society. Had there been a Spanish town council, he would have been a member. In the plebeian European community of sixteenth-century Tlaxcala, accident of birth counted for little. Nearly everyone was an immigrant, and no one was descended from a conqueror. A man like Francisco, however, created a new position; his sons (with the exception of Juan, an obrajero, who was as industrious and resourceful as his father), lived off the inherited wealth and social position. His daughters were married to men who were destined to be members of Tlaxcalan society as respected and important as himself. One son-in-law was a notary public, the other an eminent obrajero.

Pérez de Rua's sources of supply were many, reflecting the varied nature of interprovincial trade. Woolens came from the local obrajes, while cacao and indigo came from the southern provinces: Guatemala, Soconusco, Oaxaca, Coatzacualcos. Most commonly, merchants relied on carters for supplies. This could be done in either of two ways: one could commission a drayman enroute south to return with cacao and indigo purchased at a prearranged price; or one could simply rely on carters who came back on their own initiative with salable dyes and "spices." The latter was by far the more prevalent method. Yet another means was employed, however, especially by Pueblans and Mexico City residents who owned chains of which their stores in Tlaxcala were merely a link. These chains maintained resident merchant-traders in the south who regularly received goods from the central region and sent back tropical raw products. (Such agents might later move to Tlaxcala to maintain a store, and still later, if successful, open a store in Puebla.) Pérez de Rua could obtain large chests from Michoacán. These were highly prized (for the excellence of the carving and lacquering, traditions still found today), especially as wedding gifts. Flour, beans, and staples came from Tlaxcalan mills and farms. Silks, damasks, and other fine cloths, as well as Spanish wine, were purchased from large import dealers in Puebla and Mexico City. No one source was responsible for more than a small share of the provincial store's stock.

Not all merchants were as rich, socially prominent, or as versatile as was Pérez de Rua. As the Indian population continued to decline in the sixteenth century, and the Spanish citizenry increased, more and more "specialty" stores appeared. Invariably these were owned and run by Europeans. Taverns predominated numerically, but the case of the Herrera-Serrano fish store is more to the point. In early 1618 Sebastián de Herrera and Miguel Serrano, both long-time citizens of Tlaxcala, seeing the possibilities, opened a fish store on the main square. It was an equal partnership: Herrera supplied the store with fish, and Serrano concerned himself strictly with selling the catch.

The mushrooming of these specialized merchants in the early seventeenth century occurred during a low period (if not, indeed, the lowest) of Indian numbers and power. The Indian population was approaching its nadir, and in this time the province had its first non-Indian "gobernador de naturales" (Diego Muñoz Camargo, the younger). Europeans found the greatest chances yet to expand into previously native fields of economic activity, while more and more Indians were forsaking those endeavors in favor of European and European-style ones. In these years Spaniards acquired more ownership of property than in all of the sixteenth century; Spaniards moved into previously peripheral activities (like fish-mongering); and Indians came to be predominant in the Spanish trades of tailoring and hat-making.

The success of specialized merchants owed more to expanding demand within the local European and Europeanized community than to a weakening of native control of industries. Some of the specialists, probably the majority, catered almost exclusively to European tastes and needs. Francisco Hurtado de Mendoza is a prime example of a specialist attracted by the developing local European economy, in this case the ever expanding obraje industry of Tlaxcala City. Hurtado moved to Tlaxcala in 1597 as the agent of Luis de Tovar, citizen of Querétaro, and he became the principal wool broker of the initial two decades of the 1600s. Tovar would entrust Hurtado with wool in lots of 7,000-odd *arrobas* (over 85 tons); Hurtado sold that and more each year. Although technically an employee of someone else, Hurtado had enormous weight in the local economy. This, plus his education, piety, and personal qualities, gained him great social standing, despite many obstacles: he arrived very late in the development of Tlaxcala's colonial society; he had no daughters or sons to marry into the existing social system; he was of ordinary parentage and a native of Colima, Mexico. Nevertheless, he served as *síndico* or treasurer-steward of the Franciscan monastery from about 1606 until his death in 1617, and he was a respected auxiliary to the cabildo. Many mourned his passing.

Native merchants, including long-distance ones, never entirely disappeared. The tiánguiz survived, a basically Indian-run (though Spanish-administered) weekly event. Those Indian activities which existed often offer evidence of considerable strength in the face of Spanish domination. A case in point is the butchering business. Although European animals were new, animal slaughter for human consumption long antedated conquest, and when the new site of the city of Tlaxcala was laid out about 1526, Indians established a row of butcher shops. The Spaniards, following their usual practice, made the supply of cattle (though not always sheep, and certainly never pigs) a monopoly, in effect a Spanish one. Each year the sole right to distribute beef (the *abasto,* "supply") in Tlaxcala was put on the auction block. After being awarded the monopoly, the Spanish *obligado* or contractor had to do many things: get sufficient cattle; move them to Tlaxcala, which lacked cattle ranches as completely as it lacked encomenderos; guard the stock once there; and come to terms with the butchers. All the butchers were Indians. They were organized into a union or guild and bargained collectively. If a Spaniard had not met their terms he could have been ruined. The usual contract ran for one year and called for the butchers to work for the obligado only three days a week, selecting, slaughtering, dressing, and weighing. In return, each butcher received the appreciable pay of 40 pesos a year, and all of them as a unit got half of the chitterlings and all of the tripe (these parts being salable to Indian consumers).

Farmers and Ranchers

Whereas merchants were the first Spaniards to carry out civil pursuits in Tlaxcala, ranchers and farmers were the first permanent Spanish residents, beginning to settle as early as 1527 and increasing constantly in number. At first they were only a few, not needing much land and not interfering with the Indian system of land tenure. But Indian tolerance of these foreign landowners ended about 1545, when the cabildo began to wage a losing legal war against the Spaniards. For the next twenty years or so, the Indians initiated repeated legal contests challenging Spanish rights to ownership and to pasturing. They lost virtually every battle, and fewer than a dozen Spaniards were forced to vacate.

Spanish agricultural enterprises were most diverse. The most common, however, was a smallish, family-owned and -run farm (*labor*) or ranch (*estancia*). Cash crops were wheat, maize, barley, and other grains. Vegetables and other comestibles for family consumption were also grown. Those who ranched raised sheep, not cattle. There was not a single cattle ranch in the entire province. That is not to say that there were no larger livestock at all. As we have seen, a large herd of cattle was driven into the province each year, and it was pastured on community land. Each farm and ranch had a dozen or so head of cattle that were kept for butchering. Also, and more importantly, at Huamantla (the carting center) there were a number of ranches raising oxen, source of power for both carts and plows in the sixteenth century. These were the *ganado mayor* responsible for so much damage to farm crops, and against which the Indians never ceased to rail.

Nicolás de Perla's sheep ranch can serve to illustrate the nature of the smaller enterprises. Nicolás was of the most common social stock, though, like most local Spaniards in the late sixteenth century, he was literate. Coming into the province around 1570, he began to purchase some scattered pieces of land around Huamantla, pieces which never came to be a single contiguous holding. Most of the lands were bought from Indians, and often payment was made in sheep rather than in money. Nicolás usually employed an Indian shepherd to help tend the stock. The contracts ran for one year, and required him to pay the shepherd a salary (of about 19 pesos), and to clothe, feed, and shelter him. With only one resident auxiliary and a few seasonal helpers, Nicolás himself lived at the ranch and did a great deal of the work, which included tending to wheat, maize, and other crops and shearing, branding, and herding the sheep. The wool that Nicolás obtained was usually sold to Pueblan or Tlaxcalan obrajeros. Nicolás and his wife lived comfortably, but not in luxury.

Greater wealth was not unknown among the province's agriculturalists, however. Most prominent was the sharp-dealing, enterprising López Arróñez family, which, on the basis of its interests centered at Apizaco, sat at the top of local Spanish society. The founders of the dynasty, Juan López Arróñez and Beatriz Gallegos, were both born in Spain, and they settled in Tlaxcala between 1548 and 1553. At his death in the late 1560s, Juan left a legacy of several sheep ranches and farms, an obraje, a grist mill, a very substantial house at Apizaco, and slaves. There was also a mortgage, but a new marriage on the part of the widow Gallegos brought needed cash, and the empire soon expanded again. Two of the three sons of Juan López Arróñez left home and set up house on their inherited land. Both prospered. Francisco, the other brother, who was probably the middle son, remained at Apizaco. Over the years he gradually took over management of the family's affairs.[5]

Under Francisco's stewardship Apizaco took on the appearance of an integrated large estate. In addition to the farming lands, the sheep ranch was big enough to support a herd approaching 20,000 head. The grist mill served not only the López Arróñez family, but all the other farmers for a good distance around. And, of course, the obraje persisted. This aspect of the family's holdings alone was enough to assure its preeminence. Apizaco as a nearly family-owned town was one of the three economic nuclei of the province alongside Huamantla and Tlaxcala proper.[6]

Francisco also saw to it that the family's economic base was not confined within the boundaries of Apizaco. He encouraged and underwrote the expansion of his brothers' landholdings and engineered the marriage of his three sisters to prominent Tlaxcalan landowners. Inés Arróñez, for example, married Juan López de Soria and moved to Texcala, where the pair developed a small-scale Apizaco, even including an obraje. Francisco's own marriage late in life was designed to enhance the family's economic and social stance. Francisco's wife was doña María de Avila, a daughter of Gaspar Rodríguez de Villanueva—Tlaxcala's most influential notary.[7]

In sum, the López Arróñez family possessed large holdings in the province, an appreciable percentage of all Spanish-owned land. Most of it was in good-sized contiguous units. The heart of the enterprise was Apizaco, but through Francisco's siblings the family directly or indirectly owned lands near Huamantla and urban real estate in Puebla and Tlaxcala. Marriages were arranged to connect the family both with up-and-coming immigrants and with the monied, socially prestigious professional class. And although Apizaco faded by the eighteenth century, the family's upward ascent through the female line was long sustained. In 1695 the great-granddaughter of Beatriz Gallegos, Tlaxcala-born doña Inés Arróñez Maldonado, was married to don Fernando Alfonso Carrillo, the chief notary of the cabildo of Mexico City.[8] The family's success and the extent of its lands were out of the ordinary. So too was the fact that it eventually transcended the province. The marriage of a daughter to a prominent citizen of Puebla or Mexico City was an ideal that few Tlaxcalans achieved.

Blacks and Indians as well as Spaniards were active in commercial agriculture. And there were Europeans and Africans who toiled on rented land because they did not possess the capital necessary to purchase land for themselves. This is not the place for a complete discussion of land use and tenure, but some mention may be made of the role of Indians in this connection. Contemporary documents do not give the impression that the Tlaxcalan Indians suffered serious loss of lands during the time period under consideration. There was no general plundering or usurpation of Indian land by Spaniards. While Indians freely sold land, they kept enough to support the traditional crops as well as the sheep many now raised. Some Indians, mainly nobles it seems, were becoming agricultural entrepreneurs in the same fashion as the local Spaniards. In the first decades of the seventeenth century the Cerón s of Huamantla, principales and fully literate in Spanish, were in some salient ways similar to the López Arróñez clan. Don Diego and don Jorge Cerón ran the family and administered the holdings on the plains surrounding Huamantla. They specialized in sheep, but also grew wheat and maize. They, too, employed a few paid resident Indian workers and hired per diem seasonal help (from nearby towns) as needed. Grain was sold to Tlaxcalan merchants or to other local stockmen. Wool was sold to Tlaxcalan and Pueblan obrajeros. Probably over half of Tlaxcala's principales were engaged in Spanish-style agriculture (though few were as acculturated as the Cerón family).

Obrajes

The obraje is commonly depicted as a jail-like enterprise, owned by a Spaniard, producing cheap woolen cloth, employing blacks and Indians who are chained to the machinery and ill fed. This image may correspond to conditions existing from the middle seventeenth through the eighteenth centuries, but not to the earlier period.

The first obraje in the province was probably at Apizaco, set up in the 1560s by Juan López Arróñez. By 1618 close to twenty obrajes must have been operating in Tlaxcala City, plus the one at Apizaco and one at

Texcala.[9] No others are evident elsewhere in the area, not even in Santa Ana Chiautempan, today the state's most important textile town. Obrajes did indeed produce cheap woolen goods, in that they cost less than imported European cloths, but local producers had not yet given up the idea of competing in the area of quality goods. Following the lead of the Puebla industry, several local obrajes, including that at Apizaco, produced expensive, fine quality material. The cloth was woolen in view of the thousands of sheep on all sides; raw cotton was not available in quantity until about 1700, after which time obrajes produced for the most part cotton goods.[10]

The owners of obrajes were not invariably Spaniards and Portuguese (in 1616 a fourth of Tlaxcala's obrajeros were Portuguese,[11] which would be true of earlier and later times as well). Gibson has noted that mestizos were sometimes obrajeros, and this was certainly true; Diego Muñoz Camargo (the famous mestizo historian) and his brother Juan Muñoz were active in the business. But Indians were obrajeros too, and quite regularly, though their exact numbers cannot yet be pinpointed. The example of the Indian noblewoman doña María Castilan Xochitl can give us some idea of this activity.

For some time prior to October 1616 doña María had maintained an obraje in her house in Tlaxcala City. The establishment was complete with combs, spinning wheels, looms, and dye-pots. Her employees were all Indians working for her on a voluntary wage basis. Her operation was a general one, producing huipiles, cloaks, bolts of cloth, blankets, and other woolens. This very definitely was an income-producing enterprise, one she engaged in for "her support and that of her children." When she ran afoul of the obraje inspector, she appealed to the viceroy and received a license to continue her operation.[12] Unlike European obrajeros, she did not purchase her wool from European merchants or ranchers; probably she supplied herself from sheep she owned, or bought wool from other Indians. In sum, doña María owned an obraje in which she used Indian labor and which she supplied with wool obtained solely within the bounds of the Indian society and economy. And as such her operation was an important innovation, for while weaving (of cotton) did exist before the arrival of the Spaniards, the technology and organization of the obraje did not.

The persons performing the ordinary work in the Tlaxcalan obrajes were practically all Indians. I have seen only two exceptions, one mestizo and one black, both working as weavers. Of the workers whose origin is known, 98 percent were native Tlaxcalans. The remaining 2 percent came from nearby Cholula and Puebla, or occasionally from Mexico City. The number of Indians employed per obraje varied, but rarely exceeded forty. A force of half that number was more common. Except in rare cases, they worked under a contract, which usually ran for a year, established a wage (usually between 10 and 30 pesos a year), and obliged the obrajero to clothe, feed, and house the worker.[13] Exceptions to this obligation occurred when the worker already lived in Tlaxcala City or Apizaco, in which case the Indian lived at home and received a higher wage. Workers entered as novices, progressed to combing, to carding, to spinning, and finally to weaving; but while both women and men were carders or spinners, only men could be weavers. With equal inflexibility, only women were cooks.

As to working conditions, in more than twenty inventories of obrajes I have never seen evidence of a single chain—and this in an era when even nails still figure in such listings. Similarly, whereas I did encounter four or five complaints of beatings, no one ever claimed to have been kidnapped or otherwise pressed into service or to have been chained to the loom. Each obraje had its own cook especially hired for that task. Meals consisted of tortillas, beans, native fruit and vegetables, and meat twice a week. Husbands and wives often worked for the same employer, and the force often included fellow villagers. Discontent did exist, though, and Indians ran away—usually to turn up working for an obrajero in better-paying Puebla. Such physical abuse as did occur came at the hands of the shop manager, usually (but not invariably) an acculturated black slave of the obrajero.

Thus we can see that up through 1618, at least, obrajes and obrajeros were quite different from those often described. Much would change by midcentury. In 1654 the obraje at Apizaco was described as "filled with low-life people, blacks and mulattoes, hardened criminals all, . . . prisoners loaded down with irons and chains."[14]

Officials and Professionals

Sitting atop, and in some ways removed from this melange of local social types, were the professionals. They were a small cadre indeed, probably never exceeding thirty in number. Before 1540 or so, there seem to have been no resident European professionals, but as there came to be a European settlement in the province, the need for a resident notary and governor arose. Tlaxcala now had two governors: an Indian nobleman who was called "gobernador" or "gobernador de naturales"; and a European who was at first designated "corregidor," later "alcalde mayor," and after about 1585 "gobernador." In the general scheme of New Spain's colonial administration, the European was far the more powerful. He handled external relations and matters involving all segments of the province's society, while the Indian governor was concerned with the internal affairs of the indigenous community only. Similarly there were two sets of notaries: Indians for the Indians, Europeans for the Europeans.

An official interpreter was the effective legal middleman between the European and Indian communities. Beyond the officials, professionals were very few. A European barber arrived in the 1580s, and began cutting hair and performing minor surgery. The *procuradores de causas* (non-degree-holding quasi-lawyers), so common and essential in Mexico City and Puebla, did not open offices in Tlaxcala, only traveling there when necessary. European doctors and pharmacists did not begin to arrive until the second decade of the seventeenth century. Native healers, of course, were actively treating people before, during, and after the period of concern to us.

The European governor was a figure from the outside, holding office for a few years at a time. At first he was likely to be an important Spaniard who arrived too late in the conquest to receive an encomienda, but who was too prominent to be ignored completely. Later governors were mostly sons of conquerors or associates of newly arrived viceroys. In all cases their connections and loyalties were in Mexico City, of which they invariably considered themselves citizens. Similarly, their economic bases were outside Tlaxcala, though it is true that they often came to own some land or have other investments in the province. Usually not themselves encomenderos, the Spanish governors tended to make a career of provincial administration. They had often served in other provinces as governor or alcalde mayor before coming to Tlaxcala, and they left to assume yet another similar post.

The well-known Gonzalo Gómez de Cervantes illustrates the type.[15] He served in the post twice, in 1584–1585 and in 1596–1598. Born in Mexico, Gonzalo came from important conqueror-encomendero families on both sides and was married to a lady of similar background, but did not inherit an encomienda. His economic well-being was rooted in extensive agricultural enterprises in Huejotzingo, Tlaxcala, and elsewhere, and he was involved in commercial activities which extended as far as Guadalajara. Though very definitely a citizen of Mexico City, Gonzalo had social relationships in Tlaxcala, both amicable and antagonistic. For example, he was very friendly with the López Arróñez family and with Rodrigo Arias, a rancher. In fact, his association with Arias prompted the Indian community of Huamantla in 1591 to petition the viceroy to disqualify him as judge in a lawsuit between Arias and themselves. These social liaisons or friendships stopped short of marriage ties. There is no evidence that any governor (or his children) ever married a Tlaxcalan, either European or Indian. Even the wealthiest Tlaxcalans were socially unacceptable marriage partners for a governor or his family. Measured against society in Mexico City and Puebla, Tlaxcalans were found wanting. They were not descendants of conquerors or of hidalgos, not well connected at the viceregal court, not metropolitan, not vastly rich from silver mining or international commerce. They were provincial, of common immigrant stock, at best only locally wealthy, and influential only within the bounds of the province.

Spanish notaries were at times as powerful as governors.[16] They were as well educated, though socially very different. None claimed descent from a conqueror or noble. Their wives were daughters of local merchants, well-to-do ranchers, artisans, and the like. In contrast to the governors, the notaries were permanent citizens of the province, identified with it, and economically and socially totally integrated into it.

The career of Gaspar Rodríguez de Villanueva offers examples of both ordinary and extraordinary behavior for a notary. Gaspar seems to have come from a middle-level Mexico City family. He first entered Tlaxcala as a notary in the 1570s, and quickly established firm contacts with the Tlaxcalan merchants and obrajeros. Although he moved to Puebla in 1580, he continued to maintain citizenship, a residence, and a notary's office in Tlaxcala. (This move to Puebla is somewhat out of character. Usually notaries who came to the province settled there permanently. Those few who did move away severed all contacts.) Besides seeing to the duties of his office, Gaspar bought and sold wool and cochineal, lent money, served as executor of wills and guardian of children, and owned, rented, and operated several ranches and farms in the province. Far and away his closest personal connection in the province was with the López Arróñez family. Ultimately, in 1601 or so, Gaspar succeeded in arranging the marriage of his daughter doña María de Avila to Francisco López Arróñez. Soon thereafter, doña María's brother Juan de Villanueva, a secular priest, moved to the López Arróñez domain of Apizaco and assumed the post of chaplain.[17] After Gaspar's death in 1606, his son and junior partner, also named Gaspar Rodríguez de Villanueva, took over the notary's office and other affairs in Tlaxcala.

Interpreters were present in Tlaxcala long before the arrival of the Spaniards, bridging the Nahuatl- and Otomi-speaking communities. After 1550, Otomi became less and less used, and in fact, proclamations and town cries were carried out only in Spanish and Nahuatl after 1560. Despite the precedents, one may not assume that all official interpreters of the Spanish period were Indians. Most were mestizos, and a few, like Francisco Martínez de Plasencia, were Spaniards. Because of their vital function, all official interpreters were important men in the Indian community, even those who were not Indians themselves.

The mestizo Julián de Vega had been doing interpreting on an ad hoc basis for some years before 1579, when he finally received a viceregal appointment as town interpreter of Tlaxcala. In his post he assisted Indians in their transactions with Spaniards, done before Spanish notaries. He also put community complaints and petitions into correct Spanish legal form and translated Nahuatl documents into Spanish for use in court cases. Julián's prestige in both communities was enhanced by his extensive landholdings, both rural and urban, and by his alliance to the Spanish interpreter Martínez de Plasencia through the latter's marriage to his sister-in-law. It bespeaks his acceptance and prestige in both Tlaxcalan communities that in Spanish documents he is described as a "vecino" or citizen of Tlaxcala, a status bestowed on few non-Europeans, while in Indian documents he is said to be a "Spaniard." Only a few other mestizos, including the very wealthy and influential Muñoz Camargo family, were so totally accepted at this level in Tlaxcala.

Other professionals arriving from outside the province—especially after 1600—tended to be university graduates just starting their careers. They came to Tlaxcala as a town and province without resident physician, pharmacist, or the like, but with a growing European population. They often required help from monied second parties in order to set up shop. When in 1616 Juan de Alarcón came to Tlaxcala as the first pharmacist, he did so in a two-year partnership with Antonio de Lepe, a citizen of Tlaxcala City. Alarcón brought the training and skill; Lepe put up the money to rent an appropriate shop and purchase chemicals and supplies. The business prospered enough so that by December of the same year Alarcón had convinced his father, a citizen of nearby Cholula, of the viability of the venture, and he received a 600-peso loan to buy Lepe out.

Women

The purpose of this essay being to help populate the barren sixteenth-century Tlaxcalan landscape, I would be remiss were I not to introduce briefly some of the women. The types which past generations of historians preferred to write about, such as nuns and doñas, were scarce among the humble Spanish provincials of Tlaxcala. There were no nunneries and hence no resident nuns. The doñas, with one exception (doña María de Avila, wife of Francisco López Arróñez), were all wives of Spanish governors, and consequently were transitory and quite outside the local framework.

The main surface role that Hispanic society assigned to women, in Tlaxcala as elsewhere, was that of marriage partner; this function was less simple and less subordinate than it might seem. Marriage, as seen repeatedly in these pages, was the main vehicle for those social-economic alliances in terms of which Spaniards organized their lives. Each party, the woman and the man, represented a family, its status, and its property, and in this respect they met as equals. It was vital that precisely the correct match be made. In Tlaxcala this usually meant that the older, established families sought through their daughters' marriages contracts to ally themselves with more recently arrived Europeans who were newly wealthy or influential. This seems to hold true for both Indians and Europeans. Marriages were always based on mutual advantage and certain kinds of affinities, even when these are hidden. Thus the seeming anomaly of a Tlaxcalan Indian noblewoman marrying a European farmer of no notable position is explained by their similar rank and interests within colonial New Spain's society generally, even though she might be in the upper class of Indian society and he in the middle area of the European sector.

Women brought to these marriages not only their family's name and prestige, but the money and economic power represented by their dowries. The dowry was the economic leverage that women had before marriage to secure an acceptable mate, and its power did not decrease in the least afterward, since it always remained the property of the wife. It usually included some money, but (in Tlaxcala at least) it consisted predominantly of such things as ranch and farm lands, seed, herds of animals, furniture, clothing, rights to mortgages, slaves, and even public offices (notary public, town council interpreter, and so on).

Given this kind of base, it is understandable that women should have been economically very influential though not much seen in the active aspects of business, farming, real estate, and the like. They were the silent partners and movers behind the scenes in a great many colonial enterprises. Juana Pérez de Gama, daughter of the merchant Francisco Pérez de Rua, was owner of half of her husband's large obraje. Her economic support was absolutely essential, as becomes clear at times when she acted as joint purchaser of wool, machinery, or supplies. Similarly, one María Hernández was equal partner with her husband in their farm. The examples are abundant and cover every activity.

Other women were much more visibly active. As elsewhere in the Spanish world, they tended to be widows, with no one to act as front man. When put in this position, some of them did not remarry lightly. María Atienza, for example, had been married to a prominent obrajero. She never married again, but did become half-owner with Francisco Barragán in yet another obraje. But by far the most spectacular businesswoman was Mencía Pérez, later in life known as Mencía Pérez de Aragón. She began her economic ascent associated with a farm. Around 1570 she married a Basque innkeeper. Before he died in 1578, the pair had moved to Huamantla and purchased what was destined to become valuable property, consisting of urban real estate, a mill, and ranch land. Her husband's sole heir, she continued after his death to expand her holdings. She was aided in this by her second husband, Rodrigo Arias, who brought a prosperous carting and ranching business to the marriage. While married to him she retreated into the traditional silent partner role, but after his death in the late 1590s she was again hectically busy. By 1600 she was the wealthiest woman in Huamantla and among the five or six wealthiest in the entire province. In 1591 she branched out and opened a shingle business. She hired Indians to cut the shingles "on the hills surrounding this town [Huamantla]," provided the transportation, and paid other expenses. In many ways Mencía fits the stereotypes: she was illiterate, she was the "quiet money" behind her husband's enterprises, she remarried quickly when widowed young. But she was also highly successful as an independent businesswoman; she lived in Huamantla, not Tlaxcala City; and she was mestizo. The latter fact explains her place of residence and the social inferiority of her spouses, an innkeeper and a carter. It is important, however, to point out that she was called a "mestiza" by her neighbors on only one occasion, an Inquisition inquiry concerning her first husband. Her wealth and success helped elevate her well above the standing of most mestizo women.

These then are a few of the new types of people living in Tlaxcala during the first century after conquest. There were others as well, artisans in Spanish trades (virtually all Indians), carters (Europeans), blacks (many of whom were free agriculturalists), Indian nobles with strong ties to the European economy. In 1618 Indian continuities, population decline, and corporate action were one side of the province; the other was a bustling European subsociety of between 300 and 400 Spaniards, Portuguese, Italians, and blacks, connected with the rest of New Spain and increasingly rooted in general provincial life.

NOTES

1. Related to my ongoing dissertation project on early Tlaxcala, this chapter draws on archival research in several repositories of Mexico City and Tlaxcala, but most especially in the Archivo General de Tlaxcala (AGT), containing the Registro de Instrumentos Públicos (RIP), with forty-four thick volumes of notarial documents to 1618, as well as lawsuits and other litigation organized by year. The career histories of which the chapter is largely built are synthesized from hundreds of individual documentary passages, too many to reproduce usefully in the present context. Only the López Arróñez family is referenced in detail as an example of the procedure.

2. Work now underway by Pedro Carrasco, Marina Anguiano, Luis Reyes, and Thelma D. Sullivan, who have struck an apparently rich vein of early Nahuatl texts from Tlaxcala, promises to make possible a far more specific, detailed, and reliable description of Tlaxcalan Indian society both before and after conquest than is presently possible. Hugo Nutini (*San Bernardino Contla*), though concentrating mainly on a later time, is working along similar lines. The single most important published source for preconquest Tlaxcala is Diego Muñoz Camargo,

Historia de Tlaxcala. For a good though increasingly outdated general survey of preconquest Nahua culture see Jacques Soustelle, *Daily Life of the Aztecs.*

3. For Tlaxcalan Indian provincial organization and institutions at the time of the conquest and after, see Charles Gibson, *Tlaxcala in the Sixteenth Century.*

4. Museo Nacional de Antropología e Historia, Colección Antigua 340, "Actas de Cabildo de Tlaxcala," f. 149v. These sixteenth-century Nahuatl minutes of the council of Tlaxcala, when studied thoroughly, will allow a closer approximation to the careers and concerns of Indian governors, dynastic rulers, councilmen, and notaries. Some sample pages, with translation, are included in Arthur J. O. Anderson, Frances Berdan, and James Lockhart, *Beyond the Codices.* The same team is working toward a more extensive transcription and translation, as are Pedro Carrasco, Luis Reyes, et al.

5. Archivo del Ayuntamiento de Tlaxcala, legajo 1622–1753; AGT, RIP, vol. 1, ff. 50r–53v; vol. 2, ff. 28r–v (3d grouping of Gutiérrez); vol. 3, ff. 208r–209v; AGT, 1564, #3; Archivo General de la Nación (AGN), Mercedes, vol. 9, ff. 276r–v. López Arróñez was accorded the right to style himself "vecino de Tlaxcala" rather than "vecino de la provincia," even though he did not live in the city.

6. AGT, RIP, vol. 1, f. 91v, f. 309r; vol. 2, ff. 13r–14v; vol. 8, ff. 41v–42v (Medinavilla), ff. 132r–133r.

7. AGT, RIP, vol. 4, ff. 13v–14r (Medinavilla); vol. 12, ff. 159r–v; vol. 20, no foliation (Rodríguez).

8. AGN, Inquisición, vol. 492, ff. 24r–25r.

9. AGT, RIP, vol. 41, no foliation.

10. Uncatalogued MSS relating to Tlaxcalan obrajes and weaving during the eighteenth century, now in the Mexican manuscripts collection of the Philip H. & A.S.W. Rosenbach Foundation, Philadelphia.

11. AGT, RIP, vol. 41, no foliation.

12. See Silvio Zavala, ed., *Fuentes para la historia del trabajo en Nueva España,* VI:265–66.

13. A cook might earn 10 pesos a year, a novice worker 12 to 14 pesos, a skilled nonweaving worker, such as a spinner, 18 to 25 pesos, and a weaver 30.

14. AGN, Civil, vol. 76, exp. 33. I am indebted to Sam Kagan for this passage.

15. See Gómez de Cervantes, *La vida económica y social de Nueva España al finalizar el siglo XVI.*

16. With regard to the Indian notaries, their writings are only beginning to be recovered and translated in any number, and it was in those mundane pieces of paper that the intimate life stories of the Indian population were told—including the lives of the notaries. I would, nonetheless, suggest the following as a probable pattern: typically the Indian notary was a son of a principal (not a cacique), educated by the Franciscans, married to a cacica or principal, holding a notarial post in the Indian governmental system, but having sufficient economic wherewithal through his inheritance and marriage to live handsomely without having to function actively in his profession—though many did so.

17. He was personal chaplain to the López Arróñez family, but he said mass on Sundays and holy days for the entire community for miles around Apizaco. By mid-seventeenth century these people were true parishioners in the obraje-town.

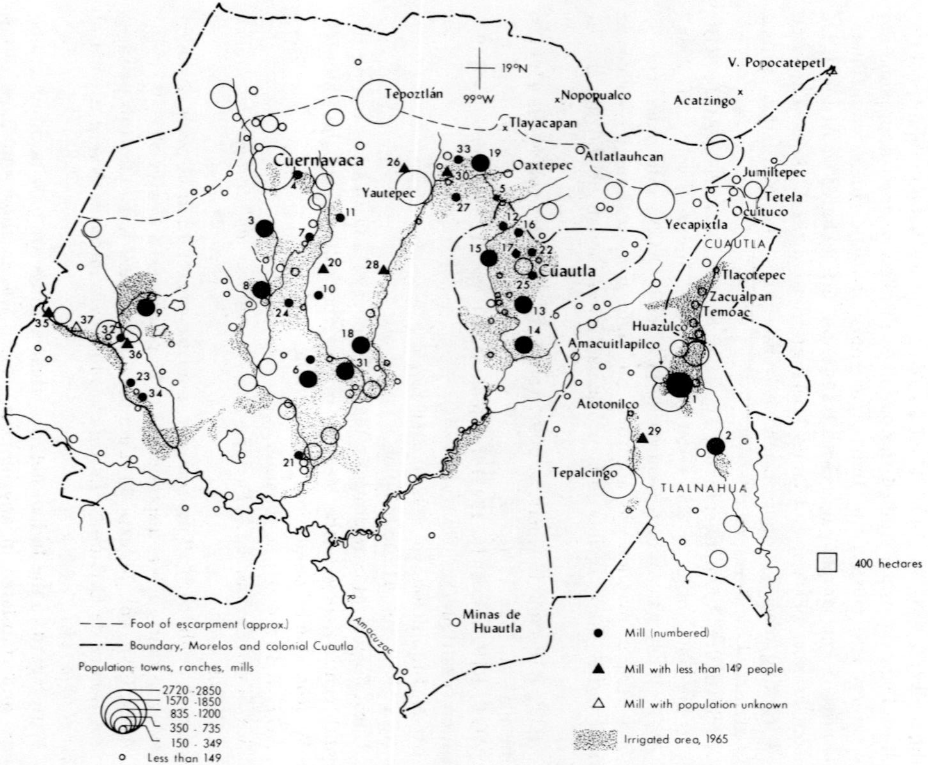

FIGURE 1. Late Colonial Morelos, with Population Centers and Sugar Mills

6. Morelos and Its Sugar Industry in the Late Eighteenth Century

Ward Barrett

The region now known as Morelos has a physical unity sufficient to define it and set it in strong contrast to other regions of Mexico.[1] This unity derives from its basin-like nature, interrupted though it is by some low ranges of hills, from its superficial geological formations, which are volcanic over much of the region, and from its location at the foot of the great escarpment of the Volcanic Plateau, which rises to Popocatepetl in the northeastern corner of the state. This location ensures that relatively abundant supplies of water drain into it from the escarpment and are available for irrigation at its base. The region is unique in Mexico, for there is no other one of similar size, offering similar advantages of climate, water, and large areas of flat land to be found elsewhere along the escarpment at the same general altitude. If we add to these attributes the great advantage of proximity to Tenochtitlan-Mexico City, in a cooler basin whose agricultural products were and still are most conveniently supplemented by those of Morelos, it is not surprising that the area should have been densely inhabited in preconquest times, become preeminent in sugar production in Mexico in colonial times, and remained so until the Revolution of the early twentieth century.

But Morelos was not a single political entity in colonial times (perhaps this is the reason why it has not received attention as a unit for that period), and in fact it did not become a state until 1869. Instead, the colonial division of the region continued to that date with two major parts, the jurisdictions of Cuernavaca and Cuautla; in addition, the jurisdiction of Tlayacapan remained separate (see Figure 1, which shows the modern boundaries of the state).[2]

The origin of the two major political divisions of the area lies in conceptions of preconquest political jurisdictions set forth by Cortés and his enemies; the colonial political map of Morelos was the outcome of their struggles.[3] The preconquest political map, here as elsewhere south of the Chichimeca frontier, was a complex mosaic of groupings of occupied, named places organized for purposes of taxation and warfare into administrative hierarchies. After the conquest, rights to services and other tribute depended, for the Spanish encomenderos and for Cortés himself, on establishment of proof of these pre-Cortesian linkages; however distorted Spanish conceptions of these may have been or become, the apparent basis of judgment was thusly entirely conservative.

Cortés claimed that the people of the region had been subject to the five principal rulers of Cuernavaca, Tepoztlán, Oaxtepec, Yautepec, and Yecapixtla, themselves subject to Moctezuma. The 1529 grant making him Marqués del Valle de Oaxaca named these five towns, and hence by implication towns subject to them, as parts of his estate. He took possession of them in 1531, but lawsuits concerning rights to Cuernavaca and Oaxtepec continued for many years. The villages of what became the jurisdiction of Cuautla Amilpas were considered by Cortés to have been subject to Oaxtepec, but in a suit begun in the 1560s the towns were taken for the crown. The jurisdiction of Yecapixtla was returned to the Marquesado in 1583, and the fourteen pueblos of the Tlalnahuas in southeastern Morelos in 1594. These events produced the split colonial jurisdiction of Cuautla. The narrowness of the belt of land connecting the two large parts of the jurisdiction of Cuernavaca was the result of another controversy in which the crown claimed domain over Tlayacapan, Atlatlauhcan, Nopopualco, and Yecapixtla. Through such arguments, ostensibly over preconquest boundaries, came about the strange shapes of the two major parts of colonial Morelos.

The Indian arrangements reflected important physical realities. The five major Indian towns were all sited near the base of the escarpment, some (Cuernavaca, Oaxtepec) near important springs, others (Yautepec, Yecapixtla) near the confluences of streams, all at points where the juxtaposition of different geological formations meant the juxtaposition of different kinds of terrain and soils. At each site, except that of Cuernavaca, fairly extensive areas of flat, irrigable land are adjacent to rocky, hilly land. From these sites, the jurisdictions of the towns extended downstream and upslope, with timber, water, and probably originally deep cultivable soils near each other.[4]

The principal towns were at about the same latitude, all in the northern parts of the valleys. Most of the aboriginal population may have been concentrated near them, or along the five major rivers that flow south, in more or less parallel fashion, to the Amacuzac. Given the advantageous physical resources, the population could have been both dense and large;

one estimate places it at 750,000, considerably larger than the rapidly growing population of 1970 (616,000).[5] This size would have made the population of the region the largest such cluster between the Valley of Mexico and Oaxaca, as it is today; and the large labor pool, the physical resources, and location of the region astride once-important trade routes from Tenochtitlan to the Pacific Coast and Central America made it attractive to Cortés and a source of controversy for years.

The population, however, as throughout Mexico, experienced a rapid decline, indicated by the decline in the number of tributaries or taxpaying heads of household in Cuernavaca (Table 1). These figures raise numerous problems, but they remain overwhelmingly the most important kind of information we have about population changes in Morelos, apart from a count or estimate of 1743 and the incomplete census of the early 1790s, which yielded totals, respectively, of 46,780 and nearly 61,000, showing an

TABLE 1. NUMBER OF TRIBUTARIES IN CUERNAVACA[a]

Date	Number	Date	Number
1585	8,108	1715	3,374
1595	7,714½	1726	7,201½
1615	4,000	1732	6,975½
1629	3,134	1739	5,765
1635	2,500	1745	6,599
1638	5,438½	1759	6,872½[b]
1651	2,013	1764	5,837[c]
1671	4,767	1769	6,429½
1680	2,110½	1775	6,668
1686	2,388	1780	6,637[d]
1696	3,342	1785	8,104½
1701	2,625½	1791	7,575½
1707	2,789	1796	8,368
		1806	9,134½

[a] From AGN, Hospital de Jesús, legajos 28 (V49), exp. 12; 132, cuadernos 2 and 3; 159; 160; 168; 179; 186, exp. 9; 215, exp. 14; 237, exp. 10, 15; 238, exp. 4, 17; 260, exp. 10; 340, exp. 27, 28, 29; García Martínez, *Marquesado del Valle,* p. 165.

[b] AGN, Hospital de Jesús, legajo 340, exp. 28, contains a royal decree directing removal of widows and spinsters from the lists.

[c] If the infirm, widows, spinsters, and *negros* were added, the total would be 6,574.

[d] If adjusted as in note [c], the total is 7,294.

increase of about a third in half a century.[6] The population of Cuautla also declined markedly; between some date in the late sixteenth century and the early seventeenth century, almost two-thirds of its tributaries disappeared, as well as more than half of those of Ocuituco.[7]

The decline in population and the disappearance of some settlements enabled the formation of sugar haciendas to proceed, and they finally came to dominate the landscape of Morelos to an extent not found elsewhere in colonial Mexico. Probably some of them were partially formed by combining small, continuous pieces of land, many with Indian names, but title to these places was established primarily through grants—from the crown in Cuautla or from the Marqués in Cuernavaca—of land claimed to be vacant, unused, or abandoned, and to a lesser extent of land purchased from Indians; ultimately, crown or Marquesado grants were mandatory. As elsewhere, title was validated through the *Composición* of the 1640s, wherein surveys of the areas of the grants were undertaken. The granting of land in the Marquesado may have lagged somewhat behind that in Cuautla, with major numbers of grants made in the former in the early seventeenth century. For irrigation and power, grants of the right to withdraw water were also necessary, and licenses were required to construct *trapiches* and *ingenios* (animal-powered and water-powered mills, respectively). Through these standard procedures and instruments, the hacienda system of Morelos came into being.[8]

Haciendas have long been discussed in terms of their origins and development, Chevalier's work being the best-known attempt to describe those in Mexico.[9] His book and its conclusions are difficult to evaluate and interpret because the work is so broad in conception and presentation. Perhaps because he saw ownership of land in rural Mexico in the present century and the nineteenth as the source of power in a two-way struggle between the government and the hacendados, Chevalier was led to conclude about the eighteenth that "[Mexico City] was like a limit set to the countryside's encroachment and a purchase point for a government that ran the risk of seeing the rest of the vast country slip from its grasp." The eighteenth-century hacendados were like warlords "in a country governed by lawyers," and the tension between these two groups was the major dialectic in the colonial history of Mexico, finding partial resolution through independence.

No clear sense emerges of the aims of these warlords, yet their motivation and values are central to Chevalier's thesis. In his words, "the landed proprietor's peculiar mentality was not conducive to thinking in terms of efficient production. He acquired land, not to increase his earnings, but to eliminate rivals and hold sway over an entire region. His scorn for extra profits sometimes went to such lengths that he destroyed perfectly good equipment on land recently purchased."[10] The hacendados are presented to us as tyrannical egomaniacs without constructive purpose; lusting for land because land was power, they sought to make the boundaries of their hacienda domains coextensive with entire regions, whatever the cost. On the other hand, Chevalier writes approvingly of the efficient way in which the religious orders managed their haciendas, contrasting their methods sharply with the disorderly ways of the hacendados, which continued to this century.[11]

The documents that form the base for these assertions and from which different inferences may be drawn are of several kinds. There are hacienda accounts, lawsuits (perhaps greatest in bulk), titles to land and water, wills, notarial records, letters (though Chevalier did not use these materials to describe the operation of units). Rarest of all are aggregated documents such as censuses, lists of plantations, ranches, and towns, or written descriptions of the working of the economy; usually the overall picture must be constructed from information about a single hacienda or several. The nature of these data tends to limit speculation about certain interesting questions. For example, I have never seen a document that would enable one to infer with certainty that the colonial hacendados of Morelos thought of themselves as a class with economic and other interests in conflict, potential or real, with those of some other clearly defined class, and in fact they were, over the centuries, persons of very diverse social and economic backgrounds and activities, many of them members of several interest groups; nor is there evidence that all of them ever banded together to act in concert about anything.

We may nevertheless use the information such documents contain to develop another way of looking at the haciendas of Morelos: we may look at them as units in a system of interrelationships and interdependencies that stemmed from their highly specialized nature, with "system" used in a loose sense and primarily to emphasize the relationships of the units to each other, to the factors of production, and to the marketing of their products. Figure 2 shows the important components of the system, and may be read as a diagram of the "hacienda system" in the sense used here, although in fact it is a flow chart showing the circulation of services and products, by value, among the units of the system. The categories used are those identified in contemporaneous accounts, so that the representation may be close to the conceptions the people within the system had of its workings, excluding, regrettably, such vitally important matters as status and ties of kinship and friendship, not to speak of the roles of graft, payoffs, coercion, and other kinds of hidden influence in its operation.

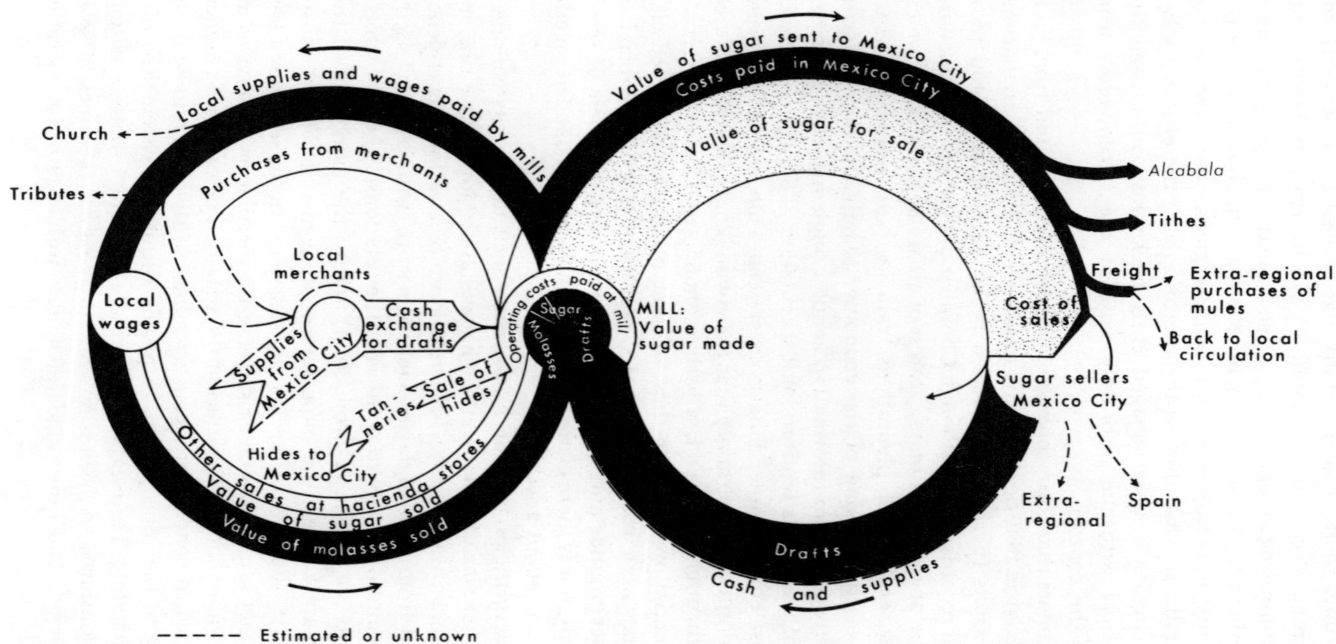

FIGURE 2. Flow Chart for a Late Colonial Sugar Hacienda of Morelos

The chart is also comprehensive: it will help us to explore the relationships of the haciendas to the towns of the region and to most of their inhabitants.

Our aim will be to examine the dimensions of this system. We need to know the total regional capacity to manufacture sugar and molasses, the costs of production, the numbers of laborers and other workers in relation to the total population of the region, and the connections with other parts of Mexico provided by trade, ownership, and the movement and consumption of sugar. The early 1790s are the principal period of investigation for a number of reasons: in one of these years, the first census of the region was taken, supplying information about the capacity of many of the mills; the period was one of approach to the apogee of the colonial industry; and there is abundant material for making comparisons, both inside and outside Mexico. The data used to estimate many of the flows are from three annual accounts (1792–1794) of the Cortés mill at Cuernavaca, wherein all the details of production, costs, and sales are to be found; extrapolation of these quantities to the other mills of Morelos will form the basis of our description of the industry.[12]

The flow chart emphasizes extraregional linkages on the right side, asserting the primacy of the flow to the principal market, Mexico City.[13] Probably much of the *panocha* produced by the small mills of the southwestern part of the state was sent to Taxco, some perhaps also to Toluca.[14] From the mills of the east, some sugar was sent to Puebla, but most of the sugar produced in Morelos, nearly all of it clayed, went to Mexico City, from whence arrived supplies not available through local production. Besides this circulation, there was also an intraregional movement, represented by the flows on the left side of the chart. The Indians, mestizos, and mulattoes who worked at the mills were paid in cash, ideally, and used their wages to buy articles at stores, both on and off the haciendas, and from itinerant peddlers; there were social expenses for them as well, many connected with the church; and it seems probable that much of their wages was used to buy *aguardiente,* the manufacture of which was made legal in 1796.[15]

Before examining the details of these flows, it may be useful to emphasize the importance of their existence. Clearly the haciendas were not autonomous, self-sufficient, and isolated; instead, we are dealing with a system of specialized producing units—sugar plantations, distilleries, tanneries, smithies, potteries, ranches, farms, villages offering lime, wood, and charcoal for sale—engaged in trade and exchange, all subject to mutual dependencies, competition of some degree in the marketplace, the vicissitudes of the weather, and other exogenous factors. These features were present from the beginning of the industry in the sixteenth century.

Sugar haciendas were business enterprises in a modern sense, run along more or less rational lines by more or less experienced and competent persons in the hope or expectation of a profit; they were not feudal or even semifeudal estates subject to the irrational whims of despotic owners. They existed in a context of widely inclusive and comprehensive sets of laws, edicts, rules, and regulations, with business and other personal relationships closely governed by contracts, customs, and routine. On the surface, at least, the accounts, records, and activities show modern purposes and spirit.

At the center of the diagram and, from our point of view, of the system, is the mill itself, of which there were thirty-seven in the late eighteenth century; only two or three more were to be founded, and they shortly thereafter. The units of the system as it was in 1910, that is, were virtually all already present by 1800, in some cases with the same boundaries. Apparently all units except one had land: Cocoyotla in the southwest was wholly dependent on the rental of Indian land, even for the site of the mill.[16] Thus we have two extremes of control over the land: on the one hand, haciendas with land sufficient for the purposes of their owners and requiring no rented land; on the other hand, a mill (not an hacienda; the distinction is made in the documents) with none at all, and between these extremes varying reliance on rented land. The demands of production could thus be met in different and even opposed ways, of which one pattern of control over land dominated, although, of course, in the Marquesado, land was held through perpetual leases, not owned in fee simple by its users.[17]

Estimate of Regional Productive Capacity

My estimate of regional productive capacity (see Table 2) is based primarily on what may be a summary of the Military Census of the early 1790s of Cuernavaca and on the manuscript Military Census of Cuautla of the same time.[18] The stated capacities of the mills ranged from 95 to 365 tons, and their population from apparently zero, at one that made only panocha, to nearly one thousand at Santa Clara Montefalco, where I have estimated a 400-ton capacity. The first ten mills in the table may have produced about 2,600 tons of sugar, or about half of the clayed sugar produced in the two jurisdictions.

Other evidence supports the individual and regional estimates. Humboldt wrote that in the jurisdiction of Cuautla Amilpas some plantations produced more than 20,000 to 30,000 *arrobas* or sugar annually (230–340 metric tons). He regarded these amounts as "very considerable" annual outputs, exceeded at the upper limit by perhaps only eight plantations

TABLE 2. PRODUCTION AND POPULATION OF THE SUGAR HACIENDAS OF MORELOS, LATE EIGHTEENTH CENTURY

Name	Capacity, Tons	Population	Name	Capacity, Tons	Population
1.[a] S. Clara	400[b]	998	21. Guadalupe	125[b]	278
2. Tenango	400[b]	660	22. Guadalupe[d]	125[b]	190
3. Temixco	365	624	23. Cuautla[e]	125[b]	182
4. Atlacomulco	265	230	24. Chiconcuac	125[b]	172
5. Cocoyoc	230	181	25. Buenavista[d]	125[b]	155
6. Treinta	200	415	26. Apanquezalco	115	70
7. S. Vicente[c]	200	223	27. S. Carlos	95	240
8. Puente	195	615	28. Xochimancas	95[b]	75
9. Miacatlán	195	562	29. Atotonilco	95[b]	65
10. Sayula	185	178	30. Michate	95	46
11. S. Gaspar	178	284	SUBTOTAL	5,438	9,705
12. Casasano[d]	175[b]	561	PRODUCERS OF PANOCHA[f]		
13. Cuahuixtla[d]	175[b]	512	31. Acamilpa	250	379
14. Tenextepango[d]	175[b]	462	32. Mazatepec	200	199
15. Hospital[d]	175[b]	419	33. Oacalco	175	174
16. Calderón[d]	175[b]	256	34. Cuauchichinola	50	182
17. S. Inés[d]	175[b]	220	35. Cocoyotla	50	130
18. Barreto	155	416	36. S. Cruz	50	130
19. Pantitlán	155	373	37. Actopan	50	—
20. Dolores	145	44	TOTAL	6,263	10,899

[a]Numbers correspond to those on map.
[b]Estimated
[c]And Matlapa
[d]In Cuautla
[e]May have made panocha
[f]All capacities estimated

on the island of Cuba, where the largest produced about 450 tons annually, only 50 more than I have assigned to the two largest mills in Cuernavaca.[19]

In addition, an anonymous pamphlet published in 1823 contains the information that the amount of (clayed?) sugar produced in Cuernavaca and Cuautla (and including a small amount from Tenancingo to the west) at about that date was 6,350 tons, nearly 1,000 tons more than the clayed sugar capacity I have estimated for 1792–94.[20] Using information about tithes paid, the same author estimated the average annual production of sugar in the Archbishopric of Mexico City (most of it from Morelos) for five-year periods. With two different values for the weight of a loaf, the pamphlet's figure of 10.58 kilograms and the recorded value of 10.0 from Atlacomulco, we get these estimates of total tonnages:

	@10.58 kgs.	@10.0 kgs.	Average
1785–1789	4,993	4,720	4,857
1790–1794	5,454	5,155	5,305
1795–1799	6,555	6,196	6,376
1800–1804	8,176	7,728	7,952

It can be argued that the use of tithes produces underestimates, some production being unreported to reduce the amount of tithe paid, and panocha may have been omitted from the pamphlet's calculations. The highest estimate for 1790–94 is nearly identical with the total of my estimates of clayed sugar capacity. Perhaps more important, the table shows that production could be expanded rapidly, increasing about 60 percent in fifteen years. We should, therefore, emphasize that the widths of the bands on the flow chart represent proportions and that they may be viewed as representative of the relative size of the flows in all of Morelos.

The production of 5,400 tons of clayed sugar probably required the cutting of about 2,700 hectares of cane, all of it irrigated; today there is much more land in irrigated cane and other crops in Morelos, showing that the colonial haciendas were far from the limits to production set by water and cultivable land.[21] Some of the cultivable land may have been in fallow, but there is little information on this point. Some land was rented to small cultivators who probably produced mainly grains, pulses, tomatoes and other vegetables for market. In the rainy season, residents of Indian villages cultivated small subsistence plots here and there, but the nonirrigated land was used primarily in the only way it could be used, as low-grade pasture, which dominated the landscape and land use outside the small, sharply contrasting irrigated fields near the rivers. The principal kinds of livestock were cattle, perhaps mostly oxen, and mules. Sheep were said not to reproduce in the region, and natural increase was inadequate to maintain the population of cattle, which, with mules, were brought from other parts of Mexico in the rainy season in customary and expected drives.[22]

The regional production of about 6,300 tons was not large by world standards. In 1791, the 792 mills of French Saint-Domingue produced about 80,000 tons of sugar; in 1780, the 1,081 estates of Jamaica produced about 45,000 tons, with production there increasing to 100,000 tons in 1805.[23] There were thus, in comparison with the trans-Atlantic sugar export industry, few mills in Morelos and production of a relatively small amount of sugar in colonial times, yet the largest mill was perhaps as large in capacity as any of its time and the average size of mills was larger than elsewhere, while the sugar haciendas controlled most of the best land and dominated the economy of the region, producing little for sale other than sugar and molasses.

Costs

The value of the sugar sent annually to Mexico City in the early 1790s was nearly one million pesos. This amount of value was small by the standards just mentioned, but within Mexico there may not have been other regions of similar size that produced an equal amount of value of crops or livestock; at the same time, this amount may have been only about 1 percent of the annual value of agricultural production in New Spain.

There were four sets of expenses of sales in the capital that were met from income of those sales: the *alcabala* (sales tax), tithes, freight, and the direct expenses incurred at the place of sale itself. Of the four items, the most expensive was the cost of freight, nearly 60,000 pesos; the other three were approximately equal at about 45,000 pesos, and the total of all four was about 200,000 pesos, or about 20 percent of the value of the sugar.

Freight.—It cost twenty reales per *carga* ("load") to ship sugar from the Cortés mill to Mexico City. This mill and Temixco, just south of Cuernavaca, were the mills nearest to the capital; the rest paid more according to the distance. To simplify calculations, I have used the rate for Atlacomulco: with an average weight per carga of 220.5 kilograms, 28,404 cargas were sent from the Morelos region to the capital at an average annual cost of 71,010 pesos.[24] In colonial times as now, freighting offered opportunities for small entrepreneurs. A small independent operator might own one or two strings of mules and carry the production of a mill on a regular basis; in this period Atlacomulco depended on three or four such carriers almost exclusively and did not use its own mules for this purpose. In fact, the arrangement was found to be sufficiently advantageous that the officials of the Marquesado were willing to lend money to one or more carriers so that they could purchase more mules, thus underlining the extreme specialization of the hacienda—they had no wish to enter the freighting business. Probably every shipment was accompanied by a letter from the administrator of the mill, in cases where the owner was a resident of the capital, and an answer was expected on the return trip, when the mules returned mostly unladen, the flow being markedly one-way in volume. The informative letters of the administrators, of which unfortunately only a very small percentage appear to have survived, discuss weather, labor, livestock, other crops, needed supplies (often sent on the return trip), the state of other plantations, and other matters of local interest.

Alcabala. — In the early 1790s, sales tax was paid at the rate of twelve reales per carga. Its total value was 42,600 pesos.

Tithes. — For the sugar industry, the "tithe" to the church was set at 4 percent of the number of loaves made; I have used instead the figure of 4 percent of the value of all sugar made, and the average price of sugar (1.38 reales per kilogram) sold in Mexico City from 1792 to 1794, to obtain an estimate of 43,200.

Sales. — Sugar from the Cortés mill was sold by a salaried employee of the Marquesado in a store owned by it, for which rent was charged to the mill. The store had "minor costs" in addition to salary and rent, and for the years 1792–1794 the average total of all its costs was 857 pesos. Nearly equal to this amount was the value of annual, regular gifts of twenty cargas of sugar to government and city officials and members of the clergy, valued at 760 pesos on average, and yielding a total average annual cost of sales of 1,618 pesos. The total of costs of sales for all the sugar sent from Morelos was thus about 45,012 pesos.

Probably most mill owners employed a different system for selling their sugar, entering into contractual agreement with a specialized seller in Mexico City, who might handle the production of several mills. There were ten such dealers in Mexico City in 1753, their places of business grouped in and near the Calle de Meleros ("Street of Honey Dealers") at the end of the aqueduct along which sugar was brought by canoe from Xochimilco. Apparently none of the ten sellers were engaged directly in sugar production in 1753, but others assumed the management of plantations at other times, as in the case of owners' bankruptcy.[25]

The relationship of seller to producer was crucial, especially in cases where the owner lived on the plantation. The seller was a general business agent who might arrange and administer all matters connected with the plantation: legal aspects, accounts, supplies, the purchase of slaves and livestock, loans and their repayment. Some sellers acted as trustees of the estates of their deceased clients, arranging for the support of their minor children and the continued operation of the plantation. Their honesty and reliability were of utmost importance to the owners of the haciendas, and the latter were not free agents when they owed advances or other debts to the sellers.

At the warehouse the sugar, which had already been weighed at the hacienda for the records of the owner or manager, was reweighed and classified by quality. Minor loss was expected and allowed on the way and more was customary in the warehouse; some of the sugar may have had to be reworked. It was sold retail for household use and in large lots to tradesmen: in 1753, for example, there were 45 *cacahuaterías* in Mexico City, 26 confectioners, 8 makers of ices, 9 *pastelerías,* and an unknown number of bakers, all of whom used or sold sugar produced in Morelos.[26]

The Flow of Cash

The costs of getting the sugar to Mexico City and selling it there represented potential diversions from the local circulation of cash. For example, additions to the stock of mules were necessarily losses, since they were not raised in Morelos; in addition, the muleteers spent money in the city and on the way. Some of the money may have found its way to Spain, as profits or in return for supplies (olive oil, wine, iron). Nevertheless, a prime responsibility of the sugar seller was to attend to the cash needs of the mill, where the workers had to be paid in cash on Saturdays.[27] Probably there was not a significant flow of cash itself from Mexico City to the plantations, as the diagram may suggest; rather, the cash was obtained from local merchants through *libranzas,* drafts or orders to pay, made out by the administrators of the mills and honored finally by the sellers in Mexico City. What we have is a large regional flow of cash from local merchants to mills, thence to workers, and at least in part back to the merchants. Money exchanged for goods and supplies purchased locally also entered this circulation, but cash wages (about 520,000 pesos per year) provided the bulk of the flow.

Some of the cash paid as wages went to the church, but this probably constituted only a small part of the total flow; in the late eighteenth century many of the cofradías of the region, for example, were described as poor or impoverished. Events of the life cycle (baptism, confirmation, marriage, and burial), as well as fiestas, took some small amount of total wages. Tributes were also relatively low: they amounted in Cuernavaca in the 1790s to about 12,500 pesos or not quite 2 percent of the total of 660,000 pesos paid for local supplies and labor.[28]

Some of the wages came back to the hacienda through sales of molasses which were then used to make aguardiente, much of it for local consumption. Some was also received through small sales of sugar at the mill, and through sales at the hacienda stores (*tiendas de raya*). The latter might be run on the account of the administrator or a relative, or sometimes the facilities were rented to a merchant who ran it on his own account. The accounts show that workers' debts, either to stores for goods or to the plantations for wage advances, were relatively small at this time, as earlier, and could not have been important in holding labor on the plantation. Some cash was received through the sale of hides of cattle to local tanneries, but the most important local source of cash was sale of molasses, a source that later was depended upon to finance entirely the cash payments to labor.

Labor

Costs and organization. —The total of labor costs at Atlacomulco, both direct and indirect, approximates the total of all costs of production, because major items (wood and other local supplies) have been converted to wages in order to estimate the number of full-time workers engaged directly and indirectly, on and off the plantation, in producing sugar (see Table 3). Three major categories of work were directly compensated in the late eighteenth century: supervisory and skilled trades, labor in the mill, and field work. The supervisors and skilled tradesmen have been included in a single category because much of the work of, for example, the skilled *maestro de azúcar* (sugarmaster) must have consisted of a mixture of supervision and labor. More than half (73 percent) of all direct costs of labor were accounted for by field work, the remainder by the other two categories.

The costs of field labor have been allocated as follows: the categories *gañanes* and *tareas,* concerned with field preparation, took one-third of all costs of field labor and its supervision; with the next two largest items, weeding and irrigation, they accounted for about 57 percent of all field costs. Less expensive were cane-cutters, muleteers, day laborers hired for planting, and *yuntas,* teams of oxen and drivers hired annually at Atlacomulco, yielding only 2.2 full-time workers. Of the group called *muchachos,* paid at half the rate received by adult males, I have assigned half to the fields and half to the mill (converting their numbers to full-time adult equivalents by dividing by two). Two slaves worked in the fields,

TABLE 3. LABOR AND LABOR COSTS

	Per 100 Tons of Sugar		Total, Morelos		
	Workers	Cost, Pesos	Percent of Labor Cost	Workers	Cost, Pesos
1. Fieldwork	76.70	6,070	58	4,832	382,410
2. Millwork	12.00	1,642	16	756	103,446
3. Supervision and trades	3.30	543	5	208	34,209
4. Support of 3	1.10	13	—	69	819
5. Local supplies	18.30	1,307	12	1,153	82,341
6. Transport	0.75	909	9	47	57,267
Totals	112.15	10,484	100	7,065	660,492

and I have calculated their costs by assuming their work was worth two reales per day, the maintenance wage for a family of four that was paid to field labor. There were four canefield guards, six oxherds, and one *jatero,* or ranchhand, all paid by the month. All of the foregoing account for 87 percent of the costs of field labor, the rest being supervisory or indirect costs.

The wage of the *aperador,* paid monthly, has been assigned to field work, although he may have had charge of equipment of both field and mill. Half of the salary of the administrator has been assigned to field work, as have all of the salaries of the *mayordomo* and field supervisor, and half the value of indirect administrative costs (the salaries of the barber-surgeon, schoolmaster, cook, tortilla maker, and the costs of rations and *gastas de casa,* or provisioning the main house of the plantation), as well as half the costs of the two skilled tradesmen who came to the mill when needed, the master carpenter and smith. The total costs of fieldwork were some 17,000 pesos annually at Atlacomulco, and the total number of full-time equivalent fieldworkers was about 200, two-thirds of all workers.

In the mills were the most highly paid workers, the *trapicheros,* in charge of milling the cane. Muchachos worked there at half pay as in the fields; there were two molasses guards, paid monthly, and the equivalent of 2.5 slaves working full time in the mill. Away from mill and hacienda were Indian and other workers who produced pottery, lime, and lumber for the mills; if the average value of their products is converted to wages at the standard rate of two reales per day, we find that, for all the mills, 1,150 full-time equivalent workers were required to satisfy the demand for these supplies.

Administrative costs include the salary of the purger, who probably kept many of the accounts, but I have assigned his salary to the mill, as well as the salary of the sugarmaster, clearly a part of milling costs, and part of the wages paid to itinerant skilled tradesmen. These assignments emphasize the differences between mill and field work; in a different context, one might wish to emphasize the relative importance of, say, supervisory work; and were this done, it would be readily apparent that the 37 mills of Morelos did not offer large numbers of opportunities for well-trained or educated persons, perhaps no more than 150 suitable positions. Nor could such persons expect to live lavishly, with large numbers of servants at their command, although the assignments made to form Table 3 understate the number of the latter. The number of men stated to have been engaged in transport (47) is clearly far too low, and may well have been ten times as large, but information is lacking about the actual numbers so engaged.

About 12 percent of the population of the region worked on or for the sugar plantations, but because of the intermittent or part-time nature of the work of many laborers, this figure is certainly an underestimate of the total number of individuals employed in a year in the industry. Table 2 shows that the population of the mills was 10,899 in the early 1790s (about 18 percent of the total population), but not all the workers lived at the mills, nor were all of their residents workers. If we assume that each worker supported three other persons, we find that some 28,000 persons, nearly half the total population, depended wholly or in part for their incomes on the sugar industry. At the moment, this simple measure is sufficient to describe the extent to which life in Morelos was bound up with work on haciendas and the production of sugar; the figure seems fairly high, consistent with the presence of a specialized regional economy, but it may not be as high as the corresponding figures for, say, some Caribbean sugar colonies at the same time. The map supports the view that the influence of the industry was pervasive and gave special character to the region; the intermixed pattern of distribution of mills and other populated places suggests that most of the inhabitants of the latter were near whatever economic opportunities the mills offered, except in the east and northwest, or at higher altitudes. In addition, Figure 2 further helps to define the regional nature of the economy by suggesting little leakage of wages from local circulation, but this impression of small loss may not be a correct one. Similarly, with wages, alcabala, tithes, and costs of freight and sales accounting for about 90 percent of the value of the sugar, little profit may have been left from sugar production (in contrast to trade) for export from New Spain, especially in view of the fact that transport costs are underestimated and the diagram says nothing about the costs of servicing the debts of the industry.

Haciendas and Pueblos

The population of Morelos was markedly clustered by the late eighteenth century, as it had been during the seventeenth and perhaps the sixteenth. Whether or not one chooses to call this an urban population depends on one's definition of the elastic word "urban." It may be useful to recall that a population cluster could not be recognized as a pueblo unless it had a consecrated church. This a great many settlements in the region had, and the pueblos shared many other features with larger towns and cities, including plazas, a pattern of streets that conformed more or less to the ideal grid pattern, common institutions of government, and corporational rights to land and water. Social and governmental functions were distributed over subregions in hierarchical fashion and hence were not present in all pueblos. Those with monastery churches may have had ecclesiastical courts, and some villages were the sites of residence of deputies (*tenientes*) of the alcaldes mayores, who themselves lived in Cuernavaca, Cuautla, or Mexico City. Given the fact that even small *pueblos de indios* shared complex organizational patterns with large cities, and contained, besides, specialized artisans, it is possible to argue that the tone of life was predominantly urban in spite of the fact that many of the males might be engaged much of the time in agricultural labor; at the least, we are not dealing with a less highly organized rural society of dispersed households, but with groups of people organized in urban ways.

It was possible for pueblos of Indians to apply for title to empty land in the same way as did Spaniards or other private persons, over whom they were by law to be preferred. Many pueblos in the Marquesado did apply for titles, many others apparently did not, and some retained both title and possession until at least the end of the colonial period. Probably most, if not nearly all, had one or more lawsuits in colonial times with neighboring haciendas, pueblos, or their own *cabeceras* or *sujetos,* over either the proper location of boundaries, or title to or possession and use of a piece of land; these lawsuits seem to have increased in frequency and intensity in Morelos in the last four or five decades of the colony, as the population increased.

Another most important relationship between towns and haciendas was formed by the opportunity the latter offered to laborers, and we have seen, in a general way, how the towns assisted in provisioning the haciendas. We cannot attempt here to gauge the coerciveness of this relationship between laborers and hacienda managers, because there is so little information on the point. Nor can we yet speak with certainty of the numbers of persons hired on a weekly or daily basis in addition to the numbers of workers already resident at the hacienda, or of the pattern of such work; that is, was it intermittent for individuals, so that most of the men who wanted to work for cash at an hacienda did so only for short periods at some or many times in their lives? This may have been the case, given the way in which day laborers were hired: each hacienda paid a group of recruiters called *capitanes* and a small commission for each *peón* (day laborer, not permanent worker) whom they brought to work there. Some of the capitanes may well have been Indians themselves, with sufficiently strong ties to one or more pueblos to be able to get laborers as they were needed.

Morelos was unique among major colonial sugar-producing areas in that its haciendas developed within a setting of previously established indigenous towns with their own claims to land and necessary water, a very different case from the Greater Antilles, where the aboriginal population had not survived and the land was more or less empty. Of course, the Indian population of Morelos was much reduced by about 1600, approximately the time when the haciendas of the region began to develop, and some towns had been abandoned, but many survived the period of depopulation and have remained to the present. By 1600 the needs of the population of the towns for land and water had diminished greatly along with their numbers, and the haciendas developed within the empty spaces that separated the towns, finally dominating land ownership in the state.

NOTES

1. For a great deal of background relevant to this chapter see my *Sugar Hacienda of the Marqueses del Valle.* The most complete bibliography of the state of Morelos is Domingo Díez, *Bibliografía del estado de Morelos.* For a later period there are John Womack, *Zapata and the Mexican Revolution,* and Felipe Ruiz de Velasco, *Historia y evoluciones del cultivo de la caña y de la industria azucarera en México.*

2. See Domingo Díez, *Bosquejo histórico geográfico de Morelos,* and his *Estado de Morelos y sus derechos territoriales*; Jesús Romero Flores, *Historia de los Estados de la República Mexicana.*

3. What follows is primarily a summary of relevant sections of Peter Gerhard, *A Guide to the Historical Geography of New Spain*; see also his "Continuity and Change in Morelos, Mexico." There is additional information in G. Micheal Riley, *Fernando Cortés and the Marquesado in Morelos, 1522–1547,* and on Tetela del Volcán in Carlos Martínez Marín, *Tetela del Volcán: su historia y su convento.*

4. Physical changes are made evident by references in many documents to swampy or marshy land that no longer has that appearance; there have also been changes due to the sugar industry (deforestation and the implied resultant changes in the regime of runoff).

5. Riley, *Fernando Cortés and the Marquesado,* p. 5.

6. Gerhard, "Continuity and Change," p. 349, estimates the population in the 1790s at 77,000.

7. The problems have been reviewed by Woodrow Borah and Sherburne F. Cook, *The Aboriginal Population of Central Mexico on the Eve of the Spanish Conquest,* and in Cook and Borah, *Essays in Population History.* Information on changes in number of tributaries and population is in Bernardo García Martínez, *El Marquesado del Valle,* pp. 163–68, and in Barrett, *Sugar Hacienda,* pp. 9–11. The data of 1743 are in José Antonio de Villaseñor y Sánchez, *Theatro Americano,* I:167–78; see Peter Gerhard, *México en 1742,* for a summary of these figures. The manuscript census of Cuautla is in the Archivo General de la Nación (AGN), Padrones 8; the populations of all inhabited places in Cuernavaca are in Manuel Mazari, "Un antiguo padrón itinerario del Estado de Morelos." The information about Cuautla is from AGN, Civil 1782, exp. 8.

8. The grants are discussed in García Martínez, *Marquesado,* pp. 95–101.

9. François Chevalier, *Land and Society in Colonial Mexico.*

10. Ibid., pp. 310–11. In this passage Chevalier shows incomprehension of the commercial imperative not to flood a small market. The hacendados' accountants,

at any rate, show interest in profits; no matter how large the size of the account, the record was kept down to the smallest necessary fraction of a *grano* ("grain"), an accounting unit that did not exist as a coin and was of very small value.

11. His opinion may have been formed in the course of editing the rather systematized, idealized *Instrucciones a los hermanos jesuitas administradores de haciendas.* A review of the actual operation of a set of Jesuit haciendas is found in Richard Blood, "A Historical Geography of the Economic Activities of the Jesuit Colegio Máximo de San Pedro y San Pablo in Colonial Mexico, 1572-1767"; he summarizes the many reasons for their success, not all of which stemmed from diligence and skill. Some enormous advantages, for example in tax rates, derived from the fact of being an ecclesiastical corporation. Anyone wishing to study the inept or unlucky management of a sugar hacienda by a religious corporation despite all its built-in advantages might look into the history of the hacienda Hospital in Cuautla. For a brief and not very useful description of a mill operated by the Jesuits in Cuernavaca, see Jean-Pierre Berthe, "Xochimancas: les travaux et les jours dans une *hacienda* sucrière de Nouvelle-Espagne au xviie siècle," pp. 88-117.

12. The accounts are in AGN, Hospital de Jesús, legajos 176; 177, exp. 6 and 8; and 185, exp. 4, 5, 6, and 8.

13. Morelos was destined, because of high land transport costs, to remain primarily a producer for internal consumption. See Juan Vicente de Guemes Pacheco de Padilla (Conde de Revillagigedo), ". . . informa en el expediente sobre averiguar si hay decadencia en el comercio . . .," in Luis Chávez Orozco, ed., *El comercio exterior y su influjo en la economia de la Nueva España (1793),* pp. 44-45.

14. Panocha is very hard dark brown sugar in small loaves, incorporating both molasses and sugar. Clayed sugar was freed of much of its molasses by slow washing with water under the flow of gravity; it was too expensive for most of the population.

15. Francisco Sedano, *Noticias de México . . . desde el año de 1756.* Before 1796, aguardiente of clandestine manufacture was called *chinguirito* or *aguardiente de la tierra* (AGN, Hospital de Jesús, legajo 381, exp. 4).

The actual amount of cash put into circulation as wages will be difficult to determine, for it includes not only silver coins but also tokens (*tlacos,* from Nahuatl "half") issued by hacienda owners to make up for the lack of copper or other coins of small denominations necessary in daily life; the abuses to which this led were reviewed by the Viceroy Conde de Revillagigedo in a letter to the king dated March 27, 1790, published in John Villasana Haggard, *Handbook for Translators of Spanish Historical Documents,* pp. 88-94; for pictures and descriptions of these tokens, see O. P. Eklund and Sydney P. Noe, *Hacienda Tokens of Mexico.* It is difficult to evaluate, but probably easy to underestimate, the importance and effects of this monetary system of coins and tokens; it could easily be, and was, used to concentrate ownership of silver coins within a few hands. A royal order of February 12, 1792, was intended to reduce its disadvantages to the poor by introducing coins of copper in the value of a quarter-real, a value still too high in light of the fact that the silver half-real, the coin of smallest value, was sufficient to supply food and drink for a person of the "ínfima clase" for a day; elsewhere, however, the Viceroy noted of tokens that "even they are better than cacao beans," which supplied the smallest change. Guemes Pacheco de Padilla, ". . . informa," pp. 53-54.

16. AGN, Tierras 2202.

17. It is not clear that this made any difference in the development of the industry.

18. Mazari, "Un antiguo padrón," for Cuernavaca; the Military Census of Cuautla is the one in AGN, Padrones 8. The summary gives the capacity of most of the mills of Cuernavaca, as well as the population of most of them, while the Padrón of Cuautla gives only the population. Since the two sets of figures from Cuernavaca show no fixed relationship between the capacity of a mill and its population, it is not possible to derive the capacity of the mills of Cuautla from the population reported for them. In addition, the capacities of the seven mills that made only panocha were not given. Of thirty-seven mills, the population of one and the capacities of twenty-one are not known. In addition, the capacities of some may not have been printed correctly. San Antonio de Atlacomulco, whose records form the basis of many other estimates I have made, was assigned an average capacity of 205 (metric) tons when, in fact, its annual average production during the three years 1792-94 was 265 tons.

The largest mill for which we have both population and capacity figures was Temixco, with a capacity of 365 tons and a population of 624; the two mills described as having perhaps the largest capacity ("de la mejor consideración") were Santa Clara Montefalco and Santa Ana Tenango, and I have assigned to each of them the capacity of 400 tons. The twelfth through fifteenth mills in the table had large populations and all had, at one time or other, the reputation of being large; I have assigned to each of them a capacity of 175 tons, as well as to the two old mills Calderón and Santa Inés. Five were assigned a capacity of 125 tons each, because none ever had the reputation of being large and their populations were similar in size, except Guadalupe's (Cuernavaca) and Buenavista's, but because the latter was at the edge of Cuautla and may have drawn workers from the town I have assigned it to this group.

Two of the seven mills that made only panocha were assigned capacities at the ratio of about one ton of capacity to one inhabitant, and the largest, Acamilpa, was limited to 250 tons. The estimated capacities of some of the panocha mills may be too high. In 1755, Cocoyotla had only 10.5 hectares in cane (AGN, Tierras 2202); in 1786, Cuauchichinola had 8.25 hectares in cane (AGN, Tierras 1948, exp. 4); on the other hand, Oacalco in 1783 had about 73 hectares in cane (AGN, Bienes Nacionales 100, exp. 62?). Guadalupe, which may have made both clayed sugar and panocha in the early 1790s, produced about 60 tons of sugar in all of 1786 and about 9,000 panochas, apparently between June and December (AGN, Tierras 1973).

19. Alexander von Humboldt, *Political Essay on the Kingdom of New Spain,* III:8.

20. A copy of this printed pamphlet is in AGN, Hospital de Jesús, legajo 219, exp. 2.

21. The yields are based on the results of the harvest of 1795 at Atlacomulco when 2 tons per hectare were obtained; Barrett, *Sugar Hacienda,* p. 130, Table

14. In 1966, there were 28,272 irrigated hectares in the state.

22. More information about the livestock industry may be found in my "The Meat Supply of Colonial Cuernavaca."

23. Noel Deerr, *The History of Sugar,* pp. 176, 198, 239-40. These may not be metric tons.

24. From 1792 to 1808, 92.5 percent of the production of Atlacomulco was sent to Mexico City. If each mule made only 50 trips annually, carrying about 100 kilograms of sugar on each trip, some 1,500 may have been engaged in the traffic. About twice as many cargas (60,000) of various goods were carried annually between Veracruz and Mexico City at this time; Guemes Pacheco de Padilla, ". . . informa," p. 25. These figures differ from those of 1805, when about 50,000 mules and 7,500 muleteers were engaged in transport on the routes between Mexico City, Acapulco, and Veracruz. The numbers were said often to have been insufficient; Eduardo Arcila Farías, *El Siglo Ilustrado en América,* pp. 84-85.

25. Eduardo Báez Macías, "Planos y census de la ciudad de México, 1753," p. 1104; a similar census of 1689, but of peninsular Spaniards only, lists a few (J. Ignacio Rubio Mañé, "Gente de España en la ciudad de México, año de 1689").

26. Eduardo Báez Macías, "Planos y census," pp. 1101-49. The Viceroy Conde de Revillagigedo suggested that a cacahuatería was a general store similar to (or identical with?) a *tienda mestiza* or *pulquería,* dealing in beverages, foodstuffs, clothing, and raw materials, and commonly a depository for stolen articles; their owners issued tokens or tlacos of small value and through them reaped large profits on the goods they sold, at great expense to the poor (Haggard, *Handbook,* pp. 88-89).

27. A lawsuit of the 1690s, apparently a time of falling sugar prices, underlines the importance of the seller in obtaining cash for the producer of sugar; the sellers in effect granted short-term loans to cover the expenses of cultivation and manufacture (AGN, Bienes Nacionales 1077, exp. 1).

28. On the state of the cofradías see AGN Diezmos 1. The tribute payments I assume to have been the same in the 1790s as in 1770, when a tributary paid 1 peso in cash, plus 4.5 reales, apparently in lieu of half a fanega of maize, if he wished (AGN, Hospital de Jesús, legajo 298, exp. 81). Table 1 shows the number of tributaries in 1791 and 1796; the average of these two figures was used to compute the annual tribute.

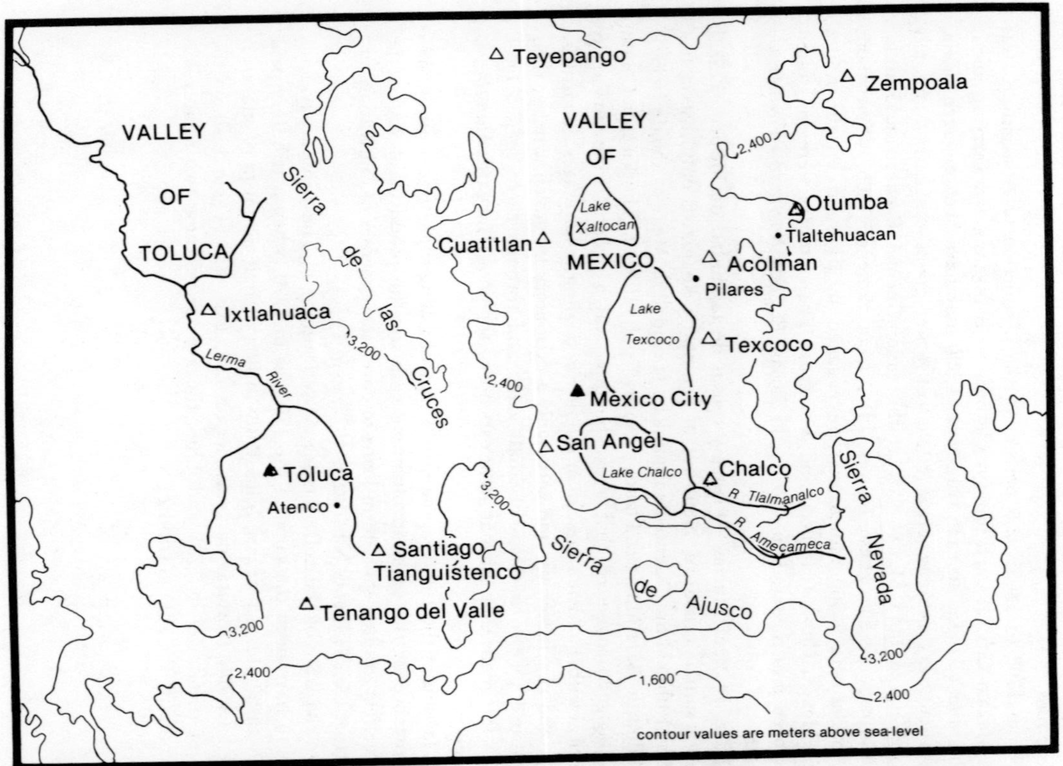

Some Provincial Centers of the Valleys of Mexico and Toluca in the Late Colonial Period, with Other Points of Reference

7. Provincial Spaniards, Indian Towns, and Haciendas: Interrelated Sectors of Agrarian Society in the Valleys of Mexico and Toluca, 1750–1810

John M. Tutino

The highland valleys surrounding Mexico City lie in the heart of Indian Mexico, and there the conquerors chose to establish their capital—situated so as best to dominate Indian society.[1] More than two centuries of Spanish rule brought complex changes to the central valleys (not the least of which was the creation of the great landed estate, the hacienda), but to the end of the colonial years the great majority of the inhabitants were agriculturalists who identified themselves as Indians, culturally distinct from the dominant Spanish minority.

The valleys of Mexico and Toluca lie adjacent at elevations above 2,200 meters, separated by a high mountain wall. During the rainy summer months, both basins annually receive around 800 millimeters of precipitation. This is generally sufficient for agriculture, but because the waters are drawn by the higher mountains at the southern end of the valleys, aridity becomes a problem to the north. In addition, in the valley of Toluca, which is above 2,800 meters elevation, the frosts of early autumn limit the summer growing season.[2]

In such an environment, agriculture was hazardous. Only in the limited areas favored with irrigation (allowed by the Lerma River at Toluca and numerous small streams and springs in the Valley of Mexico) were environmental insecurities partially overcome. Reports from estate administrators at numerous locations during the late eighteenth century reveal no year wholly spared from natural hazards to agriculture. During the worst years the rains never came, irrigation waters eventually disappeared, and crops withered. More regularly, rains began late, or ended early, or ceased for several weeks during the growing season, or came in such force that they destroyed maturing plants. Moreover, problems which delayed crop fruition increased susceptibility to autumn hail and frosts. In sum, there was rarely a good agricultural year in the central highland valleys—only more or less bad ones.

This precarious countryside environment was primarily the home of Indian agriculturalists. At the end of the colonial period Indians still constituted over 80 percent of the census population of the Valley of Mexico outside Mexico City itself, where the proportions were nearly reversed.[3] Over the course of the eighteenth century, Indian numbers in the Valleys of Mexico and Toluca had tripled from the low figures of the century previous. The great majority of those designated as Indians remained residents of the corporate, landholding Indian communities which were by far the most numerous settlements in the valleys. On the eve of national independence, these communities held 90 percent of a much enlarged Indian tributary population as measured by census.[4] They continued to control significant areas of agricultural lands, but while their populations expanded, their landholdings could not, leading inevitably to the proliferation of tensions; land disputes initiated in the Valleys of Mexico and Toluca during the eighteenth century increased at a rate even faster than the population.[5] The growth of population and of agrarian tensions underlay much of provincial life in the highland valleys during the last colonial years.

Spanish Townsmen

The various sections of the valleys were tied to the viceregal capital, Mexico City, through a number of substantial towns. Centers such as Texcoco, Toluca, and Otumba served as the seats of provincial administration and justice in addition to being the hubs of regional commerce. If in the course of time the commercial center had shifted from the ordained legal center of a certain area, these two critical town functions would still seek each other out. At both Chalco and Tetepango, the royal administrator (*subdelegado*) chose to live in the principal commercial town rather than the official seat of justice.

The major provincial towns were characterized by the presence of local oligarchies of Spanish townsmen. These included merchants and agriculturalists along with colonial administrators, tax collectors, and clergymen. Most often, influential townsmen held multiple roles simultaneously. As a group they produced foodstuffs which they sold in the local towns as well as in Mexico City; they traded between the outlying areas and the capital; and they served the institutional needs of state and church. In so doing they mediated between the dominant urban metropolis and the general population of the hinterland.

To consider an example, a figure most typical of this mingling of functions, and indeed typical in everything but his exceptional success, was one don Juan Garrido, who was tithe collector, merchant, and agriculturalist at Texcoco during the 1780s and 1790s. He used his official access to tithe income to fund speculative private commerce and to operate haciendas which he leased. He also engaged in the short-term financing of other estates in the Texcoco region. During this time Garrido characterized himself as a merchant of Texcoco. In the first decades of the next century he moved his base of operations to Mexico City. There he could hope to enter the fringes of the colony's most powerful and prestigious oligarchy. His place at Texcoco, meanwhile, was assumed by don Francisco Menéndez Valdés, a newly appointed subdelegado who was also a merchant and estate agriculturalist.

Provincial clerics and royal officials were transferred from one town to another regularly and frequently. Thus they stood to gain little from the purchase of local agricultural properties. Instead, they preferred to lease lands which could be worked for profit during an appointment, then abandoned. The Condes de Santiago, the owners of numerous estates in the Valley of Toluca, expected that the arrival of each new royal justice or parish priest would quickly bring a request for the lease of lands. Most often they granted the request, in the hope that the arrangement would orient the administration of justice and religion to the favor of the landed clan.

Official position was no absolute requirement, however, and many provincial families attained local prominence without involvement in the hierarchies of state or church. At Santiago Tianguistenco, in the southern Valley of Toluca, a clan with the name of Garduño operated a store, owned one modest hacienda, and leased several properties from larger estates in the area. The combination of commercial and agricultural pursuits, with capital newly acquired in commerce moving toward the land, typified the provincial townsmen, much as it did the far wealthier and more powerful elite families of Mexico City. This continuing fusion supported the durability of many provincial families. At Otumba, a small number of extended families—the Espinosas, the Lazcanos, the Sandovals—engaged in local commerce, owned some small agricultural properties, and leased yet others, while they perpetuated their local hegemony through judicious intermarriage.

How wealthy were these prominent provincials? Their agricultural estates were generally valued at under 40,000 pesos, with most falling between 10,000 and 20,000 pesos. Entire patrimonies ranged in value from 20,000 to 70,000 pesos. This was wealth of a much lower order than that of the Mexico City elite, whose haciendas were rarely valued below 50,000 pesos; their patrimonies usually exceeded 100,000 pesos and often reached into the millions. A few provincials did amass estates valued about 100,000 pesos and yet chose to remain in the towns.[6] Although they might have followed the common path to the metropolis, they apparently decided to remain where they were more socially prominent and economically secure.

The groups of prominent townsmen of the Valleys of Mexico and Toluca were miniature replicas of the Mexico City elite. Merchants were landowners, too, or in the process of becoming landowners. These people also became provincial officials and clerics. But while emulative of the Mexico City oligarchy, the townsmen were also quite subordinate to it. That is why most provincials fortunate enough to acquire substantial wealth moved to the metropolis. The most striking example of such a career is that of don Manuel Rodríguez de Pedroso. Early in the eighteenth century Rodríguez de Pedroso came as an immigrant to join his uncle, member of a provincial landed clan based at Zempoala, and, as so often, he married a cousin of his there. Trading successfully and pioneering in the hacienda production of pulque, he made a fortune in less than thirty years. On the basis of that, he moved his family to Mexico City, entailed his landholdings, obtained the title of Conde de San Bartolomé de Jala, and entrenched his descendants as members of the oligarchy of the viceregal capital.

Most provincial townsmen, however, never saw wealth such as that amassed by the Conde de Jala. Rather they continued to live and work in the provinces, tied to the Mexico City elite by varying relations of dependence. Institutionally, every provincial justice, tax collector, and priest reported to a superior in the capital. Such bureaucratic links were often complemented by personal relations of dependence. In 1802, for example, don Juan Felipe Mugarrieta, subdelegado at Santiago Tianguistenco, referred to don Domingo de Lardizaval, a prominent Mexico City bureaucrat, as "my protector."[7] Most provincial traders were also subordinate to urban interests. At San Angel, in the southwestern corner of the Valley of Mexico, a don Miguel Duarte managed a store as agent for don Isidro de Icaza, a merchant of Mexico City, as well as for the Condes de Santiago, landowners also based in the capital. Nearby, a doña Juana María Cumano traded under the auspices of don José Sánchez Espinosa, another Mexico City merchant and landowner.

Since provincial wealth flowed toward the metropolis, the merchant-landowner fusion, a basic process of self-reinforcement for the urban elite, was much less effective for the townsmen. The most successful traders among them departed, while only a portion of the earnings of the rest remained with them in the towns. Provincial commerce, too, reinforced the urban elite, with only the leavings bolstering the town oligarchies.

Yet despite their subordination to the greatest of colonial elites, the townsmen were themselves elite in the provincial context. Above all, they were intermediaries, living with a tryingly ambivalent situation. In striving to improve his position, a townsman's only recourse was often his link to an urban oligarch. He thus sought to use his dependence to escape from it. The attempt was inherently contradictory, and few found success. Rather, most Spanish townsmen remained within local clans which for generations lived in the provinces, serving urban interests as intermediaries between the most powerful colonials and the less fortunate mass of provincial population.

Small-Scale Spanish Agriculture

At the fringe of the culturally Spanish sector of society in the central valleys were a number of agriculturalists living and working on small estates, usually called "ranchos." Some owned their holdings, either alone or in conjunction with one or more kinsmen. More often, ranchos were leased, either from haciendas or from landholding Indian communities. The rancheros occupied small niches interspersed at wide intervals among the predominant haciendas and the Indian communities. Ethnically, the rancheros were similarly marginal. Approximately half of them claimed Spanish status; the rest were of mixed ancestry, usually Spanish and Indian. Culturally, their language and their economic life placed them squarely within the Spanish sector, though at its very edge and in close contact with much that was Indian.

Although operating on a small scale, the rancheros were commercial farmers. In the Otumba region, they each annually harvested from 150 to 300 fanegas of maize, well in excess of familiar subsistence needs and enough to earn a modest profit. Harvests, and agricultural earnings along with them, were at the mercy of the fluctuating climate, but the seasonal nature of farming allowed the rancheros to engage in supplemental activities. Most prominent among them was the maintenance and operation of mule trains; the ranchero was often also the *arriero* (muleteer). Hauling especially grains and pulque, the rancheros enhanced their own incomes while providing the region's agricultural economy with an elastic transportation capability.

Through this combination of economic activities the ranchero-arrieros of the central valleys lived at a level below that of the Spanish townsmen, but well above the poverty of minimum subsistence. They were tied into Spanish society through the extension of the relations of economic dependence which characteristically integrated that sector. Rancheros funded their agriculture through credit extended by the townsmen, who were in turn funded by urban entrepreneurs. As arrieros, they sold their services primarily to the haciendas, thus entering into the service of the colony's landed elite. Further, rancheros and members of their families were an important source of skilled and supervisory workers for the great estates. Though at the margin of Spanish society, in multiple and complex ways the ranchero-arrieros were tied to its principal social and economic institutions.

Indian Corporations

Corporate Indian communities were the most numerous and populous components of provincial society in the central highland valleys. Although Indian towns and villages were diversified and complex social units, including artisans, laborers, and agriculturalists, the aspects that interest us here are the communities' control of agricultural resources and the way they were allocated. The amount of land available to a given community and the nature of its allocation played a large role in structuring Indian society.

Land surveys and census materials do not provide a complete aggregate picture of Indian land retention in the central valleys, but a large number of local surveys and many more scattered references indicate that Indian communities generally controlled significant arable holdings. Though there were frequent complaints of shortage of pastures, subsistence lands were in various degrees available to community members across most of the Valleys of Mexico and Toluca.[8]

Widespread retention of agricultural lands by Indian communities did not guarantee their allocation as subsistence plots to the inhabitants. In the more important towns where large numbers of Spaniards lived, there was considerable land retention, more in fact than elsewhere; but much was turned over to properties producing income for the support of local government. What led to this? The answer must be sought in the role of the governors of Indian communities.

The Indian communities of late colonial Mexico were sharply differentiated between the few who controlled the allocation of resources and the majority dependent on their decisions. I would thus challenge Charles Gibson's conclusion that "the effect of Spanish colonialism on the class stratification of Indian society was to equalize and compress, to move all classes toward a single level and condition."[9] Though Gibson correctly emphasizes the exclusion of Indians from the highest socioeconomic and political levels of colonial society, the fact that they were thus restricted did not forge an equality within the village community.

A report prepared by the bishop of Michoacán at the end of the eighteenth century emphasized the sharp stratification of the Indian communities.[10] As given to crude stereotypes in his opinions on Indians as he was with other Mexican ethnic groups, he saw the eight or ten notables in each village (who were often the only Spanish speakers, he thought) as an idle, parasitic group, conniving to keep the rest in "ignorance" and "barbarism." Yet the bishop's analysis contains some truth. The offices of corporate government were repeatedly monopolized by a small, self-perpetuating group of the powerful and noble, as they had been from preconquest times. Although these leaders were legally Indian (they had to be in order to qualify for office), their frequent knowledge of Spanish and use of Spanish patronyms (whereas most Indians still used a Christian name or a religious term as a surname) indicate a cultural position combining the Spanish with the Indian. Surely many were of mixed ancestry. Linked by kinship within their communities, they also cemented ties with leaders of neighboring villages, another pattern with preconquest origins. These interlocking groups of nobles were long the most powerful political force within Indian society, and they had considerable control over the distribution of corporate agricultural resources.

Such elites can be studied only in local context; here, attention will be given to the leaders of Acolman and Otumba.[11] The two towns lie not far apart in the northeastern quadrant of the Valley of Mexico, but they occupied very different environments. Nonetheless, they developed essentially similar social configurations, which may represent a basic common denominator of Indian social organization in the central valleys.

To the end of the colonial years, Acolman was an exceptionally Indian community. Few Spaniards lived among the numerous Indian agriculturalists. The local elite consisted of a small group of prosperous Indian families. Their struggles for control of life at Acolman have left sufficient documentation to reconstruct an outline of the lifestyle and values of an Indian elite.

The leading families of Acolman, who rotated in community office, had come to hold an exceptionally large amount of land within the community, whether through allocation, purchase, or inheritance. Each elite clan held numerous plots, their households averaging from four to ten apiece. They annually harvested from 40 to 80 fanegas of maize (well in excess of the familial subsistence minimum of 10 fanegas). They also raised small quantities of wheat and beans, made pulque, and kept modest herds of livestock. For example, the widow doña María Francisca inherited from her late spouse eight agricultural plots, 43 animals, and over 80 fanegas of maize in storage. The value of her nonlanded property was estimated at over 500 pesos.[12] In late colonial Mexico such an estate was not wealth, but it was not poverty either.

The Indian elite at Acolman treated their holdings as private property, as Indians had been doing throughout central Mexico from the sixteenth century. Contracts for both sales and rentals are noted in the surviving records. When those practices were denounced before the Spanish courts as illegal, the situation was lamented, but allowed to continue as long as transactions were confined to members of the corporate community which legally held the properties.[13]

The apparent adoption of Spanish institutions was often rather an adaptation of a preconquest one or a merging of the two. The Acolman elite's holdings were a great deal like those which before the conquest Valley nobles maintained within the framework of communities. It was the same in other aspects of culture. The nobles of Acolman were like Indians all over central Mexico in devoting fields, flowers, and candles to saints' images kept at home; and among the images, by the eighteenth century, there was always Our Lady of Guadalupe.[14]

Something of the lifestyle of a young member of the Acolman elite emerges from a unique document which was composed in response to the Spanish courts' demand for an accounting of four years' expenditures on the part of a certain Agustín Basilio. In question was the patrimony amassed by don Baltasar Lucio, late governor at Acolman. It included seven plots of agricultural land, numerous stands of maguey, and livestock. Agustín Basilio was one of two heirs to this Indian fortune; the

TABLE 1. FOUR YEARS' LIVING EXPENSES OF AGUSTIN BASILIO, c. 1804–1808

	Total[a]	Mean per Year
Food: at 1½ reales per day	274/6	68/6
Pulque: at 1½ reales per day	274/6	68/6
Clothing: 5 pairs of pants, 3 shirts, 2 belts, and 2 hats	39/2	9/7
Worship: pilgrimages and candles	32/1	8/0
Taxes: parochial obventions, 3.2; royal tributes, 5.2; exemption from corvee labor on drainage works at Huehuetoca, 4 pesos; obventions and pensions of pueblo, 10.1	22/5	5/6
Marriage	54/0	
Housing: reconstruction of his room	5/4	
Total	703/0	161/1

Source: AGN, Tierras, vol. 2526, exp. 5, fol. 5–6, 1809.
[a] Amounts in pesos and reales (1 peso equals 8 reales).

kind of life it gave him, as specified in the document, is summarized in Table 1. He clearly did not struggle at the margins of subsistence. His expenditures on food, clothing, and taxes comprised less than half of the total. The cost of his food suggests that he consumed more than did many entire Indian families, for it alone was valued at more than the average income of a poor Indian family (less than 50 pesos a year). The other half of his expenses—for worship, marriage, and especially for pulque—went beyond biological necessities, though of course even the poorest families spent something in these areas. Most of the extra expense went to his drinking allowance. Agustín Basilio was a member of the Indian elite, well connected within his community and able to live considerably above the subsistence level. But he had no avenue of advance, little to gain beyond what he already had. The product of his fight for community power and resource control, as his expenditures indicate, was an increased consumption of the intoxicant pulque.

Though only a short distance to the northeast of Acolman, Otumba was a quite different Indian community. It lay in a far more arid environment where irrigation was impossible, agriculture uncertain, and pulque production the principal economic activity. Otumba had also acquired a substantial population of non-Indians. While corporately still an Indian community, it was simultaneously a major Spanish provincial town. In some important ways Otumba's Indian elite was quite similar to that at Acolman. Both were quite close to being mestizo, and both combined political office with direct control of a large proportion of community resources. But at Otumba, the greater penetration of Spaniards brought a far more divisive factionalism to Indian politics and led to the allocation of community lands to favored members of the local Spanish community.

From at least 1750 until early in the 1790s, two powerful clans, with the names Cortés and Ramírez, shared control of the principal Indian offices at Otumba. Repeatedly they were accused of electoral fraud, theft of community funds, and extreme favoritism in land allocation. The charges were usually well founded, and the offenders were often reprimanded by the Spanish authorities. Nothing, however, was done to diminish their community power. Finally, late in the 1780s, at a time when community life was severely disrupted by a combination of famine and epidemic, a rival group headed by the López and Vázquez families challenged the long entrenched rulers of Otumba. Early in the 1790s, following several years of dispute, the newcomers triumphed. They soon entrenched themselves in office, stripped the old leadership of their many properties, and redistributed them to forge a new support coalition.

Such political machinations were possible partly because of the minority participation in community government which had been the norm in central Mexico since preconquest times. Voting for office was limited to the quasi-noble stratum of Indians—those called principales in the sixteenth, seventeenth, and early eighteenth centuries, and sometimes *vocales* in the latter colonial period. At Otumba in 1775, 45 men selected the rulers of a community of 595 Indian families and 2,260 persons.[15] The limited franchise facilitated the perpetuation of larger properties within the group of the powerful; those enfranchised gave their support to the leadership, which in turn favored them over the ordinary members of the community.

The unequal distribution of lands among Indians characterized both Acolman and Otumba. In the latter, large amounts of the best agricultural land were also allotted to non-Indians. This coincided with the involvement of influential Spaniards in Indian politics at Otumba. In a disputed election in 1775, the alcalde mayor openly supported one faction of Indian leaders, while the parish priest (following a classic pattern) backed the opposition.[16] Closely tied to Spanish provincials, the "Indian" leaders at Otumba were quite Hispanized by the late colonial years; they even conducted community business in Spanish. If the leaders at Acolman were mestizo, leaning toward the Indian, those at Otumba were mestizo with a Spanish emphasis.

Over the centuries of colonial rule, the Indian leadership at Otumba, as in other towns, had cooperated in the permanent alienation of community properties. During the late eighteenth century, however, leasehold alienations were a factor of more immediate consequence than sales, giving Spanish townsmen and rancheros the use of agricultural lands legally belonging to Indian society. The income thus generated supported local government and especially local religion. An account of the expenditures of four communities in the Otumba jurisdiction in 1794 reveals that the bulk of the proceeds from leases eventually went to the provincial clergy as payment for services, especially during major local fiestas. The leasing of Indian lands thus benefited the Spanish sector of provincial society in more ways than one.

What was left to the majority of Indian agriculturalists? If despite unequal distribution and alienations they had adequate subsistence lands, little damage was done to the traditional Indian lifestyle, based in good part on family subsistence agriculture. By the late eighteenth century, however, the growth of the Indian population combined with the political allocation of limited community lands left the majority of Indians, though living in landed communities, unable to meet their subsistence needs with the plots they had. Quantitative information detailing the distribution of community lands in the four towns of the Otumba jurisdiction, combined with a contemporaneous census of the Indian population there, revealed the following trend.[17] In the larger towns where Spanish residence and influence were greatest, so too was Indian corporate strength and the retention of community lands—but many of them were turned to the benefit of non-Indians, leaving the Indian majority in need. In smaller or more remote towns, though direct Spanish influence was much less, community lands were also scarce, so that Indians found themselves short of subsistence lands there too. The majority of Indians at Otumba held lands, but rarely enough to provide full subsistence support.

The situation at Otumba paralleled that prevailing at Chalco and is consistent with the less complete information relating to other areas of the Valleys of Mexico and Toluca. The following scheme generally characterized Indian access to land within the communities there during the late colonial years: a sizable minority held nothing more than their house lots; half the community members or a little more had additional agricultural plots, but insufficient to produce subsistence for the average family; another minority enjoyed generally adequate subsistence holdings; and a tiny elite had extensive lands. Thus the great majority of Indians could not rely on community resources to provide their basic needs. They had to seek other means of support; in most cases this meant working for wages and purchasing foodstuffs. The Spaniards' haciendas were the principal employers of labor and producers of foodstuffs in the central valleys, so that in the late colonial years the haciendas became as essential to the subsistence of provincial Indian life as they long had been to the urban Spanish sector.

Haciendas

Interspersed among the Indian communities of the central valleys, haciendas were numerous, large, and economically diversified; most were owned and operated by members of the Mexico City elite. Their earnings derived from sales of foodstuffs and other rural products to those Mexicans who could pay for them. The market of the hacienda was above all the urban mass of Mexico City, but also the provincial town dwellers and much of the Indian population. Though the estates of the Valleys of Mexico and Toluca were principally oriented to supporting an urban oligarchy by filling the needs of the urban populace, they were major institutions of rural society, since they were closely intertwined with a provincial population which absorbed an important, though secondary, portion of hacienda produce and provided the workers needed to maintain hacienda operations.

The estates of the central valleys usually combined the production of staple grains, livestock, and the intoxicant pulque. These activities required two types of labor, one more skilled and permanent, the other more shifting. Care of animals and the fermentation of pulque from the sap of the maguey cactus called for the constant attention of a small number of persons. Some additional workers were hired seasonally to supplement them in the transplanting of maguey and the slaughtering, branding, and shearing of livestock. The cultivation of staple grains—the maize, wheat, and barley which predominated on most central haciendas—also required a small nucleus of permanent workers. The seasonal demands of grain agriculture, however, were much more extreme, creating a demand for large numbers of workers who could be employed on a short-term basis.

The dual need for a few permanent and numerous temporary workers was met in the haciendas of this time by three categories of laborers beneath the foreman level. An upper group, consistently called *sirvientes* (literally "servants") or *sirvientes meseros* (*mesero* is "paid by the month") consisted mostly of Spaniards or culturally Spanish mestizos. They worked regularly, received monthly salaries, and occupied the more administrative and skilled positions at the estates. Indian workers residing permanently on the haciendas were called *gañanes* ("field hands"). Despite their permanent residence, they were employed less regularly than were the sirvientes and were paid at a daily rate for performing more laborious tasks. Finally, Indians living in corporate communities and working at the haciendas on a day-to-day basis were called *peones* (literally "people on foot") or *peones alquilados* (*aquilado* is "hired temporarily" or "rented"). Their employment was most irregular, and they also were paid at a daily rate. The peones were by far the largest group of estate workers, providing an elastic source of labor which could be employed when needed and ignored for the rest of the year.

The more Spanish sirvientes formed the elite of hacienda labor. They monopolized most tasks in the care of livestock, as well as those demanding agricultural skills. On a modest rancho there might be as few as three or four sirvientes; on a large hacienda they would number several score. Their position within the Spanish sector is confirmed by their inclusion in the militia census of 1792, which excluded all Indians. Those living on the haciendas of two sample jurisdictions (Otumba and Tetepango) were half Spaniards and half ethnically mixed.[18] All had Spanish surnames and communicated in Spanish—a requisite of permanent hacienda employment.

Among hacienda workers only the sirvientes were offered permanent full-time work. They earned a monthly salary, usually of about four pesos. In addition, they received a weekly ration of maize that covered the basic needs of their families and was guaranteed no matter what the state of the harvest or the prevailing price. In times of scarcity, the sirvientes saw the monetary value of their recompense increase along with maize prices, at the time when most provincials braced against dearth.

Fully guaranteed subsistence while serving the estate, the sirvientes were thus solidly within the pyramid of personal dependence which began at the pinnacle of the urban elite, passed through the estate administrators, and encompassed these most favored workers. As the name "sirviente" so clearly implies, to enjoy such security the worker had to serve faithfully the interests of the estate. This was to be insured through close supervision. As one member of the landed elite instructed her estate administrator, "lesser dependents require that their superiors constantly watch them and verify their activities; if this is neglected even the good turn bad."[19] The essence of social dependence was the exchange of service for security.

Few late colonial provincials chose to remain long in this role. Estate records document the often brief tenure of sirvientes on the haciendas of the Valleys of Mexico and Toluca.[20] Rather than forming a closed group long dependent on the haciendas, the more Spanish workers were a part of the broader stratum of rancheros and arrieros. Individual families would often have some members laboring for themselves on ranchos, others working for the haciendas. And many a youth labored for the estates before trying his hand at independent farming.

To the families living on the provincial fringe of the culturally Spanish sector of colonial society, two roles were thus commonly available. Life as a sirviente on a great estate offered dependent security; the operation of a small rancho, often combined with transport work, allowed a more independent life, though subject to the unpredictability of climate, markets, and rural credit. Independence seems to have been the preferred position when it was a possibility. Hacienda service was seen as a way-station toward that goal. Youths often supplemented their parents' earnings before making an attempt at independent farming.

The permanent workers of the second category, the gañanes or Indian workers living with their families on haciendas, were the laborers least important to estates of the central valleys during the last colonial years. On modest properties located near Indian communities which provided sufficient workers, gañanes were often not present at all.[21] They were more common on larger estates, especially on those in less densely populated areas, where they usually numbered some twenty-five families per hacienda. Their terms of employment were quite unfavorable. Though estate residents like the sirvientes, the gañanes were not guaranteed regular employment, nor were they given weekly maize rations. Rather they were allowed to purchase maize from the estate with their wages. The latter, as calculated on a daily basis, were generally about

25 percent lower than those paid to laborers who were Indian community residents and came to the haciendas only for short-term stints.[22]

In return for residence on the estates, gañanes did receive guaranteed access to maize and to credit. The latter, in the form of either wage advances or distribution of goods through hacienda stores, has often been seen as a form of quasi-bondage. This view, applied to both Spanish sirvientes and Indian gañanes, deserves discussion, for it has dominated much of the literature on estate labor relations in Mexico.

Debts—essentially stemming from payment by an estate for services not yet rendered—could not alone be coercive. Bondage could not derive merely from the existence of a continuing relation of debtor and creditor, but could only be institutionalized by the creditor's ability and willingness to force the debtor to clear his account through either labor or cash payment. Thus the prevalence of any system of oppressive "debt peonage," so called, is not proved by the widespread existence of debts owed by workers to estates; for that, evidence of the systematic use of coercion to force the honoring of those debts would be necessary.

During the last half century of colonial rule, no such systematic coercion prevailed in the central valleys. Rather, workers commonly received goods and money from estates on the promise of future labor, but never fully performed the work or paid off the debt either. The estate had little recourse but to carry the debt perpetually, or to write it off as an inevitable labor expense. Wage advances were used to lure workers to the estates when they were scarce or otherwise especially needed. Such advances rarely hampered the mobility of the workers. More and more evidence points to the generalization that during the last colonial years wage advances to workers signified above all else their bargaining power in the labor market.[23]

This is well illustrated in the experience of the Condes de Santiago, a landed clan based in Mexico City and holding numerous haciendas in the southern Valley of Toluca. When control of these estates changed hands within the family in the first years of the nineteenth century, the two parties fell to bickering over the disposition of about 500 pesos of debts owed by the haciendas' sirvientes and gañanes. Neither faction of the elite clan wished to retain the obligations. They shared the belief that any attempt to collect would bring in little money and only cause the exodus of most of the resident families. The greatest of landed families of late colonial Mexico thus acted on the assumption that in the central valleys debts were an unrecoverable expense incurred by estate owners in order to obtain workers.

The largest number of residents of the Valleys of Mexico and Toluca working at the haciendas were Indians living in corporate communities.

They labored seasonally to meet the estates' fluctuating labor demands. As population growth caused the expansion of that portion of the Indian population which was unable to meet its own subsistence needs, seasonal hacienda labor increasingly provided the necessary supplemental income. But while the work thus obtained was both seasonal and supplemental, it was not casual. It was organized by community labor bosses, called *capitanes,* who assembled work gangs (*cuadrillas*), bargained for their services with estate administrators, and supervised the work. The system shielded the mass of Indians from direct dealings with the haciendas. It simultaneously gave another avenue of local wealth and power to the community elites, the cultural mestizos described earlier. These leaders thus were heavily involved in both the allocation of corporate lands and the procurement of hacienda labor. The two essential supports of Indian life lay within their grasp.

Mediated by the community elites and generally responsive to the haciendas' fluctuating labor demands, the provision of workers to late colonial estates cemented a symbiosis between the two principal institutions of provincial life. An analysis of the labor accounts of two estates reveals that work opportunities meshed well with the needs of the residents of Indian communities. The minority of Indians who were left entirely landless by the intersection of population growth and community politics could labor for the haciendas on a regular basis. That meant laboring over 140 days each year to earn, at the standard wage of 2 reales daily (1 peso equaled 8 reales), at least 35 pesos. Nearly a third of that income then had to be spent on the purchase of the 10 fanegas of maize which constituted the minimal base of a family diet. The larger number of Indians who held lands ranging from highly insufficient to all but enough for full familial support could also find work at the haciendas to suit their needs. They might labor from less than 20 days to nearly 140 and earn anywhere from a few pesos in supplemental income to half of their family's support. It was this large and varied group of Indians—practicing subsistence agriculture above all else, but impelled by late colonial circumstances to labor for wages—that provided the pool of workers essential to haciendas characterized by fluctuating labor needs.

The institutional symbiosis between haciendas and Indian communities should not be mistaken for equality. The estates had large amounts of a scarce resource—land—which was becoming ever scarcer relative to rising population. And the benefits of estate agriculture were channeled primarily to support a small urban elite. The Indian people within the corporate communities, on the other hand, were becoming ever more plentiful in late colonial Mexico, pressing ever harder against limited community resources. The benefit this increasing group received from the symbiosis between the hacienda and the Indian community was continued subsistence.

The relationship could be extremely delicate. Though arising at the intersection of estate labor demands and Indian subsistence needs, its local configurations derived from the many bargains struck between numerous hacienda administrators and even more numerous community elite groups. A failure in bargaining jeopardized the labor relation. Many communities in the central valleys gained access to estate pastures and woodlands in exchange for the regular provision of labor. In several instances in which they were denied that accustomed privilege, the flow of workers to the estate was stopped.

More often, the relation collapsed because of the effects of natural disasters. Every time epidemic disease crippled a large portion of Indian society, haciendas found workers exceedingly scarce. Conversely, when drought or frost, or their combination, caused scarcities of maize and brought famine near, Indian agriculturalists found subsistence difficult to maintain. Their subsistence crops failed, and, though usually to a lesser extent, so did those of the haciendas. An Indian's hirability diminished just when he needed work most. As conditions worsened, Indian life was severely disrupted by workers traveling ever longer distances in search of employment. In the late eighteenth century, when population pressed ever harder against the land, such subsistence crises struck the central valleys on the average of once per decade.[24]

The last colonial century brought notable changes to provincial life in the Valleys of Mexico and Toluca. During the seventeenth century, when Indian population was at its postconquest nadir, Spaniards based in Mexico City had institutionalized their control of extensive lands, not then needed by Indian society, to create the hacienda as a specific estate form. When in the eighteenth century the Indian population tripled, spurring a new demand for lands, they were not available. Instead, ever-increasing numbers of Indians became progressively less able to rely on subsistence agriculture and more dependent upon commercial relations between estate and laborer. The change brought growing profits to the Mexico City oligarchy which continued to control the haciendas. It insured a comfortable life to the provincial Spaniards who served that elite. The change was also turned to advantage by the Indian leaders who had so strong a role in the allocation of community lands and the channeling of labor supplies. But for the majority of the provincial population, Indians living at the edge of subsistence and depending upon local leaders for both land and labor opportunities, there was change without benefit. They remained living dangerously close to the level of minimum subsistence, while shifting away from the relative autonomy of

ORDER NUMBER

PO NYAATP08

BOOK NUMBER

9783561

BAY NUMBER

7195-6

AUTHOR	Altman, I (ed)
TITLE	Provinces of Early Mexico: Variants of Spanish American Regional Evolution (UCLA Latin

DESCRIPTION

Volume 36. This is an ex-library book and may have the usual library/ used-book markings inside.This book has hardback covers. Book contains pen & pencil markings. In poor condition, suitable as a reading copy. No dust jacket.

subsistence agriculture toward greater economic dependence as wage workers in the Spanish economy. The trend brought increasing dependence upon their community elites and upon the precarious hacienda-community symbiosis. Each time nature caused it to break down, the suffering that resulted could only reinforce the need for its quick re-establishment and continued maintenance. Only thus could landowners prosper and Indians subsist.

NOTES

1. This chapter forms part of a larger investigation into the Mexico City elite, its members' haciendas, and their relations with the Indian communities of the valleys surrounding the viceregal capital during the late colonial and early national years. The core of this work is contained in my doctoral dissertation, "Creole Mexico: Spanish Elites, Haciendas, and Indian Towns, 1750-1810." A preliminary study, focusing on one region within the Valley of Mexico, has appeared as "Hacienda Social Relations in Mexico: The Chalco Region in the Era of Independence"; it contains a more detailed portrait of the city-dwelling owners than is called for in the present context.

The underlying research involves the compilation of biographical and other information found primarily in the surviving records of several landed families. Some basic collections are the Papeles de los Condes de Regla (hereafter cited PCR) preserved in the Library of Washington State University, Pullman, Washington; the Papeles de los Condes de Santiago Calimaya (hereafter CSC) in the Biblioteca Nacional, Mexico City; records of the hacienda operations of don José Sánchez Espinosa, in the Latin American Collection Library of the University of Texas at Austin, catalogued under his name (hereafter JSE); and an invaluable set of account books for two properties held by the Gudiel Roldán family, in the Archivo General de la Nación, Mexico City (AGN), Vínculos 53, 54, 55.

Family papers are supplemented with the resources of the AGN. Most important to this inquiry were the sections Tierras and Indios, which for the Valleys of Mexico and Toluca have been catalogued in Mario Colín, ed., *Indice de documentos relativos a los pueblos del Estado de México: Ramo de Tierras del Archivo General de la Nación* and *Ramo de Indios del Archivo General de la Nación.* The analysis here also depends heavily upon important antecedent studies, especially Charles Gibson, *The Aztecs under Spanish Rule,* and Enrique Florescano, *Precios del maíz y crisis agrícolas en México, 1708-1810.* A large number of informative related studies have been compiled in Florescano, ed., *Haciendas, latifundios, y plantaciones en América Latina.*

2. Claude Bataillon, *La ciudad y el campo en el México central,* pp. 15-43.

3. Gibson, *Aztecs,* table 11, p. 146; AGN Historia 523, f. 145, 1793.

4. Gibson, *Aztecs,* table 18, p. 254.

5. Calculated from Colín, *Ramo de Tierras.*

6. Values are derived from estate auctions advertised in the *Gazeta de México,* 1784-1821.

7. PCR, vol. 124, f. 3, 13 Jan. 1802.

8. For Chalco, see AGN Tierras 1518, exp. 1, ff. 22-32; for Texcoco, AGN Indios 80, ff. 7-27; for Acolman, AGN Tierras 1702, exp. 1, ff. 1-51; for Otumba, Luis Chávez Orozco, ed., *Documentos para la historia económica de México,* vol. V; for the northern Valley of Mexico, PCR uncatalogued materials, "Posesión de San Javier, 1777"; for the southern Valley of Mexico, CSC, "Ayuntamientos, Alcaldes, y Ciudadanos . . . 21 June 1826"; for Malinalco, AGN Indios 80, ff. 154-89.

9. Gibson, *Aztecs,* p. 153.

10. Alexander von Humboldt, *Ensayo político sobre el reino de la Nueva España,* p. 71.

11. The sources for this inquiry were all documents in AGN Tierras and Indios pertaining to Otumba and Acolman between 1750 and 1820; they can be located through Colín, *Ramo de Tierras* and *Ramo de Indios.*

12. AGN Tierras 2525, exp. 1, ff. 1-26, 1817.

13. AGN Tierras 1615, exp. 1, 1793; Tierras 2315, exp. 1, ff. 8, 19, 1781.

14. AGN Tierras 2514, exp. 3, 2nd part, f. 4, 1748.

15. Gibson, *Aztecs,* pp. 176-177; AGN Indios 65, ff. 17-19, 1775; AGN Bienes Nacionales 403, Padrón de Otumba, 1792.

16. AGN Indios 65, exp. 16, ff. 17-19, 1775.

17. Chávez Orozco, *Documentos,* V; AGN Bienes Nacionales 403, Padrón de Otumba, 1792.

18. AGN Padrones 12, ff. 154-174; 18, ff. 9-17.

19. PCR, vol. 124, f. 51, 23 June 1802.

20. On this point, my materials are corroborated by James D. Riley, "Santa Lucía: Desarrollo y administración de una hacienda jesuita," pp. 265-66.

21. See, for example, Delfina López Sarrelangue, "La hacienda de San José de Coapa," in Florescano, *Haciendas, latifundios, y plantaciones,* pp. 239-40.

22. For corroboration of this view of gañanes, see Riley, "Santa Lucía," p. 267.

23. See also Gibson, *Aztecs,* pp. 253-56; François Chevalier, ed., *Instrucciones a los hermanos jesuitas administradores de haciendas,* pp. 128-29; Riley, "Santa Lucía," pp. 265-66; Richard W. Blood, "A Historical Geography of the Economic Activities of the Jesuit Colegio Máximo de San Pedro y San Pablo in Colonial Mexico, 1572-1767," pp. 182-85.

24. Florescano, *Precios del maíz,* pp. 180-95.

Part III: The North

The North is so vast, especially as we conceive of it here, including everything beyond the old Aztec and Tarascan domains, and so varied, that selectivity imposes itself. We present here three studies concerning different types of regions: (1) one of the great silver mining districts of the kind that gave impetus to northward expansion and a viable money economy to the rest of Mexico—Zacatecas; (2) one of the reasonably fertile and well-located areas of the nearer North where lively agrarian-commercial activity came into being over time—Querétaro; and (3) one of several huge, far distant, nearly empty fringe areas where a small number of settlers attempted to raise livestock in the face of many obstacles, from lack of water to Indian raids—Nuevo León-Coahuila.

If the North has great variety, it also has its sameness. All the major settlements studied here are new foundations, in this respect typical of the entire macroregion. The settlers of the area relate directly to aspects of a physical environment—silver deposits or agricultural conditions—rather than primarily to a landscape of permanent Indian structures, as in the Center and South. The Hispanic element is much more straightforwardly dominant than elsewhere in the country. But along with the Spanish settlers there always come Indians from the Center, enough of them to establish their own long-lasting community life: in barrios around Zacatecas, inside the town of Querétaro, in formally organized corporations even as far north as Nuevo León. Note in the chapter on Zacatecas how many mining terms are Nahuatl. In fact, there are more such words than Bakewell has occasion to mention, and for very basic things related to the industry: *malacate,* "windlass, hoist," from *malacatl,* "spindle, something revolving on itself"; *tepetate* "slag," from *tepetlatl* "hard rock"; *tenate,* "hide bag for carrying ore," possibly from the root *tematl-,* "sling"; and even this does not exhaust the loans. In all three of our Northern areas we find another constant, an especially close contact with and reliance on Mexico City. One might say this is true everywhere; nevertheless, it is far more pronounced here than in the South. The North's flatness and ease of transportation, its lack of populous hinterlands, and of course the silver wealth of parts of it, all favored this result. Zacatecas looked to Mexico City for finance and supply; both the nearer Querétaro and the more distant Nuevo León looked there for markets and social-economic alliances.

After reading this section, one would do well to consult also the work of David Brading, who has contributed greatly to both the mining and the agrarian history of the region.[1] His studies of the mining industry of Guanajuato, a district which eclipsed Zacatecas in silver production in the eighteenth century, and of the related agricultural areas of the western Bajío, are all in all quite consonant with those here, by Bakewell and Super, which concentrate on the immediately preceding period. The general techniques and organization of both mining and agriculture stayed much the same. The turnover of personnel at the upper levels, and more especially in mining, remained high, and the laborers of both mines and rural estates were mobile as before. The tie to Mexico City was basically as strong as ever, and of the same kind. There are also some differences, not contradictions or distinctions of kind, but expectable changes as trends become cumulative. The scale of mining operations and the extent of joint investment, growing in the seventeenth century, grew yet more in the eighteenth. The tendency of merchant-financiers to take a more and more active part in the industry is also a cumulative trend. Growth in scale and extent, as the industry reached an all-time peak of production in the late colonial period, created the desire for, and partial, precarious, temporary attainment of, financial independence from Mexico City. The mine workers of the North were somewhat Hispanized in the sixteenth century, more so in the seventeenth, and in the eighteenth their descendants were no longer Indians at all, but mestizos, mulattoes, and Spaniards who had so completely forgotten the line of evolution as to have conceived the notion that Indians were not good mine workers. Among hacienda workers this development had not gone as far, and the *indio vago* or mobile non-pueblo Indian was still important. The maturation and relative consolidation of estates in the western Bajío occurred along lines familiar from Querétaro and elsewhere, but at a different time, and naturally so, since the factor there was more the late rise of nearby Guanajuato as a market than any changes in Mexico City.

It is not as though the areas unmentioned in this section of the book loomed as large in the Mexican social and economic fabric as they do on the map. Humboldt, when he discussed the North, liked to tell how (even in his late time, the early nineteenth century) a given Northern jurisdiction's extension equaled that of some huge European country and its population was less than one of the smallest. Emptiness has its significance, of course. For Mexico of the colonial period, the far North was largely irrelevant, tending to be a (minor) financial-administrative burden and a late, sporadic strategic worry, if also a place of potential growth in some far distant future.

One major area not included here may fall rather outside the patterns triangulated by our chapters: Guadalajara in the near northwest. We do know that Hispanic agrarian development roughly comparable to and coeval with Querétaro's took shape in the area, directed on the one hand towards relatively close Zacatecas and on the other towards Mexico City.[2] But Guadalajara had many special characteristics. The area contained significant enclaves of settled peoples, so that encomiendas were more than negligible. As a Spanish municipality with elements of a fixed Indian hinterland, the city bore some resemblance to those of the Center and South. Moreover, Guadalajara was set up as the capital of the North, the seat of a bishop and an Audiencia whose jurisdictions included vast stretches of more northward mining and livestock country; to some extent the city could draw on the entire macroregion. It failed handsomely to rival Mexico City as an attraction and source of support; but even so there was an accretion. By the late colonial period there had taken place an impressive growth in social and commercial strength, the sources of which are not yet well understood. Some presently ongoing dissertation projects will doubtless throw much light on the matter.[3]

J. L.

NOTES

1. *Miners and Merchants in Bourbon Mexico*; "The Structure of Agricultural Production in the Mexican Bajío during the Eighteenth Century"; and, with Celia Wu, "Population Growth and Crisis: León, 1720–1860."

2. See Jesús Amaya, *Ameca, protofundación mexicana: el origen de su propiedad rural.* I draw this conclusion also from my own preliminary survey of early notarial records in Guadalajara.

3. I am thinking especially of work being done at this writing by Eric van Young at Berkeley and Richard Lindley at the University of Texas.

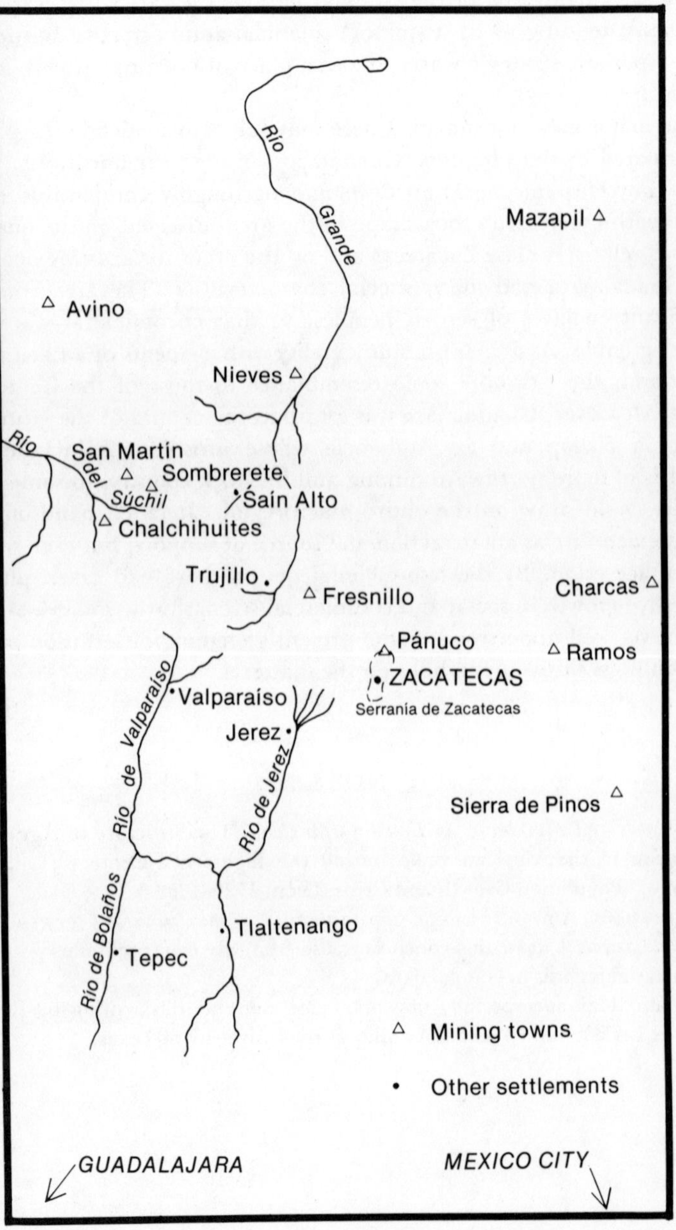

The Zacatecas District

8. Zacatecas: An Economic and Social Outline of a Silver Mining District, 1547–1700

P. J. Bakewell

The appearance of a piece of ore far from where it should have been began the history of silver mining in Zacatecas.[1] In early 1547 Juan de Tolosa, exploring for mines, found or was shown a fragment of Zacatecan ore at the Indian town of Tlaltenango, eighty miles southwest of Zacatecas and eighty miles due north of Guadalajara. He went on to the future site of Zacatecas, discovered more ores, had them assayed, found them to be worth exploiting, and, together with a small number of Spanish companions, started to establish a town near the deposits. Discoveries in 1548, within a few miles of Zacatecas, made the town thenceforth a major producer of silver.

During the 1550s and 1560s continuing searches for mines, starting from Zacatecas, revealed useful deposits farther north: San Martín (1556), Chalchihuites (1556), Avino (probably before 1558), Sombrerete (about 1558), Fresnillo (1556), Mazapil (1568), Nieves (1574), and Charcas (about 1574). These were the most significant deposits near Zacatecas and were included within the jurisdiction of the office of the royal treasury (*caja real*) that was founded in the town in 1552 or soon after. For the purposes of this essay, the mining district of Zacatecas will be taken as the area circumscribed by these deposits. These more northerly discoveries were the result of prospecting by early settlers of the town—notably Tolosa himself—but they must also be seen as an episode in the general northward exploration and settlement of New Spain that included the discovery of Zacatecas itself. The movement built on previous Spanish expansion from central Mexico outwards, especially the occupation of the Guadalajara area and the subsequent defeat of the Caxcan Indians in the Mixtón war of 1540-42; the Caxcanes held the steep-sided valleys to the north of Guadalajara that led directly to Zacatecas. As a rich mining center Zacatecas was then both an object achieved and a stepping-off point for further exploration.

The ore deposits in the north of the Zacatecas district produced much silver at various times—especially Sombrerete in the third quarter of the seventeenth century—but the output of the mines in the close vicinity of Zacatecas itself was greater than all the others combined during the century and a half considered here. The principal mines were opened in the Serranía de Zacatecas, a small, low range of bare and rounded hills rising out of the great flatness of the north Mexican plateau. The richest silver veins lay between Zacatecas and Pánuco, a mining village seven miles to the north.

Zacatecas was built in a basin in the hills, at about 8,000 feet, in a geographical and human wilderness. The land was uncultivated. To the north of the Serranía stretched the *altiplanicie,* high, cold, dry, poor of soil, and covered with scrub. Though inhospitable, the land presented no physical obstacles to travel. Water filled occasional streams and water holes for most of the year and could be used for irrigation in certain areas where the soil was more fertile. Indian inhabitants of the area at the time of settlement were scattered bands of hunter-gatherers whom the Spaniards called collectively Chichimecas, as the Aztecs had before them. There were several distinct groupings of these Indians around Zacatecas: Zacatecos to the north, Huachichiles to the east, Tepeques to the west, Tepehuanes to the northwest. These were the people overcome in the thirty years of the Chichimec wars, lasting from the early 1560s until about 1590.[2] The conflict was inevitable as Spanish settlement moved northward. The discovery of Zacatecas accelerated that northward movement and so precipitated the conflict. There was never danger of the town's destruction by direct Indian attack, but some of the smaller mining towns further north were made uninhabitable. In an attempt to dislodge the Spaniards from Zacatecas, the Indians took to harassing trade and communications. This tactic caused shortages of mining materials and food in the town, and prices rose. No direct connection can be made between the Chichimec war and the decline in silver production during the last quarter of the sixteenth century, however, since output continued to fall in the 1590s, when the fighting was over.

By the last decade of the sixteenth century Chichimec opposition to Spanish settlement had been destroyed—first by military conflict and then by assimilation. The Chichimecas were wooed with free supplies of food and clothing, and consented to be settled into towns. After that (about 1590) they all but disappeared from view. Their wandering way of life was gone. Living, as they did thereafter, cheek by jowl with Spaniards and with sedentary and agricultural Indians whom the Spaniards took to the north to form frontier settlements, the identity of the Chichimecas dissolved. Writing in the mid-seventeenth century, Tello observed that since 1614 the Chichimecas around Zacatecas seemed to have disappeared.[3]

Like most mining towns in Spanish America, Zacatecas was founded informally. There was no notarized act of establishment. The town began life as a mining camp built to house those who came to work ores of uncertain extent and performance. In effect, the establishment of Zacatecas was largely an entrepreneurial and commercial venture undertaken by two settlers of wealth and experience, Cristóbal de Oñate and Diego de Ibarra. Oñate was a veteran of the conquest of New Galicia[4] and of the Mixton war. He had also served as lieutenant governor of the province and at the time of the Zacatecas strike was probably the richest man in it. He had interests in mines elsewhere in New Galicia and may have used profits from these in establishing Zacatecas. Ibarra, Spanish-born like Oñate, was also a veteran of the Mixton war. After the war he began exploring northward in New Galicia in company with an uncle. Possibly the two Ibarras, as well as Tolosa, who actually made the discovery at Zacatecas, were part of a general enterprise of mining exploration organized by Oñate.

News of the strike spread quickly. But the mines did not seem rich at first, and Zacatecas was located in remote Indian territory, so there was difficulty in attracting settlers. Tolosa and Ibarra built a fortified house immediately after the discovery, to defend their bands of followers and slaves from a threatened attack by the Huachichil Indians. Ibarra is then said to have written to friends and acquaintances in settled areas, urging them to come to Zacatecas. According to a report of Ibarra's services, at times he was supporting seventy to eighty Spaniards. Oñate reported that his own employees had wished to leave Zacatecas because the ores were poor and there was a lack of food, but Ibarra persuaded them to stay. Oñate himself may have been in Mexico City part of the time in the early years after the foundation of Zacatecas, though witnesses attesting to his services claim that he was the oldest and principal settler of the mines and also fed and housed poor people on their arrival. Whatever the accuracy of these reports, it seems quite evident that the establishment of Zacatecas was a piece of speculative private enterprise. Exploration and settlement took place entirely without official support. The crown showed no interest in Zacatecas until the size of its deposits became apparent in the early 1550s. Like the later development of the mining industry (especially the construction of plants for amalgamation), the settlement was essentially a capitalist undertaking, in the simple sense that it was a conscious application of accumulated wealth for the purpose of increasing that wealth. Ibarra and Oñate spent their money in an attempt to attract and retain men who would work the mines. They themselves hoped to, and did, benefit from the expansion of mine working. They both made considerable fortunes in the 1550s.

Occurrence of silver ore determined the pattern of settlement beyond Zacatecas. Tolosa and Ibarra's nephew, Francisco de Ibarra, explored to the north and located the other large ore deposits of the district. Diego de Ibarra financed Francisco's expeditions from his early profits at Zacatecas.[5] The major mines had been found and settled within about twenty-five years of the Zacatecas strike. By 1582 the figures for refining plants (*haciendas de minas*) and adult male Spaniards in the district were as follows:

Location	Plants	Spaniards
Zacatecas and Pánuco	25	800
Sombrerete	12	200
Fresnillo	11	150
San Martín	6	80
Nieves	5	30
Chalchihuites	4	30
Mazapil	3	100

Charcas is reported as being just settled in 1582. There is evidence that an effort to work it had been made in the early 1570s, but the attempt was frustrated by Indian hostility. Ranchos had by 1582 been abandoned because of Indian attacks.[6] A notable, indeed extraordinary, feature of mining at Mazapil was that much ore was sent for refining to mills 150 miles away, since Indian hostilty prevented construction of refineries at that remote northern outpost. The ores must have been of great richness to make freighting over such a distance worthwhile. There is no space here to follow the history of each of the minor towns. Their growth was not as sustained as that of Zacatecas proper, and in the seventeenth century all suffered a decline in mining. Sombrerete recovered in the middle of the century, but many of the others did not. A manuscript of 1671 describes Fresnillo as then being much declined; Ramos as long abandoned; Sierra de Pinos (a mining town founded about 1603, 70 miles to the southeast of Zacatecas) as being almost abandoned; and Charcas as abandoned for many years, though now being resettled from San Luis Potosí, because of a new mine discovery.[7] No silver was produced at Mazapil for an unknown period before 1655, when mining resumed on a small scale.[8]

The Town of Zacatecas

During the sixteenth century Zacatecas grew beyond the stage of a temporary agglomeration to become a Spanish city, a mining and trading center of considerable complexity. From the earliest recorded time it had a Spanish town council rather than an Indian one, and in 1585 it received the title of City. By the early seventeenth century it was considered by the citizens to be the second city of New Spain, an opinion in some ways justified, however much inhabitants of Puebla might have quibbled with it. Five major religious orders had establishments in Zacatecas, substantial two-story residences characterized the center of town, and the thriving shops and markets, feeding on Zacatecas silver at its source, far outstripped their equivalents in most provincial towns.

Active mining entrepreneurs lived in Zacatecas itself, not abandoning it in favor of Mexico City as did the landowners and encomenderos of some other regions. The reason may be in part that mines and their refineries demanded the owners' constant attention since technical and financial decisions had to be made frequently and quickly, and owners were perhaps unwilling to leave matters of such urgent importance to majordomos and technicians, however expert. The remoteness of Zacatecas from Mexico City may have been another reason. Not only was the distance physically great, but its influence may have encouraged the development of a self-contained society in Zacatecas, in which the rich miner or merchant could achieve enough status to satisfy his social ambitions. Bishop Mota y Escobar, visiting Zacatecas in the first years of the seventeenth century, found men there whom he considered *nobles.*[9] His criterion for judging their nobility was, apparently, that they maintained horses and arms. Obviously there were other associated qualities which he fails to mention. Among this group of noblemen there were, he said, only a few who were rich, and they were miners. It can be guessed that those considered noble at that time were the descendants of the founders and of the early, rich settlers of the town. Mota y Escobar does not comment on the absence in Zacatecas of encomenderos, who in the cities of central Mexico constituted the core of a nobility.

The social framework of Zacatecas was built by Spaniards; but in addition to its Spanish inhabitants, wealthy and poor, the town of course contained Indians, who came from the south like the Spaniards themselves, to make up for the lack of local workers. The first wave of southern Indians, arriving in the 1550s and 1560s, found themselves in an unfamiliar town, set in unfamiliar terrain, far from the fertile and cultivated lands of the Valley of Mexico, Cholula, Tlaxcala, and Michoacán. Zacatecas at that time was a mere mining camp, but it had been created wholly by Spaniards. It is entirely possible that in Zacatecas, for the first time since the conquest of Anahuac, Spaniards in New Spain found themselves on more familiar ground (almost "home" ground) than did the sedentary Indians of central Mexico. The Spaniards had created a town on the north Mexican plateau where none had existed before. In every new region of central Mexico that the Spaniards entered and began to settle, they found an urban-agricultural way of life which, through a mixture of influence, persuasion, imposition, and force, they slowly bent to their own use and advantage. In Zacatecas, the bending was much simpler. Here in the north the only preexisting Indian culture was that of the Chichimecas, which was so different that the Spaniards could not adapt it to their use and instead set about destroying it. The immigrant Indians from the south brought with them to Zacatecas much of their way of life and tried to establish it there. But the physical and much of the psychological basis of that way of life could not be transported. They must have felt distressingly uprooted.

Nevertheless, the immigrant Indians did retain a corporate sense, grouping themselves according to origin in a number of townships around the periphery of Zacatecas. The Tlaxcalans formed a barrio called Tlacuitlapan (Nahuatl, "in the back of things") on the northwest edge of the town. Near there, the Mexica gathered in Mexicapan, named after them. To the south, Indians from Texcoco created a barrio "El Niño Jesús." The Tarascans of Michoacán formed two townships to the west: San José and Tonala Chepinque (also Nahuatl, "wet in the dry time"). The formation of barrios was evidence of the Indians' natural desire to maintain their culture as much as possible in an alien place by congregating like with like. How far they succeeded would be hard to measure even if much information were available, which it is not. The distinct townships still persisted at the end of the seventeenth century, which indicates that Indians from the different regions still felt the need for a familiar enclave in Zacatecas.

Techniques of Mining and the Output of Silver

The central activity of Zacatecans, both Spanish and Indian, was extracting silver ore in the diggings and reducing it in the refining works that lined the creek running through the town. After the early years, the central technique was the amalgamation or patio process.

The ores worked in the Serranía de Zacatecas in the years just after the discovery were rich. The early miners of Zacatecas, like their counterparts in most silver mining areas of colonial Spanish America, found concentrated silver oxides awaiting them in the weathered parts of the veins, close to the surface. These ores were cheap to extract and could be smelted at low cost. Abundant wood near Zacatecas fired the furnaces.

Later miners looked back on this time as a golden age. But by the mid-1550s the surface ores had been seriously depleted. Smelting became less profitable as the yield of the ores fell, for this method could not process large amounts of lower-grade ore.

The situation was saved by the introduction of refining by amalgamation, in which mercury's peculiar property of combining with other metals, even when they are in chemical compounds, was exploited. Mercury could extract even the small proportion of silver that was contained in the lower-quality ores of the late 1550s. Amalgamation was being used in Zacatecas by August 1557, and it remained the mainstay of silver processing there until the late nineteenth century. Consequently mercury supply was a vital matter, as we will see later. A rise in output resulted from the innovation, lasting into the 1570s. The 1560s were the true period of foundation of the Zacatecas industry. Smelting had required little investment and little new technology. In contrast, amalgamation demanded heavy capital spending and familiarization with an entirely new technique, for the process had never before been used on a large scale. Indeed, the miners of early Mexico virtually invented amalgamation as an industrial process, for although the properties of mercury had been known since Roman times, they had never been exploited except in a trivial way. There is a report that by 1562 the miners of Zacatecas had spent over 800,000 pesos on the buildings and machinery (*ingenios*) necessary for amalgamation. To render the process feasible in the dry northern plateau, Mexican miners developed what may be called a dry technique, involving the use of mules instead of water for power, and reuse of water in special washing vats. All refineries in Zacatecas proper were mule-powered, and water power was rare in the whole district.

Amalgamation was not a panacea, however. It solved some problems of refining, but problems of extraction were also great. By the early 1570s the increasing depth of the mines was causing difficulties in cutting and removing ore. At these greater depths flooding began to occur. And the further the miners went below the surface, the lower the silver content of the ores fell. When amalgamation was introduced, 100 pounds of ore (a *quintal*) had yielded 3 to 5 ounces of refined silver; by 1572 a quintal gave only 1¼ to 1½ ounces. It was at such low levels of ore yield that the Zacatecas industry operated from then on. Much better ores were, of course, found from time to time in rich pockets of the Serranía, and at other mining centers. But the general run of ores yielded 1 to 2 ounces of silver per quintal.

After these major early innovations there was no further technical advance in refining during the period under consideration here, apart from the introduction of pyrites (called *magistral* by the miners) as a reagent in amalgamation. Advances in extractive technique were not great either. Little planning of underground workings took place. Haphazard and probably inefficient tunneling in pursuit of the vein was the commonest practice. The contemporary procedure of claiming mines led to a proliferation of small, separate workings along a vein. Not until the 1640s, when an innovating and highly successful Zacatecan miner, Bartolomé Bravo de Acuña, interconnected four mines on the rich Veta Grande, did a semblance of rational and planned exploitation of the veins appear. Some form of water extraction had been necessary since the 1570s. By the early seventeenth century, bucket chains and wooden lift pumps were being used. Little information is to be had about drainage, so any improvements there must remain unknown. In ore extraction, the late seventeenth century may have seen one important technical development: blasting. Mining documents of the time are silent about the use of powder underground, but blasting was certainly being carried out by the 1730s; together with plentiful mercury, it may well have played a large part in Zacatecas's early eighteenth-century boom.

As a result of the interplay between these techniques and the factors of mercury supply, ore deposits, and finance, the course of silver production in the Zacatecas district was far from smooth, as Figure 1 shows.[10] There were periods of high output at intervals of about fifty years (1570–75, 1610–35, 1675–90), separated by periods of slump. Another high point seems likely to have come after 1720, but research on output has not been carried beyond that year. It may be possible to fit the output curve of Zacatecas into some general cyclical pattern, but there appear to be quite specific reasons why output varied as it did. The seventeenth century, it will be noted, cannot be characterized as a time of general decline despite the slump of midcentury, since it contains two such significant high periods.

Miners' Holdings

Though veins and mining shafts were important, the real core of the mining industry was the hacienda de minas, which was not merely a refining mill, but a social and economic unit as distinctive as the more commonly known agricultural hacienda. Within its confining wall, it contained stamp mills, washing vats, patios for incorporation, sheds for machinery, storerooms, stables for horses and mules, rooms to house workers and their families, a dwelling house for the owner, and a chapel. It was the base for the miner's *cuadrilla* or labor gang, and there workers received a supply of meat and maize as part of their wage. It is unclear whether the refineries housed both refining workers and mine workers, or whether the latter lived in hamlets or huts close to the entrance of their mine. Surviving manuscripts from Zacatecas reveal all too little, in fact, about the life and working conditions of the Indian mine laborer.

The term "miner" (*minero*) denoted a person owning the means, or part of the means, of producing silver. Those who owned mines, but no refining mill, were occasionally referred to as miners, and those who owned a refinery always were; most commonly, miners owned both. In 1626, at the height of the early seventeenth-century boom, the numbers of owners and refineries in the district were as follows:[11]

Locations	Owners	Refineries
Zacatecas and Pánuco	40	46
Ramos	15	17
Fresnillo	9	9
Sierra de Pinos	7	7
Sombrerete	3	5
Avino	3	3
Nieves	2	2
Charcas	2	2
Chalchihuites	1	1

All together there were eighty-two owners of ninety-two refineries. They produced perhaps a third of the silver of New Spain.[12]

As well as his refinery, the miner might own land around Zacatecas where he bred mules to power his machinery and grew grain to feed his laborers and his animals. He usually occupied a substantial, sometimes truly large, house in the center of Zacatecas, generally close to the main square of the town and the parish church. The house would be well furnished, sometimes with Turkish carpets and Chinese silks. He would marry into an existing mining family.

A miner's estate.—The unusually large range of possessions of one mid-seventeenth-century miner can serve to illustrate the complex for us. Francisco de Escobedo, born in Toledo, made his will in Zacatecas in October 1646.[13] He left two refineries. One was three miles outside town. It was an amalgamation plant in working order, with two mills for crushing ore and one powered paddle wheel and vat for washing amalgam. Forty mules provided the necessary energy. There were also fifty donkeys, probably used for carrying ore to the refinery from the various mines forming part of Escobedo's estate. At the entrance to one of the mines were six *aposentos* ("rooms, lodgings")—presumably huts to shelter the mine workers. There were three slaves—one black, one mulatto, and one *chino*. ("Chinos," quite common as slaves in seventeenth-century Zacatecas, were brought from the Philippines on the Manila galleon.) The dwelling house of the refinery had one large room (*sala*) and three smaller aposentos. It had a flat roof of hard-packed earth (*terrado*).

Escobedo owned another refinery at Tepec, 100 miles southwest of Zacatecas, on the Bolaños river. This was a mixed smelting and amalgamation works that contained two sets of double smelting furnaces with power-driven bellows. There was a walled yard (*incorporadero*) for amalgamation, and a washing vat. In this refinery were five slaves—three black men and one woman, and one chino. There were also Indian wage-workers, twenty in number (all men), fourteen of them married. There were twenty-three mules—fourteen to drive the bellows, six for freighting, and three for riding; also, eight donkeys. Associated with the refinery were several mines of unstated location, but presumably in Tepec itself.

Apart from his refining plants, Escobedo owned a rural hacienda, called "San Andrés," in the valley of Tlaltenango. San Andrés was a notable complex of agriculture, stockraising, and cart building. It had a carpenter's shop where nine carts were under construction. There were three separate "estancias," two with barns, one with a chapel, and each with a small dwelling. No mention is made of grain in the barns, but in that valley the crop was probably maize. There were also lands for stock raising. The complement of animals was large: 160 oxen for pulling the carts and for plowing; 68 horses; 80 riding mares; 92 unbroken mares; 18 pack mules; 3 donkeys. Thirty-one free workers were employed at San Andrés—mostly Indians, but a few mulattoes also. Sixteen slaves and one black freedman completed the labor force (five black men and four women; four mulatto men and three women). The hacienda house was large: three salas, nine aposentos, some with terrado roofs and some with wooden shingles (*tlajamaniles*), a kitchen, two patios and one small pen or corral. There were various other aposentos, doubtless to house the workers and slaves. Possibly Escobedo lived at San Andrés; he is unusual for a miner in not having a town house in Zacatecas. His estate is more imposing and diverse than that of most of his mining companions in Zacatecas at the time, but otherwise it resembles them in achieving a considerable degree of vertical integration.

Miners' Careers

The four men traditionally considered the founders of Zacatecas—Juan de Tolosa, Cristóbal de Oñate, Diego de Ibarra, and Baltasar Temiño de Bañuelos—had careers which proved typical, though on a magnificent scale, of those of the dominant Spanish group in Zacatecas during the sixteenth and seventeenth centuries. They were all immigrants from Spain. They sought and found wealth through mining in Zacatecas.

That wealth gained them social status and enabled them to attract highborn and well-connected wives. They obtained high military and civil offices, also through wealth. They left influential sons.

Oñate, for example, even before the Zacatecas discovery, married the daughter of the first *factor* (manager) of the royal treasury of New Spain. He left one illustrious son in don Juan de Oñate y Salazar, conqueror, *adelantado* and governor of New Mexico. Another son, don Alonso de Oñate y Salazar, was a miner in Zacatecas, and then became solicitor general (*procurador general*) for all the miners of New Spain, New Galicia, and New Biscay. Oñate, it is true, had other distinctions besides wealth from Zacatecas.

The three other founders, however, used their wealth from Zacatecas as the major support of their social advance. Tolosa married doña Leonor Cortés Moctezuma, daughter of Hernando Cortés and doña Isabel Moctezuma, herself the daughter of Moctezuma. Don Juan Cortés Tolosa Moctezuma, Tolosa's son, was an active miner and cabildo member in Zacatecas until his death in 1624.

Diego de Ibarra achieved possibly even more powerful connections. He married the daughter of don Luis de Velasco, viceroy of New Spain. Velasco's son, also named don Luis, became viceroy in his turn, his first term of office running from 1589 to 1595, when Ibarra was still alive, though an elderly man. What economic advantages he may have derived from being brother-in-law of the chief executive of New Spain are unknown. But his social standing in Zacatecas must have been enhanced by the connection.

Bañuelos, unlike the others, took a wife from Zacatecas itself. He married doña María de Zaldívar Mendoza, one of a family of rich miners and early settlers of Zacatecas. For a time Bañuelos held the influential but highly expensive post of lieutenant captain-general of New Galicia, to direct and finance the campaign against the Chichimecas.

There was much intermarriage in the second generation of these families, creating a powerful and cohesive group of mine and land owners in Zacatecas in the late sixteenth century and the early seventeenth.[14] The family names survived later in the seventeenth century, but the descendants lost the luster and the wealth of the founders, pulled down by the general decline of mining in those decades. A Juan de Vargas, who was in Zacatecas about 1650, said that he had seen grass (*zacate*) being sold from a cart in the streets for the maintenance of the widow of the *maestre de campo* Vicente de Zaldívar Mendoza.[15] This Zaldívar, as recently as 1616, had paid for the building of a large Jesuit college and church in Zacatecas, reputedly donating 100,000 pesos for the construction and as endowment.

Immigration

Nearly all the miners mentioned so far were born in Spain. In this they were not atypical. Many of the most active miners in the second half of the seventeenth century were first-generation immigrants. Because of the lack of pre-1640 records, it cannot be said whether this was equally true earlier. It is difficult, also, to demonstrate specific family or regional links between the immigrants and existing Zacatecan families; more research might show them. The immigrants came from a variety of Spanish regions, but mainly from a central block running north-south across the Iberian peninsula: the Basque country, Old Castile, New Castile, Extremadura. Their wills show them generally to have been successful miners, which is the more notable in that they prospered in the depressed conditions of the midcentury. With few exceptions, they fared better than miners originating in Zacatecas. This may have been in part the success of the energetic newcomer, untrammeled by conventions and preconceived ideas; but the immigrant also may have held an economic advantage over the old Zacatecan families.

Immigration is one aspect of a clearly marked tendency among Zacatecan mining families—their lack of durability. Almost without exception, they declined rapidly after their rise to wealth. The north-of-England saying "clogs to clogs in three generations," which has its counterparts in many other countries, was well exemplified in Zacatecas. It would be wrong, however, to condemn the third generation out of hand, because the fluctuations of Zacatecas's silver output, caused in large part by exterior influences, made it inevitable that families would periodically decline. Again, the conventional Hispanic pattern of inheritance of that time, by which estates were divided up more or less equally among all the heirs, made it difficult for an economic unit such as a refinery to survive for long periods. The slump after 1630 put the immigrants at a large initial advantage in mining, for prices and rents of refineries and mines fell to a tenth of the level they had reached during the first quarter of the seventeenth century. If the immigrant came with even a small amount of capital, therefore, he could buy himself into silver mining cheaply, and he had the great advantage of not having to repay or service old mercury debts to the royal treasury. That may have been the key to his indisputable success in many instances.

Miners and Landholding

The establishment of the minor towns of the district was accompanied by the granting of agricultural and grazing lands to settlers near them. Two especially productive agricultural areas began to be exploited immediately after the discovery of nearby ores: the Súchil river valley to the west of San Martín, and the lands bordering the Río Grande to the west and north of Fresnillo. In both these areas, irrigation was employed. Full advantage could not be taken of these lands until the Chichimec conflict ended, but they were always a useful source of wheat, maize, and meat for Zacatecas and the other district towns.[16] The small, early land grants gradually accreted into larger haciendas.

As already mentioned, possession of land was a common characteristic of the miners of Zacatecas. In the early years of mining, settlers and miners received grants (*mercedes*) of land near the new mining towns, especially in the river valleys just mentioned. Grants were also made in the area immediately to the south of Zacatecas, as far as an area known as the Monte Grande, some 20 miles to the south, which was a well-used source of wood and charcoal. These early landholdings provided food (mainly grain) for the mining towns, that, undoubtedly, being the purpose for which the grants were sought. During the late sixteenth century, many holdings were gathered together into the hands of a few owners, and the large rural hacienda of north Mexico began to assume its characteristic form.

A vast hacienda.—The prime example of an early large hacienda within the Zacatecas district, owned by a citizen of the town, is Diego de Ibarra's estate of Trujillo. Ibarra was rich from the early proceeds of the Zacatecas mines. Besides the power that wealth gave him, he held great political power, having succeeded his nephew Francisco de Ibarra as governor of New Biscay after Francisco's death in 1575. Wealth and authority no doubt combined to enable him to amass the huge Trujillo holdings which, in 1611, consisted of eighty-four sitios falling in a triangle between Zacatecas, Valparaíso, and Sombrerete.[17] The central Trujillo holding itself lay on the Río Grande almost directly west of Fresnillo.

Though much research remains to be done on land tenure in the Zacatecas district, it seems unlikely that such large holdings as Ibarra's were typical of tenure. The large estates undoubtedly occupied a considerable part of the land surface, but they were few. If the characteristic holding is taken as being that possessed by most owners, then quite a small rural estate was the rule. It may be that if and when the necessary research is done, the typical rural property owned by the Zacatecan miner will prove to be like that described by one Melchor Caldera in his will of 1659.[18]

An ordinary hacienda.—Caldera had: an "hacienda del monte" (position unstated) where he cut wood, made charcoal, and kept 3 carts, 236 oxen, and 100 horses; a sitio in the jurisdiction of Aguascalientes called San Nicolás de los Mezquites, adjoining another half-sitio, where he had altogether 300 cattle and 300 horses; and an additional sitio, about which he gave no information. Caldera was in that medium category to which most miners belonged in Zacatecas—owning a single refinery and living in a decent house near the middle of town. His rural possessions were similarly neither large nor small. It is evident that miners of his sort used their lands to provide supplies for their mining operations—in Caldera's case, wood, charcoal, animals to use as an energy source, and possibly meat and leather. Any surplus may have been sold in Zacatecas. Francisco de Escobedo, whose will was quoted above, used his lands similarly. Here, as in other cases we have seen, mines, refining plant, and rural property constituted an economic whole. Ownership of land may have brought some increase in social standing, or at least was regarded as a desirable attribute for a successful miner. But the economic reasons for land ownership—ensuring one's own supplies for mining and refining—were strong as well.

In the well-known interpretation of François Chevalier,[19] the decline of silver mining led to a consolidation of the rural hacienda. The falling-off of mining activity caused the market for hacienda produce at the mines to decline, and also brought about a fall in the general level of economic activity in Mexico. In that difficult situation, the haciendas are supposed to have retreated into economic self-sufficiency and isolation. Chevalier, in fact, did not advance this sequence of events with complete certitude, and he even suggests that haciendas may in some cases have been *destroyed* by the penury of their owners, not merely forced into a static self-sufficiency. This was certainly what happened to the rural estates of some miners of Zacatecas. The very large estates, with which Chevalier was primarily concerned, conceivably may have survived in self-sufficiency. But some of the lesser holdings owned by Zacatecan miners did not. The usual cause of their destruction, as Chevalier hinted, was the indebtedness of their miner owners, either to the royal treasury for mercury or to private individuals for loans and supplies.

A dissolving estate.—An example of this dissolution of landholdings is the story of the San Pedro estate of one Vicente de Zaldívar Mendoza, a highly regarded and prosperous miner in Zacatecas in the early seventeenth century and already referred to above. In the Súchil valley, west of Sombrerete, he had a considerable tract of land centered on the hacienda of San Pedro, where he produced grain, cattle, and horses, probably to supply his mines at close-by San Martín. By the mid-seventeenth century, financial troubles weighed heavily on this estate. Zaldívar's widow, doña María Oñate Cortés, rented out most of the Súchil land, keeping only the sitio of San Pedro itself. In 1664 her son, the Adelantado don Nicolás de Zaldívar y Oñate, renewed the lease. Fifteen years later, all his goods had been confiscated by the treasury for his debts, and the treasury had caused all his lands to be leased. The debt owing on the family estate was over 300,000 pesos. Much of the land at Súchil had been sold. Failure in mining was the cause of the family's poverty.[20] The royal treasury thus had no hesitation in seizing and forcibly leasing out lands when the debtor had no other resources to set against his debts.

A consolidating estate.—The case of the Zaldívar estate is far from uncommon in seventeenth-century Zacatecas. Yet if dissolution of land-holdings was taking place on the one hand, reformation occurred on the other. The Bravo family was gathering land at the same time as the Zaldívar's were losing it. Bartolomé Bravo de Acuña appeared in Zacatecas in the early 1640s. Beginning in a small way in mining by renting a refinery, he became by the time of his death, in 1661, one of the most successful Zacatecan miners of the century. His principal feat was to restore workings on the Veta Grande, four miles north of Zacatecas, to production. In this project he invested over 100,000 pesos. In the latter part of his life he was alcalde ordinario of Zacatecas, then alcalde mayor of Fresnillo. Exactly how he succeeded as a miner in a period of general decline is not clear, nor is the source of his capital. Undoubtedly, technical imagination and expertise in clearing four mines on the Veta Grande and linking them by underground galleries was at the root of his wealth. The first surviving record of a modest land purchase by him dates from 1653. After then his son, don Juan Bravo de Medrano, and later his widow, doña Catalina de Oñate, continued to buy and take leases on land in the same area, between Jerez and Juchipila. Don Juan was as successful a miner as his father and in 1691 bought the vacant Spanish title of Conde de Santa Rosa, becoming the first citizen of Zacatecas to hold a title of nobility. This assembling of lands by the Bravo family was not a unique occurrence, though again it must be said that more research is needed to determine firm patterns of development in Zacatecas land tenure. It would be a good beginning to know how the entailed Trujillo estate fared throughout the mining depression.

Labor in the Mining Industry

It does not appear that Zacatecas suffered from labor shortage at any time as a result of the decline of the Indian population of central Mexico; no correlation is apparent between changes in the size of that population and variations in silver output in the Zacatecas district. The overall Indian population was undoubtedly falling rapidly while production of silver tended upwards from the mid-sixteenth century to about 1620; production then fell for reasons not connected with labor shortage—lack of mercury and finance and decline of ore quality. At the height of Zacatecas's first boom, in 1625, the number of Indian workers employed in extraction and refining at Zacatecas and Pánuco was probably about 1,700. It is unlikely, therefore, that the total number of Indians working in mining in the whole district could have exceeded 5,000 at any time during the seventeenth century, a very small proportion of whatever minimum the Indian population of central Mexico may have fallen to in that century.

Local circumstances affected production more for brief periods. In 1576–77, for example, many Indian workers at Zacatecas perished in the devastating *matlazahuatl* epidemic (probably typhus). One report, of 1577, stated that over 2,500 Indians—certainly a large proportion of the mining labor force of the time—had died in the town. Just how long the resulting labor shortage depressed mining after the epidemic is hard to know. The president of the Audiencia of New Galicia reported some months later that the mines of the province, including Zacatecas, were being repopulated as Indians settled in them.

As interesting as numerical considerations related to labor is the question of how Indians were employed in the mining industry. The fact that Zacatecas lay far to the north of existing Spanish settlement in 1547 and, in particular, the fact that it was the first mining center in New Spain to be established outside the area inhabited by the sedentary Indian peoples of central Mexico meant that the labor systems it employed at the start were peculiar to it. Later those systems were to become increasingly common over the whole of the mining north, so that Zacatecas figures as a precursor in labor matters.

The lack of a sedentary agricultural population near Zacatecas had considerable social and economic consequences. In central Mexico, in the sixteenth and seventeenth centuries, unskilled labor for mining was drawn from Indian towns by repartimiento (forced rotary labor). But this was not possible in Zacatecas; regular quotas of mine workers could not be drawn from nomads, especially from belligerent nomads. It was similarly impossible to exact tributes from such Indians. Thus they could not be used as a basis for even the modified form of encomienda that survived after the New Laws of 1542; hence that characteristic social figure of sixteenth-century Mexico, the encomendero, was all but unknown in Zacatecas.

How, then, were the mines worked? In the early years, Indian slaves were much used. In 1557, a judge of the Audiencia of New Galicia reported to the king that there were Indian slaves in Zacatecas, as well as other Indians who were not slaves, though the miners claimed they were. These other Indians had made agreements with the miners to work for a certain period; when it elapsed, the miners would not release them and kept them as if they were slaves.[21] Some Indian slavery at Zacatecas persisted into the late seventeenth century. But after perhaps the first ten years of Zacatecas's existence, such slaves formed an insignificant portion of the labor force. Zacatecas relied largely on those Indians who freely contracted to work for miners.

Immediately after the discovery of ores, Indians from various parts of central Mexico began to stream northwards to Zacatecas: Aztecs, Tlaxcalans, Cholulans, and Otomis. Shortly afterwards there came workers from Michoacán and the Pueblos de Avalos. These Indians hired themselves out to Spanish employers, mainly to dig and carry ore (two separate tasks). Their right to do so freely, without interference or direction from Spanish justices, was declared in an order of 1550, given by a member of the Audiencia of New Galicia. Though research has not revealed any examples of labor contracts made between Spaniards and Indians, a system of hired labor, with previously agreed wage rates and perquisites, clearly prevailed in Zacatecas during the sixteenth and seventeenth centuries. Each worker performed a set daily task or *tequío* (from Nahuatl "quota, task"). Effective wage rates are impossible to calculate since, in addition to receiving a cash wage, mine workers were permitted to extract for themselves a small amount of ore, the *pepena* (from Nahuatl "choose, glean"), which they might smelt or sell; and employers provided food for their workers, apparently as part of the wage.

Although it is clear that in the long term lack of labor was not a major determinant of silver output in the Zacatecas region, there is no doubt that there were occasional shortages. This is revealed by competitive bidding for labor in, for example, the 1590s. Possibly in an effort to retain their workers, miners in various towns of the district were paying wages in advance. But at least some Indians promptly disappeared with their money (and in some cases, their advance food rations) to other mining towns where, presumably, wages and conditions were better. That advance payment was a singularly ineffective way of retaining laborers is clear from repeated orders that Indians should be forced to serve out time for which they had been paid and that advance wages should be limited. There is little evidence for any generalized use of "debt peonage" among miners of the district. Miners' wills, for example, do not show that Indians owed many or large debts to their employers.

Mobility and instability of labor thus characterized the Zacatecan industry. Not only did Indian labor there move readily from one employer to another, and from one town to another, but it migrated from the south to Zacatecas and back again in a fluid manner. In April 1622 the vicar of the Franciscan monastery observed that 904 Indians were then resident in the part of Zacatecas where the Franciscans exercised parochial duties (the northern end of town); but that in times when rich pepenas were to be had in the mines, this number might rise to over 2,000. If the observation is correct, then it is a further demonstration that the holding of labor by debts, if attempted, was ineffective. It also demonstrates that Zacatecas could secure abundant labor if it could offer the right price. When miners complained of lack of labor, they meant lack of sufficient *cheap* labor. One effect of the easy ebb and flow of workers to and from the district may have been to increase the abruptness of total rises and falls in production. It can be imagined that when rich ores were found, labor poured in to mine them; and when it appeared that they were exhausted, labor left just as fast. The rapid drop in production of the 1630s may owe something to this effect. If Zacatecas had had steady repartimiento labor, rises and falls might have been more gentle.

One typical labor institution of Zacatecas tended to counteract the instability of the work force. Many Indians were hired for mining and refining not on a temporary basis, but as members of apparently quite permanent work teams—the miners' cuadrillas. The cuadrilla is first mentioned in Zacatecas in 1550, but the specialized work team is obviously not a Zacatecan invention. It was used previously in mines in central Mexico and may have originated in Spain. In its 1550 appearance, the term seems to refer to a team of slaves (whether black or Indian is not stated). By 1568 the cuadrillas evidently consisted of hired Indians, working at least semipermanently for Spaniards in mines and refineries. A list of 1622 gives the numbers of Indians employed in April of that year by the owners of fourteen refining works in the north of the town. The largest employer (don Juan de Oñate) had a cuadrilla of 85 Indians (46 in the refinery and 39 in his mines); the smallest had 12 Indians in his refinery and 6 in his mines. Altogether the fourteen miners employed 664 Indians—an average of 47.4 each. The cuadrilla system probably provided the miner and refinery owner with a more readily accessible and compact labor force than he would have obtained if he had had to hire Indians on daily, weekly, or even monthly contracts. Tello, writing of the early decades of the seventeenth century, refers to the customary fighting among Indians that took place on feast days "because of the rivalries that there were between those [Indians] of some mining haciendas and those of the others." These fights (called locally "sasemís," apparently from Nahuatl *ça cemi,* "for the last time, once and for all") often led to eight, twelve or twenty deaths. The civil authorities of Zacatecas were powerless to stop them. But in 1626 the bishop of Guadalajara, when visiting the town, determined to put an end to them. As one of his countermeasures "he had to take from them their brotherhoods (*cofradías*) and the insignias of the Holy Christs which each cuadrilla takes out every year, accompanied by music, on Holy Thursday, from the monastery of San Francisco and that of San

Agustín . . ." There are references to such fighting in manuscript sources as well as in Tello, so that his account is probably to be believed. The occurrence of these fights and the existence of religious brotherhoods in the mining works indicate a sense of community within them. This feeling may also have benefited the miner by tending to stabilize his labor force.

The refineries were also home, undoubtedly, to a number of black and mulatto slaves. Mota y Escobar, who visited Zacatecas between 1602 and 1605, found some 800 slaves, blacks and mulattoes, men and women, in the town. Assuming that half this number were men, black and mulatto slaves formed about a fifth of the mining industry's labor force at that time, since Mota y Escobar estimated that there were 1,500 Indian mining workers in Zacatecas. As in silver mining everywhere in Spanish America, black slaves were employed mostly in refineries rather than underground. Freedmen, black and mulatto, according to Mota y Escobar, hired themselves out as workers on ranches and farms, and in the mining industry. How many freedmen there were is not known.

It can be guessed that one result of the uprooting of Indian workers was that they were more easily molded into a skilled and permanent labor force than would have been possible if Zacatecas had been sited further south and the Indians taken for employment straight from their native lands and towns. The central relationship, indeed, between Spaniard and Indian in Zacatecas was from the start one of employer and employee. Spaniards in Zacatecas were not fundamentally concerned with the Indian as a grower of food, as a seller of artifacts, as a domestic servant, as a payer of tribute, but as a laborer for mine and hacienda. So not only was the immigrant Indian in Zacatecas separated from the environment to which he had been accustomed historically, but also he found himself in a far simpler economic relationship with the Spaniard than that with which most Indians in central Mexico were faced. He was a *naboría* or full-time employee of Spaniards, the position of only a minority in the older areas.

It may well be that the uprooting of Indians, together with the directness of the employer-laborer relationship, facilitated the formation of cuadrillas and the settlement of whole families in the refining works. The resulting relative fixedness of the labor force would mean the growth of a body of skilled workers, which would have happened less quickly and efficiently if labor had been conscripted, as under repartimiento. The labor force was by no means wholly stable, of course, as has already been pointed out. But without the special circumstances of Zacatecas, stability might have been far less than it was. Undoubtedly, as the northward journey to the mines and experience of labor there became more common, Indians had less sense of dislocation. If many went to Zacatecas when times were good and then left again, occasional employment there in mining must have become part of the normal way of life of many Indians from central Mexico. But the fundamental structure of employment in Zacatecas, laid down in the years before 1560, persisted. Wage-labor performed by free Indians, organized into work teams and directly supported by their employers, was established within ten or fifteen years of the discovery of the ores.[22]

The impression given by the manuscript sources describing labor in Zacatecas is that there was, on the whole, more cooperation than antagonism between the Indian workers and their Spanish employers. Also, many important jobs in the mining industry, between the extremes represented by the hacienda owner and the carrier of ore, were shared among Spaniards, people of black origin, and Indians—for instance, the essential tasks of building and maintaining haciendas and their machinery. Mota y Escobar found that of all the workers in "mechanical offices," carpenters and "masters of making machines" were the best paid in Zacatecas. Spaniards, mulattoes, and Indians exercised these trades.[23]

Merchants

Somewhat apart from the mining industry proper and the corps of owners and workers, there stood another powerful economic group, the merchants of the town. As a social group, merchants are rather less visible than the miners. Mota y Escobar declared that all the merchants of the town were "middling people" (*gente intermedia*)—that is to say, not "nobles." But many of them were rich (even by Zacatecan standards), with fortunes of 20,000 pesos upwards, and three or four with over 100,000 pesos. None of these merchants, added Mota y Escobar, were "of Spain" (de España)—that is, they did not deal directly with Spain but bought their goods in Mexico City. They did not belong, he implied, to the group of socially prominent trans-Atlantic traders of the capital, and in some cases in fact they were the latters' representatives.

The middle years of the seventeenth century saw the rise of a small but powerful group of merchant-financiers, the *aviadores* ("outfitters") and *mercaderes de plata* ("silver merchants"). The aviadores were normally general merchants whose businesses were in the mining towns and who supplied goods and materials to regular miner customers. The silver merchants were buyers of refined but uncoined silver and operated mostly in Mexico City.

From the beginning there had been a close connection between mining and commerce. Before the crown assumed a monopoly of the distribution of mercury in New Spain in 1572, merchants had supplied it to miners on credit. There are many complaints from miners in Zacatecas during the late sixteenth century about the distressing rates of interest charged by the merchants for loans and for goods supplied on credit. In fact, the real profits of the merchants were probably not exorbitant. The supply of credit, and perhaps of risk capital, by merchants to miners undoubtedly continued throughout the early seventeenth-century boom of Zacatecas. Merchants probably made money as output rose and lost it when it collapsed. Their fortunes at this time cannot be followed for lack of specific documentation, but it is evident that by the middle of the century the merchants had come to play a more important role than ever in mining. This may have been because they had become the only source of credit; before 1634 it had been possible to obtain large loans in the form of mercury supplied on credit from the royal treasury. Moreover, after 1634, the crown tried to collect old debts on mercury and thus drained large sums of cash from Zacatecas. Given the chronic shortness of liquid cash, the aviador insinuated himself firmly into the production process of silver. In practice, the debts owed to him by the miner were paid before the debts that the miner owed to the crown. If the treasury officials tried to collect the crown's debts first, the aviador would abandon the miner. In these circumstances, the treasury officials were bound to yield and allow the aviador his priority, in order to avoid ruining the miner and losing not only the debts owed, but also the tax the miner paid on the silver he produced and the price he paid for his mercury.

In view of this precedence over the crown in debt collection that the aviadores acquired, it seems at first sight odd that in the second half of the seventeenth century miners apparently paid their mercury debts to the crown far more quickly than they had in the first. Before 1650 it had normally taken the treasury ten years or more to collect payment on a consignment of mercury that had been distributed to the miners. But after that date, payment was collected in a few months. The reason for this rapid payment is undoubtedly that the miners were borrowing from the aviadores in order to pay the treasury in full. They came to owe their aviadores more money than they ever had owed to the crown. In November 1677 their debt to the merchants was over a million pesos, whereas their debt to the crown for mercury had been 401,252 pesos in 1603, 273,000 in 1625, and some 438,000 around 1660.

What was the source of the aviadores' funds? One partial answer is local trading profits. Another is the merchants' mining activities. While they never bought or ran mines themselves, the aviadores did have a large interest in refining. As early as 1576 merchants were reported to be smelting ores in Zacatecas, using bellows and furnaces in their own houses and employing as many as ten to twenty Indians to work them. They were said to be sending Indians to the mines to steal good ores and to have caused the collapse of seventeen of the best mines in Zacatecas and Pánuco because their Indians took ore from the pillars left by miners to support the workings. Merchants also bought from Indian mine workers the good ore they took as a supplement to wages, the pepena. Local trading and refining thus provided some funds which the Zacatecan merchants could reemploy in mining.

It is clear, though, that a major part of the funds being used in Zacatecas was capital raised in Mexico City. As Viceroy Cerralvo wrote in leaving office in 1636, the merchant community (*comercio*) of Mexico City played an essential role in the economy of New Spain. It supplied funds to miners, agriculturalists, stock breeders, sheep farmers, obraje owners, and sugar refiners. The merchants of the capital city sought to make profitable investments of funds that otherwise lay idle between the comings and going of the trans-Atlantic trading fleets. Interest rates on these funds varied according to the state of commerce in general: if good, interest was low; if bad, high.

Funding from Mexico City is very much in evidence in Zacatecas during the second half of the seventeenth century. Joseph de Villarreal, an immigrant merchant of Zacatecas and almost certainly the largest mining creditor in Zacatecas in that century, was at bottom an agent for two pairs of silver merchants in Mexico City (all four of them with "Captain" before their names): Joseph de Retes and Dámaso de Zaldívar, and Juan de Urrutia Retes and Luis Sáenz de Tagle. On their behalf Villarreal bought unminted silver with coin. From 1659 to 1669 he received 609,805 pesos from Urrutia Retes, and returned to Mexico City 601,755¾ pesos in refined silver. The Retes family later had a similar trade with don Andrés de Estrada, corregidor of Zacatecas from 1678 to 1684; supplying materials and credit (collectively known as *avío*) was a common practice among corregidores of Zacatecas. Estrada was said, in June 1684, to have received 2,500,000 pesos in coin from his suppliers in Mexico City during his term of office. Thus Zacatecan mining undoubtedly depended on Mexico City for much of its working and investment capital, especially after the collapse of the first boom of the early seventeenth century. But the situation was really one of interdependence. Silver was New Spain's main export commodity. Without it, the colony's trade with Europe (and with the Orient) could hardly have continued. The merchants of the capital would have been fewer and their profits lower. It was therefore in their own interest to invest in mining and encourage the future production of silver.

A merchant financier.—Joseph de Villarreal's career in Zacatecas shows to what extent the merchant-financier could dominate mining and indeed the political and social life of the town. His, of course, is the extreme case. But other, lesser aviadores must have enjoyed something of the power and prestige that he acquired, in proportion to the extent of their financing activities. In 1669, Villarreal, who like so many important merchants was always styled "Captain," was described as the biggest buyer of silver and ores in Zacatecas and all New Spain, and as "one of the rich and powerful men of the kingdom."[24] When making his will in 1680, Villarreal declared that there were debts owing to him of 149,000 pesos and that he himself owed only 7,400 pesos, all to his correspondents in Mexico City. Well before his avío activities become apparent, he can be seen to have made his mark in Zacatecas, buying in 1654 the office of *alguacil mayor,* or chief constable, in the cabildo. The office may have been the most powerful of all those comprising the cabildo, since the alguacil mayor was the chief executive officer of the law. Whereas the higher-placed corregidor held office for a maximum of seven years, the alguacil mayor held his for life and might create a position of more lasting personal power. Villarreal was alguacil mayor a full thirty years, from 1654 to 1684. By the 1660s he was a powerful person in Zacatecas. He was supplying avío to more than twenty miners and refiners—probably about half of all such people in the town, to judge by lists of miners from those years. Furthermore, he was buying silver from over thirty other people in various parts of the district. Some of these thirty themselves bought from miners on a smaller scale; others produced smelted silver with furnaces in their houses. One such was Villarreal's son-in-law, Joseph Ramírez. Like many aviadores before him, Villarreal was accused of passing off the smelted silver that he had bought as silver produced by miners (and taxed at a lower rate), thus defrauding the crown of its tax. There can be little doubt that he did so.

Villarreal's establishment matched his wealth and political preeminence. He owned at least twelve houses in Zacatecas, large and small, as well as his own assay office. He had nine black and mulatto slaves and a carriage drawn by four mules (a rarity, as far as can be seen, in Zacatecas).

A general merchant.—Zacatecas had more dealers in goods than dealers in silver. In that sense a trader more typical than Villarreal was Juan Domingo de Vargas, a native of Cuenca in Spain, who died in 1654. At that time he owed 14,476 pesos in large debts, plus a few smaller sums within Zacatecas. Of this total, 11,977 pesos were owed to Joseph de Retes and Joseph de Quesada, silver merchants of Mexico City, with whom Villarreal also dealt heavily. Vargas estimated that the stock of his shop in the Calle de Tacuba, the main trading street of Zacatecas, was worth 20,000 pesos. Other items of his estate were a sum of 1,640 pesos which he had sent to Puebla, to buy goods there, and 750 pesos owed to him by Bartolomé Bravo de Acuña, the price of two slaves. He lived in a large house. He held a 6,000-peso share in a trading partnership with his son-in-law. His wife, doña Catalina de Ayala (possibly a member of a mining family of Zacatecas called Ayala), had brought a dowry of 1,500 pesos. Vargas declared that at the time of his marriage he possessed 10,000 pesos in capital. He had four children, of whom the eldest son had studied in Mexico City and was *bachiller de artes.* His sole executor was Bartolomé Bravo. Here, evidently, is a well-to-do immigrant merchant who had managed to prosper in Zacatecas while mining declined. His appointment of Bravo as executor suggests that he was well connected among the influential citizens.

Smaller dealers and other types could also be illustrated, but this is not the place for a full portrait of the Zacatecan merchant. Yet while documentation becomes full only for the second half of the seventeenth century, there are enough instances of immigrants from Spain to show that the immigrant merchant, like the immigrant miner, was an identifiable type, even though he may in reality have been outnumbered in his profession by native-born inhabitants of New Spain or Zacatecas. According to their wills, at least one merchant came from each of the following towns or regions of Spain: Cuenca, Biruega (near Toledo), La Mancha, Osuna, La Guarda (Galicia), the *montaña de Burgos,* Madrid, Seville. Another was probably from the Basque country. Like the miners, then, immigrant merchants came mainly from a series of central provinces running north-south across Spain. Like the miners also, immigrant merchants achieved very differing degrees of success in their business.

A distinction between those merchants and miners of whom records remain is that none of the merchants, not even Villarreal, owned land (at least they made no reference to it in their wills). It may be that land ownership was not an accepted adjunct of the merchant's way of life, while it was of the miner's. But an economic explanation of the difference seems more obvious. The miner needed land to provide supplies to his mining enterprise; the merchant lived by liquidity and did not need ranching or agricultural produce.

Miners, Merchants, and the Cabildo

The auction of cabildo office did not keep the membership of that body from reflecting the economic balance of power in Zacatecas. Whichever mining families were most prosperous at the moment were usually represented there. Voting members were nearly all miners until mid-seventeenth century, when with the growing importance of merchant financiers not only Villarreal, but Captain Joseph de Arroyo Santerbaez, another aviador, entered the cabildo. Arroyo was a man of lesser means and smaller economic influence. His entry to the cabildo in 1660 is, therefore, possibly an even clearer sign of the rising power of the merchant in Zacatecas. What is yet more impressive is the fact that Villarreal and Arroyo, from 1663 to 1666 and from 1668 to 1670, when membership and attendance were at a low point, constituted half the voting membership of the cabildo at the annual elections of the two alcaldes ordinarios (first-instance justices) of the town. This situation could have provided, and perhaps did provide, quite extraordinary advantages for the merchants, because the alcaldes ordinarios were powerful officers of the law. To have them inclined to take one's own views could be most profitable, whether any litigation arose or not. Arroyo was himself alcalde ordinario several times during his period of office as a councilman. After the disappearance of Arroyo and Villarreal from membership of the cabildo in 1684, presumably caused by their deaths, dominance of miners returned. Attendance at elections rose, and no known merchants held office. It is tempting, and probably correct, to connect this reaffirmation of the mining interest with the resurgence of mining in Zacatecas after 1670.

The Role of Mercury and the Crown in Silver Production

Nothing could have been of more lively interest to the Spanish crown than an industry producing so much revenue in such an eminently liquid form. Therefore the crown participated more actively in the business of silver mining than was its wont with the society and economy in general. Once the wealth of Zacatecas was apparent, its corregidor came to be appointed directly from Spain. And when the crucial role of mercury in the amalgamation process became clear, the crown was quick to make mercury supply a royal monopoly. The availability of an important factor of production thus lay in part within administrative decision. Though officials sent the most mercury where the greatest production was going on or expected, the supply of mercury became in itself an important variable affecting production.

Indeed, mercury supply seems to have been the single largest determinant of output in the first half of the seventeenth century. In that century Zacatecas, like the other mines of New Spain, received the great majority of its mercury from European sources. Mercury exports from Europe to New Spain in the years 1600–1630 were higher than at any other time in the sixteenth and seventeenth centuries. The major European source was Almadén, in southern Spain, which was highly productive in these years. Arrivals of mercury at Zacatecas, similarly, were larger from 1610 (when records begin) to 1630 than in the rest of the century.

These large supplies seem to have been the basic cause of the first great silver boom at Zacatecas. It is true that ore yields were better than average, though not spectacularly high, until around 1620, and that one evidently important technical innovation came into general use between 1600 and 1605: the addition of pyrites to the amalgam during ore processing. But it seems likely that, above all, the availability of large supplies of mercury led to the increasing production of the first two decades of the seventeenth century. And not only did the miners have large amounts of mercury at their disposal; they also received it from the crown, the monopoly supplier, on the easiest of terms. In an attempt to maximize the production of silver, the crown allowed the miners substantial credit on their purchases of mercury. At Zacatecas this policy certainly brought returns in these early decades of the seventeenth century, when mercury was plentiful. In the 1620s, however, ore yields in Zacatecas began to fall. Production remained high until about 1630, but it seems likely that through the mercury credit scheme the crown was in effect subsidizing a growing number of basically unprofitable mines. This cannot be demonstrated conclusively for lack of accounts of mining undertakings; and even if account books had survived, it is improbable that they would have shown profit or loss unequivocally. Nevertheless, the decline in ore yields during the 1620s, coupled with a decline in production and a growing debt for mercury, suggests that overall profitability was falling.

The collapse of silver output in the 1630s was undoubtedly in part a result of the fall in ore yield and also, if profitability was indeed decreasing, of insufficient investment, especially in prospecting for new mines and in underground extension of existing ones. But the collapse resulted more directly from a lack of mercury. By this time, mercury production at Huancavelica, the great Peruvian mine, was falling. To maintain levels of silver output in South America, where production was far greater than in New Spain, the crown diverted supplies of European mercury from New Spain to Peru. At the same time, credit sales were reduced, and continual efforts were made at Zacatecas in the 1640s, 1650s, and 1660s to collect the old debts. When, as usually happened, the owners of mines and refining plants could not pay, the properties were confiscated. An effort was normally made by the treasury to lease them out, the rent being paid to the crown against the debt owed for mercury. But in this period of general depression of Zacatecan mining, the rents obtained were usually small, and the debts declined very little. Indeed, between 1625 and the early 1660s, the total debt actually increased, mainly because of credit given on mercury between 1625 and 1634, after which credit was denied. In 1625 the total mercury debt of Zacatecas and its district stood at

273,000 pesos; in 1659 Zacatecas alone owed 248,670 pesos, while four years later, in December 1663, the rest of the district owed 189,149 pesos. Attempts to collect the mercury debt, ineffective as they were, nevertheless drained considerable sums from the mining industry between 1640 and 1670, at a time when it needed an increased supply of capital for exploration and expansion of mines.

There is a mysterious period in the middle decades of the seventeenth century: mercury supplies to Zacatecas declined very steeply between 1640 and 1660, yet silver production did not drop correspondingly, but rather flattened off at about the average level of the sixteenth century. The reason appears to be that the miners reacted to mercury shortage by returning to the smelting techniques of a century before. They did so above all at Sombrerete, which enjoyed a period of glory between 1650 and 1690. The first document indicating Sombrerete's resurgence is dated 1646. Smelting required ores of a richness not seen in the district since the 1550s. Exactly how these ores were found at Sombrerete and why they were found at that particular time are the central puzzles of Zacatecan mining in the seventeenth century. Was it luck, or the result of new prospecting and new investment—a classic case of response to a challenge? Probably smelting became more common also at Zacatecas itself, though there the miners still relied basically on amalgamation. From Figure 1 it can be seen that Sombrerete, from 1683 to 1690, produced over half the output of the entire district. There is reason to think that it yielded a similar proportion in the 1670s also. After 1690 Sombrerete's output fell rapidly, causing a sharp decline in the total production of the district. The reason was, without doubt, a fall in the quality of ores. By the start of the eighteenth century Sombrerete had declined greatly.

Zacatecas evidently recovered from about 1660 onward, contributing its share to the extraordinarily rapid rise of the district's total output between 1665 and 1680. Perhaps the recovery was due in part to a return to smelting, but even more to an increase in the mercury supply between 1665 and 1685. By the early 1680s, the level of mercury arrivals at Zacatecas had reached that of the 1640s, though it was still only about half that of the first three decades of the century. Mercury supply again fell in the last fifteen years of the seventeenth century, probably causing the temporary decline in the amount of silver taxed at Zacatecas in the 1690s (see Figure 1). After 1700, Zacatecas's output rose rapidly again. Research on mercury supply has not been taken beyond 1700. But it is known that the mercury output at Almadén increased sharply at the start of the eighteenth century, probably the impetus for Zacatecas's new boom.

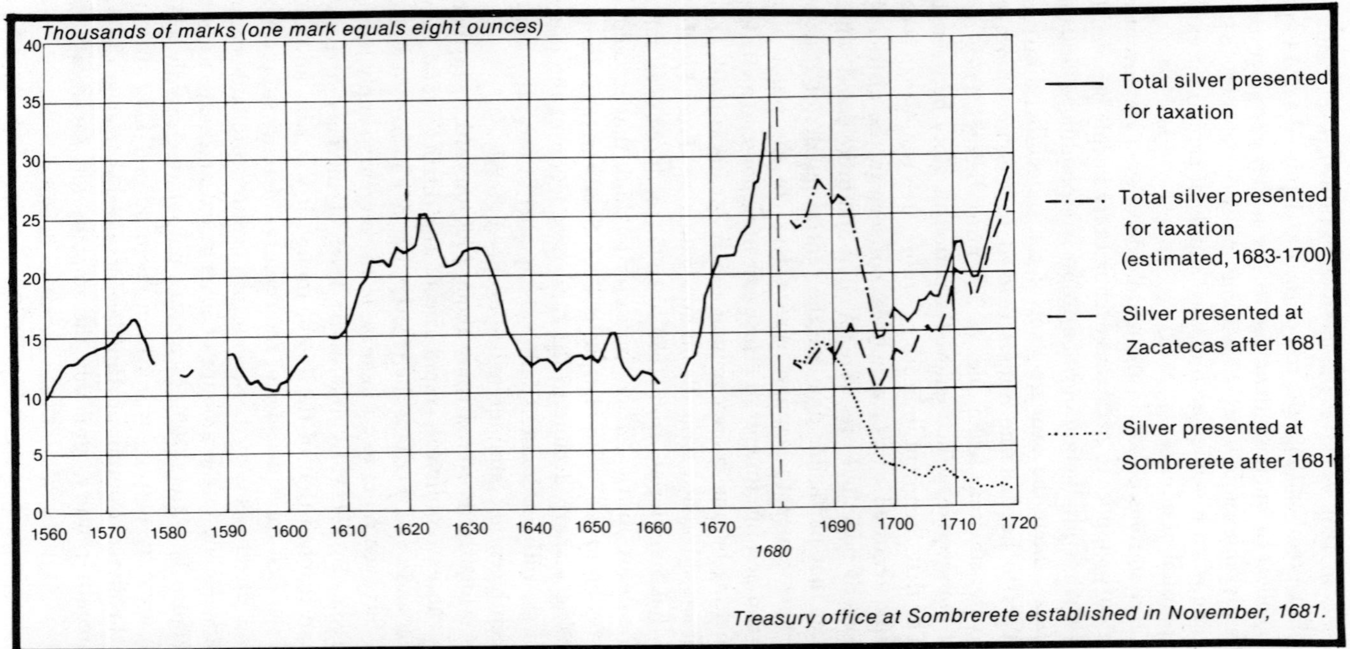

FIGURE 1. Three-year Moving Mean of Registered Silver Production in the Zacatecas Region, 1560–1719

Zacatecas in the Mexican Economy

Extractive industries in many countries today are often seen as economic enclaves—enterprises which employ few people, which touch little on the life of the majority of the population, and whose product is in large part exported. It is difficult, however, to view the silver-producing industry of Zacatecas in that way, even though the number of workers employed in the industry was small, and a very large part of their output was exported, either to Europe or the Orient. One of the most striking aspects of the Zacatecan industry is the extent to which it was embedded in the economic fabric of New Spain. The part of silver output taken by the crown was remitted directly to Spain. But the remaining portion of output, some 80 percent, entered mercantile economic circuits of varying length before it was exported. Much was sent directly to Mexico City as repayment of loans or as payment for supplies of goods, helping to give the Mexico City market its great power in interregional trade. Some was sent to a great number of other places in New Spain from which Zacatecas drew its necessities—to the Bajío and Aguascalientes for grain, for example; to Michoacán for grain, sugar, and fish; to Parras, north of Mazapil, for wine; to surrounding areas of the plateau for meat and leather. Most of this silver, to be sure, was eventually gathered by the major trans-Atlantic traders of Mexico City to pay for New Spain's imports. But a proportion of it was redistributed to diverse parts of the colony as capital and credit for productive processes. Some of this silver, indeed, returned to Zacatecas, through the silver merchants especially, as funds for the maintenance of mining. This funding became progressively more important to Zacatecas as the seventeenth century progressed and as the crown's hidden subsidizing of mining through mercury credit was withdrawn. The internal generation of capital for mining is a sign of a growing economic autonomy of New Spain in the seventeenth century.

Another aspect of Zacatecas's integration into New Spain is its dependence on more southerly regions for labor. Even when well established, the town and the district were as incapable of creating an adequate supply of workers in times of heavy exploitation of the mines as they were of raising sufficient local capital for their industry. Again, as was hinted in the previous paragraph, Zacatecas could not feed itself without bringing in supplies from a very large area to the south. The district's own grain lands were far from adequate to the demand, so that large amounts of wheat and maize were imported from the region of Aguascalientes, the Bajío, and Michoacán in normal years; and in times of poor harvests, grain was sought as far away as Toluca. It is likely that the rise of the northern mines in the sixteenth century, especially Zacatecas, was in part responsible for the development of the Bajío as a grain-producing area.

Zacatecas was, therefore, inextricably fused into the economic whole of New Spain; being thus fused, it was economically dependent on other regions. But at the same time, it was depended upon. Without it—the major silver-producing area of the time in New Spain—the merchants of Mexico City would have found their trading opportunities much reduced for lack of silver to export. A large market for goods of many kinds would have been removed, with consequent ill effects for New Spain's producers, especially for agriculturalists. Zacatecas, like other Mexican silver-mining areas in the colonial period and beyond, may be considered to have been ultimately dependent on its European mercury source and on the final markets for silver in Europe and the East; but its economic relationship with other parts of New Spain was more one of symbiosis than of dependence.

NOTES

1. My *Silver Mining and Society in Colonial Mexico: Zacatecas 1546–1700* is a full-scale treatment of Zacatecas in narrative, political, economic, and social terms. Its exhaustive referencing precludes the necessity of such in the present chapter, which states succinctly some of the book's salient points and gives additional material on types of careers and holdings for mining entrepreneurs and merchants.

2. For the war, see the lucid and well-documented work of Philip Wayne Powell, *Soldiers, Indians, and Silver: The Northward Advance of New Spain, 1550–1600*.

3. Fray Antonio Tello, *Cronica . . . de la Santa Provincia de Jalisco,* p. 776.

4. New Galicia was the name given to the area north and west of central Mexico, with a separate Audiencia in Guadalajara, though under the viceroy of New Spain. New Galicia included Zacatecas itself, though in the long run the influence of Mexico City was stronger than that of Guadalajara, as will be seen.

5. There is an account of Francisco de Ibarra's doings in J. Lloyd Mecham, *Francisco de Ibarra and Nueva Vizcaya.*

6. These figures are from Vargas Rea, ed., *Relaciones de los pueblos del Nuevo Reino de Galicia,* vol. V.

7. Archivo de la Tesorería de Zacatecas (hereafter ATZ RO), correspondence of treasury officials (William L. Clements Library, Ann Arbor, Michigan) 26, report of 4 December 1671. It is illustrative of the rise of Sombrerete that the officials remarked that many shops (retail businesses) had moved there from Zacatecas because of the lack of mercury and consequent decline of Zacatecan mining.

8. ATZ RO 19, declaration of collectors of revenues in various district towns, 1651–1652.

9. Alonso de la Mota y Escobar, *Descripción geográfica de los reinos de Nueva Galicia, Nueva Vizcaya y Nuevo León,* a source of great value for its detailed general description of Zacatecas.

10. The graph, showing a three-year moving average of the registered silver production of the Zacatecas district, represents the amount of silver presented for taxation at the Caja Real of Zacatecas and at the Caja of Sombrerete after its establishment in November 1681. There are no reliable tax figures for the years before 1560, and occasional gaps in the surviving Caja accounts cause some breaks in the graph. The accounts are confused in the period 1681-1700, so it has been possible to calculate only rather arbitrary averages for those years. Nevertheless, there is no doubt that the trend is correct. It is unlikely that the graph shows total production. Miners were obliged to pay the crown a total of 10.9 percent of the silver produced in return for access to subsoil deposits, which in Spanish law belonged to the monarch. The record of the amounts of this tax collected is the only continuous indication of production. Although there were frauds in payment and collection, there is nonetheless good reason to believe that the tax record accurately shows the changing trends in production; and the trends are what interest the historian, not absolute production figures.

11. Archivo General de Indias (AGI) Guadalajara 33, *visita* by Francisco de Villarreal to Zacatecas, section headed "Depósitos de azogues."

12. In various years of the seventeenth century, Zacatecas took a quarter to a half of the total amount of mercury used in New Spain.

13. ANZ 1644 (marked "No. 1").

14. See the family trees in José Ignacio Dávila Garibi, *La sociedad de Zacatecas en los albores del régimen colonial.* This mainly genealogical work is a useful tool for studying the early society of Zacatecas.

15. AGI México 37, R. 1.

16. The manuscript sources for studying land tenure in the Zacatecas district are numerous and scattered, and the author does not claim to have investigated this topic more than superficially. For early land grants (of estancias and sitios) in the district, see, for example, the legajo in Archivo del Ayuntamiento de Zacatecas marked "Títulos de propiedades. Pág. XIV"; and Archivo General de la Nación (AGN) Tierras 700, ff. 370-93.

17. Depending on what sort of sitios the 84 of Trujillo were, the estate's area could have been anywhere from 162,000 to 364,000 acres, or even larger, given the often poor definition of sites.

18. ANZ (notarial book of) Felipe de Espinosa 1659, ff. 271v.-272v.

19. *Land and Society in Colonial Mexico: The Great Hacienda.*

20. ANZ Felipe de Espinosa 1656, f. 244; also ANZ José de Laguna 1676-80, ff. 185v-188v.

21. AGI Guadalajara 51, Dr. Morones to crown, 17 Aug. 1557.

22. The employer-employee relationship between Spaniard and Indian, with the consequences suggested here, must have been characteristic of most of the mining towns of the plateau—San Luis Potosí, Durango, Parral, for example. But Zacatecas came first.

23. Mota y Escobar, *Descripción geográfica,* p. 66.

24. AGI México 78, "1669 años. Testimonio de los autos, declaraciones e informaciones . . ."; see f. 12, testimony of don Pedro Fernández de Cabrera.

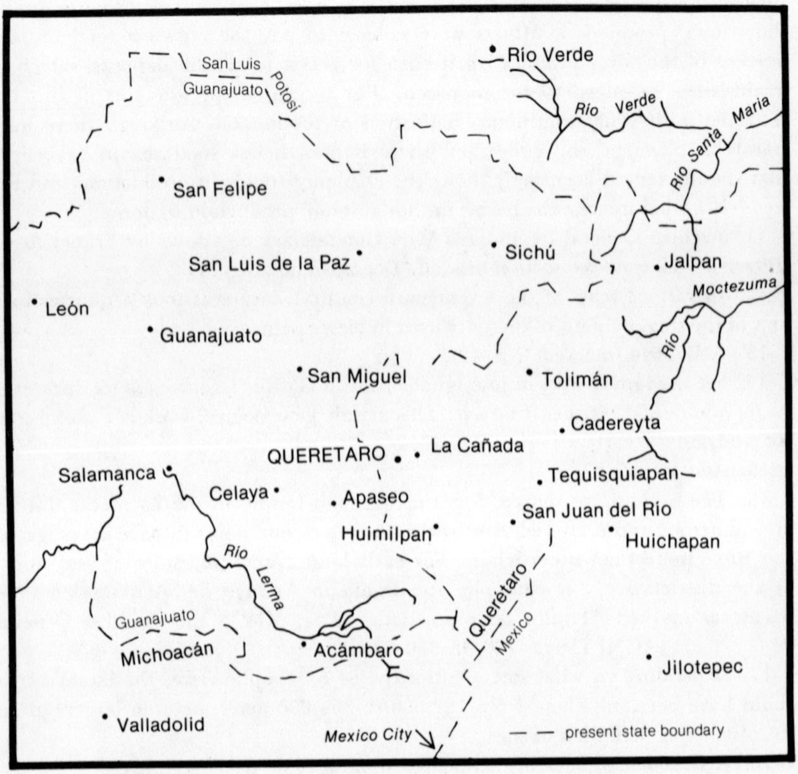

Sites Important to Querétaro's Early Development

9. The Agricultural Near North: Querétaro in the Seventeenth Century

John C. Super

The basic forms of European colonization were broadly similar throughout Mexico, but at the regional and local levels numerous variations and subtle alterations occurred, depending on location, resources, and the nature of the pre-Spanish population.[1] The town and province of Querétaro lie in the eastern end of the temperate basin called the Bajío, about 120 miles northwest of Mexico City. The area's location between the northern mining settlements and the heavily populated Valley of Mexico foretold its development into an important trading center. Fertile crop land and open pastures, rather than silver deposits or wet lowlands propitious for the sugar industry, constituted the primary resources of the area and gave impetus to a particular type of estate formation. The lack of a large, sedentary Indian population at the time of the conquest also influenced future social and economic relationships, limiting the importance of encomiendas and Indian communities. The effect of these three factors can be seen in the Spanish institutions established in the province, the organization of the town, the types of economic pursuits, and the forms of social arrangements.

The Town of Queretaro

Combined Spanish and Indian forces, led by the encomendero of Acámbaro, Hernán Pérez de Bocanegra, head of a family that remained important in the Bajío for a century, and don Hernando de Tapia, an Otomi Indian leader whose descendants were to have extensive economic interests in the Bajío until the 1620s, founded Querétaro in 1531. During the decades immediately thereafter, Querétaro functioned primarily as a frontier outpost, serving as a buffer between the Chichimecas to the north and the sedentary country to the south; specifically, the settlement protected the incipient trade routes connecting the southern Bajío with the central valley. Such a role was not a new one for the eastern Bajío, since the region had previously been the outer fringe of the Toltec and Aztec empires. However, the true orientation of the local Spanish presence quickly became evident with the increasing value of stock raising and commerce. By the last decades of the sixteenth century, an inchoate commercial-agricultural structure far overshadowed the military aspects of the town.

Legally, the town of Querétaro passed through three distinct phases. Six years after its foundation it received the designation of "pueblo de indios," or Indian village. In 1655 it seems to have become a Spanish villa or town, and in the following year it was designated a city. The appellation of "city" represented late political recognition of circumstances that had prevailed since the first years of the seventeenth century. While officially an Indian village, Querétaro had developed into a relatively large, economically wealthy, and politically important Spanish city. The word "pueblo" should not obscure the social and economic diversity found in the town, nor the constant, overriding importance of Europeans in it, even though they lacked the formal recognition found in other major centers. In most respects Querétaro was a European community, although a relatively large, ethnically diverse Indian population lived there through the colonial period.

After the 1580s, the town entered a period of sustained physical and demographic growth. Observers estimated that 50 Spaniards lived in Querétaro in 1582; in 1586 that number had risen to 70. By 1624 possibly 500 *vecinos,* or householders, resided in the town. By the mid-seventeenth century, the European population of the town must have approached 2,000. Important physical changes took place during the same period. The first decades of the century witnessed the growth of residences, stores and artisan shops, textile plants, and monasteries and convents. In 1643 the town contained at least 320 Spanish-owned houses and 28 general stores. The spatial distribution of the new buildings conformed to the original plan of the town designed in 1550 (the town site of 1531 was moved in 1550). During the middle decades of the eighteenth century the town experienced another period of physical growth with the construction of new religious and political buildings and private mansions. Scores of shops, stores, and craft stalls stood in the shadow of the imposing religious edifices; textile mills, tanneries, and the tobacco factory gave the town an industrial air; and over 2,000 houses lined the 272 streets in the city. By 1810 possibly 50,000 people inhabited Querétaro, of whom perhaps a third were Indians.

The degree of corporate differentiation corresponded to the stages of demographic and physical growth. For the first hundred years the town lacked many of the corporate symbols of social distinctions so important in other places. For example, until the 1620s, the community supported only one widely recognized *cofradía,* membership in which conferred little status, since residents from most ethnic and economic groups belonged to it. Later, cofradías for Indians (Otomi and Tarascan), blacks, and mulattoes operated alongside those for Spaniards. Whether the town's late-developing guild system followed the same course is uncertain.

Querétaro originally lacked the formal, segregated residential patterns of some central Mexican cities. Indians, mestizos, blacks, and Spaniards lived next to each other, and during the early years some Indians resided in the more prestigious parts of town. As Querétaro grew, however, status distinctions began to be reflected in residence patterns. Indian barrios—almost unknown in the early seventeenth century—were recognizable labeled components of the city by the eighteenth century. Increased urban land prices and social considerations had forced the Indian from the core of the city. But even those areas properly considered Spanish included some Indians, and areas described as Indian, such as north of the river flowing through the town, included Spaniards. Economic considerations and a growing urban population were chiefly responsible for the development of the barrios in Querétaro.

The town had immense cultural impact on many aspects of Indian life, but was far from omnipotent. The existence of the settlement itself depended on factors which reinforced the primacy of Indian languages and families, such as the continual migration of Indians to the town from the surrounding country and from further away. The number of temporary Indian residents also contributed to the population of Querétaro. Many came from satellite communities for short stays, but some traveled from distant towns and worked for months in the province. The latter, best described as seasonal workers, formed temporary associations with the permanent Indian population, usually based on occupational contacts. This type of Indian, with his mobility, different work experiences, and interaction with different ethnic groups, often possessed more Hispanic traits than permanent Indian residents.

In contrast to Indians living on rural estates or in Indian villages, those living in town faced a complex economic structure, fully controlled by Spaniards. The range of occupations open to them was much larger; similarly they interacted with a broader range of ethnic groups. Life in the town meant adjusting to Spanish currency, legal codes, and language. But adaptation to Spanish society did not mean total assimilation. Indian languages, family solidarity, and customs maintained remarkable resiliency, especially among the Otomis, even under continual pressures from the Spanish community. And newly arrived Indians, from the Valley of Mexico or from Michoacán, formed subgroups within the town and preserved their cultural identity. Indians could live in houses flanked by Spaniards' homes, work in Spanish-controlled occupations, and participate in Spanish religious services while still retaining their own languages and naming patterns and marrying within their own ethnic groups. A primary factor determining the response of Indians to urban life was the presence or absence of kin and personal associates speaking the same language. Those Indians who had family ties in Querétaro—regardless of how long the family had lived there—had less need to speak Spanish or to interact with the Spanish community.

The traditional, formal manifestations of Indian corporate culture—markets, social differentiation, political institutions—underwent more modification than did family organization. Indian life mirrored Spanish life in numerous ways. Indians adopted Spanish law and customs for regulating litigation, commercial transactions, dowries, and church donations. And the importance of private property in its application to land and livestock was as great among Indians as among Spaniards.

As the political and religious center of the province, Querétaro had standardized, formal relationships with subordinate communities. The local Spanish officials, consisting first of an alcalde mayor and his staff, then, after 1656, a cabildo with its alcaldes, councilmen, and lesser officials, had legal jurisdiction over the area from San Juan del Río in the south to San Pedro Tolimán in the north, towns designated as cabeceras with their own local administrators, but still dependent on Querétaro. Church organization closely paralleled that of political life. Querétaro served as the headquarters of the regular clergy, who linked the outlying villages to the town through the *doctrina,* or rural parish. And because of the town's growing reputation as a spiritual center, local convents and monasteries attracted novitiates and endowments from throughout the Bajío, creating strong personal and financial allegiances to Querétaro. Through its parish work, land ownership, and popular support, the church acted as an important integrative force in the province.

Economic ties between towns were stronger than institutional ones. The commercial connection with Mexico City was the most intense interurban relationship, but other towns in the Bajío and in the north also maintained close, continuous contact with Querétaro. These ties were expressed clearly in the temporary migration of people and capital between Querétaro and these towns. For example, the mining town of Sichú, located in the easternmost tip of the state of Guanajuato, drew frequently on Querétaro's resources. During the first part of the seventeenth century, Sichú served almost as an urban appendage of Querétaro (where there was no mining), attracting money, goods, and labor. In addition to mining-related personnel, shopkeepers, artisans, and agricultural workers moved back and forth between Sichú and Querétaro. Sichú provided an outlet for agriculturally generated wealth, thus adding a new dimension to the economic structure of Querétaro. The very nature of the relationship—and relationships with other mining communities—meant that it would be temporary, dependent primarily on the productivity of the Sichú mines. More permanent links existed between Querétaro and other Bajío communities. Based on trade, agriculture, politics, and religion, these contacts spanned the seventeenth and eighteenth centuries.

Two other types of settlements, distinguished partly by size and degree of dependence, surrounded Querétaro. First, small communities, most simply Indian villages, sprang up in the province. Whether they were entirely new or based in part on older settlements is uncertain; that so many had a saint's name only, and no Indian name, points to new foundation. None grew into significant population centers, nor did any achieve a level of economic specialization or production competitive with Querétaro proper. They served as a labor reservoir for Querétaro and a secondary market for the town's products. The substantial labor needs of the town's textile mills drew workers from neighboring communities, and part of the local economy was always directed to outlying villages. Second, Querétaro spawned new Spanish communities as its resources and needs matured. In a manner reminiscent of the earliest years of colonization, the town served as the platform upon which new settlements were based. For the first years of their history, these new towns relied almost entirely on Querétaro for political legitimacy, economic resources, and manpower.

Querétaro's influence spread deeply through the province, preventing a purely rural existence. Similarly, the countryside affected the town in numerous ways. From the settlement's foundation a close—and at times reciprocal—relationship, expressed in the movement of people, capital, forms of organization, and values, tied the town to the hinterland. The two can best be viewed as a single unit created by interlocking urban and rural patterns. Dichotomization effectively obscures provincial history by creating barriers which simply did not exist. The early history of the town is perforce the history of the province.

Perhaps the inhabitants' own expressed notions of local cohesion best illustrate this. When urban residents voiced their praise of the "glories" of the town, they spoke not only of its well-planned streets, magnificent architecture, and religious devotion, but of its productive hinterlands, which they alleged to be the most fertile in the viceroyalty. Contemporaries thus implicitly viewed the town and the country as a unit. The values and social needs of the inhabitants of the town corresponded with those of the country-dwellers; neither group viewed itself as an isolated entity with peculiar social and economic patterns. Of course factors including occupation, residence, and different social arrangements did distinguish some country-dwellers from some town-dwellers, but such factors did not create separate social systems, mainly because of the frequent and far-ranging interaction between the two sectors. Except for pure Indian villages, if such ever existed, the differences between town and country were in degree, not in kind.

Economic Activity in the Province

Estates.—During much of the colonial period the provincial money economy rested primarily on crop production and animal husbandry. In the early years the local population was small and there was not yet a developed production and distribution system in relation to the more distant southern markets (which themselves took time to develop), so that until the last decades of the sixteenth century agricultural output was restricted. Nevertheless, the products of the land, especially wool and mutton, provided the basis for the first accumulation of wealth and for increased trade with other regions in Mexico.

As everywhere, animal husbandry represented the first stage in the province's development of a Spanish agriculture. Perhaps 200,000 sheep grazed south of Querétaro in the 1580s, a number that increased substantially in the following decades. As pasture lands became scarce, the industry expanded northward, with Querétaro residents acquiring vast estates in areas as remote as San Miguel, San Luis Potosí, and even farther north. The availability of local and distant pastures (the Querétaro sheep industry was partially transhumant) and the growing southern markets made pastoral activities a natural investment. Official land grants (mainly for grazing lands) received by Querétaro residents supported the early pastoral inclination of the economy.

Crop lands of various types were in production from the earliest period, but it was not until the 1630s and 1640s that such holdings came to be as numerous as stock enterprises. The seventeenth century as a whole saw a slow shift from an agricultural economy based on livestock to one based mainly on crops. As the large flocks of sheep moved farther north, lands in the valley were planted in wheat, maize, and citrus. By the eighteenth century, the provincial agricultural economy relied more heavily on crops, and the types of estates owned by residents reflected this change. The word "estancia" had once meant a stock-raising enterprise, but now estancias were converted to other purposes. The change of primary emphasis from stock to crops occurred slowly and naturally, responding partly to heavier external demands—the market needs of Mexico City and other towns—and partly to internal demands.

All ethnic groups supplied workers for agriculture, with Indians, blacks, and mulattoes dominating during the early period. Mestizos became more conspicuous toward the end of the seventeenth century. Workers came to the estate as slaves, free contract workers (seasonal and permanent), and indebted servants. Various leasing arrangements also provided workers. (Textile plants used the same techniques and types of workers as estates, but during the seventeenth century relied more heavily on black and mulatto slaves.)

Terms used by Querétaro residents to describe different types of agricultural enterprises derived from primary land use. The terms "hacienda" and "estancia"—and their various combinations—between them covered much of the productive land. Most haciendas, usually specified as *de pan llevar* ("grain producing"), *de labor* ("farming"), or *de riego* ("irrigated"), specialized in wheat production, yet some of them raised a limited amount of stock as well as crops. Stock raising was found mainly on estancias, the basic units of sheep and cattle ranching, although some estancias included agricultural land. Neither the hacienda nor the estancia thus pursued true specialization, but estancia operations were closer to it than those of the hacienda.

Many smaller agricultural units lay interspersed among the haciendas and estancias. For some of these, no special nomenclature was applied, and an appreciation of their importance comes only from inventories. The proprietors of these farms fell somewhere between the social categories of husbandman/shepherd and rancher/agriculturalist. Owning only one or two of the smallest grants, *caballerías,* or parts of one, they often specialized in truck farming or citrus production and served the needs of a local clientele. When lands of this sort had markets and irrigation, they could be financially successful, providing their owners with a temporarily sound social and economic position; but, because of their size, they faced the prospect of absorption by larger units.

Title to all types of estates in Querétaro changed hands frequently during the first century of colonization. Two patterns of buying and selling emerge from the history of individual estates. In the first, an individual dealt in numerous properties, manipulating them, refashioning units; some owners bought and sold for speculation, others to consolidate lands already owned, and still others to move in and out of rural business. Most property transactions occurred in the course of such operations. The second pattern represents the sale of lands that had been held as a unit by a single family for more than one generation. Typically this family had moved to Querétaro in the late sixteenth century and through property accumulation had established itself in the town. By the 1630s estates owned by these families began to collapse due to accumulated pressures: financial indebtedness, overexpansion, church liens, and numerous heirs.

Early estates usually encompassed dispersed lands located throughout the valley, or, in some cases, in places as far east as Michoacán and as far north as Nuevo León. Owners often rented out or sold their distant parcels, especially if these did not fit in with the productive orientation of centrally located properties. But when distant lands served the estates, for example as grazing lands for sheep ranches, owners administered them directly. The geographic diversity of estates so evident in the sixteenth century began to change in the seventeenth century, as owners strove to develop geographically contiguous properties.

Regardless of their type or size, Querétaro estates did not approximate traditional descriptions of the classic hacienda. Seldom did they operate in isolation or achieve self-sufficiency. The value and production of land conformed to broader economic trends. The existence of rural estates involved a combination of variables—owners and workers, markets and prices, merchants and transporters—all of which point to integration rather than isolation.

Manufacture.—Until the 1580s the limited size of local manufacturing enterprises dictated Querétaro's almost total reliance on Mexico City for even the most basic of manufactured commodities. From that time, small artisan shops, usually with a staff of fewer than three or four, began to appear, but they produced only the simplest of items, such as shoes and ordinary clothing. The subsequent increase of the town's population and that of nearby communities gave artisans a larger, more diversified market. Local artisan ranks swelled in response to the new demand, and new types, like those specializing in silk garments or in certain aspects of the building trades, found buyers for their products. The proliferation of artisans in Querétaro was a natural response to an increasing, more demanding, provincial market. But even though the town's artisan population increased and became more diversified, the original dependence on Mexico City for specialty items continued.

Manufacturing on a larger scale closely followed the establishment of artisan shops. For much of the town's history, manufacturing meant textile production in obrajes or textile mills. Querétaro, like most Spanish American communities, also produced cloth in the home and in *trapiches* (small textile shops), but the obraje most characterized Querétaro's urban industry. The abundance of wool, the availability of markets, and the lack of local high-value export resources combined to make the obraje a singular provincial institution. During the early seventeenth century, the formative period of the industry, ownership and labor patterns, credit relationships, and markets took shape. Some further changes occurred in the eighteenth century, related to market shifts and competition, but these were more adjustments to the maturity of the obraje system than substantial alterations in the organization of the industry.

In the late eighteenth century another industry, represented by the royal tobacco factory, began operations in Querétaro. Second in size to that of Mexico City, by the 1790s the factory came to employ almost as many urban workers as all local textile factories combined. The decision to locate the factory in Querétaro must have been in part, at least, a recognition of the town's manufacturing tradition. Successful operation of the tobacco factory and of obrajes depended on a long-established, relatively effective transportation system, and on the proximity of large markets.

Commerce.—Agriculture and urban economic activities supported a large mercantile group that supplied credit to provincial businessmen and arranged the flow of goods in and out of the province. From the discovery of silver and the opening of a serviceable road between the northern mines and the Valley of Mexico, commerce was instrumental in Querétaro's development. Yet the orientation of the whole provincial commercial structure, the stamp which it received during the 1580s and 1590s, and then carried into the eighteenth century, depended only indirectly on silver production. Querétaro's economy pointed south rather than north, and commercial exchange with Mexico City and other central Mexican towns occurred more regularly than with northern mining centers. The central valley consumed Querétaro's raw materials and in return supplied the province with consumer goods and with capital.

Provincial commercial organization included three distinct yet closely related networks of trading, each contributing in a separate way to the region's development. The first had its base in Mexico City and simultaneously served many towns in the Bajío. This trade, which was wholesale only and showed a high degree of standardization, relied on the merchant-factor method of sales and distribution. Mexico City companies placed personal representatives in Querétaro who were responsible for sales, delivery, and payments. Often representatives would live in Querétaro for as long as ten years, serving one or more Mexico City commercial houses. Variations of the permanent merchant-factor method, some of them displaying a remarkable persistence, strengthened the economic bonds between Mexico City and the province. Mexico City residents who served political stints in the province afterward returned to the capital, using their previous bureaucratic associations for commercial purposes. Although the goods entering Querétaro showed a high degree of diversity, they clustered around three items: wine, dry goods, and slaves, the last almost exclusively controlled by Mexico City traders. In the other direction, the Mexico City merchants shipped wool, obraje cloth, and livestock from Querétaro to Mexico City.

The second type of trading network was provincial or local. Although it shared many characteristics with the Mexico City system, such as reliance on factors, minor political posts, and the company to facilitate trade, the provincial network rested squarely on the resources of the province. Perhaps the most important function of local commercial elements was as a credit source for industry and agriculture. As lending agencies, local firms invested heavily in agricultural production and in return received preferential treatment in the purchase of the valley's products for resale. The next step was for merchants to become land and stock owners themselves, as some did. Many commercial firms acted similarly to those in Mexico City, trading with smaller communities in the Bajío as well as inside Querétaro. Others developed as specialists in local products. Without doubt wool was the most important product during the first part of the seventeenth century. Although most merchants participated in the wool trade, only a small number can be classified as wool merchants, specializing in the purchase of Bajío wool for sale to middlemen in Mexico City. Silver also called forth specialized trading, but no rich silver merchants developed in early seventeenth-century Querétaro.

Retail selling, the third level of trade in the province, grew substantially from the late sixteenth century. Retail stores could be owned by provincial merchants, thereby providing an outlet for the goods they imported, or by obrajes, for the sale of wool and cloth, but most owners were simply shopkeepers by profession. Even though Mexico City merchants influenced retail selling in Querétaro, they seldom directly owned retail stores. The stores operated in all parts of the town, either as parts of homes or hostelries or as independent units. Large stores carried a wide assortment of items, with emphasis on dry goods; they served numerous clients and employed a staff of relatives and slaves. Other stores, usually smaller, seemed to concentrate on one or two products, selling to a restricted clientele. Among urban businesses, retail stores may have been the most susceptible to economic reverses and bankruptcy. Some stores began with very modest inventories, survived for a couple of years, and then met financial ruin. Even the large stores, due to the necessity of extending credit in over-the-counter transactions, often became insolvent. Still, the number and types of stores continued to grow, fulfilling a significant role within an increasingly complex provincial economic structure. Stores never monopolized the retail business—small agriculturalists retailed some products in the market, for example—but they became the common intermediary between producer and consumer.

The Organization of Society

The range of social types, or groups sharing common patterns of behavior, expanded greatly as the population and economy of the province became more diversified. This section describes four groups within the province—estate owners, merchants, blacks, and mestizos—as well as treating the topics of social status, mobility, and patriarchalism.

The diversity of estate types and methods of tenure resulted in a landholding group that encompassed owners of sprawling northern pastoral ranches, medium-sized wheat farms, and small truck and citrus farms. Owners of Querétaro land could be principally ranchers and farmers or they could be merchants, manufacturers, or political officials—and local landowners were often residents of other towns in Mexico. Corporate entities such as convents, monasteries, cofradías, and hospitals also owned land.

Through much of the seventeenth century, the *criador de ganado menor,* or wealthy sheep rancher, occupied the apex of the estate hierarchy. During the eighteenth century the hacendado, or owner of integrated rural enterprises with a concentration on agriculture, replaced the criador. Although the change corresponds to a slight shift in emphasis in the rural economy, both terms in their time implied wealth, status, and political influence. These individuals had prestigious family ties with merchants and other landowners through the Bajío and south to Mexico City, ties that also served their business interests. Moreover, proprietors of large estates typically owned slaves and valuable urban properties and had the ability to provide large dowries for their daughters. One of the major distinctions between large landowners and others was the former's identification with Mexico City, both socially, through various church donations and the ownership of residential property, and financially, through the location of business associates in the capital. Owners of smaller estates attempted to emulate the life style of the hacendados and criadores, but due to their lack of direct representation in other cities, they had limited credit and market options, which reinforced their isolation and provincialism.

Absentee ownership increased during the seventeenth century. Before that time, Querétaro residents owned and worked most of the region's farms and ranches. The entry of Mexico City residents into provincial agriculture, while reflecting the closer integration of the Bajío and the center, did not appreciably alter the techniques of property management and the objectives of estate owners. Owners treated their property as productive enterprises to be worked in the most acceptable contemporary manner (this did not prevent some cases of mismanagement). Here there was little difference between the types of owners and the estates of different sizes. Landlords attempted to keep all productive land in continuous use, either directly or through leasing the land. Very little productive land lay fallow long. In managing their estates, owners relied first on relatives for the most responsible positions, and then on professional estate foremen. Mexico City owners would choose younger relatives, quite often nephews, to reside in the province and oversee their properties. Wealthy local landowners, whose daughters promised attractive dowries, selected future sons-in-law with definite managerial skills. For those agriculturists who did not have extended family ties (many of them Portuguese immigrants), compatriots substituted for relatives. The new immigrant from Spain or Portugal, starting at the bottom by leasing a farm or buying a small rural property, was a persistent figure in Querétaro.

As seen, by the mid-seventeenth century, owners were consciously pruning distant fragments of land in the hopes of obtaining more integrated estates. This effort rested at least partially on economics, since geographically unified properties were easier to manage. But the interest in estate consolidation did not lead to the use of formal mechanisms for preserving estates. The creation of *mayorazgos,* or entails, remained the privilege of a very limited number, and never became a common characteristic of the region's estate owners.

In a manner similar to the landowning group, Querétaro's merchant population consisted of numerous subgroups, defined by products, clientele, range of operations, and social position. The occupation of "mercader" did not imply a static social and economic position, and residents of varying levels of wealth, involved in distinct market situations, fell under the generic label. The highest-placed type of merchant was the one who concentrated on interprovincial trade. With his headquarters in Querétaro, he had agents in other towns in the Bajío and Mexico City, close personal associations with local landed interests, and strong enough credit and capital reserves to participate in the buying and selling of most items of value in the province. This type of merchant was capable of purchasing local political offices (usually that of alguacil mayor), owning four or five slaves, providing large dowries for his daughters, and living in an expensive urban house. A sharp distinction existed between the provincial trader and the numerous retailers in Querétaro. Whereas a prosperous retailer could diversify his economic interests and gain status in the community, most retailers remained behind the counter, selling small quantities of dry goods and depending on the provincial trader for their stock.

Provincial merchants lived and worked in a manner similar to the town's obraje owners—frequently the same individual was a merchant and factory owner. Owners shared the aspirations and successes of merchants, and they used many of the same techniques for conducting business. By the beginning of the eighteenth century some of the wealthiest, most politically influential residents of the town were obraje owners.

As to blacks and mulattoes, they seldom achieved the social position of even the poorest landowners, merchants, and obraje owners. Blacks mostly appeared as slaves; consequently the details of their lives remain unknown to us. From the first years of the seventeenth century Querétaro had a large black population, possibly equaling the size of the European community during the 1630s and 1640s. Many residents owned one or two slaves, whom they employed as domestic servants; the wealthy ostentatiously owned five or six household slaves. Both urban and rural economic activities used slave labor. Blacks worked primarily in the town, where they labored in artisan-related tasks, transportation or in the textile production, which in some cases relied completely on slave labor in the seventeenth century. In the countryside, they worked mainly at specialized tasks in ranching and horticulture. By 1700 the association between slaves and specific types of employment began to diminish, and slaves worked in most occupations.

Fewer mulattoes than blacks lived in the town during the period, but, as usual in Latin America, they formed the largest percentage of the free colored population. Like blacks, mulattoes were first associated with urban occupations, especially textile work and transportation. In the few cases where the behavior of mulattoes can be determined, they appear as marginal figures in the Spanish world, modest in wealth and status. But their associations differed sharply from those of Spaniards. Mulatto social contacts centered on the Indian population of the town rather than on poor Spanish groups.

The lives of mestizos, or more correctly, those addressed as mestizos in local records, differed little in the essentials from the lives of mulattoes. Until the middle of the seventeenth century, the identifiable mestizo population was very small; for example, a list of houses in the town in 1643 mentions only seven mestizos as owners or renters. It is likely, however, that many individuals of mixed blood avoided being called mestizos. Persons so labeled invariably fit within a low social and economic category. Occupationally they worked as artisans or in textile mills, usually at poorly paid tasks. They seldom found opportunities in the more financially rewarding levels of agriculture and commerce. In their associations, mestizos had more informal contacts with Indians and mulattoes than with Spaniards; their circles did not extend beyond the marginal social and economic groups in the town. All this naturally contributed to a stereotyped suspicion and disrespect for "mestizos." Reinforcing this was their criminal record, for many of them had been in jail at one time or another, and this in turn contributed to their dependent economic status. Regardless of the low social and economic situation of the group, it had a well-defined, integrated position within the social order. Descriptions of a large, disruptive, vagabondish mestizo population do not apply to the early history of the province.

To assess the relative social level of the above groups, and of the entire population of the province, the concept of social position or status seems more useful than concepts such as class, estate, and corporation. Such factors bore on status, but their unqualified use as set categories obscures the multiplicity of factors determining an individual's or group's relative position in provincial society. Each identifiable group and subgroup in Querétaro had definite status attributes and avenues for acquiring them, distinct from those applying to other members of the society. Rather than attempting to define the status qualities of each group, the following discussion treats selected criteria of status which had broad applicability to the province. Phrased more directly, on what qualities did provincial society place high value? Although these qualities primarily affected the status of Spaniards, they carried more social significance for Indians as well in an area like Querétaro than in areas of dense Indian population.

Both formal and informal designations of status existed, but in practice they showed close interdependence, one often flowing from or coinciding with the other. The admixture of such qualities resulted in a social hierarchy based on numerous distinctions, though these distinctions lacked the clarity necessary for a categorical differentiation or stratification.

Formal status in Querétaro depended partly on traits legally sanctioned. The marks of status most highly valued consisted of different titles of honor, government positions, and military rank. (Designations such as vecino, *residente,* and *estante* referred to degrees of citizenship and had no visible effect on social position.) The terms "don" and "doña" conveyed considerable distinction in Querétaro during its early history, but by the eighteenth century they had lost much of their significance. Though still not used indiscriminately, they no longer gave much of a clue to an individual's status. During the first years of the seventeenth century, however, the acquisition of these appellations by the children of new families was an important step in the families' social legitimization. As the population and wealth of the province increased, formal titles of nobility became more evident. These then commanded the respect which earlier might have been accorded a "don." The appearance of a titled nobility in Querétaro represented an important transition in the social history of the province. Formal recognition of social position and real or imagined lineage through titles which were recognized also outside of the province added another dimension to the social scale, making it as complete as those found in larger, wealthier urban centers. With the location of a nobility in the town, and the creation of new titles, such as the Conde de la Sierra Gorda, the social hierarchy had reached full maturity.

Local bureaucratic posts conferred social prestige and political power. For influential families in the province they offered a traditional vehicle for gaining social recognition and material emoluments. Access to bureaucratic office reflected social and economic arrangements which lay at the very base of provincial organization. Those groups with major interests in land and stock, commerce, and manufacturing—the main economic activities of the province—might aspire to and obtain posts. During much of the seventeenth century, however, the possibilities for merchants and obraje owners were limited. In the pre-1656 period, members of these two groups often occupied the posts of alguacil mayor (chief constable), teniente de alcalde mayor (deputy of the alcalde mayor), and *alférez real* (royal ensign), but they did not become alcalde mayor, a position reserved for ranchers and Mexico City citizens. Even though local commercial groups did not receive the most powerful political offices, they effectively participated in the power system through intermarriage and economic alliances. Interoccupational exclusivity diminished in the eighteenth century, since merchants and industrialists by then occupied most levels of government.

Military titles, a third type of formal status, had less social consequence than titles of nobility or political office. A Querétaro captain or colonel commanded respect, but not in the same sense as the military figures of the far north, where such titles suggested enormous estates, political power, groups of retainers, and the highest social prominence. Most "military" men in Querétaro acquired their rank during the early Chichimec campaigns, and after their stints of service they continued to use the titles in an honorific way. Some of these veterans achieved substantial social recognition in Querétaro, but their military titles only underscored titles of "don" or political office. No specific distinguishing patterns of behavior can be attributed to retired military personnel or to those who sported military titles without previous military service; the social matrix in which they lived was essentially that of other comparable social groups. Military titles did come to reflect an occupational role in Querétaro during the eighteenth century, as part of general changes in Mexico and the Spanish empire. Even then, a military man had a more general status in the community which was only partly based on his military position.

Besides titles, government offices, and military rank, which were often merely a legal or conscious recognition of other realities of social life, numerous other variables affected an individual's position in the social hierarchy: lineage, occupation, wealth, convent and cofradía affiliation, residence location, land ownership, and personal associations. The potential social force of each of these elements was situational, since each could be a partial cause or result of any other, and most often they all coincided at a certain level. Further, their meaning changed through time, as it must have done in all of Spanish America, given similar conditions. For example, it appears that residence patterns had more social meaning in the eighteenth century than in the sixteenth, when there was less residential segregation. Of all of these esteemed qualities, wealth consistently had the most potential for shaping an individual's social position. It did not automatically confer prestige or honor in itself, but it acted as a generative force leading to the acquisition of symbols of respectability and to the alteration of life styles.

Other marks of social position, more difficult to define because so embedded in the rest of life, existed in the province. One of the most accepted of these was the ability to provide satisfactory dowries for daughters, an obligation consciously recognized and assiduously pursued by most socioeconomic groups. The fulfillment of this obligation, often jointly undertaken by many relatives and associates, brought familial honor and esteem from peers. Associations, in the broadest sense, corresponded to social rank. During the early years, the small size of the Spanish community created a social context in which economic and personal contact occurred frequently among most Europeans, almost regardless of social position. Hence "social" engagements between the wife of the single encomendero of the town and the wife of a petty merchant, or between an artisan and a political official, were common patterns of behavior at that time. But increases in population and in economic and social diversity changed this openness, and purely social interaction became more restricted, limited to individuals of relatively equal social and economic position, or to associations of a pronounced patron-client nature.

No one criterion defined any group exclusively. A person's position within the social order depended on the possession of a combination of qualities. These same status determinants applied in varying degrees to Indians (as well as to mestizos and free mulattoes and blacks) living in the province. Occupation, wealth, and official titles—and the network of personal associations influenced by these—appeared as the strongest criteria for social differentiation among Indians.

Three conclusions can be drawn from this discussion. First, the conditions of social stratification stemmed from the specific historical experience of the province as well as from general Spanish American social traditions. Second, provincial society of the colonial period lacked rigid social distinctions which sharply and exclusively delineated one group from another.

Differences were often blurred because of the subtleties and multiplicities of the determinants of social status. Third, an individual's position in the social hierarchy did not flow entirely from ascription—status was both ascribed and achieved.

Social mobility, or more specifically, the ability of an individual to move from one group to another through the acquisition of new status criteria, was a feature of Querétaro life. To label the society as open would be fallacious, but a certain amount of mobility existed for all social and economic groups. Because of the limitations of the documentation, most evidence of mobility applies to Spaniards. For the resident of the province, the period up to the 1640s offered various opportunities for social advancement. The availability of resources (land and livestock) at that time appreciably enhanced an individual's chances for success. Provincial and interprovincial trade offered a means to wealth. And for the individual who lacked assets to participate in these, the ranks of artisans (including the transportation industry) remained unrestricted. Although the largest number of artisans were Spaniards, many mestizos and blacks participated in this part of the economy. For blacks and mulattoes, though, economic success—and the resultant social conditions, such as a house in town—came above all from the transportation business, in which free blacks often worked as muleteers. Some blacks also became independent agricultural workers; their success here is impossible to determine.

Much of the evidence for vertical social mobility comes from the activities of Spaniards in the rural economy. Land and stock, particularly sheep, constituted the essentials of the rural economy until the middle of the seventeenth century. Until this time, access to these items was not unduly limited. Of the different methods available for obtaining land and stock, and consequently of securing additional symbols of status, the following are the most noticeable: leasing rural property, marrying into propertied families, and acquiring property while working as a rural majordomo. Each of these, or a combination of them, permitted non-propertied residents to acquire agricultural estates. Becoming a proprietor did not automatically elevate a person socially, but it did act as one precondition for such a shift.

For the Querétaro newcomer, social legitimization often followed success in a rural enterprise. The children of persons who entered the province in the 1580s and 1590s acquired the status denied their parents. Titles of don and doña and the marriage patterns of children visibly demonstrated the change. The title of doña and a large dowry, which may have included land and stock, allowed women to marry into prominent families outside of the province. After two generations, the family position could have improved substantially, with evidence of the rise displayed in titles, marriages, urban property, and church bequests. Economic decline, however, often followed social ascendancy. Following the period of quick growth, the original estate of the family could become smaller and less valuable due to different liens, economic reversals, and fragmentation. When this occurred, the family's prestige and reputation usually returned to its former level—all within two or three generations. Except for those sons and daughters who had at least partially disengaged themselves from the family enterprise, through either marriage or the pursuit of another occupation, the decline of the family estate also meant a decline in status.

Commerce and manufacturing offered numerous opportunities for social movement. Here advancement did not require a change in economic role, although the switch from merchant to rancher was by no means rare. The acquisition of land and stock, through either purchase or marriage, may have been a social ideal for merchants, but it was also a natural extension of business interests. Merchant buying, selling, and loaning revolved around local landed groups. The close financial connections between the two, which often entailed social relations, resulted in merchant ownership of land. And, at times, this interest could extend to a change in primary economic role from merchant to landowner, with the possibility of corresponding changes in status designations. The change from merchant to landowner occurred gradually; as an individual's strictly mercantile transactions decreased, investments in land and stock increased.

Whereas landownership may have opened new social vistas for merchants, those who spent their lives in the commercial profession could achieve a social position in many ways equivalent to the most esteemed estate owners. There was no moral or cultural stigma attached to the merchant profession. Often merchants lacked the prestige of estate ownership, but they could readily correct that condition through the purchase of land. It is true that they were excluded from holding the highest local political office, that of alcalde mayor. Successful merchants possessed many of the criteria of social distinction: slaves, a fine residence, important family associations, and the like. To obtain the highest success, one usually had to meet certain preconditions. These included ties with an influential family, generally one that had direct influence with the landed elite; connections with local political figures; and access to credit in the province and in Mexico City. Those individuals who possessed or could develop these relationships encountered few obstacles on the road to social eminence. On the other hand it was almost inconceivable that a newcomer with only enough capital to open a small dry goods store on the fringe of the town could ever become the owner of a provincial trading company.

Agriculture and commerce, two of the most inclusive occupational categories in the province, entailed a substantial amount of fluidity in their organization, offering Querétaro residents chances to change their socioeconomic circumstances. Opportunities for financial success and social prestige in land generally have been considered more limited than opportunities in commerce because of the supposed barriers of entail, land monopoly, and the association of land with elites. The early history of Querétaro suggests the opposite. Land offered more chances for upward social mobility than commerce. Newcomers found it easier to acquire land and stock, which gave them a defined status and an opportunity for improvement, than to acquire the prerequisites for success in commerce.

Social movement within other occupational groups and among Indians, blacks, and mestizos is more difficult to trace. Movement certainly took place within these groups, but vertical changes were probably not as substantial as among Spaniards in land and commerce. A great deal of horizontal mobility occurred, mainly expressed in occupational shifts. This type of change, whether limited vertical mobility (tailor to master tailor) or horizontal mobility (field laborer to textile worker), need not have been devoid of significant social consequences.

Provincial social mobility found expression in various ways. Both intragenerational and intergenerational mobility occurred, with the strongest signs of social advancement in the latter. Besides the mobility of individuals, it appears that entire occupational categories changed status, particularly the military. Certainly the status of a military officer during the Chichimeca campaigns in the sixteenth century, or of an officer in the late eighteenth century when the military received renewed support, differed from that of military officers during most of the seventeenth century, a period of minimal emphasis on defense. Similarly, the addition of new occupational groups or of new honor groups, like the titled nobility, affected the social hierarchy.

Regardless of the economic role or social position of individuals, patriarchalism, or the complex of personal relations that depended on and owed primary allegiance to the father, has often been assumed to be an important aspect of early Mexican social structure. For a society to be organized patriarchally, certain social conditions must be present. At first glance, Querétaro appears to have been organized in a typical patriarchal fashion, as the legal and cultural traditions supporting the household fit a patriarchal mold. But Querétaro's social and economic orientation prevented the development of a pure type of patriarchalism. The economy of the province, in both its manufacturing and agricultural forms, was based on the continual flow of money, commodities, and labor in and out of the region. Members and nonmembers of the family, often located in distant areas, held responsibility for the economic success of families. This authority often originated from the family head, but because of the complexity of the business world, it assumed an independent character that functioned outside of the purview of the family head. The appendages of patriarchal power became centers of authority themselves.

Querétaro households generally speaking did not conform to the *casa poblada* image, with the numerous retainers, servants, and multigenerational relatives. The lack of large integrated households undermined the extent of any one individual's personal authority. Sons and daughters, married or of marriageable age, and brothers, sisters, and grandparents frequently lived in separate households. Even so, those households did not function independently of each other. Kinship ties remained strong, and often members of the family participated in the same economic enterprises. But even with this type of integration, the household of a relative assumed its own characteristics, which in turn prevented an extended patriarchally-based social system.

Several factors operated counter to patriarchal authority within the household. Perhaps the most important of these was the influence retained by women. Married women, often the source of financial success for families, maintained direct control over resources that they brought into the marriage. They could delegate responsibility for this wealth to male members of the family, or they could hold it throughout the marriage. This included the right to determine, or at least influence, the transmission of properties to succeeding generations. Married women and widows exercised a considerable amount of control over many aspects of the family and over social and economic arrangements indirectly related to the family. The common division of inheritance among all children male and female was another equalizing factor.

For most families, the patterns of marriage, the scattered households, and the conditions for economic success precluded patriarchalism of an ideal type. It may have existed, however, as a conscious social objective. An analysis of selected families reveals a stronger patriarchal tendency among families of high social and economic rank. The families of the local encomendero and the cacique especially seem to have fit a patriarchal mold. These two individuals, whose titles symbolically represented a specific way of life that originated with the conquest, strove to maintain their traditional family dominance. Other families, some of them more successful economically than those of the cacique and encomendero, showed only hints of patriarchal organization. For merchant families in particular, such a principle of family organization might have inhibited the flexibility and independent authority needed for success.

Social relationships and economic trends in Querétaro took a definite mold during the late sixteenth and early seventeenth century, a period of substantial growth for the province. The rural estate forms, urban industrial pursuits, and network of trade which were established during this time carried into the eighteenth century. Similarly, provincial society, partly marked by fluidity and mobility, assumed a more complete and unified shape. By the middle years of the seventeenth century Querétaro was a regional center with a clearly defined social and economic structure based on provincial integration and on integration with other parts of Mexico.

NOTE

1. This chapter is based principally on Querétaro notarial records from the 1590s to the 1720s. The most intensive research was on documents from the first half of the seventeenth century. Local notarial records are housed in the Archivo de Notarías (Palacio de Gobierno) in Querétaro. Large sections of this archive and others have been microfilmed (52 rolls) and are available in the Museo Nacional de Antropología, microfilm section, Querétaro series. The Querétaro notary performed the same service as notaries in the capital, formalizing in a legal way the daily activities of residents of the town. Further information came from the Archivo General del Estado de Querétaro and from the Archivo de la Notaría Parroquial de Santiago de Querétaro (available on microfilm in the Archivo Microfílmico de Genealogía y Heráldica, Mexico City). The Archivo General de la Nación also contains important data on Querétaro; the most important ramo is Tierras, followed by Civil, Indios, Inquisición, Mercedes, General de Parte.

Some of the themes mentioned in this chapter are more extensively studied and documented in my "Querétaro: Society and Economy in Early Provincial Mexico, 1590-1630." An analysis of manufacturing in the province can be found in my "Querétaro Obrajes: Industry and Society in Provincial Mexico, 1600-1810." Few other published works on the early history of the province are available. For a partial list of contemporary works and a description of the city's archives see Bernardo García Martínez and Andrés Lira González, "Querétaro: la historia y sus instrumentos." Rafael Ayala Echavarri provides a complete bibliography of the state's history in *Bibliografía histórica y geográfica de Querétaro*.

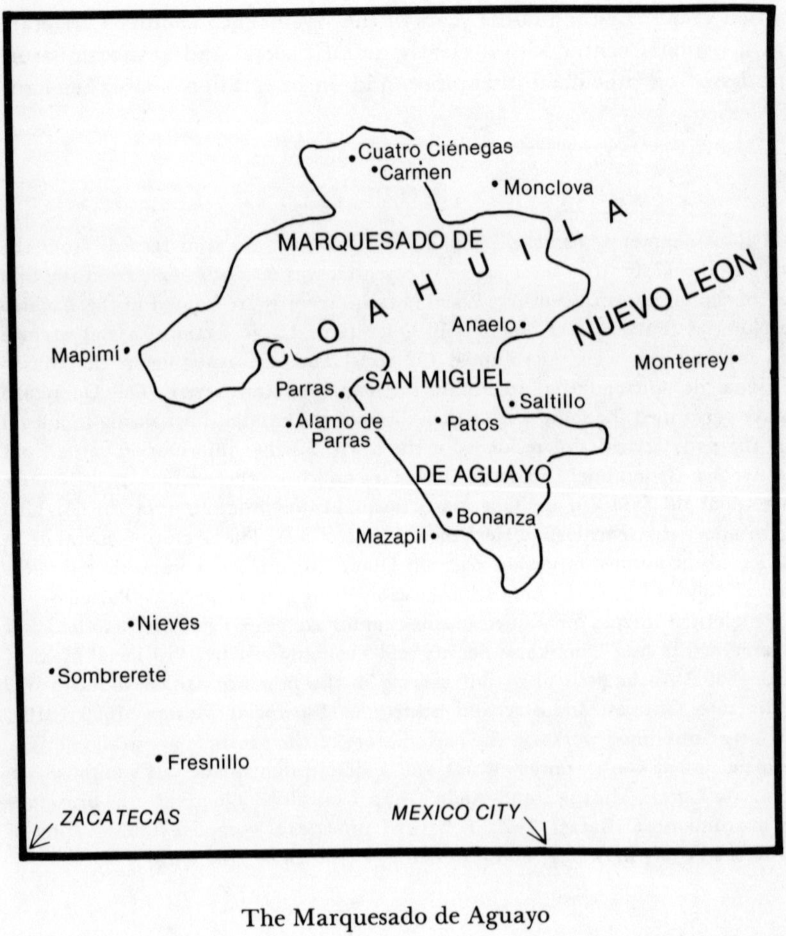

The Marquesado de Aguayo

10. A Family and Region in the Northern Fringe Lands: The Marqueses de Aguayo of Nuevo León and Coahuila

Ida Altman

The northern provinces of Nuevo León and Coahuila offered few attractions to potential settlers.[1] The region was barren, broken by mountain chains, and dry, with very few rivers that supplied water the year around. Nomadic and seminomadic indigenous groups, many of whom showed hostility to newcomers in their territory, constituted the sparse population of the area. Pockets of sedentary population were small and scattered and could not support an encomienda system in any way comparable to that which developed further south.

The possibility of finding mineral wealth probably inspired the initial efforts of Spaniards to explore and settle Nuevo León and surrounding areas of northern New Spain in the middle decades of the sixteenth century. Indeed, silver was discovered at Mazapil on the edge of the Zacatecas district in the last quarter of the century, but this find and others made in the region were secondary compared with strikes made to the south in Zacatecas, or later to the west in Hidalgo del Parral.

The Indian slave trade (i.e., the business of capturing allegedly hostile Indians for sale elsewhere) dominated the first phase of Nuevo León's history, shaping the future development of the province in a number of ways. It accounted for the foundation of the two most important provincial cities, Saltillo and Monterrey, before the end of the sixteenth century; fostered the early development of routes for transportation and communication; ensured the hostility of local Indian groups; and focused the attention of many Spaniards on a shifting and tenuous commodity rather than on a more permanent type of settlement. The region was, after all, far from utterly lacking in natural resources. It was well suited to the raising of a variety of livestock, and a number of locations permitted irrigation and agriculture. But markets being so distant and at that time still small, the marginal Indian slave trade predominated, as in comparable areas as far away as southern Chile and São Paulo; settlement for the most part thus retained a token, transitory nature throughout the sixteenth century. Although Monterrey was founded for the second time in 1596 with the chimerical hope that it would become a center of trade and communications between Zacatecas and the coast, the well-established Mexico City-Veracruz route prevailed.

One student of early Nuevo León is at pains to establish the presence of a substantial number of Sephardic Jews among the early settlers of the province.[2] His work lends support to the conclusion that the settlers of the marginally attractive north of New Spain were correspondingly marginal individuals socially and economically. In the early years Jews and foreigners (mainly Portuguese) were going there, attracted by the slave trade and small mining strikes or pushed out of the richer areas of the country by their failure to command social or economic resources. Most of the individuals who stayed in the region ended up in Saltillo or Monterrey, acquiring small landholdings in the immediately surrounding area. Simultaneously, Indians from central New Spain founded new settlements in the province, such as the Tlaxcalan pueblo of Santa María de las Parras in 1598; their holdings in land were similarly circumscribed.

In this manner the way was left open for title to land in the *despoblado*, or unpopulated regions, of Nuevo León to become concentrated in the hands of a very small group of individuals. They saw in stock raising—an activity which, as practiced in the Mexican north, relied on the extensive availability of land—the potential for future fortunes. This style of ranching required the seasonal or transhumant movement of stock, with vast landholdings compensating for the aridity of the terrain.

A Basque immigrant of a somewhat different type from the early slave hunters, Francisco de Urdiñola, succeeded in establishing for himself an economic stronghold in the region of Nueva Vizcaya, or Nuevo León and southern Coahuila.[3] Born in Guipúzcoa, he was present in the area of Mazapil, Saltillo, Zacatecas, and Río Grande from perhaps the 1570s. His first success in Nueva Vizcaya was in mining; he owned and worked mines in Bonanza, Mazapil, Ramos, and Río Grande, in the region of Nieves. Very early, however, Urdiñola began to acquire land, probably both to supply his mines and to invest in the future stability of his family's fortunes; later these lands were to be the basis and core of the Marquesado de San Miguel de Aguayo. The grant for the estancia of San Francisco de los Patos was obtained in 1583, and other titles go back still farther.

Appointed governor of Nueva Vizcaya in 1603 by the viceroy of New

Spain, Urdiñola took advantage of his governmental position to acquire yet more land. Lands granted to other individuals during his term of governorship often passed into his possession soon thereafter. Urdiñola's holdings were primarily suited to stock raising, though it is doubtful that in his time the market for meat and wool could support anywhere near the kind of extensive sheep ranching that would characterize the estate in the eighteenth century. In addition to pastures, Urdiñola also owned some of the best agricultural land in the region. The haciendas of Patos and Parras grew maize and wheat in the late sixteenth century. A small amount of this produce was sent as far as Zacatecas, though most of it must have gone to the more easily accessible mines of Mazapil and Sombrerete. Vineyards at Parras allowed the production of wine and brandy, and, by one account at least, a textile obraje at Patos also goes back to Urdiñola's time.

Francisco de Urdiñola, then, exemplified many of the factors that shaped early Nuevo León. A late-arriving Basque immigrant, he went to a remote and uninviting region seeking a base for his fortunes. His involvement in mining reflects the early, if ephemeral, importance of this activity in the province. The ease with which he acquired extensive landholdings substantiates the relative lack of interest that most other individuals in the area had in this most available, if seemingly least productive, resource that the province had to offer. Prominent for his wealth in a marginal and sparsely populated area, he held a succession of military and governmental positions—first as lieutenant governor and captain general of New Galicia and then as governor of Nueva Vizcaya—which underlined his economic power in the province.

The overall picture of Nuevo León in the late sixteenth and early seventeenth centuries is that of small Spanish towns, Indian colonies, and minor mine sites in the midst of an immense despoblado. Title to the vacant land was gradually being taken up by a few powerful individuals; the province remained isolated from the wealth of the capital city and unattractive as compared to a thriving mining center like Zacatecas. Although the export of Indian slaves was still a principal economic activity in the early seventeenth century, by this time a certain development and permanence were evident. Monterrey already had about a thousand inhabitants and was the commercial center for Nueva Vizcaya. Established transport routes went toward Mexico City, through Zacatecas on the one hand, and San Luis Potosí and Querétaro on the other. One author estimates that by the end of the sixteenth century Nuevo León had something on the order of half a million head of sheep. But the province was almost constantly on a war footing throughout the seventeenth century. This factor possibly favored the large landowners, who could afford some protection for themselves and furthermore were not threatened by the ambitions of smaller landowners, who probably preferred the relative safety of holdings near Saltillo or Monterrey.[4]

Thus the large estates of Nuevo León developed in a degree of isolation from the Spanish cities nearer the core of Mexico. Yet with their dominant economic role in the region, the estates ultimately came to link the northern provinces to Mexico City and to other regions by sending local products to outside markets, virtually dictating the course of regional development. In examining Urdiñola's descendants and their provincial estates, this essay will attempt to explicate these relationships by showing how the family and estates were tied to the provinces on the one hand and to Mexico City on the other. The articulation of these factors of provincial development, family history, and estate operation should show that the mature Hispanic traditions of family and estate formation that characterized the central region of New Spain were operative also in the northern provinces, adapting to whatever land, people, and resources the region offered and tying the whole back to the core once again.

The Marqueses de Aguayo

The family before the title: second generation.—When Urdiñola died in 1618 on his hacienda of Santa Elena in Nuevo León, his properties passed almost intact to the elder of his two daughters, doña Isabel de Urdiñola, who married twice. By her first marriage she had a daughter, later her heiress. Her second marriage was to an immigrant named Alvear y Salazar who, like Urdiñola, served as governor of Nueva Vizcaya.

Third generation.—Doña Isabel's daughter and Urdiñola's granddaughter, doña María de Alcega, again married a Spanish immigrant, by the name of Valdés y Rejano, who also apparently at some time served as governor of Nueva Vizcaya. This generation of the family is the first known to have lived at Santa María de las Parras, close to Santa Elena, where a daughter's birth was recorded in 1645. Doña Francisca de Valdés Alcega y Urdiñola, Urdiñola's great-granddaughter, became the third in the line of females to inherit the estates, and she too followed the tradition of marrying an immigrant, who, however, soon left her a widow and childless.

The first Marqueses.—Doña Francisca's second marriage, in 1669, was with yet another immigrant, by the name of don Agustín de Echeverz Espinal y Subiza, born in Navarre. From the time of his arrival in New Spain, probably in 1664, Echeverz y Subiza had served in a series of minor offices in Nuevo León. First appointed by the viceroy as protector of the Tlaxcalan and Huachichil Indians in the pueblo of San Esteban de Nueva Tlaxcala near Saltillo, he was promoted in 1666 to the office of "protector and war captain" for the frontier of Mazapil. Following his marriage he was named lieutenant to the captain general, a position much like the post of alcalde mayor which he held in the district of Saltillo or Parras through the 1670s. These official positions of his early career were all fairly minor.

Echeverz y Subiza seems to have taken a greater interest in the family estates than had the immigrant males who were his predecessors. Local missionaries sharply criticized him for hunting down Coahuilan Indians and forcing them into slavery on his estates, apparently a common practice of local landholders at the time. His attempted interference with the Franciscan colonization of Coahuila, in which the Franciscans intended to establish settlements for relocated or subjugated local Indians without the participation of the Spanish landholders, also illustrates his interest in preserving a source of labor for his estates and in preventing the infringement of others on lands he might want. Failing, however, to obstruct the settlement or to take by force the Coahuilan Indians who had been gathered for this purpose, he capitulated on the issue and cooperated to a certain extent with the bishop of Guadalajara in the recruitment of Tlaxcalan settlers for Coahuila.[5]

Don Agustín and his wife doña Francisca had greater ambitions than to remain relatively obscure landholders and local dignitaries in the northern provinces. They traveled together to Spain in 1682 where, with the aid of testimonials Echeverz y Subiza had prepared in 1678 and the (not impressive) sum of 562,000 maravedís in payment, they obtained from the crown the titles of Marqués and Vizconde of the Villa de San Miguel de Aguayo y Santa Olaya, only the fifth such title of nobility to be granted to an individual residing in New Spain. Echeverz y Subiza returned in 1683 to serve as governor of Nuevo León. His career in the post was quite undistinguished, his only impact on provincial affairs being his organization of a local militia in 1684 and two successive expeditions in 1686 and 1687 to seek out the allegedly encroaching French. He also sponsored the founding of two new Tlaxcalan settlements in Coahuila, neither of which received any material aid beyond the usual grants of land. Echeverz y Subiza served only until 1687, rejoining his family in Spain because of the illness of his wife. It was after that, in Pamplona in 1693, that an entail of the Marquesado estates was effected.

After returning to Spain in 1682 the family remained at Pamplona some twenty-five years. Of all the immigrant Spaniards who had married into the family, Echeverz y Subiza alone fulfilled the stereotyped immigrant's dream: he acquired wealth and social position in the New World and returned to his native land to enjoy the fruits of his ambition and hard labor.

The second Marqueses.—The first Marqueses de Aguayo, like previous generations, produced a sole heiress to the title and entail, doña Ignacia Javiera de Echeverz y Valdés. Twice married to members of the Spanish nobility, twice widowed, in 1704 she married don José Ramón de Azlor y Virto de Vera, second son of the Conde de Guara.

During the family's residence in Spain the estates had remained under the care of administrators, one of whom was probably Echeverz y Subiza's brother don Pedro Fermín. Following the birth in 1707 of doña María Josefa Micaela, the future third Marquesa, the family moved to New Spain and established residence on the estates of the Marquesado, where the birth of a second daughter was recorded at the hacienda of San Francisco de los Patos in 1715. A few years later, in 1722, the family took up residence in Mexico City.

Upon their arrival in Mexico the second Marqués and Marquesa undertook the personal management, consolidation, and expansion of their estates in Nuevo León and Coahuila. *Composición* procedures were initiated in 1714, and soon thereafter the Marqueses began to acquire new land titles, mostly in Coahuila, for quite nominal fees (note the lateness of these procedures compared with central Mexico). These token payments were justified in petitions on the basis of the expense and risk the Marqueses would have to undertake in order to maintain a force of *escolteros* (a private armed guard) to protect the area, and the high costs of transportation that effective settlement would impose. In 1727 a second entail was created.

The rapid acquisition of new land titles and attempted consolidation of holdings brought the Marqueses de Aguayo into frequent conflict with the other residents of the province. The Indians of Santa María de las Parras, who a hundred years before had almost been stripped of their water rights by Urdiñola's daughter, were told that they faced fines if their cattle grazed on the lands of the Marquesado. The pueblo itself possessed very little land, a situation which, together with the difficulty of obtaining water even on a fee basis, created real hardship. Even more indicative of the local impact of the Marquesado's expansion in the early eighteenth century were the protests of the Tlaxcalans of the pueblo of San Francisco de Coahuila and of the Spaniards of the nearby villa of Monclova; both parties pointed out that the granting of such extensive tracts of land to the Marqués de Aguayo had given him a monopoly of the well-watered sites in the province, had forced residents to buy or rent from him lands and water rights which had been available previously for public use, and would in the future discourage potential settlers from coming to the province. These arguments were of no effect.

In 1719 the second Marqués further enhanced his prestige and upheld a family tradition by becoming governor of Coahuila and Texas. In this position he financed and led an expedition north to the area of present-day San Antonio, attempting to reestablish a small cluster of missionary settlements which had been virtually abandoned because of threats from the

French. After living in Mexico City a number of years, the second Marqués and Marquesa died in the mid-1730s and were buried in Parras.

The third Marquesa. —The elder daughter, doña María Josefa Micaela, inherited the title and estates. In 1725, at Patos, she married don Francisco de Valdivielso y Mier, the first Conde de San Pedro de Alamo, a Montañés immigrant and financier. Valdivielso, who had made his fortune in silver banking at Zacatecas and as a merchant-aviador in Guanajuato and Pachuca, also owned mines at Mazapil and Zacatecas and extensive sheep-ranching estates in Nuevo León. He was a widower, having previously married doña Luisa Sánchez de Tagle, daughter of the second Marquesa de Altamira, who had brought him a huge dowry and possibly had inherited the silver bank which her grandfather, the first Marqués de Altamira, had founded.

The third Marquesa's younger sister, doña María Ignacia, chose a religious career and distingushed herself in the upper class society of Mexico City by founding, in 1757, under the authority of the archbishop, the convent of Nuestra Señora de Pilar, Compañía de María, commonly known as "la Enseñanza." M. María Ignacia ran this school, which educated the daughters of the best families of the capital, until her death in 1777. The archbishop had granted her the right of patronage, to continue after her death in the hands of the Marqueses de Aguayo. The financing of the Enseñanza undoubtedly became rather costly, but its sponsorship must have contributed to the family's prestige.

The third Marquesa and her husband the Conde seem to have spent little time on their northern estates, residing instead in Mexico City, where their two sons were born. They did, however, pursue certain land claims in Coahuila that were pending at the time of the death of the second Marqués, Azlor y Virto de Vera. When Valdivielso died in 1749 (following the death of his wife), both sons were minors. An agreement effected in 1764 gave the elder son the father's title, that of Conde de San Pedro de Alamo, and the younger, the mother's, that of Marqués de San Miguel de Aguayo. The details of this settlement are not clear, though it appears to have been fairly amicable. At the time, the *mayorazgo* of the Marqués de Aguayo was worth over 900,000 pesos, compared with 300,000 for the Conde de Alamo; the former, however, was allegedly debt-ridden, the latter solvent. The two halves of the family remained close and intermarried considerably in the years to come, and the brothers undertook certain legal actions jointly.

The fourth Marqués. —The lifetime of the fourth Marqués de Aguayo, don Pedro Ignacio de Echeverz y Valdivielso, spanned the second half of the eighteenth century and the period of Mexican independence. In many ways don Pedro Ignacio exemplified the stereotype of the wealthy creole absentee landowner living in the capital city. Holding a number of titles and offices in the viceregal government, probably honorary, he also took an active part in public affairs relevant to his role as a landowner, serving at times as the unofficial representative of the interests of those of his class who were not living in Mexico City. He also continued to make at least annual visits to his estates in Nuevo León and Coahuila, generally staying at Parras or Bonanza. It seems likely that don Pedro Ignacio's residence in the capital conferred on him a certain political leverage that he would have lacked had he remained in the provinces.

The financial difficulties that afflicted the estates and the family of the Marqués in the late eighteenth and early nineteenth centuries probably cannot be attributed directly to absentee ownership or mismanagement by the administrators who supervised the provincial estates. Although obviously the fourth marqués had less interest in the expansion or management of the estates than had his predecessors, his inheritance already was beset with financial difficulties when he succeeded to it. Financial reform measures taken by the crown in the early nineteenth century compounded those problems considerably. By the terms of the law of Consolidación in 1804, a rigorous measure that the Marqués de Aguayo and other affected landowners vehemently opposed, don Pedro Ignacio was required to pay 450,000 pesos over a period of ten years. It is not known how much he actually paid before the law was rescinded at the end of 1808. In the first decade of the nineteenth century new taxes were also imposed on the sale in Mexico City of liquor and meat, two of the principal products of the northern estates of the Marquesado. The end of the long association of family and estates came around the time of independence, in the 1820s, when don Pedro Ignacio's heir lost possession of the estates of the marquesado to a group of creditors.

The Marquesado Estates

The estates attained their highest level of development and productivity at almost the same time they faced their most severe financial difficulties, in the second half of the eighteenth century and early years of the nineteenth. The Marquesado reached its greatest extent in the 1760s, encompassing some 14,688,634 acres or 22,950 square miles. The flocks of sheep were estimated at between 200,000 and 300,000 head. An inventory of March 1761, including houses and other buildings, wells and irrigation works, vines, gardens, livestock, factories, and equipment, came to a total of 1,100,776 pesos, of which 674,283 pesos represented the value of the lands.

From the beginning the principal foci of the estates of the Marqués de Aguayo were the haciendas of Santa María de las Parras and San Francisco de los Patos. The first was famed for its vineyards and production of wine and brandy, which were shipped to Mexico City for sale. The farms around Parras also produced maize, wheat, and beans which were used to supply the establishment at Parras, the hacienda of Patos, and the livestock, as well as the employees at the hacienda of Bonanza. The hacienda of San Francisco de los Patos was the sheep-ranching center for the estates. It was the location for the main obraje, which had forty looms and a fulling mill and produced for sale as well as supplying workers of the estate. Another center for the estates was the hacienda of Bonanza, located near Mazapil, important for both mining and stockraising and headquarters for a large area. Other haciendas, especially those near Monclova in the northeast, such as Anaelo, Castaños, and Cuatro Ciénegas, were more tenuously established, plagued by erratic water supply and hostile Indians.

Extensive availability of land was the key to the large-scale, mobile style of sheep ranching practiced in Nuevo León and Coahuila. As has been indicated, the Marqueses de Aguayo possessed title to a huge tract of land in the northern provinces, and through other formal and informal mechanisms succeeded in gaining access to more lands yet for the pasturage of their flocks. By the eighteenth century the estates had a hierarchical staff with an *administrador general* at the top, staying mainly in the area of the holdings, coordinating and making decisions for the whole operation. Under him were the *mayordomos,* each in charge of one of the individual haciendas or ranches. The structure of the staff under the mayordomo seems to have varied considerably from one place to the next; there might be several *caporales* or foremen responsible for the livestock, then subforemen, *vaqueros,* each of whom would be in charge of three shepherds and their flocks.

The variety of economic functions of the estates suggests a corresponding variation in the nature of the labor force. Agriculture and industry required larger year-round labor forces than did ranching; populations were greatest where labor requirements were highest, such as at Parras and Patos, the latter having a population of 1,201 persons in 1765. The proportion of what could be called "debt laborers" among the permanent work force of the estates is not known. Very likely the lack of alternative economic opportunities was as strong a holding factor as debt, but a certain turnover is evident. Shepherds were undoubtedly more mobile than agricultural workers because of their relatively responsible and independent positions, and they seem to have had little hesitation in leaving one employer for another. A small number of black slaves worked on the estates in addition to the hired laborers, holding skilled or supervisory positions as overseers of obrajes, weavers, or shoemakers. The estates also utilized temporary labor, chiefly in the lambing season and at shearing time. Apparently the Tlaxcalans from the pueblos around Monclova would hire themselves out for this purpose.

Meat and wool were the chief products of the estates. Mexico City was the major outlet for meat, although this market was not a consistently dependable one. The outlets for wool are not specifically known, though the annual fair held in Saltillo in September was probably the major occasion for sales and Puebla, with its textile production, one of the principal destinations. Possibly some wool made its way to the capital city as well. The manufacture of wine and brandy, while definitely secondary, was not unimportant, as the hacienda of Parras was considered not only the major supplier of liquor to northern New Spain but one of the largest producers in the entire country.

The problems that typically affected the functioning of the estates in the eighteenth century were much the same as those of centuries before. The destruction caused by the raids of hostile Indians, together with the droughts so characteristic of the north Mexican climate and the occasionally devastating effects of plant and animal disease, constituted a set of problems so recurrent throughout the entire period of the history of these estates that they could be considered normal conditions of ranching and agriculture in Nuevo León and Coahuila. These factors of course did take their toll on the profitability of the estates in terms of both revenues and lives lost; but the word "normal" is used to suggest that adaptations and alternative solutions were devised so as to permit the maintenance of day-to-day operations. One such adaptation to the danger from Indians was the use of forces of escolteros in particularly vulnerable areas; another was the tendency to withdraw, completely or in part, from dangerous sites where the costs of maintaining defenses and normal production became prohibitively high. Several ranches along the road from Saltillo to Monclova were abandoned for this reason in the late eighteenth century.

Indian depredations, causing much damage to the outlying northern and eastern haciendas of the Marquesado, plagued the province, with only short intervals of peace, during the entire eighteenth century and far on into the nineteenth. Raiding Indians killed and captured laborers or their children, destroyed or carried off metal equipment, took large numbers of livestock, and burned granaries and crops. The token defense efforts of the royal government in New Spain were wholly inadequate to the needs of the province; Coahuila had only three understaffed presidios. Governmental efforts were generally in the traditional direction of encouraging the keeping of arms by individuals; one governor in the 1790s fined landowners and administrators who failed to provide weapons for their employees, as well as those employees who neglected to carry available arms.

When it became more expensive for an owner to maintain the defenses of an isolated hacienda than to abandon it altogether, he would choose the latter course, as did the Marqués de Aguayo in several instances. These deserted areas would then in turn become bases for Indian activity, the result being an increased threat to the welfare of all residents of the province. This circular process produced continuing complaints by local owners that the government would do nothing, and by high officials that the owners would not take measures to defend themselves.

The effects of climate and disease could also be cumulative, piling misfortune upon misfortune. A severe drought of the 1770s ended in 1778, to be followed in the course of the next year or so by a large-scale epidemic among the flocks of sheep. The years 1784–1785 brought another drought. Still another drought in 1801 was compounded by a destructive plague of crickets that wrought havoc on the grain fields; at Patos the wheat crop was afflicted by a plant fungus called *chauistle* (from Nahuatl *chayauiztli,* the falling to the ground of grains). When the drought broke in 1802, heavy flooding followed; a hailstorm in May of that year, just before harvest time, further reduced the grain yield at Patos, to a third of what it had been in 1801.

The enormous size and multiple resources of the Marquesado enabled it to cope with the extreme problems of the far north; faced with similar circumstances, a smaller holding would have suffered much more. Nevertheless, such difficulties must have had their effect, particularly when coupled with new factors like the rise in taxes on produce or the disruption associated with the independence movement. Certain ranches were abandoned and never reoccupied, representing lost income. Loans taken out by the family were never repaid, converting minor financial setbacks into long-term problems of credit and debt. But as long as the estate was able to continue extensive and large-scale operations, overall production could be maintained at levels high enough to compensate for normal problems and support the upper-class lifestyle of the Marqueses de Aguayo.

The Marquesado and the Provinces

Francisco de Urdiñola's descendants were firmly rooted in the northern provinces for all that they had become an upper-class family in Mexico City society by the eighteenth century. The ties were of two kinds: first, connections that were direct and personal, and second, the effect of the presence and operation of the Marquesado estates on the life of the provinces.

In the first category were the governmental and military positions held by the family members from the time of Urdiñola onward. As mentioned above, five male members of the family served as governors—three of Nueva Vizcaya, one of Nuevo León, and one of Coahuila and Texas. Appointment to the office of governor seems to have been virtually a function of ownership of the provincial estates, and the position was more than just honorary, since it provided some leverage on local affairs and politics.

Urdiñola took advantage of his office to proceed with his acquisition of land titles, and his daughter's husband attempted to exert the power of his position to obtain a monopoly of water rights near Parras. Even the minor offices Echeverz y Subiza held in Nuevo León conferred a certain local status and allowed him to develop a familiarity with provincial affairs. The military aspect of his governorship and later that of Azlor y Virto de Vera in Coahuila and Texas also brought them into closer contact with the local populace—from which they drew their militia groups and military expeditions—than might otherwise have been the case.

The factor of residency was another obvious and continuing tie between family and province. Urdiñola and probably his daughter lived at Santa Elena; the move in the third generation to Santa María de las Parras suggests the increasing importance of the Coahuilan part of the estates. On their return from Spain, the second Marqués and Marquesa came first to the hacienda of Patos before they established residence in the capital city, and the ties to the provincial estates remained strong, as both were buried at Parras, and their daughter was married at Patos in 1735. For the remainder of the colonial period the family was more firmly entrenched in the capital; but even the fourth marqués, don Pedro Ignacio, continued to make regular visits to the estates, as was the common practice among absentee landowners resident in Mexico City.

The almost continual conflict between the family and the other elements of the province—Indian pueblos, Spanish towns, missionaries—is a more complex but probably also more crucial area of contact. The nature of these clashes, the battles, legal and otherwise, that were lost and won, reflect the state of the provincial economy and society and reveal the direct impact thereon of the almost unobstructed growth of the estates. The battles were, naturally, over the control of and access to resources: water, since Nuevo León and Coahuila boasted relatively few well-watered locales; land, which had seemed so abundant in the sixteenth century but came increasingly to be at issue; and labor. But disputes generally involved more than one factor.

The early clash between doña Isabel and the Indian pueblo of Santa María de las Parras was a case in point. Having previously been stripped of all pasture land in the vicinity, the charterless Indian community was now threatened with loss of the water supply to its *huertas* (orchards or intensively cultivated large gardens), since doña Isabel proposed to divert the water exclusively to the hacienda at Parras. It may have been her intention, at least in part, to force the Indians of Parras into labor service on her estates by this action, as they would have no other recourse to support their community. The dispute over the pasturage of cattle and the pueblo's continued difficulty in obtaining access to water in the time of the second Marqueses reveal the hardships that the proximity of the Marquesado over time imposed on the pueblo of Parras. The latter did, however, score a minor victory in 1730 in a clash over the founding of a new settlement in the area of La Laguna. The Indians of Parras wanted to found a new community at a site that had been granted to the brother of the first Marqués, don Pedro Fermín de Echeverz, in 1700. The Marqueses de Aguayo claimed the lands and opposed the new foundation, but the Indians succeeded in invalidating the claim by proving that the marqueses had never populated the site or even paid the required amount to clear the grant.

Echeverz y Subiza's conflict with the missionaries in Coahuila has a certain blustering quality; it is difficult to believe that he could have seen the missions as a real threat to his social and economic position in the provinces. Perhaps he was resentful of the friars' criticism of his slave-hunting activities and their clearly-voiced preference for colonizing Coahuila without secular participation. In the end he hit upon the ideal—from his point of view—solution to the problem of the missions and new foundations of Indian pueblos; coexisting with them and giving little aid could stymie their success as effectively as could open opposition.

The early eighteenth-century conflicts over the extensive land grants to the Marqueses de Aguayo and over depopulated sites to which they had title form an even more serious area of dispute, focusing the attention of local residents on the issue of present and future provincial development. The protests of the Indians of San Francisco de Coahuila and the Spaniards of Monclova in the 1730s indicate their awareness that the increasing dominance of the Marqueses de Aguayo and their monopolization of available resources constituted not only a contemporary threat to their livelihood but would have a strong negative effect on the course of the general development of the region. They justifiably feared a future when all resources would be in the hands of a small number of powerful landowners, preventing settlement and colonization by a more modest class of individuals.

Here again the Marqueses de Aguayo triumphed. Title to huge tracts of land was granted them during the middle decades of the eighteenth century. Local residents in the 1770s pointed out that many of these sites, granted over their protests, either had never been effectively occupied or, if they had, had become depopulated, and proposed, with the Coahuilan governor's support, that they should settle them. The fourth Marqués de Aguayo hedged, maintained he would reoccupy the sites soon, in the usual fashion blamed the viceregal government for providing inadequate defenses, and in the end agreed that individuals might settle on the abandoned sites, but only so long as they were prepared to leave upon notice (the viceroy had previously barred the governor of Coahuila from dividing any lands belonging to the Marquesado).

These conflicts point to the most basic way in which the estates, and therefore the Marqueses de Aguayo, were tied into provincial life—through the local circumstances of daily life which the estates shared with all provincial residents. For almost everyone in Nuevo León and especially in the more northern province of Coahuila, daily life was difficult. Fray Agustín de Morfí reported that the residents of the hacienda of Anaelo lived in constant fear of Indian attack and at the slightest sign of an approach would climb the chapel roof to comparative safety. Harassment from hostile Indians caused the Marqueses to abandon ranches and haciendas in the late eighteenth century, fostering yet greater threats to the estates and to other residents of the provinces. Transportation was often erratic and unreliable, in part because the Indian problems discouraged the independent muleteers who worked the routes from Mexico City to Saltillo and Monclova, on which almost everyone in the provinces—including the Marqueses de Aguayo—relied. Difficulties in transportation encouraged the Marqueses to decentralize supply; the mayordomo of the hacienda of Carmen, for example, relied far more heavily on the store owned by the Sánchez Navarro family in Monclova than on the central hacienda of Patos for supplies.

Certain aspects of land tenure also brought provincial residents into contact with the Marquesado. Having monopolized an enormous amount of the available land in the area, the Marqueses did lease out some holdings. Individuals who rented farms from the Marquesado were, however, generally poor, and their rented lands were located in the least profitable or most dangerous areas of the Marquesado. With scarcely any leverage in rental agreements, these tenants were little more than de facto dependents of the estates; indeed they were in perhaps a worse position than servants, exposed to all risks with no assurances of steady employment. In some cases, rental of lands allowed the Marqués to maintain title to holdings for which he had no actual current use. Considering how marginal the majority of individuals were who rented from the Marqués, most of them working tiny farms or breeding a few cattle, it is apparent that rentals were a form of minimal exploitation representing not a source of income but a kind of insurance by which lands not actually in use could be kept secure for the Marquesado and prevented from passing into other hands. In this way they helped assure the economic preeminence of the Marqueses in the area.

The managerial structure of the estates and the nature of the labor force they utilized were sketched briefly above. Here, of course, the estates and provincial society in a sense merge, as the individuals employed by the

Marqueses de Aguayo resided in the provinces, in many instances were similar to other provincial residents independent of the great estates, and in some cases played more or less prominent roles in local society. The similarity between the positions of tenants and of permanent laborers has been commented upon. Turnover and mobility in the labor force strongly suggest that in the area of labor, at least, the Marquesado did not exercise a very complete regional monopoly; laborers and shepherds apparently found local employment elsewhere with some ease.

Although specific and detailed information about the lives of the laborers on the estates is difficult to glean, one can glimpse something of the managerial group or middle-level staff, their daily lives and functions, their integration into provincial life and society. Information about three cases reveals rather different career patterns and social relationships.

In the second half of the eighteenth century an individual named Francisco de Mata acted as a mayordomo of the Marqués de Aguayo for some three decades. Several factors reveal a position of some responsibility: his long period of service on the ranches of Carmen (near Monclova) and Anaelo (between Saltillo and Monclova); his mobility; and his relative independence in details of decision making in matters of ranching operations and minor financial and business transactions. He had attained some financial independence as well, keeping a flock of his own sheep at Carmen, and possibly purchasing land at one time. Mata was a close friend and compadre of the cleric don José Miguel Sánchez Navarro, with whom he had many business dealings and kept in close touch. The Sánchez Navarro family ran a store in Monclova that had a virtual monopoly on local supply; at this time they were beginning to go into sheep ranching, and were soon to emerge as leading stock raisers in Coahuila. Although employed by the Marqués de Aguayo, Mata remained extremely close to Sánchez Navarro, in fact siding with him on one occasion against his employer by reporting to the governor of Coahuila that the Marquesado administrator was illegally working a newly discovered salt mine at Cuatro Ciénegas.

A contemporary of Mata was don Juan Antonio Caviedes. Serving as "administrador general" for the Marqueses de Aguayo for some fifteen years, Caviedes's participation in legal affairs, his handwriting, and the customary use of the title "don" with his name (unlike Mata for example) indicate he was an individual of some education and status in local society. He lived at Patos and in Parras, where he died in 1775. There seems little doubt that an individual occupying the position of general manager of the Marquesado must have attained a considerable degree of power and social prestige, and probably was considered a member of the upper class in local provincial society.

Another employee of the estates, José Gerónimo Cacho, was both more educated and more ambitious than Mata. An administrator of Patos around the turn of the nineteenth century, Cacho exhibited a notable kind of social mobility, attaining financial independence and marrying into the family that was on the rise in Coahuila, the Sánchez Navarros. It is not clear how long Cacho was employed at Patos, but from 1802 on he was in close touch with the Sánchez Navarros regarding matters of mutual interest. By 1807 he was living in Saltillo, working for the Sánchez Navarro family and allied to it by marriage, and was a landowner in his own right.

José Gerónimo Cacho is an interesting figure not only in that he succeeded in establishing financial independence from his former employers, but because his life spanned and symbolically linked two stages basic to the evolution of Coahuila. After serving as an employee of the Marquesado de Aguayo, the then largest family estate of the northern provinces, Cacho became attached to an ambitious and energetic provincial family which was to help change Coahuila and Nuevo León from a region strictly secondary to Mexico City and central New Spain into one that could claim a certain economic independence and internal social cohesion. The eclipse of the Marquesado's economic and social dominance in the area by the Sánchez Navarros was translated into individual and human terms in the life of a man such as Cacho, or even of Francisco de Mata. Although the regional transformation was far from complete, and the Sánchez Navarros were also to become *the* estate-owning family and frequent governors, they were more than just the successors of the Marqueses de Aguayo; rather they represented the move to a second stage of Coahuilan provincial development.[6]

Familial and Interregional Patterns

The foregoing discussion of the estates and provincial ties of the Marqueses serves to illustrate almost equally well the manner in which the family and estates were integrated into the economy and society of New Spain as a whole and connected to the capital city in particular. The estates functioned as producers of raw materials for central Mexican manufacturing centers and for consumption in the capital city; thus the northern provinces remained, for the most part, in a secondary position to central New Spain, which absorbed their products while providing Nuevo León and Coahuila with supplies and the great landowners with profits. In other words the northern provinces were to Mexico City much as New Spain was to Spain throughout the colonial period, each an outlying area, marginal and isolated in relation to a metropolis, looking to the metropolis as a primary market and source of wealth and growth. On such a basis the Marqueses de Aguayo were able to develop a lifestyle that increasingly integrated them into the Mexico City upper class. As the central Mexican markets grew in power and the products of Nuevo León and Coahuila went from marginal in the late sixteenth and seventeenth centuries to significant by the mid-eighteenth century, the descendants of Urdiñola altered their status from that of a provincial upper-class family to one well established in upper-class society in the capital. Marriage patterns, holding of governmental positions, acquisition of the title and entail in the seventeenth century, shift of residence in the eighteenth, the establishment and support of the Enseñanza, and the fourth Marqués's political influence all serve to underline this upward mobility.

The pattern of marriage of creole females to immigrant males from northern Spain was so strong in the family as to have been literally the rule for marital alliance up to the generation of the fourth Marqués, when succession by two sons broke the pattern. The origins of these immigrants indicate that ties of kinship or friendship, or at least a sense of regional cohesion, were operative. Such ties could serve the newcomer as a point of entry into a society in which he had no other or major stable base. The motivations for the family members to make such marriages are not completely clear, since not all the matches show a preoccupation with wealth and security as clearly as the marital alliance with the Conde de San Pedro de Alamo; such factors as the preferences dictated by Basque fathers may have figured in the choice.

In a sense the in-marrying of immigrants served as an invigorating or renewing force, counterbalancing the isolation and stagnation that could have engulfed an upper-class family geographically removed from the mainstream of New Spanish society. By the late eighteenth century the family that had acquired the title of Marqués de San Miguel de Aguayo was an old one; but in every generation the acceptance into its ranks of Spanish immigrants effected a kind of renewal. Chance alone determined that in each generation the successor to the holdings would be female; but more than chance figured in the marriages they made. The successive generations of in-marrying immigrants were notably energetic, ambitious, and upwardly mobile individuals who invigorated the family and assured its continuation by constantly improving its position in the provinces. At least four of these men were instrumental in accumulating, expanding, and consolidating the landholdings of the Marquesado (Urdiñola, Echeverz y Subiza, Azlor y Virto de Vera, and Valdivielso). Many such individuals had reason to seek to better their position. Echeverz probably came from an impoverished, if respectable, family in Spain; hence his migration, and that of his brothers, to the New World. Azlor y Virto de Vera was the second son of a count and ineligible to succeed his father; through his marriage he acquired a title and wealth.

The customary haste with which upper-class females were remarried in colonial society also figured in the marriage pattern. Urdiñola's heiress married twice; the first Marquesa de Aguayo was twice married; her daughter married three times in Spain before immigrating to the New World; and the third Marquesa, although she married only once, was wed within a year of her father's death. The huge family holdings, successively inherited by the female line for many generations, were never long under the exclusive control of a creole heiress.

The recurrent feature of upward mobility among generations of males marrying into the family suggests another aspect of colonial society: the relationship of wealth to social status. In the case of the descendants of Urdiñola, the two are identical; wealth was both the indicator of and the means to economic and political power, which in turn signified social status. Echeverz y Subiza's wealth through marriage, rather than his services, allowed him to acquire a noble title. The second Marqués distinguished himself in the service of the crown in Texas by drawing on his financial resources and, again, the family's revenues maintained the prestigious "Enseñanza" in the capital. The obvious inseparability of wealth and social status in this family, with its provincial origins and ties and wealth from sheep ranching, suggests that the connection between economic assets and upward social mobility was not a phenomenon unique to any one group, region, or time of the colonial period. In Spanish society, wealth and status always went hand in hand.

Similarly, the distinction of upper-class colonial "elites" by sectors of the economy—commerce, mining, agrarian production—must inevitably break down. In colonial society power and status were determined by the holding of wealth, regardless of its source. Rather than delineate elites, it is more instructive to see a versatile upper class which, while operating in different sectors of the economy, either singly or through a multiplicity of involvements, was basically a unit in terms of social status, shared values, marital alliances, and power capabilities. The lives of the members of the family discussed here—their career patterns, economic resources, marriages—illustrate the closeness and fluidity of social and economic groups that as an aggregate formed the upper class of New Spain.

If the conclusion that the Marqueses de Aguayo were fully integrated members of the upper class of New Spanish society is accepted, then another notion often associated with the northern provinces, the question of whether this was a "frontier" society, can be discounted easily. The early development of the provincial estates in the time of Urdiñola, the existence of a standard estate structure identical to that found in central New Spain, the acquisition of a title of Castilian nobility, the family's adoption of residence in Mexico City in the early eighteenth century, all show that society in the provinces developed precisely along the lines indicated by the development of New Spain. Circumstantial differences, such as the dryness and sparse indigenous population of the north, fostered new economic adaptations (hence the prevalence of stock raising rather than agriculture); but these innovations did not generate the creation of a radically new or different society. Not only were provincial life and society long subordinate to the capital, but despite the absence of one social group—the large indigenous sector—social and economic organization in the northern provinces conformed closely to the model of the center. Whereas the men of this landowning family responded to their economic and social situation with energy and enterprise, they had no desire or need to reject the larger society of which they were the product and of which they remained a part; they helped shape the province in the image of the center.

NOTES

1. This chapter is based largely on my master's thesis at the University of Texas, "The Marqueses de Aguayo: A Family and Estate History." The principal archival source for the thesis was the Sánchez Navarro Papers (University of Texas Latin American Collection), which contain considerable information on the Marqueses and their estates (titles, estate inventories, correspondence, and so on). This collection formed the basis for Charles H. Harris's *A Mexican Family Empire: The Latifundio of the Sánchez Navarros, 1765–1867,* a study of the family that succeeded the Marqueses de Aguayo in the area of Nuevo León-Coahuila, which was also consulted. The other major sources for the thesis were Vito Alessio Robles's three-volume history of Coahuila and Texas, consisting of *Coahuila y Texas en la época colonial,* and the two volumes of *Coahuila y Texas desde la consumación de la independencia hasta el tratado de paz de Guadalupe Hidalgo*; the same author's biographical study *Francisco de Urdiñola y el norte de la Nueva España*; and fray Juan Agustín de Morfí's *Viaje de indios y diario del Nuevo Mundo,* which provides much detailed information on the provinces in the late 1770s. Supplemental material on Nuevo León and Saltillo was found in Eugenio del Hoyo's lengthy *Historia del Nuevo Reino de León (1577–1723).* Genealogical information on the family of the Marqueses was drawn chiefly from Frederick C. Chabot's short study "Los poderosos Aguayos" and Ricardo Ortega y Pérez Gallardo's *Historia genealógica de las familias más antiguas de México.*

2. See Hoyo, *Historia,* pp. 234-41.

3. Modern authors commonly give Urdiñola the title of "don" in view of his prominence, and indeed there is a painting of him from the late colonial period that does so in its caption. But documents of his time, including those signed by

himself, invariably call him only "Francisco de Urdiñola" or "Capitán Francisco de Urdiñola"; and Morfí writing in the latter eighteenth century still does not title him "don." Even more striking is the fact that Urdiñola's wife, Leonor de Lois or Leonor López de Lois, though related to a northern "captain" somewhat like Urdiñola himself, did not bear the much more liberally used title "doña." (See Alessio Robles, *Francisco de Urdiñola y el norte de la Nueva España,* frontispiece, and pp. 2-5, 67-76, 105, and 249-73.) Urdiñola claimed hidalgo status, perhaps without too great exaggeration, but his beginnings must be judged modest.

During Urdiñola's time, the archdiocese of Nueva Vizcaya, which was under the jurisdiction of the audiencia of Guadalajara, encompassed most of the area later to become the province of Coahuila (in the late eighteenth century). In the late sixteenth and the seventeenth centuries Mapimí, Parras, Saltillo, and Anaelo were all within the jurisdiction of Nueva Vizcaya, whereas Mazapil and Zacatecas to the south were included in Nueva Galicia. Nuevo León was apparently always considered a separate province, whereas the provinces of Coahuila and Texas (which were often linked, particularly through dual governorships) were creations of a later period.

4. Most of the information on the province in this time period comes from Hoyo, *Historia* (see pp. 397-406 in particular). Israel Cavazos Garza makes population estimates in his *Cedulario autobiográfico de pobladores y conquistadores de Nuevo León.*

5. David B. Adams, "The Tlaxcalan Colonies of Spanish Coahuila and Nuevo León: An Aspect of the Settlement of Northern Mexico," is the source of most of this material.

6. See Harris, *A Mexican Family Empire,* and also his *Sánchez Navarros: A Socio-Economic Study of a Coahuilan Latifundio, 1846–1853.*

Bibliography

In a sense the published literature relevant to the set of topics dealt with in this book is vast. If, however, we consider only works which involve distillation, analysis, and re-creation, the quantity becomes much smaller. Indeed, in the body of the book our authors have already referred to the majority of such works in existence. In the notes to the chapters and in the introductions to the three sections, the reader will find some pertinent remarks on the most significant items in this body of writing.

Two works may be singled out. The greatest of the travelers, and one of the first of the scholars, was Alexander von Humboldt. In the *Political Essay on the Kingdom of New Spain* his Nordic, early nineteenth-century European biases and blindnesses are in strong evidence, and the organization of the encyclopedic book is resolutely nonregional, but one may reasonably expect to find there a considerable amount of more or less reliable information on different aspects of any region of late colonial Mexico.

As a research and reference tool, Peter Gerhard's *Guide to the Historical Geography of New Spain* stands out. Jurisdictions are its forte. Its author never intended it to have the completeness and accuracy of a phone book, and if the reader bears this in mind he can find there a jurisdictional, demographic, and bibliographical introduction to a great many Mexican subregions of the colonial period, including obscure ones. Gerhard's extensive but selective general bibliography can also do much to point the reader further.

What follows here is simply a listing of published items referred to in the body of this book.

Adams, David B. "The Tlaxcalan Colonies of Spanish Coahuila and Nuevo León: An Aspect of the Settlement of Northern Mexico." Doctoral dissertation, University of Texas, 1970.

Alessio Robles, Vito. *Coahuila y Texas desde la consumación de la independencia hasta el tratado de paz de Guadalupe Hidalgo.* 2 vols. México, 1945–56.

______ . *Coahuila y Texas en la época colonial.* México, 1938.

______ . *Francisco de Urdiñola y el norte de la Nueva España.* México, 1931.

Altman, Ida. "The Marqueses de Aguayo: A Family and Estate History." Master's thesis, University of Texas, 1972.

Alva Ixtlilxochitl, don Fernando de. *Obras históricas*. 2 vols. México, 1965.

Amaya, Jesús. *Ameca, protofundación mexicana: el origen de su propiedad rural*. México, 1951.

Anderson, Arthur J. O., Frances Berdan, and James Lockhart, trans. and eds. *Beyond the Codices*. UCLA Latin American Studies Series 27. Berkeley and Los Angeles, 1976.

Arcila Farías, Eduardo. *El Siglo Ilustrado en América*. Caracas, 1955.

Ayala Echavarri, Rafael. *Bibliografía histórica y geográfica de Querétaro*. México, 1949.

Bakewell, P. J. *Silver Mining and Society in Colonial Mexico: Zacatecas 1546–1700*. Cambridge, 1971.

Báez Macías, Eduardo. "Planos y census de la ciudad de México, 1753." *Boletín del Archivo General de la Nación* VIII (1967).

Barrett, Ward. "The Meat Supply of Colonial Cuernavaca." *Annals of the Association of American Geographers* LXIV (1974):525-40.

______. *The Sugar Hacienda of the Marqueses del Valle*. Minneapolis, 1970.

Bataillon, Claude. *La ciudad y el campo en el México central*. México, 1972.

Berthe, Jean-Pierre. "Xochimancas: les travaux et les jours dans une *hacienda* sucrière de Nouvelle-Espagne au xviie siècle." *Jahrbuch für Geschichte von Staat, Wirtschaft und Gesellschaft Lateinamerikas* III (1966):88-117.

Blood, Richard. "A Historical Geography of the Economic Activities of the Jesuit Colegio Máximo de San Pedro y San Pablo in Colonial Mexico, 1572-1767." Doctoral dissertation, University of Minnesota, 1972.

Borah, Woodrow. *New Spain's Century of Depression*. Ibero-Americana 35. Berkeley and Los Angeles, 1951.

______. "Race and Class in Mexico." *The Pacific Historical Review* XXII (1954): 331-42.

Borah, Woodrow, and Sherburne F. Cook. *The Aboriginal Population of Central Mexico on the Eve of the Spanish Conquest*. Ibero-Americana 45. Berkeley and Los Angeles, 1963.

______. "A Case History of the Transition from Precolonial to the Colonial Period in Mexico: Santiago Tejupan." Paper presented at the International Conference of Americanists, Mexico City, 1974.

Brading, D. A. "Government and Elite in Late Colonial Mexico." *Hispanic American Historical Review* LIII (1973):389-414.

______. *Miners and Merchants in Bourbon Mexico, 1763–1810*. Cambridge, 1971.

______. "The Structure of Agricultural Production in the Mexican Bajío during the Eighteenth Century." Paper presented at the XLI International Congress of Americanists, Rome 1972.

Brading, D. A., and Celia Wu. "Population Growth and Crisis: León, 1720-1860." *Journal of Latin American Studies* V (1973):1-36.

Campbell, Leon G. *The Military and Society in Colonial Peru*. American Philosophical Society, Philadelphia, forthcoming.

Carrasco, Pedro. "La casa y hacienda de un señor tlalhuica." *Estudios de Cultura Náhuatl* X (1972):225-54.

Cavazos Garza, Israel. *Cedulario autobiográfico de pobladores y conquistadores de Nuevo León.* Monterrey, 1964.

Chabot, Frederick C. "Los poderosos Aguayos." *Anales del Museo Nacional de Arqueología, Historia y Etnografía,* cuarta época, VII (1931):127-46.

Chance, John K. "Race and Class in a Colonial Mexican City: A Social History of Antequera, 1521-1800." Doctoral dissertation, University of Illinois, 1974.

Chávez Orozco, Luis, ed. *Documentos para la historia económica de México,* vol. V. México, 1934.

______. *El comercio exterior y su influjo en la economía de la Nueva España (1793). Colección de documentos para la historia del comercio exterior de México,* vol. IV. México, 1960.

Chevalier, François. *Land and Society in Colonial Mexico: The Great Hacienda.* Berkeley and Los Angeles, 1970.

Chevalier, François, ed. *Instrucciones a los hermanos jesuitas administradores de haciendas.* México, 1950.

Colín, Mario. *Indice de documentos relativos a los pueblos del Estado de México: Ramo de Tierras del Archivo General de la Nación* (México, 1966) and *Ramo de Indios del Archivo General de la Nación* (México, 1968).

Cook, Sherburne F., and Woodrow Borah. *Essays in Population History: Mexico and the Caribbean.* 2 vols. Berkeley and Los Angeles, 1971-74.

______. *The Population of the Mixteca Alta 1520–1960.* Ibero-Americana 50. Berkeley and Los Angeles, 1968..

Dávila Garibi, José Ignacio. *La sociedad de Zacatecas en los albores del régimen colonial.* México, 1939.

Deerr, Noel. *The History of Sugar.* London, 1950.

Díez, Domingo. *Bibliografía del estado de Morelos.* México, 1933.

______. *Bosquejo histórico geográfico de Morelos.* Cuernavaca, 1967.

______. *Estado de Morelos y sus derechos territoriales.* México, 1932.

Durán, fray Diego. *Historia de las Indias de Nueva España e islas de la Tierra Firme.* 2 vols. México, 1967.

Durbin, Thomas E. "Aztec Patterns of Conquest as Manifested in the Valley of Toluca." Doctoral dissertation, UCLA, 1970.

Eklund, O. P., and Sydney P. Noe. *Hacienda Tokens of Mexico.* New York, 1949.

Florescano, Enrique. *Precios del maíz y crisis agrícolas en México,* 1708-1810. México, 1969.

Florescano, Enrique, ed. *Haciendas, latifundios, y plantaciones en América Latina.* México, 1975.

Florescano, Enrique, and Isabel Gil, eds. *Descripciones económicas generales de Nueva España, 1784–1817.* México, 1973.

Ganster, Paul B. "A Social History of the Secular Clergy of Lima During the Middle Decades of the Eighteenth Century." Doctoral dissertation, University of California, Los Angeles, 1974.

García Martínez, Bernardo. *El Marquesado del Valle: tres siglos de régimen señorial en Nueva España.* México, 1969.

García Martínez, Bernardo, and Andrés Lira González. "Querétaro: la historia y sus instrumentos." *Historia Mexicana* LXX, no. 2 (Oct.-Dec. 1968).

Gerhard, Peter. "Continuity and Change in Morelos, Mexico." *Geographical Review* LXV (1975):335-52.

______. *A Guide to the Historical Geography of New Spain.* Cambridge, 1972.

______. *México en 1742.* México, 1962.

Gibson, Charles. *The Aztecs under Spanish Rule.* Stanford, 1964.

______. *Tlaxcala in the Sixteenth Century.* New Haven, 1952.

Gómez de Cervantes, Gonzalo. *La vida económica y social de Nueva España al finalizar el siglo XVI.* Edited by Alberto María Carreño. México, 1944.

Haggard, John Villasana. *Handbook for Translators of Spanish Historical Documents.* Austin, 1941.

Hamnett, Brian R. *Politics and Trade in Southern Mexico 1750–1821.* Cambridge, 1971.

Harris, Charles H. *A Mexican Family Empire: The Latifundio of the Sánchez Navarros, 1765–1867.* Austin, 1975.

______. *The Sánchez Navarros: A Socio-Economic Study of a Coahuilan Latifundio, 1846–1853.* Chicago, 1964.

Hoyo, Eugenio del. *Historia del Nuevo Reino de León (1577–1723).* 2 vols. Monterrey, 1972.

Humboldt, Alexander von. *Ensayo político sobre el reino de la Nueva España.* México, 1966.

______. *Political Essay on the Kingdom of New Spain.* 4 vols. London, 1811.

Hunt, Marta Espejo-Ponce. "Colonial Yucatan: Town and Region in the Seventeenth Century." Doctoral dissertation, University of California, Los Angeles, 1974.

Karttunen, Frances, and James Lockhart. *Nahuatl in the Middle Years: Language Contact Phenomena in Texts of the Colonial Period.* University of California Publications in Linguistics 85. Berkeley and Los Angeles, 1976.

Katz, Friedrich. "Labor Conditions on Haciendas in Porfirian Mexico: Some Trends and Tendencies." *Hispanic American Historical Review* LIV (1974): 1-47.

Landsberger, Henry A., ed. *Latin American Peasant Movements.* Ithaca, 1969.

Lockhart, James. "Encomienda and Hacienda: The Evolution of the Great Estate in the Spanish Indies." *Hispanic American Historical Review* XLIX (1969): 411-29.

______. "Españoles entre indios: Toluca a fines del siglo XVI." In Francisco de Solano, ed. *Estudios sobre la ciudad iberoamericana.* Madrid, 1975. Pp. 435-91.

Lockhart, James, and Enrique Otte, eds. *Letters and People of the Spanish Indies, Sixteenth Century.* Cambridge, 1976.

MacLeod, Murdo J. *Spanish Central America: A Socioeconomic History, 1520–1720.* Berkeley and Los Angeles, 1973.

Martínez Marín, Carlos. *Tetela del Volcán: su historia y su convento.* México, 1968.

Marzahl, Peter. "The Cabildo of Popayán in the Seventeenth Century: The Emergence of a Creole Elite." Doctoral dissertation, University of Wisconsin, 1970.

______. "Creoles and Government: The Cabildo of Popayán." *Hispanic American Historical Review* LIV (1974):636-56.

Mazari, Manuel. "Un antiguo padrón itinerario del Estado de Morelos." Sociedad Científica "Antonio Alzate," *Memorias* XLVIII (1927):149-70.

Mecham, J. Lloyd. *Francisco de Ibarra and Nueva Vizcaya.* Durham, N. C., 1927.

Miranda, José. *La función económica del encomendero en los orígenes del régimen colonial. Nueva España (1525-1531).* México, 1965.

Molina Solís, J. F. *Historia de Yucatán.* 4 vols. Mérida, 1896-1927.

Morfí, fray Juan Agustín de. *Viaje de indios y diario del Nuevo Mundo.* Edited by Vito Alessio Robles. México, 1935.

Mota y Escobar, Alonso de la. *Descripción geográfica de los reinos de Nueva Galicia, Nueva Vizcaya y Nuevo León.* Guadalajara, 1966.

Muñoz Camargo, Diego. *Historia de Tlaxcala.* México, 1892.

Nutini, Hugo. *San Bernardino Contla.* Pittsburgh, 1968.

Ortega y Pérez Gallardo, Ricardo. *Historia genealógica de las familias más antiguas de México.* 3 vols. México, 1908-1910.

Osborne, Wayne S. "Indian Land Retention in Colonial Metztitlan." *Hispanic American Historical Review* LIII (1973):217-38.

Otte, Enrique. "Die europäischen Siedler und die Probleme der Neuen Welt." *Jahrbuch für Staat, Wirtschaft und Gesellschaft Lateinamerikas* VI (1969):1-40.

Paso y Troncoso, Francisco del, ed. *Epistolario de la Nueva España, 1505-1818.* México, 1939-42.

Planos de ciudades iberoamericanas y filipinas sacados del Archivo de Indias. 2 vols. Madrid, 1951.

Pomar, Juan Bautista. *Relaciones de Tezcoco.* México, 1891.

Powell, Philip Wayne. *Soldiers, Indians, and Silver: The Northward Advance of New Spain, 1550-1600.* Berkeley and Los Angeles, 1952.

Rea, Vargas, ed. *Relaciones de los pueblos del Nuevo Reino de Galicia,* vol. V. México, 1952.

Riley, G. Micheal. *Fernando Cortés and the Marquesado in Morelos, 1522-1547.* Albuquerque, 1973.

Riley, James D. "Santa Lucía: Desarrollo y administración de una hacienda jesuita en el siglo XVIII. *Historia Mexicana* XXIII (1973).

Romero Flores, Jesús. *Historia de los Estados de la República Mexicana.* México, 1964.

Roys, Ralph L. ed. *The Titles of Ebtun.* Washington, D. C., 1939.

Rubio Mañé, J. Ignacio. *Alcaldes de Mérida de Yucatán: 1542-1941.* México, 1941.

______. *Archivo de la historia de Yucatán, Campeche y Tabasco.* 3 vols. México, 1942.

______. "Gente de España en la ciudad de México, año de 1689." *Boletín del Archivo General de la Nación* VII (1966):5-406.

Ruiz de Velasco, Felipe. *Historia y evoluciones del cultivo de la caña y de la industria azucarera en México.* México, 1937.

Sedano, Francisco. *Noticias de México . . . desde el año de 1756.* Edited by Joaquín García Icazbalceta. 2 vols. México, 1880.

Service, Elman R. "The Encomienda in Paraguay." *Hispanic American Historical Review* XXXI (1951):230-52.

Shanin, Teodor, ed. *Peasants and Peasant Societies.* Middlesex, 1971.

Soustelle, Jacques. *Daily Life of the Aztecs.* London, 1961.

Spalding, Karen. "Indian Rural Society in Colonial Peru: The Example of Huarochirí." Doctoral dissertation, University of California, Berkeley, 1967.

Spores, Ronald. "The Zapotec and Mixtec at the Spanish Contact." In Robert Wauchope, ed. *Handbook of Middle American Indians,* III, Part 2. Austin, 1965. Pp. 962-87.

Stephens, John L. *Incidents of Travel in Yucatan.* 2 vols. New York, 1963.

Super, John C. "Querétaro Obrajes: Industry and Society in Provincial Mexico, 1600-1810." *Hispanic American Historical Review* LVI (1976):197-216.

______. "Querétaro: Society and Economy in Early Provincial Mexico, 1590-1630." Doctoral dissertation, University of California, Los Angeles, 1973.

Taylor, William B. *Landlord and Peasant in Colonial Oaxaca.* Stanford, 1972.

Tello, fray Antonio. *Crónica . . . de la Santa Provincia de Jalisco.* Guadalajara, 1891.

Tutino, John M. "Creole Mexico: Spanish Elites, Haciendas, and Indian Towns, 1750-1810." Doctoral dissertation, University of Texas, 1976.

______. "Hacienda Social Relations in Mexico: The Chalco Region in the Era of Independence." *Hispanic American Historical Reiview* LV (1975):496-528.

Villaseñor y Sánchez, José Antonio de. *Theatro Americano.* 2 vols. México, 1746-48.

Womack, John. *Zapata and the Mexican Revolution.* New York, 1969.

Zavala, Silvio, ed. *Fuentes para la historia del trabajo en Nueva España.* 8 vols. México, 1939-46.

Index